1001 BEST

CROCKPOT

RECIPES OF ALL TIME

EMMA KATIE

D1620431

Copyright © 2016 Emma Katie

All rights reserved.

This book is licensed for your personal enjoyment only. This book may not be re-sold or given away to other people. If you would like to share this book with another person, please purchase an additional copy for each recipient. If you're reading this book and did not purchase it, or it was not purchased for your enjoyment only, then please return to your favorite retailer and purchase your own copy. Thank you for respecting the hard work of this author.

No part of this book may be reproduced in any form or by any electronic or mechanical means, including information storage and retrieval systems, without written permission from the author, except for the use of brief quotations in a book review. If you would like to use material from the book (other than just simply for reviewing the book), prior permission must be obtained by contacting the author at emma.katie@outlook.com.

Check out more books by Emma Katie at:
www.amazon.com/author/emmakatie

CONTENTS

Introduction.. xxv

Appetizers

Candied Kielbasa 3
Bacon Wrapped Chicken Livers 3
Cocktail Meatballs 3
Sausage Dip 4
Cheesy Beef Dip 4
Tropical Meatballs 4
Glazed Peanuts 5
Spiced Buffalo Wings 5
Ham and Swiss Cheese Dip 5
Mexican Dip 6
Spanish Chorizo Dip 6
Asian Marinated Mushrooms 6
Nacho Sauce 7
Five-Spiced Chicken Wings 7
Queso Verde Dip 7
Party Mix 8
Caramelized Onion Dip 8
Molasses Lime Meatballs 8
Bourbon Glazed Sausages 9
Sweet Corn Crab Dip 9
Blue Cheese Chicken Wings 9
Rosemary Potatoes 10
Creamy Spinach Dip 10
Cheesy Bacon Dip 10
Artichoke Dip 11
Zesty Lamb Meatballs 11
Cheese and Beer Fondue 11
Chili Chicken Wings 12
Chipotle BBQ Meatballs 12
Chipotle BBQ Sausage Bites 12
Cheesy Chicken Bites 13
Stuffed Artichokes 13
Pork Ham Dip 13
Honey Glazed Chicken Drumsticks 14
Cranberry Sauce Meatballs 14
Cheeseburger Dip 14
Bacon Crab Dip 15
Curried Chicken Wings 15

Wild Mushroom Dip 15
Mediterranean Dip 16
Bacon New Potatoes 16
Bean Queso 16
Pizza Dip 17
Green Vegetable Dip 17
Spicy Enchilada Dip 17
Mixed Olive Dip 18
Spicy Asian Style Mushroom 18
Three Cheese Artichoke Sauce 18
Mexican Chili Dip 19
Boiled Peanuts with Skin On 19
Spicy Glazed Pecans 19
Cheesy Mushroom Dip 20
Taco Dip 20
Swiss Cheese Fondue 20
Spicy Chicken Taquitos 21
Quick Layered Appetizer 21
Oriental Chicken Bites 21
Sweet Corn Jalapeno Dip 22
Pretzel Party Mix 22
Maple Syrup Glazed Carrots 22
Balsamico Pulled Pork 23
Carne Asada Nachos 23
Bacon Black Bean Dip 24
White Bean Hummus 24
Spicy Monterey Jack Fondue 24
Tahini Cheese Dip 25
Tahini Chickpea Dip 25
Roasted Bell Peppers Dip 25
Charred Tomato Salsa 26
Pimiento Cheese Dip 26
Eggplant Caviar 26
Sausage and Pepper Appetizer 27
Bacon Baked Potatoes 27
French Onion Dip 27
Teriyaki Chicken Wings 28
Goat Cheese Stuffed Mushrooms 28
Pepperoni Pizza Dip 28
Creamy Potatoes 29
Beer BBQ Meatballs 29
Baba Ganoush 29
Beer Cheese Fondue 30
Mozzarella Stuffed Meatballs 30
Marinara Turkey Meatballs 30
Four Cheese Dip 31
Quick Parmesan Bread 31
Cranberry Baked Brie 31

Classic Bread in a Crock Pot...32
Caramelized Onion and Cranberry Dip...32
Cheeseburger Meatballs...32
Bacon Wrapped Dates...33
Parmesan Zucchini Frittata..33
Hoisin Chicken Wings...33
Ranch Turkey Bites...34
Turkey Meatloaf..34
Artichoke Bread Pudding...34
Bacon Chicken Sliders...35
Chili Corn Cheese Dip...35
Southwestern Nacho Dip..35
Marmalade Glazed Meatballs...36
Creamy Chicken Dip..36

Soups

Butternut Squash Creamy Soup...39
Cajun Black Bean Soup..39
Creamy White Bean Soup...40
Ham White Bean Soup...40
Creamy Bacon Soup...40
Pinto Bean Chili Soup..41
Black Bean Soup..41
Three Bean Soup..41
Posole Soup...42
Provencal Beef Soup..42
Sausage Bean Soup..43
Curried Lentil Soup...43
Tuscan Chicken Soup...43
Mixed Bean Vegetarian Soup...44
Tomato Beef Soup..44
Coconut Squash Soup..45
French Onion Soup...45
Shrimp Soup..45
Creamy Potato Soup..46
Italian Barley Soup..46
Quick Lentil Ham Soup..47
Split Pea Sausage Soup..47
Zucchini Soup...47
Beef Taco Soup..48
Southwestern Bean Soup..48
Spicy Black Bean Soup...49
Chicken Sausage Soup...49
Beef Cabbage Soup..49
Beef Vegetable Soup..50
Sweet Corn Chowder...50

Chicken Enchilada Soup..50
Italian Barley Soup 51
Ham Bone Cabbage Soup 51
Lima Bean Soup...52
Okra Vegetable Soup 52
Mexican Beef Soup..52
Hungarian Borscht 53
Chicken Rice Soup...53
Ham Potato Chowder 54
Potato Kielbasa Soup 54
Curried Corn Chowder 54
Two-Fish Soup 55
Creamy Cauliflower Soup 55
Stroganoff Soup 55
Winter Veggie Soup 56
Spiced Creamy Pumpkin Soup 56
Kielbasa Kale Soup 56
Lemony Salmon Soup 57
Creamy Noodle Soup 57
Asparagus Crab Soup 58
Orange Sweet Potato Soup..58
Cream of Broccoli Soup...58
Ham and White Bean Soup 59
Cheesy Broccoli Soup...59
Chunky Potato Ham Soup 59
Leek Potato Soup 60
Creamy Leek and Potato Soup..60
Lentil Soup with Garlic Topping 61
Minestrone Soup 61
Roasted Bell Pepper Quinoa Soup..62
Red Chili Quinoa Soup..62
Corn and Red Pepper Chowder...62
Chunky Mushroom Soup..63
Curried Vegetable Soup 63
Mixed Veggies Coconut Soup...64
Pumpkin Hearty Soup 64
Chunky Pumpkin and Kale Soup 64
White Chicken Chili Soup...65
Italian Veggie Pasta Soup 65
Garam Masala Chicken Soup 66
Orange Salmon Soup 66
Creamy Tortellini Soup...66
Spicy Chili Soup with Tomatillos 67
Portobello Mushroom Soup...67
Bouillabaisse Soup..68
Pork and Corn Soup 68
Creamy Tomato Soup with Flour Dumplings...68
Curried Turkey Soup..69

Ham and Sweet Potato Soup...69
Indian Cauliflower Creamy Soup..70
Moroccan Lentil Soup...70
Black Bean Mushroom Soup...70
Three Bean Quinoa Soup...71
Garlicky Chicken Soup..71
Vegetable Chicken Soup..72
Summer Squash Chickpea Soup...72
Tomato Fish Soup...72
Beef Mushroom Soup...73
Hungarian Goulash Soup..73
Moroccan Lamb Soup..74
Shredded Beef Soup...74
Chicken Sweet Potato Soup...74
Hot and Sour Soup...75
Swedish Split Pea Soup..75
Chicken Chickpea Soup...76
Quinoa Soup with Parmesan Topping..76
Turkey Tortellini Soup...76
Pork Applesauce Soup...77
Smoked Sausage Lentil Soup...77
Salmon Fennel Soup..78
Smoked Sausage Cabbage Soup..78
Creamy Edamame Soup...78
Pork Edamame Soup..79
Chicken Pearl Barley Soup..79
Roasted Tomato Soup..79
Summer Vegetable Soup..80
Bean Medley Soup...80
Spiced Pork Soup...81
Meatball Soup..81
Creamy Carrot Lentil Soup..82
Roasted Chicken Stock..82
Fish Sweet Corn Soup..82
Creamy Mediterranean Soup...83
Chicken Chickpea Soup...83
Curried Prawn Soup...83
Three Cheese Broccoli Soup..84
Bacon Potato Soup...84
Beef Bacon Barley Soup..84
Pesto Chicken Soup...85
Herbed Chickpea Soup..85
Spicy White Chicken Soup..85
Chicken Gnocchi Soup..86
Beef Tortellini Soup..86
Chicken Sausage Rice Soup...87
Spinach Sweet Potato Soup...87
Thick Green Lentil Soup..87

Herbed Spinach Lentil Soup 88
Kale Potato Soup 88
Chicken Parmesan Soup 88
Basil Tomato Soup 89
Lasagna Soup 89
Chicken Tortellini Clear Soup 90
Creamy Spinach Tortellini Soup 90
Minestrone Soup 90
Bean and Bacon Soup 91
Bacon Cheeseburger Soup 91
Grits Potato Soup 91
Smoky Sweet Corn Soup 92
Simple Chicken Noodle Soup 92
Cream of Chicken Soup 92
Stuffed Bell Pepper Soup 93
Chicken Wild Rice Soup 93
Thai Chicken Soup 93
Chicken Taco Soup 94
Cheddar Garlic Soup 94
Meatball Tortellini Soup 94
Tuscan Kale and White bean Soup 95
Garlicky Spinach Soup with Herbed Croutons 95
Comforting Chicken Soup 96
Tuscan White Bean Soup 96
Vegetable Chickpea Soup 96

MAIN DISHES

Vegetables

Spinach Bean Casserole 101
White Bean Spinach Enchiladas 101
Layered Spinach Ricotta Lasagna 101
Summer Squash Lasagna 102
Vegetable medley Stew 102
Quick Zucchini Stew 103
Spicy Sweet Potato Chili 103
Sweet Potato Curry 103
Bean Tomato Stew 104
Cocoa Black Bean Chili 104
Barley Black Bean Stew 104
Couscous with Vegetables 105
Zucchini Bean Stew 105

Three Bean Chili 105
Rice Bean Stew 106
Cuban Beans 106
Tofu Chickpea Curry 107
Curried Coconut Chickpeas 107
White Bean Artichoke Ragout 107
Marinara Sauce 108
Pinto Bean Chili with Butternut Squash 108
Veggie Chickpea Curry 109
White Bean Casoulet 109
Saucy Tomato White Bean Stew 109
Kidney Bean Chili with Crunchy Corn Chip Topping 110
White Bean Chili over Creamy Grits 110
Roasted Bell Pepper Stew 111
Quinoa Black Bean Chili 111
Parsnip Butternut Squash Stew 111
Quick Lentil Stew 112
Chipotle Lentil Chili 112
Cauliflower Lentil Stew 113
Leek Potato Stew 113
Madras Lentils 113
Vegetarian Gumbo 114
Butternut Squash Curry 114
Vegetarian Fajitas 115
Sweet and Spicy Vegetable Curry 115
BBQ Tofu 116
Hoisin Braised Tofu 116
Mushroom Stroganoff 116
Greek Rice Stew 117
Coconut Bean Curry 117
Wild Rice Veggie Stew 117
Cauliflower Mashed Potatoes 118
Spring Mashed Potatoes 118
Lemony Artichokes 118
Lentil Stuffed Bell Peppers 119
Greek Stuffed Zucchini Boats 119
Roasted Bell Pepper Cannellini Stew 119
Vegetarian Jambalaya 120
Pearl Barley Mushroom Stew 120
Spicy Vegetarian Chili 120
Mediterranean Stew 121
Tomato Chickpea Stew 121
Autumnal Stew 122
Vegetarian Coconut Curry 122
Marinated Mushrooms 122
Hearty Vegan Chili 123
Pumpkin Spinach Stew 123
Quick Okra Stew 123

Southwestern Style One Pot Meal 124
Creamy Mushroom Stew 124
Eggplant Casserole 124
Slow Cooker Ratatouille 125
Kitchen Sink Stew 125
Chickpea Curry 125
Layered Vegetable Stew 126
Mexican Vegetable Casserole 126
Cheesy Potato Casserole 127
Barley and Bean Tacos 127
Wild Rice Stuffed Bell Peppers 127
Red Lentil Dal 128
Spicy Red Lentil Curry 128
Fennel Tomato Pasta Sauce 128
African Sweet Potato Stew 129
Chipotle Bean and Quinoa One Pot Stew 129
Butternut Squash Chili 130
Bulgur Chili 130
Buffalo Cauliflower 130
Cauliflower Mashed Sweet Potato 131
Roasted Slow Cooker Chili 131
Curried Potato Stew 131
Indian Spiced Lentils 132
BBQ Lentils 132
Bourbon Baked Beans 133
Creamy Butternut Squash Coconut Chili 133
Spinach Lentil Stew 133
Mashed Sweet Potato with Lentils 134
Quinoa Black Bean Chili 134
Spinach Potato Stew 134
Puttanesca Pizza 135
Vegetable Pot Pie 135
Tofu Eggplant Stew 136
Teriyaki Tofu 136
Mushroom Barley Risotto 136
Wild Mushroom Barley Risotto 137
Creamed Sweet Corn 137
Spring Vegetable Farro 137
Whole Roasted Cauliflower 138
Fava Bean Stew 138
Garlicky Lentil Stew 138
Orzo Enchilada Sauce 139
Oriental Chickpea Stew 139
Curried Tofu Lentils 139
Quinoa Tofu Veggie Stew 140
Zucchini Rolls in Tomato Sauce 140
Summer Lasagna 141
Tofu Broccoli Rice 141

Oat Sweet Potato Chili..141
Tofu Korma..142
Vegetarian Bolognese Sauce..142
Black Eyed Peas Stew..142
Mango Tofu Curry...143
Eggplant Tapenade...143
Asian Eggplant Stew...143
Citrus Black Bean Stew...144
Spicy Chickpea Stew...144
Mediterranean Chickpeas..144
Collard Greens Stew...145
Red Wine Vegetable Stew..145
Jamaican Red Bean Stew...146
Noodle Stroganoff..146
Pumpkin Apple Stew...146
Indian Chickpea Curry...147
Spiced Lentil Stew..147
Thai Style Butternut Squash Tofu Stew..147
Creamy Lentil Stew..148
Green Pea Tomato Stew..148
Slow Cooker Steamed Rice..148
Spinach Casserole...149
Quinoa Butternut Squash Casserole...149
Mung Bean Stew..149
Vegetable Shepherd's Pie...150
Herbed Barley Casserole..150
Chickpea Tikka masala..150
Indian Style Tofu Stew..151
Root Vegetable Risotto...151
Red Wine Braised Tempeh...152
Tofu Ratatouille...152
Mexican Quinoa...152
Indian Spiced Quinoa Stew..153
Crock Pot Jambalaya..153
Butternut Squash Balls...153
Chinese Hot Pot..154
Stuffed Onions..154
Boston Baked Beans..154
Fennel Risotto...155
Asparagus Barley Stew...155
Black Bean Portobello Chili..155
Creamy Chickpea Stew...156
Asian Marinated Eggplants...156
Cheesy Three Bean Chili...157
Herbed Risotto..157
Summer Squash Casserole..157
Tomato Crouton Stew...158
Pinto Bean Sloppy Joes..158

White Bean Chard Stew 158

Dried Tomato Stew 159

Mediterranean Crock Pot Stew 159

Tofu Vegetable Hot Pot 160

Pineapple Slow Cooked Tofu 160

Three Bean Cornbread Casserole 160

Spicy Fried Beans 161

Tomato Sauce Beans over Milky Grits 161

Tempeh Butternut Squash Stew 161

Paste Veggie Stew 162

Tempeh Quinoa Stew 162

Quinoa Corn Stew 163

Lime Bean Stew 163

Jamaican Red Bean Stew 163

Herbed Vegetable Meatloaf 164

Mixed Lentil Spicy Stew 164

Pineapple Baked Beans 164

Broccoli Rice Pilaf 165

Creamy Potatoes 165

Veggie Refried Beans 165

Layered Sweet Potatoes 166

Stuffed Butternut Squash 166

Vegetarian Fajitas 166

Spinach Cottage Cheese Casserole 167

Green Bean Casserole 167

Seitan Chow Mein.. 167

Chinese Tofu Kung Pao 168

Five Spice Marinated Tofu 168

Bok Choy Shiitake Crock Pot Fry Up 168

Indian Mixed Veggie Curry 169

Seitan Rice Pilaf... 169

Savory Sweet Potato Apple Casserole 169

Spanish Rice Pilaf..170

Tempeh Carnitas 170

Curried Rice and Lentils..170

Eggplant Parmigiana..171

Asparagus Casserole 171

Ravioli Stew... 172

Vegetarian Hungarian Goulash.. 172

Ginger Glazed Tofu.. 172

Artichoke Black Olive Tagine 173

Beans Bourginon 173

Tofu Dumpling Stew.. 173

Hearty Sweet Potato Stew..174

Hominy Casserole 174

Garden Crock Pot Chili..175

Mexican Tortilla Chip Casserole 175

No Fuss Vegetarian Chili..175

Ricotta Veggie Lasagna 176
Bean and Spinach Enchilada Sauce 176
Parmesan Biscuit Pot Pie 176
Hearty Black Bean Quinoa Chili 177
Farro Pumpkin Stew 177
Madras Vegetable Curry 178
Simple Potato Stew 178
Meatless Pasta Sauce 178
Balsamic Vegetable Sauce 179
Couscous Cauliflower Stew 179
Mediterranean Chickpea Feta Stew 179
Eggplant Caponata 180
Provence Summer Veggie Stew 180
Asiago Chickpea Stew 181
Enchilada Orzo 181
Broccoli with Peanuts 181
Layered Eggplant Parmesan Bake 182
Ginger Teriyaki Eggplant 182
Honey Orange Glazed Tofu 182
Chunky Pasta Sauce... 183
Parmesan Artichokes 183
Glazed Beets 183
Hoisin Tofu.. 184
Bacon Brussels Sprouts 184
Balsamic Roasted Root Vegetables.. 184
Cranberry Sauce 185
Alfredo Green Bean Casserole 185
Peppercorn Artichoke Casserole 185
Spicy Salsa Red Beans 186
All Green Asparagus Casserole.. 186
Mustard Baked Potatoes 186
Molasses Baked Beans 187
Bacon Baked Beans 187
Ketchup Bean Stew... 187
Black Eyed Peas and Okra Stew 188
Green Onion Barley Risotto 188
Cumin Red Cabbage 188
Buttered Broccoli... 189
Herbed Broccoli Soufflé 189
Layered Carrot Pudding.. 189
Orange Marmalade Glazed Carrots.. 190
Butter Spring Vegetables 190
Carrot Spinach White Bean Stew 190

Chicken Recipes

Chicken Layered Potato Casserole 193
Creamy Chicken Stew 193
Orange Glazed Chicken 193
Spiced Chicken over Wild Rice 194
Chicken Garbanzo Curry 194
Chicken Barley Squash Salad 194
Chicken Cauliflower Gratin 195
Vegetable Braised Chicken 195
Parmesan Chicken 195
Thai Chicken Vegetable Medley 196
Cider Braised Chicken 196
Multigrain Chicken Pilaf 196
Chicken Sweet Potato Stew 197
Cream Cheese Chicken 197
Pulled Chicken 197
Cheesy Chicken 198
Garden Chicken Stew 198
Swiss Cheese Saucy Chicken 198
Garlicky Butter Roasted Chicken 199
Brown Sugar Glazed Chicken 199
Chicken Tikka Masala 199
Green Pea Chicken with Biscuit Topping 200
Creamy Chicken and Mushroom Pot Pie 200
Curry Braised Chicken 200
Bacon Chicken Stew 201
Soy Braised Chicken 201
Fennel Braised Chicken 202
Sesame Glazed Chicken 202
Sweet Glazed Chicken Drumsticks 202
Chicken Shrimp Jambalaya 203
Chicken Black Olive Stew 203
Chicken Stroganoff 203
Adobo Chicken with Bok Choy 204
Creole Chicken 204
Lemon Garlic Roasted Chicken 204
Paprika Chicken Wings 205
Spinach Chicken 205
Spiced Butter Chicken 205
Cordon Bleu Chicken 206
Red Wine Chicken and Mushroom Stew 206
Tomato Soy Glazed Chicken 206
Medley Vegetable Chicken Stew 207
BBQ Chicken 207
Spicy Hot Chicken Thighs 207
Cream Cheese Button Mushroom Chicken Stew 208

Thai Style Chicken...208
Chicken Taco Filling...208
Chicken Mole...209
White Chicken Cassoulet...209
Lemon Pepper Chicken..209
Honey Garlic Chicken Thighs with Snap Peas..210
Mexican Chicken Stew..210
Whole Orange Glazed Chicken...210
Red Salsa Chicken...211
Arroz Con Pollo..211
Cheesy Chicken Chili...211
Hoisin Chicken..212
Teriyaki Chicken...212
Jamaican Jerk Chicken...212
Greek Orzo Chicken..213
Mango Chicken Sauté..213
Artichoke Chicken Casserole...213
Italian Fennel Braised Chicken...214
Buffalo Chicken Drumsticks..214
Blue Cheese Chicken...214
Cashew Chicken...215
Turmeric Chicken Stew..215
Peanut Braised Chicken...215
Alfredo Chicken..216
Herbed Chicken and Mushrooms...216
Caramelized Onions Chicken Stew..216
Coq au Vin..217
Cacciatore Chicken...217
Pear Roasted Chicken..218
Deviled Chicken..218
Greek Style Chicken Ragout..218
Chicken and Sweet Potato Spiced Stew...219
Rich Chicken Rice Stew..219
Stout Carrot Chicken Stew..219
African Inspired Chicken Stew..220
Honey Orange Glazed Chicken Drumsticks...220
Chicken Ravioli In Tomato Sauce..220
Bourbon Braised Chicken..221
Mexican Shredded Chicken...221
Cheesy Chicken Burrito Filling...221
Coconut Ginger Chicken...222
Banana Chicken Curry..222
Lemon Garlic Whole Roasted Chicken...222
Tarragon Chicken..223
Balsamic Braised Chicken with Swiss Chard..223
Lemonade Chicken..223
Spice Rub Chicken..224
Chicken Pasta Bake...224

Lime Cilantro Chicken..224
Fiesta Chicken Stew...225
Honey Sesame Glazed Chicken...225
Veggie Medley Chicken Meatloaf 225
Creamy Salsa Verde Chicken...226
Cheesy Chicken Pasta..226
Korean BBQ Chicken 226

Pork Recipes

Red Salsa Pork Tenderloin...229
Sweet and Spicy Pulled Pork...229
Brazilian Pork Stew...229
BBQ Pork Ribs...230
Apple Bourbon Pork Chops...230
Red Wine Braised Pork Ribs 230
Onion Pork Tenderloin...231
Fennel Infused Pork Ham 231
Country Style Pork Ribs 231
Chili Verde...232
Mexican Pork Roast...232
Balsamic Roasted Pork 232
Pineapple Cranberry Pork Ham 233
Italian Style Pork Shoulder 233
Apple Butter Short Ribs...233
Ginger Beer Pork Ribs...234
Teriyaki Pork Tenderloin..234
Sauerkraut Cumin Pork 234
Herbed Roasted Pork 235
Chili BBQ Ribs..235
Lemon Roasted Pork Tenderloin..235
Sour Cream Pork Chops...236
Hawaiian Pork Roast..236
Black Bean Pork Stew..236
Honey Glazed Pork Ribs..237
Mango Flavored Pulled Pork 237
Maple Glazed Pork Tenderloin 237
Pork Sausage Stew...238
Harvest Pork Stew..238
Sweet Potato Pork Stew 238
Roasted Bell Pepper Pork Stew 239
Red Chile Pulled Pork..239
Blackberry Pork Tenderloin...239
Havana Style Pork Roast..240
Creamy Dijon Pork Shoulder...240
Marsala Pork Chops...240
Chipotle Pork Chili..241

Slow Cooked Pork in Tomato Sauce 241
Pork Sausage Ragu 241
Sweet and Sour Pork Chops 242
Pork Potato Stew 242
Tomato Sauce Pork Roast 242
Bacon Potato Stew 243
Miso Braised Pork 243
Red Bean Pork Stew 243
Smoked Ham and Lima Bean Stew 244
Spiced Plum Pork Chops 244
Green Enchilada Pork Roast 244
Navy Bean Stew 245
Ham Scalloped Potatoes 245
Ginger Slow Roasted Pork 245
Provencal Pork Stew 246
Smoky Pork Chili 246
Pork Cannellini Bean Stew 246
Curried Roasted Pork 247
Asian Style Pot Roast 247
French Onion Roasted Pork Chop 247
Cuban Pork Chops 248
Red Beans Rice 248
Thyme Flavored White Bean Pork Cassoulet 248
Apricot Glazed Gammon 249
Pork Chickpea Stew 249
Spiced Pork Belly 249
Veggie Medley Roasted Pork Tenderloin 250
Peanut Butter Pork Belly 250
Lemon Vegetable Pork Roast 250
Ham and Green Pea Stew 251
Hearty BBQ Pork Belly 251
Pork Taco Filling 251
Pork Belly over Smoky Sauerkraut 252
Red Cabbage Pork Stew 252
Cheddar Pork Casserole 252
Vietnamese Style Pork 253
Mushroom Pork Stew 253
Golden Maple Glazed Pork Chops 253
Autumn Pork Roast 254
Onion Pork Chops with Creamy Mustard Sauce 254
Szechuan Roasted Pork 254
Cola BBQ Pork Roast 255
Filipino Adobo Pork 255
Garlic Roasted Pork Belly 255
Sticky Glazed Pork Ribs 256
Kahlua Pulled Pork 256
Jerk Seasoning Pork Roast 256
Fruity Pork Tenderloin 257

Caribbean Sticky Pork Ribs...257
Pizza Pork Chops..257
Apple Cherry Pork Chops...258
Mango Chutney Pork Chops..258
Smoky Apple Butter Pork Chops...258
Roasted Rosemary Pork and Potatoes..259
Three Pepper Roasted Pork Tenderloin...259
Intense Mustard Pork Chops...259
Cuban Style Pork Roast over Simple Black Beans............................260
Honey Apple Pork Chops...260

Beef Recipes

Korean Beef Stew...263
Beef Salsa Chili...263
Caramelized Onion Beef Pot Roast...263
Italian Beef Spaghetti Sauce...264
Old Fashioned Beef Stew..264
French Onion Sandwich Filling..265
Layered Enchilada Casserole..265
Beef Roast with Shallots and Potatoes...265
Beef Roast with Shiitake Mushrooms..266
Tangy Italian Shredded Beef...266
Southern Beef Pot Roast...266
Beef Rice Stuffed Bell Peppers...267
Beef Zucchini Stew..267
Beef Sloppy Joes...267
BBQ Beef Brisket...268
Vegetable Beef Roast with Horseradish..268
Cowboy Beef..268
Sweet and Tangy Short Ribs...269
Hungarian Beef Goulash..269
Bavarian Beef Roast..269
Beef Stroganoff..270
Pepperoncini Beef Stew..270
Corned Beef with Sauerkraut..270
Mexican Braised Beef..271
Beef Cabbage Rolls...271
Bell Pepper Steak..271
Button Mushroom Beef Stew...272
The Ultimate Chili..272
Tomato Beef Stew..272
Beef Curry Stew...273
Beef Roast au Jus..273
Coffee Beef Roast..273
Root Vegetable Beef Stew...274
Beef Bolognese Sauce...274

Hamburger Beef Casserole 274
Texas Style Braised Beef 275
Mediterranean Beef Stew 275
Beef Three Bean Casserole 275
Garlicky Beef Pasta Sauce 276
Crouton Beef Stew 276
Swiss Steaks 277
Carne Guisada 277
Red Wine Onion Braised Beef 277
Beer Braised Beef 278
Cabbage Rice Beef Stew 278
Marinara Flank Steaks 278
Ground Beef BBQ 279
Beef Okra Tomato Stew 279
Beef Barbacoa 279
Caribe Pot Roast 280
Cajun Beef Stew 280
Everything But the Kitchen Sink Beef Stew 280
Stuffed Flank Steaks 281
Hominy Beef Chili 281
Mexican Beef Stuffed Bell Peppers 281
Beef Macaroni 282
Apple Corned Beef with Red Cabbage 282
Sweet Potato Shepherd's Pie 283
Chunky Beef Pasta Sauce 283
Hot Corned Beef 283
Mediterranean Beef Brisket 284
Sriracha Style Corned Beef 284
French Style Braised Beef Sirloin 284
Classic Osso Buco 285
Curried Beef Short Ribs 285
Beef Barley Stew 285
Beef Pot Roast with Turnip Greens 286
Gruyere Flank Steaks 286
Collard Green Feet Sauté 286
Autumn Red Beef Curry 287
Saffron Beef Tagine 287
Jalapeno Braised Beef Flank Steaks 287
Veal Paprikash 288
Curried Yogurt Braised Beef 288
Ginger Rump Roast 288
Garden Beef Stew 289
Roasted Garlic Shredded Beef 289
Beef Nacho Casserole 289
Bacon Wrapped Beef Tenderloin 290
Coffee Sriracha Roasted Beef 290
Hard Cider Beef Pot Roast 290
Tangy Pomegranate Beef Short Ribs 291

Asian Style Beef Short Ribs 291
Ginger Ale Beef Ribs 291
Rich Stout Beef Casserole 292
Five-Spice Beef Short Ribs 292
Fruity Veal Shanks 292
Beef Lentil Stew with Goat Cheese 293
Red Wine Braised Oxtail 293
Spiced Beef Tenderloin 293
Beef Strips with Egg Noodles 294
Fennel Osso Bucco 294
Apple Parsnip Beef Steaks 294
Hearty Beef Burry 295
Spicy Beef Ragu 295
Beef Broccoli Sauté 296
Jalapeno Mushroom Steaks 296
Herbed Beef Tenderloin 296
Kale White Bean Stew 297
Dijon Beef Stew 297
New Potato Beef Stew 297
Rosemary Garlic Beef Stew 298
Moroccan Beef Short Ribs 298
Cuban Flank Steaks 298
Oriental Beef Brisket 299

Dessert Recipes

Peach Cobbler 303
Lavender Blackberry Crumble 303
Raspberry Brownie Cake 303
Banana Chunk Cake 304
Apple Butter 304
Pineapple Upside Down Cake 304
Pure Berry Crumble 305
Apple Sour Cream Crostata 305
Cranberry Stuffed Apples 305
Autumnal Bread Pudding 306
Creamy Coconut Tapioca Pudding 306
Rich Chocolate Peanut Butter Cake 306
Black Forest Cake 307
One Bowl Chocolate Cake 307
Oat Topped Apples 307
Apple Cinnamon Brioche Pudding 308
Apple Cherry Cobbler 308
Nutty Pear Streusel Dessert 308
Pumpkin Croissant Pudding 309
Strawberry Fudgy Brownies 309
Caramel Pear Pudding Cake 309

Walnut Apple Crisp..310
Pumpkin Cheesecake..310
Lemon Berry Cake..310
Silky Chocolate Fondue...311
Orange Ginger Cheesecake..311
Mocha Chocolate Brioche Pudding..312
Chocolate Chips Peanut Butter Cake...312
White Chocolate Apricot Bread Pudding..312
Coconut Poached Pears...313
Chocolate Walnut Bread..313
Chocolate Pear Crumble..313
Ginger Fruit Compote..314
Gingerbread Cake..314
Egyptian Rice Pudding...314
Molten Chocolate Cake..315
Amarena Cherry Cola Cake..315
Crock Pot Crème Brulee...315
No Crust Lemon Cheesecake..316
Fudgy Peanut Butter Cake...316
Spiced Rice Pudding..316
Spiced Poached Pears..317
White Chocolate Apple Cake..317
Tiramisu Bread Pudding...317
Amaretti Cheesecake...318
Brandied Brioche Pudding..318
Vanilla Bean Caramel Custard...318
Pineapple Coconut Tapioca Pudding..319
Cardamom Coconut Rice Pudding..319
Rocky Road Chocolate Cake..319
Carrot Cake...320
Lemon Poppy Seed Cake...320
Peanut Butter Cheesecake...321
Ricotta Lemon Cake..321
Sour Cream Cheesecake..322
Chocolate Chip Brownies...322
Maple Roasted Pears...322
Apple Granola Crumble..323
Mixed Nuts Brownies...323
Turtle Cake..323
Peanut Butter Chocolate Chips Bars..324
Cream Cheese Brownies..324
Golden Raisin Brioche Pudding..324
Coconut Condensed Milk Custard..325
Peppermint Chocolate Clusters..325
Buttery Chocolate Cake...325
S'Mores Fondue...326
Double Chocolate Cake..326
Saucy Apple and Pears..326

Blueberry Dumpling Pie...327
Dried Fruit Rice Pudding..327
Hazelnut Liqueur Cheesecake...327
S'Mores Brownies...328
Chai Poached Pears..328
Sticky Cinnamon Rolls...328
Crustless Peach Pie..329
Monkey Bread...329
Pumpkin Streusel Cake..330
Spiced Raisins Tapioca Pudding...330
Coconut Blueberry Crumble..330
Blueberry Preserve...331
Mango Tapioca Pudding...331
No Crust Lemon Cheesecake...331
Upside Down Banana Cake..332
Dulce de Leche...332
Fudge Raspberry Cake...332
Gluten Free Blueberry Cake..333
Caramel Peanut Butter Cheesecake...333
Fudgy Raspberry Chocolate Bread Pudding..............................333
Pear and Apple Butter..334
Cinnamon Coffee Cake..334
Spiced Applesauce Cake..334
Red Velvet Brioche Pudding..335
Caramel Mocha Cheesecake...335
Butterscotch Self Saucing Pudding..336
Creamed Rice Pudding...336
Lemon and Lime Quick Pudding...336
Dark Cherry Chocolate Cake...337
Overnight Plum Pudding..337
Golden Syrup Pudding...337
Chocolate Chip Cookie Bars...338
Browned Butter Pumpkin Cheesecake.......................................338
Butterscotch Cake..338
Rich Bread Pudding...339
Dulce de Leche Chocolate Pie..339
Grand Marnier Soufflé...340
White Chocolate Cheesecake Soufflé...340
Chocolate Mocha Bread Pudding...340
Chunky Pumpkin Cake...341
Coconut Oatmeal Brownies..341
Swirled Peanut Butter Cake..341
Lemon Buttermilk Cake...342
Apple Dump Cake...342
Butter Lime Cake..342
Caramel Apple Crisp..343
Pear Blueberry Cake..343
Amaretto Pear Butter...343

Cherry Dump Cake...344
Cardamom Carrot Cake..344
Hot Fudge Chocolate Cake...344
Cinnamon Rolls..345
Slow Cooker Fudge..345
Spiced Plum Butter...346
Slow Cooked Chocolate Cream..346
S'Mores Baked Sweet Potatoes..346
Sweet Potato Chocolate Cake..347
Dark Chocolate Almond Cake..347
Honey Yogurt Cake...347
One Large Vanilla Pancake..348
Lemon Bars..348
Hazelnut Crumble Cheesecake...348
Mexican Chocolate Cake...349
Boozy Bread Pudding...349
Banana Walnut Cake..350
Raspberry Poached Pears..350
Saucy Peach and Apple Dessert...350
Turtle Upside Down Cake..351
Indian Almond Pudding..351
Triple Chocolate Brownies...351
Pepita Pumpkin Cake...352
Pumpkin Bread..352
Cinnamon Banana Bread..353
Caramel Sauce Poached Pears..353
Caramel Peach Crisp..353
Grain Free Chocolate Cake...354
Gluten Free Coconut Cake..354
Cranberry Walnut Bread..354
Tipsy Pumpkin Bread Pudding..355
Nutella Bread Pudding..355
Pear Walnut Cake...355
Chocolate Chip Cookie Bars...356

Beverages

Mulled Wine...359
Cranberry Spiced tea...359
Rosemary Mulled Cider..359
Gingerbread Hot Chocolate..360
Gingerbread Mocha Drink..360
Salted Caramel Milk Steamer..360
Apple Chai Tea..361
Ginger Pumpkin Latte..361
Hot Caramel Apple Drink..361
Spiced White Chocolate..362

Apple Bourbon Punch..362
Maple Bourbon Mulled Cider..362
Autumn Punch..363
Hot Spicy Apple Cider...363
Boozy Hot Chocolate...363
Vanilla Latte...364
Apple Ginger Delight...364
Eggnog Latte..364
Citrus Bourbon Cocktail..365
Lemonade Cider...365
Spiced Pumpkin Toddy..365
Raspberry Hot Chocolate...366
Nutella Hot Chocolate...366
Mulled Cranberry Punch..366
Citrus Green Tea..367
Whiskey Pumpkin Drink..367
Mulled Pink Wine..367
Black Tea Punch...368
Cherry Cider...368
Chocolate Hot Coffee...368
Spiced Coffee...369
Kahlua Coffee..369
Peachy Cider..369
Pomegranate Cider...370
Ginger Tea Drink..370
Spiced Lemon Cider Punch..370
Brandied Mulled Wine...371
Hot Whiskey Sour..371
Caramel Hot Chocolate..371
Hot Marmalade Cider...372
Peppermint Hot Chocolate...372
Orange Brandy Hot Toddy...372
Spicy Mulled Red Wine...373
Lemon Lime Jasmine Tea..373
Party Cranberry Punch...373
Caramel Cider..374
Hot Cranberry Toddy...374
The Ultimate Hot Chocolate..374
Buttered Hot Rum..375
Irish Cream Coffee..375

Conclusion..**377**

1 INTRODUCTION

Although decades ago cooking was a necessity, nowadays food is available everywhere, from huge supermarkets that display a wide range of products, to small restaurants and pubs found at every corner of the street. And in these conditions, cooking is being looked at like something that takes too much time and sometimes may not worth it. But why does this happen?! When have we lost the pleasure of cooking?! It does make me worry sometimes because there's plenty of people out there who prefer to buy any super processed food than take some time and cook for them and their families every day. And that is such a shame because on the long run, home cooking is healthier, cheaper and it has the ability to create emotions and memories. I still remember what food my grandmother used to spoil me with or what my mother used to make me when I was ill. Food brings people together around the table to share the same meal, talk about their day and connect with each other and for that reason I believe home cooking should be an important part of our lives!

Nothing compares to a freshly made stew or a rich soup or even a properly made dessert, that's for sure! And that is when slow cooking steps in, helping you to balance the lack of time with the desire of providing your family with a healthy, tasty, delicious meal that is made with love. And although it has a fancy name, a slow cooker is not just another kitchen gadget that you will buy and store in your cupboards without using, trust me! It will become an important part of your life, helping you cook a wide range of dishes, from simple soups to hearty stews, delicious appetizers and amazing desserts or tasty beverages. So keep reading and learn why a slow cooker is important in a household, how to choose the best one, how to use it and read 1001 amazing recipes designed to fit everyone's tastes!

Everything You Need to Know About Slow Cookers

A slow cooker is an electric machine consisting of a ceramic pot, either round or oval, covered with a lid, usually made of glass so you can see through. The machine is designed in such way that it can be left working while you are out. A small electric current evenly heats the ceramic pot so the food inside gets cooked. Although some people worry that the electricity in the pot may cause harm to their houses, do know that the electrical unit has such a low power that it is safe to leave it on while out. In fact, a lamp may have a higher power than a crock pot, that low and safe it is!

The slow cooker, also known as a crock pot, was invented in the 1936 when Irving Naxon submitted an application for a food heating equipment. One year later he received the patent and named his device the Naxon Beanery. The idea of the pot came to Naxon after talking to his mother; she told him about a technique of re-heating the food that took hours and hours so he thought it might be a good idea to come up with a device that does it by itself, a device that would help his mom re-heat his favorite dish and many other people to do the same thing. In the 1970s, Rival bought the patent from Naxon and re-named it the crock pot. Interesting enough, the advertisement of the first crockpot said: "cooks all day while the cook is away" – enough said!

Although safe, there are a few rules that need to be followed when using a slow cooker:

- Don't fill the container of the pot over the 2/3 full mark.
- During cooking, keep the lid sealed and in straight position, making sure the steam remain trapped inside and cook the food accordingly.

- Test the crock pot from time to time to make sure the pot is working properly and the unit heats correctly.
- When testing the crock pot, fill it 2/3 with water and cook for 8 hours then measure the temperature – a temperature higher than 185F means the heating element is as brand new, but a lower temperature may indicate a fault.
- Don't spill liquids outside the ceramic insert. If it does happen, clean carefully with a cloth and allow to dry before turning the pot on, making sure the electrical unit hasn't been damaged.
- Don't use the slow cooker to re-heat the food – re-heating food changes its properties and may allow bacteria to form, especially with the low temperature that a slow cooker has.
- Avoid cleaning the pot with abrasive solutions or chemicals.
- Soak food the night before if needed – beans and grains cook easier and quicker if they have been soaked in water the night before.
- Clean the pot right after cooking, otherwise food will start to dry out and bacteria may form.
- Due to the sealed lid, liquid barely evaporates, therefore not much liquid is needed in the recipes.
- If you want to thicken the food, you have to roll the ingredients through flour or cornstarch before slow cooking them.

The Benefits of a Crock Pot

Economical – the slow and long cooking time allows you to use cheaper cuts of meat or you can even add less meat and more veggies for a healthier dish.

You don't need as much fat – cooking in a slow cooker doesn't require any additional fat because the food, if it has enough moisture, won't stick to the bottom of the pot. As for taste, fattier doesn't mean better in most cases – the slow cooking time allows flavors to develop so fat is not needed to enhance the taste

The food is tastier – the slow cooking time allows flavors to develop properly without turning mushy or fall apart.

You can leave it unsupervised – you can turn the pot on just before going on then come back home to a bowl of hot soup or warm stew without worrying about safety or taste. You can leave it on while you sleep. How amazing would it be to wake up to a bowl of warm, rich oatmeal or any other breakfast dish?!

You don't need special cooking skills – all you need to do when it comes to slow cooking, is to chop a few ingredients and throw them in the pot then allow it to do its magic for a few hours.

You are in total control of what you're cooking, when, with what ingredients and for how long – the versatility of slow cooking comes in handy every single day!

It saves you time and effort – for once, cooking can stop being a chore and become a pleasure because it's done incredibly easy with a slow cooker.

What to Cook in a Crock Pot

Crock pots can be used for a wide range of recipes, as proven in this book. Hot soups, rich stews, delicious appetizers and amazing desserts are just a few of the dishes that make the crock pot such an amazing and versatile kitchen gadget.

By definition, slow cookers allow you to use any ingredient, but the most common one seems to be meat, being known the fact that meat usually has a more complex cooking process and sometimes can be tough and packed with fibers instead of juicy and tender. The crock pot takes care of that aspect and cooks the meat in such way that it becomes melt-in-your-mouth. While most recipes call for simply throwing the meat in the pot, some ask you to first fry the meat on all sides – this is done to add flavor to the dish and it's not compulsory, but recommended. When cooking meat, you need to remember to add some sort of moisture to the pot in order to keep the piece of meat juicy and tender.

Cooking vegetables is easier than cooking meat, although it does take more prepping time. Usually vegetables need to be peeled and chopped or diced, but it's a simple and straight forward task, nothing that can't be done in a few spare minutes. Also, don't forget that you can find plenty of mixed frozen veggies at the store to make your life easier and your cooking richer!

Apart from meat and veggies, you can also cook grains, sea food, spreads and dips in a crock pot, but desserts need to have a category of their own as well. Chocolate cake, bread puddings or tapioca pudding have never been easier and tastier!

How to Choose a Slow Cooker

Slow cookers nowadays are incredibly cheap and reliable and there's just two things to keep in mind when buying one: the size and the price.

Slow cookers come in various sizes, but they have been established by counting the volume found in the pot. To know if it's the right pot, you need to consider how many servings you will be sending out to the table and from there, find the right crock pot for you. For instance, a 2-quarter slow cooker is enough for 2 people, but not large enough for 4 and the list can go on. I'd recommend having a small slow cooker and a larger one for those times when you have guest over or need to cook larger quantities of food.

In terms of money, slow cookers are incredibly cheap nowadays. It doesn't even matter what brand it is because the conception nowadays is buying from individuals and not from brands. What this means it that the reviews of a product talk more about the product itself than any seller might. In addition to this, crock pots have the same basic principles of working so it doesn't really matter if it's a well-known brand or one you've never heard of.

Appetizers

Candied Kielbasa

Time: 6 1/4 hours   Servings: 8

Ingredients:
2 pounds kielbasa sausages
1/2 cup brown sugar
1 cup BBQ sauce

1 teaspoon prepared horseradish
1/2 teaspoon black pepper
1/4 teaspoon cumin powder

Directions:
Combine all the ingredients in a slow cooker, adding salt if needed.
Cook on low settings for 6 hours.
Serve the kielbasa warm or chilled.

Bacon Wrapped Chicken Livers

Time: 3 1/2 hours   Servings: 6

Ingredients:
2 pounds chicken livers

Bacon slices as needed

Directions:
Wrap each chicken liver in one slice of bacon and place all the livers in your crock pot.
Cook on high heat for 3 hours.
Serve warm or chilled.

Cocktail Meatballs

Time: 6 1/2 hours   Servings: 10

Ingredients:
2 pounds ground pork
1 pound ground beef
4 garlic cloves, minced
1 shallot, chopped
1 egg
1/4 cup breadcrumbs
2 tablespoons chopped parsley
1 tablespoon chopped cilantro

1/2 teaspoon chili powder
2 tablespoons cranberry sauce
1 cup BBQ sauce
1/2 cup tomato sauce
1 teaspoon red wine vinegar
1 bay leaf
Salt and pepper to taste

Directions:
Combine the cranberry sauce, BBQ sauce, tomato sauce and vinegar, as well as bay leaf, salt and pepper in your slow cooker.
In a bowl, mix the two types of meat, garlic, shallot, egg, breadcrumbs, parsley, cilantro and chili powder. Add salt and pepper to taste.
Form small meatballs and place them all in the sauce in the slow cooker.
Cover and cook on low settings for 6 hours.
Serve the meatballs warm or chilled with cocktail skewers.

SAUSAGE DIP

Time: 6 1/4 hours   Servings: 8

Ingredients:

1 pound fresh pork sausages   1 can diced tomatoes
1 pound spicy pork sausages   2 poblano peppers, chopped
1 cup cream cheese

Directions:

Combine all the ingredients in a crock pot.
Cook on low settings for 6 hours.
Serve warm or chilled.

CHEESY BEEF DIP

Time: 3 1/4 hours   Servings: 8

Ingredients:

2 pounds ground beef   1/2 cup white wine
1 pound grated Cheddar   1 poblano pepper, chopped
1/2 cup cream cheese

Directions:

Combine all the ingredients in a crock pot.
Cook on high settings for 3 hours.
Serve preferably warm.

TROPICAL MEATBALLS

Time: 7 1/2 hours   Servings: 20

Ingredients:

1 can pineapple chunks (keep the juices)   1 pound ground beef
2 poblano peppers, chopped   4 garlic clove, minced
1/4 cup brown sugar   1 teaspoon dried basil
2 tablespoons soy sauce   1 egg
2 tablespoons cornstarch   1/4 cup breadcrumbs
1 tablespoon lemon juice   Salt and pepper to taste
2 pounds ground pork

Directions:

Mix the pineapple, poblano peppers, brown sugar, soy sauce, cornstarch and lemon juice in a slow cooker.
Combine the ground meat, garlic, basil, egg and breadcrumbs in a bowl. Add salt and pepper to taste and mix well.
Form small meatballs and place them in the sauce.
Cover and cook on low settings for 7 hours.
Serve the meatballs warm or chilled.

Glazed Peanuts

Time: 2 1/4 hours   Servings: 8

Ingredients:

2 pounds raw, whole peanuts
1/4 cup brown sugar
1/2 teaspoon garlic powder
2 tablespoons salt

1 tablespoon Cajun seasoning
1/2 teaspoon red pepper flakes
1/4 cup coconut oil

Directions:

Combine all the ingredients in your slow cooker.
Cover and cook on high settings for 2 hours.
Serve chilled.

Spiced Buffalo Wings

Time: 8 1/4 hours   Servings: 8

Ingredients:

4 pounds chicken wings
1 cup BBQ sauce
1/4 cup butter, melted
1 tablespoon Worcestershire sauce
1 teaspoon dried oregano
1 teaspoon dried basil

1 teaspoon onion powder
1 teaspoon garlic powder
1/2 teaspoon cumin powder
1/2 teaspoon cinnamon powder
1 teaspoon hot sauce
1 teaspoon salt

Directions:

Combine all the ingredients in a slow cooker.
Mix until the wings are evenly coated.
Cook on low settings for 8 hours.
Serve warm or chilled.

Ham and Swiss Cheese Dip

Time: 4 1/4 hours   Servings: 6

Ingredients:

1 pound ham, diced
1 cup cream cheese
1 can condensed cream of mushroom soup

1 can condensed onion soup
2 cups grated Swiss cheese
1/2 teaspoon chili powder

Directions:

Combine all the ingredients in a slow cooker.
Cook on low settings for 4 hours.
Serve the dip preferably warm.

Mexican Dip

Time: 4 1/4 hours

Servings: 10

Ingredients:

2 pounds ground beef
1 can black beans, drained
1 can diced tomatoes
2 poblano peppers, chopped

1/2 teaspoon chili powder
2 cups grated Cheddar cheese
Salt and pepper to taste

Directions:

Combine all the ingredients in a slow cooker.
Adjust the taste with salt and pepper if needed.
Cook on high settings for 4 hours.
The dip is best served warm.

Spanish Chorizo Dip

Time: 6 1/4 hours

Servings: 8

Ingredients:

8 chorizo links, diced
1 can diced tomatoes
1 chili pepper, chopped

1 cup cream cheese
2 cups grated Cheddar cheese
1/4 cup white wine

Directions:

Combine all the ingredients in your slow cooker.
Cook the dip on low settings for 6 hours.
Serve the dip warm.

Asian Marinated Mushrooms

Time: 8 1/4 hours

Servings: 8

Ingredients:

2 pounds mushrooms
1 cup soy sauce
1 cup water

1/2 cup brown sugar
1/4 cup rice vinegar
1/2 teaspoon chili powder

Directions:

Combine all the ingredients in your slow cooker.
Cover the crock pot and cook on low settings for 8 hours.
Allow to cool in the pot before serving.

Nacho Sauce

Time: 6 1/4 hours

Servings: 12

Ingredients:

2 pounds ground beef
2 tablespoons Mexican seasoning
1 teaspoon chili powder
1 can diced tomatoes

2 shallots, chopped
4 garlic cloves, minced
1 can sweet corn, drained
2 cups grated Cheddar cheese

Directions:

Combine all the ingredients in your slow cooker.
Cook on low settings for 6 hours.
This dip is best served warm.

Five-Spiced Chicken Wings

Time: 7 1/4 hours

Servings: 8

Ingredients:

1/2 cup plum sauce
1/2 cup BBQ sauce
2 tablespoons butter
1 tablespoon five-spice powder

1 teaspoon salt
1/2 teaspoon chili powder
4 pounds chicken wings

Directions:

Combine the plum sauce and BBQ sauce, as well as butter, five-spice, salt and chili powder in a crock pot.
Add the chicken wings and mix well until well coated.
Cover and cook on low settings fir 7 hours.
Serve warm or chilled.

Queso Verde Dip

Time: 4 1/4 hours

Servings: 12

Ingredients:

1 pound ground chicken
2 shallots, chopped
2 tablespoons olive oil
2 cups salsa verde
1 cup cream cheese
2 cups grated Cheddar

2 poblano peppers, chopped
1 tablespoon Worcestershire sauce
4 garlic cloves, minced
1/4 cup chopped cilantro
Salt and pepper to taste

Directions:

Combine all the ingredients in your slow cooker.
Add salt and pepper to taste and cook on low heat for 4 hours.
The dip is best served warm.

PARTY MIX

Time: 1 3/4 hours

Servings: 20

Ingredients:

4 cups cereals
4 cups crunchy cereals
2 cups mixed nuts
1 cup mixed seeds
1/2 cup butter, melted

2 tablespoons Worcestershire sauce
1 teaspoon hot sauce
1 teaspoon salt
1/2 teaspoon cumin powder

Directions:

Combine all the ingredients in your slow cooker and toss around until evenly coated.
Cook on high settings for 1 1/2 hours.
Serve the mix chilled.

CARAMELIZED ONION DIP

Time: 4 1/2 hours

Servings: 12

Ingredients:

4 red onions, sliced
2 tablespoons butter
1 tablespoon canola oil
1 cup beef stock
1 teaspoon dried thyme

1/2 cup white wine
2 garlic cloves, chopped
2 cups grated Swiss cheese
1 tablespoon cornstarch
Salt and pepper to taste

Directions:

Heat the butter and oil in a skillet. Add the onions and cook over medium flame until the onions begin to caramelize.
Transfer the onions in your slow cooker and add the remaining ingredients.
Season with salt and pepper and cook on low settings for 4 hours.
Serve the dip warm with vegetable sticks or your favorite crunchy snacks.

MOLASSES LIME MEATBALLS

Time: 8 1/4 hours

Servings: 10

Ingredients:

3 pounds ground beef
2 garlic cloves, minced
1 shallot, chopped
1/2 cup oat flour
1/2 teaspoon cumin powder
1/2 teaspoon chili powder
1 egg

Salt and pepper to taste
1/2 cup molasses
1/4 cup soy sauce
2 tablespoons lime juice
1/2 cup beef stock
1 tablespoon Worcestershire sauce

Directions:

Combine the molasses, soy sauce, lime juice, stock and Worcestershire sauce in your slow cooker.

In a bowl, mix the ground beef, garlic, shallot, oat flour, cumin powder, chili powder, egg, salt and pepper and mix well
Form small balls and place them in the sauce.
Cover the pot and cook on low settings for 8 hours.
Serve the meatballs warm or chilled.

BOURBON GLAZED SAUSAGES

Time: 4 1/4 hours   Servings: 10

Ingredients:
3 pounds small sausage links   1/4 cup maple syrup
1/2 cup apricot preserves   2 tablespoons Bourbon

Directions:
Combine all the ingredients in your slow cooker. Cover with its lid and cook on low settings for 4 hours.
Serve the glazed sausages warm or chilled, preferably with cocktail sticks.

SWEET CORN CRAB DIP

Time: 2 1/4 hours   Servings: 20

Ingredients:
2 tablespoons butter   1 cup sour cream
1 cup canned sweet corn, drained   1 can crab meat, drained
2 red bell peppers, cored and diced   1 teaspoon Worcestershire sauce
2 garlic cloves, chopped   1 teaspoon hot sauce
2 poblano peppers, chopped   1 cup grated Cheddar cheese

Directions:
Mix all the ingredients in your slow cooker. Cover the pot with its lid and cook on low settings for 2 hours.
Serve the dip warm or chilled.

BLUE CHEESE CHICKEN WINGS

Time: 7 1/4 hours   Servings: 8

Ingredients:
4 pounds chicken wings   1 tablespoon Worcestershire sauce
1/2 cup buffalo sauce   1 cup sour cream
1/2 cup spicy tomato sauce   2 oz. blue cheese, crumbled
1 tablespoon tomato paste   1 thyme sprig
2 tablespoons apple cider vinegar

Directions:
Combine the buffalo sauce, tomato sauce, vinegar, Worcestershire sauce, sour cream, blue cheese and thyme in a slow cooker. Add the chicken wings and toss them until evenly coated.
Cook on low settings for 7 hours.
Serve the chicken wings preferably warm.

ROSEMARY POTATOES

Time: 2 1/4 hours   Servings: 8

Ingredients:
4 pounds small new potatoes
1 rosemary sprig, chopped
1 shallot, sliced
2 garlic cloves, chopped

1 teaspoon smoked paprika
1 teaspoon salt
1/4 teaspoon ground black pepper
1/4 cup chicken stock

Directions:
Combine all the ingredients in your slow cooker.
Cover with its lid and cook on high settings for 2 hours.
Serve the potatoes warm or chilled.

CREAMY SPINACH DIP

Time: 2 1/4 hours   Servings: 30

Ingredients:
1 can crab meat, drained
1 pound fresh spinach, chopped
2 shallots, chopped
2 jalapeno peppers, chopped
1 cup grated Parmesan
1/2 cup whole milk

1 cup sour cream
1 cup cream cheese
1 cup grated Cheddar cheese
1 tablespoon sherry vinegar
2 garlic cloves, chopped

Directions:
Combine all the ingredients in your slow cooker.
Cover with its lid and cook on high settings for 2 hours.
Serve the spinach dip warm or chilled with vegetable stick or your favorite salty snacks.

CHEESY BACON DIP

Time: 4 1/4 hours   Servings: 20

Ingredients:
1 sweet onions, chopped
1 teaspoon Worcestershire sauce
1 teaspoon Dijon mustard
1 cup cream cheese

10 bacon slices, chopped
1 cup grated Gruyere
1/2 cup whole milk
Salt and pepper to taste

Directions:
Combine all the ingredients in a slow cooker.
Adjust the taste with salt and pepper and cover with its lid.
Cook on low settings for 4 hours.
Serve the dip warm or chilled with vegetable sticks, biscuits or other salty snacks.

ARTICHOKE DIP

Time: 6 1/4 hours   Servings: 20

Ingredients:

2 sweet onions, chopped
1 red chili, chopped
2 garlic cloves, chopped
1 jar artichoke hearts, drained and chopped

1 cup cream cheese
1 cup heavy cream
2 oz. blue cheese, crumbled
2 tablespoons chopped cilantro

Directions:

Mix the onions, chili, garlic, artichoke hearts, cream cheese, heavy cream and blue cheese in a slow cooker. Cook on low settings for 6 hours. When done, stir in the cilantro and serve the dip warm or chilled.

ZESTY LAMB MEATBALLS

Time: 7 1/4 hours   Servings: 10

Ingredients:

3 pounds ground lamb
1 shallot, chopped
2 garlic cloves, minced
1 tablespoon lemon zest
1/4 teaspoon five-spice powder
1/2 teaspoon cumin powder
1/4 teaspoon cumin powder
1/4 teaspoon chili powder

1/2 cup raisins, chopped
1 teaspoon dried mint
Salt and pepper to taste
2 cups tomato sauce
1 lemon, juiced
1 bay leaf
1 thyme sprig
1 red chili, chopped

Directions:

Mix the tomato sauce, lemon juice, bay leaf, thyme sprig and red chili in your slow cooker. Combine the remaining ingredients in a bowl and mix well. Season with salt and pepper and give it a good mix. Form small balls and place them in the sauce. Cover with its lid and cook on low settings for 7 hours. Serve the meatballs warm or chilled.

CHEESE AND BEER FONDUE

Time: 2 1/4 hours   Servings: 10

Ingredients:

4 tablespoons butter
1 shallot, chopped
2 garlic cloves, minced
2 tablespoons all-purpose flour
2 poblano peppers, chopped

1 cup milk
1 cup light beer
2 cups grated Cheddar
1/2 teaspoon chili powder

Directions:

Melt the butter in a saucepan and stir in the shallot and garlic. Sauté for 2 minutes then add the flour and cook for 2 additional minutes. Stir in the milk and cook until thickened, about 5 minutes. Pour the mixture in your slow cooker and stir in the remaining ingredients. Cook on high settings for 2 hours and serve the fondue warm with biscuits or other salty snacks.

CHILI CHICKEN WINGS

Time: 7 1/4 hours

Servings: 8

Ingredients:

4 pounds chicken wings
1/4 cup maple syrup
1 teaspoon garlic powder
1 teaspoon chili powder
2 tablespoons balsamic vinegar

1 tablespoon Dijon mustard
1 teaspoon Worcestershire sauce
1/2 cup tomato sauce
1 teaspoon salt

Directions:

Combine the chicken wings and the remaining ingredients in a slow cooker.
Toss around until evenly coated and cook on low settings for 7 hours.
Serve the chicken wings warm or chilled.

CHIPOTLE BBQ MEATBALLS

Time: 7 1/2 hours

Servings: 10

Ingredients:

3 pounds ground pork
2 garlic cloves, minced
2 shallots, chopped
2 chipotle peppers, chopped

Salt and pepper to taste
2 cups BBQ sauce
1/4 cup cranberry sauce
1 bay leaf

Directions:

Mix the ground pork, garlic, shallots, chipotle peppers, salt and pepper in a bowl.
Combine the BBQ sauce, cranberry sauce, bay leaf, salt and pepper in your slow cooker.
Form small meatballs and drop them in the sauce.
Cover the pot with its lid and cook on low settings for 7 hours.
Serve the meatballs warm or chilled with cocktail skewers or toothpicks.

CHIPOTLE BBQ SAUSAGE BITES

Time: 2 1/4 hours

Servings: 10

Ingredients:

3 pounds small smoked sausages
1 cup BBQ sauce
2 chipotle peppers in adobo sauce

1 tablespoon tomato paste
1/4 cup white wine
Salt and pepper to taste

Directions:

Combine all the ingredients in your slow cooker.
Add salt and pepper if needed and cover with a lid.
Cook on high settings for 2 hours.
Serve the sausage bites warm or chilled.

Cheesy Chicken Bites

Time: 6 1/4 hours

Servings: 10

Ingredients:

4 chicken breasts, cut into bite-size cubes
1/4 cup all-purpose flour
Salt and pepper to taste
1 cup cream cheese

2 roasted red bell peppers
1 cup shredded mozzarella
1/4 teaspoon chili powder

Directions:

Mix the cream cheese, bell peppers, chili powder, salt and pepper in a blender and pulse until smooth.
Pour the mixture in your slow cooker and add the remaining ingredients.
Cook on low settings for 6 hours.
Serve the chicken bites warm or chilled.

Stuffed Artichokes

Time: 6 1/2 hours

Servings: 6

Ingredients:

6 fresh artichokes
6 anchovy fillets, chopped
4 garlic cloves, minced
2 tablespoons olive oil

1 cup breadcrumbs
1 tablespoon chopped parsley
Salt and pepper to taste
1/4 cup white wine

Directions:

Cut the stem of each artichoke so that it sits flat on your chopping board then cut the top off and trim the outer leaves, cleaning the center as well. In a bowl, mix the anchovy fillets, garlic, olive oil, breadcrumbs and parsley. Add salt and pepper to taste. Top each artichoke with breadcrumb mixture and rub it well into the leaves. Place the artichokes in your slow cooker and pour in the white wine. Cook on low settings for 6 hours. Serve the artichokes warm or chilled.

Pork Ham Dip

Time: 6 1/4 hours

Servings: 20

Ingredients:

2 cups diced ham
1 pound ground pork
1 shallot, chopped
2 garlic cloves, chopped
1 teaspoon Dijon mustard

1 cup tomato sauce
1/2 cup chili sauce
1/2 cup cranberry sauce
Salt and pepper to taste

Directions:

Heat a skillet over medium flame and add the ground pork. Cook for 5 minutes, stirring often.
Transfer the ground pork in a slow cooker and add the remaining ingredients.
Adjust the taste with salt and pepper and cook on low settings for 6 hours.
Serve the dip warm or chilled.

HONEY GLAZED CHICKEN DRUMSTICKS

Time: 7 1/4 hours   Servings: 8

Ingredients:

3 pounds chicken drumsticks
1/4 cup soy sauce
1/4 cup honey
1 teaspoon rice vinegar

1/2 teaspoon sesame oil
2 tablespoons tomato paste
1/2 teaspoon dried Thai basil

Directions:

Combine all the ingredients in your slow cooker and toss them around until the drumsticks are evenly coated.
Cover the pot with its lid and cook on low settings for 7 hours.
Serve the chicken drumsticks warm or chilled.

CRANBERRY SAUCE MEATBALLS

Time: 7 1/2 hours   Servings: 12

Ingredients:

3 pounds ground pork
1 pound ground turkey
1 egg
1/2 cup breadcrumbs
1 shallot, chopped
1/2 teaspoon ground cloves

Salt and pepper to taste
2 cups cranberry sauce
1 cup BBQ sauce
1 teaspoon hot sauce
1 thyme sprig

Directions:

Mix the ground pork, turkey, egg, breadcrumbs, shallot, ground cloves, salt and pepper and mix well.
In the meantime, combine the cranberry sauce, BBQ sauce, hot sauce and thyme sprig in your slow cooker.
Form small meatballs and drop them in the sauce. Cook on low settings for 7 hours.
Serve the meatballs warm or chilled.

CHEESEBURGER DIP

Time: 6 1/4 hours   Servings: 20

Ingredients:

2 pounds ground beef
1 tablespoon canola oil
2 sweet onions, chopped
4 garlic cloves, chopped
1/2 cup tomato sauce

1 tablespoon Dijon mustard
2 tablespoons pickle relish
1 cup shredded processed cheese
1 cup grated Cheddar

Directions:

Heat the canola oil in a skillet and stir in the ground beef. Sauté for 5 minutes then add the meat in your slow cooker.
Stir in the remaining ingredients and cover with the pot's lid. Cook on low settings for 6 hours.
The dip is best served warm.

Bacon Crab Dip

Time: 2 1/4 hours   Servings: 20

Ingredients:

1 pound bacon, diced
1 cup cream cheese
1/2 cup grated Parmesan cheese
1 teaspoon Worcestershire sauce

1 teaspoon Dijon mustard
1 can crab meat, drained and shredded
1 teaspoon hot sauce

Directions:

Heat a skillet over medium flame and add the bacon. Sauté for 5 minutes until fat begins to drain out.
Transfer the bacon in a slow cooker.
Stir in the remaining ingredients and cook on high settings for 2 hours.
Serve the dip warm or chilled.

Curried Chicken Wings

Time: 7 1/4 hours   Servings: 10

Ingredients:

4 pounds chicken wings
1 cup tomato sauce
1/4 cup red curry paste
1/2 cup coconut milk

2 shallots, chopped
1/2 teaspoon dried basil
Salt and pepper to taste

Directions:

Combine all the ingredients in a slow cooker and toss around until evenly coated.
Adjust the taste with salt and pepper and cook on low settings for 7 hours.
Serve the chicken wings warm or chilled.

Wild Mushroom Dip

Time: 4 1/4 hours   Servings: 20

Ingredients:

1 pound wild mushrooms, chopped
1 can condensed cream of mushroom soup
1 cup white wine
1 cup cream cheese
1 cup heavy cream

1/2 cup grated Parmesan
1 teaspoon dried tarragon
1/2 teaspoon dried oregano
1/2 teaspoon ground black pepper
Salt and pepper to taste

Directions:

Combine all the ingredients in your slow cooker.
Adjust the taste with salt and pepper and cook on low settings for 4 hours.
Serve the dip warm or chilled.

MEDITERRANEAN DIP

Time: 6 1/4 hours   Servings: 20

Ingredients:

2 tablespoons canola oil
1 pound ground beef
2 shallots, chopped
2 garlic cloves, chopped
4 ripe tomatoes, peeled and diced
1/2 cup Kalamata olives, pitted and chopped

1/2 cup black olives, pitted and chopped
1/2 teaspoon dried oregano
1 teaspoon dried basil
1/4 cup white wine
1/2 cup tomato sauce
Salt and pepper to taste

Directions:

Heat the oil in a skillet and stir in the beef. Cook for 5 minutes then add the shallots and garlic and cook for 5 additional minutes.

Transfer the mixture in your slow cooker and add the remaining ingredients.

Season with salt and pepper and cook on low settings for 6 hours.

Serve the dip warm or chilled.

BACON NEW POTATOES

Time: 3 1/4 hours   Servings: 6

Ingredients:

3 pounds new potatoes, washed and halved
12 slices bacon, chopped
2 tablespoons white wine

Salt and pepper to taste
1 rosemary sprig

Directions:

Place the potatoes, wine and rosemary in your slow cooker.

Add salt and pepper to taste and top with chopped bacon.

Cook on high settings for 3 hours.

Serve the potatoes warm.

BEAN QUESO

Time: 6 1/4 hours   Servings: 10

Ingredients:

1 can black beans, drained
1 cup chopped green chiles
1/2 cup red salsa
1 teaspoon dried oregano

1/2 teaspoon cumin powder
1 cup light beer
1 1/2 cups grated Cheddar
Salt and pepper to taste

Directions:

Combine the beans, chiles, oregano, cumin, salsa, beer and cheese in your slow cooker.

Add salt and pepper as needed and cook on low settings for 6 hours.

Serve the bean queso warm.

Pizza Dip

Time: 6 1/4 hours

Servings: 20

Ingredients:

1 pound spicy sausages, sliced
1/2 pound salami, diced
1 red bell pepper, cored and diced
1 yellow bell pepper, cored and sliced
1 onion, chopped
2 garlic cloves, minced

2 cups tomato sauce
1/2 cup grated Parmesan
1 cup shredded mozzarella
1/2 teaspoon dried basil
1/2 teaspoon dried oregano

Directions:

Layer all the ingredients in your slow cooker.
Cook on low settings for 6 hours, mixing once during the cooking time to ensure an even distribution of ingredients.
Serve the dip warm.

Green Vegetable Dip

Time: 2 1/4 hours

Servings: 12

Ingredients:

10 oz. frozen spinach, thawed and drained
1 jar artichoke hearts, drained
1 cup chopped parsley
1 cup cream cheese
1 cup sour cream

1/2 cup grated Parmesan cheese
1/2 cup feta cheese, crumbled
1/2 teaspoon onion powder
1/4 teaspoon garlic powder

Directions:

Combine all the ingredients in your slow cooker and mix gently.
Cover with its lid and cook on high settings for 2 hours.
Serve the dip warm or chilled with crusty bread, biscuits or other salty snacks or even vegetable sticks.

Spicy Enchilada Dip

Time: 6 1/4 hours

Servings: 8

Ingredients:

1 pound ground chicken
1/2 teaspoon chili powder
1 shallot, chopped
2 garlic cloves, chopped
1 red bell pepper, cored and diced

2 tomatoes, diced
1 cup tomato sauce
Salt and pepper to taste
1 1/2 cups grated Cheddar cheese

Directions:

Combine the ground chicken with chili powder, shallot and garlic in your slow cooker.
Add the remaining ingredients and cook on low settings for 6 hours.
Serve the dip warm with tortilla chips.

Mixed Olive Dip

Time: 1 3/4 hours   Servings: 10

Ingredients:

1 pound ground chicken
2 tablespoons olive oil
1 green bell pepper, cored and diced
1/2 cup Kalamata olives, pitted and chopped
1/2 cup green olives, chopped

1/2 cup black olives, pitted and chopped
1 cup green salsa
1/2 cup chicken stock
1 cup grated Cheddar cheese
1/2 cup shredded mozzarella

Directions:

Combine all the ingredients in your slow cooker.
Cover with its lid and cook on high settings for 1 1/2 hours.
The dip is best served warm.

Spicy Asian Style Mushroom

Time: 2 1/4 hours   Servings: 8

Ingredients:

1/4 cup hoisin sauce
1/4 cup soy sauce
2 garlic cloves, minced

1/2 teaspoon red pepper flakes
2 pounds fresh mushrooms, cleaned

Directions:

Mix the hoisin sauce, soy sauce, garlic and red pepper flakes in a bowl.
Place the mushrooms in your slow cooker and drizzle them with the sauce.
Cook on high settings for 2 hours.
Allow the mushrooms to cool in the pot before serving.

Three Cheese Artichoke Sauce

Time: 4 1/4 hours   Servings: 16

Ingredients:

1 jar artichoke hearts, drained and chopped
1 shallot, chopped
2 cups shredded mozzarella
1 cup grated Parmesan

1 cup grated Swiss cheese
1/2 teaspoon dried thyme
1/4 teaspoon chili powder

Directions:

Combine all the ingredients in your slow cooker.
Cover the pot with its lid and cook on low setting for 4 hours.
The sauce is great served warm with vegetable sticks or biscuits or even small pretzels.

Mexican Chili Dip

Time: 2 1/4 hours

Servings: 20

Ingredients:
1 can black beans, drained
1 can red beans, drained
1 can diced tomatoes
1/2 teaspoon cumin powder

1/2 teaspoon chili powder
1/2 cup beef stock
Salt and pepper to taste
1 1/2 cups grated Cheddar

Directions:
Combine the beans, tomatoes, cumin powder, chili and stock in your slow cooker.
Add salt and pepper to taste and top with grated cheese.
Cook on high settings for 2 hours.
The dip is best served warm.

Boiled Peanuts with Skin On

Time: 7 1/4 hours

Servings: 8

Ingredients:
2 pounds uncooked, whole peanuts
1/2 cup salt

4 cups water

Directions:
Combine all the ingredients in your slow cooker.
Cover and cook on low settings for 7 hours.
Drain and allow to cool down before servings.

Spicy Glazed Pecans

Time: 3 1/4 hours

Servings: 10

Ingredients:
2 pounds pecans
1/2 cup butter, melted
1 teaspoon chili powder
1 teaspoon smoked paprika
1 teaspoon dried basil

1 teaspoon dried thyme
1/4 teaspoon cayenne pepper
1/2 teaspoon garlic powder
2 tablespoons honey

Directions:
Combine all the ingredients in your slow cooker.
Mix well until all the ingredients are well distributed and the pecans are evenly glazed.
Cook on high settings for 3 hours.
Allow them to cool before serving.

Cheesy Mushroom Dip

Time: 4 1/4 hours   Servings: 16

Ingredients:

1 can condensed cream of mushroom soup
1 pound mushrooms, chopped   1/2 teaspoon chili powder
1 teaspoon Worcestershire sauce   1 cup grated Cheddar cheese
1/4 cup evaporated milk   1 cup grated Swiss cheese

Directions:

Mix the cream of mushroom soup, mushrooms, Worcestershire sauce, evaporated milk and chili powder in your slow cooker.
Top with grated cheese and cook on low settings for 4 hours.
Serve the dip warm or re-heated.

Taco Dip

Time: 6 1/2 hours   Servings: 20

Ingredients:

2 pounds ground beef   1 cup tomato sauce
2 tablespoons canola oil   1 tablespoon taco seasoning
1 can black beans, drained   2 cups Velveeta cheese, shredded
1/2 cup beef stock

Directions:

Heat the oil in a skillet and add the beef. Cook for 10 minutes, stirring often.
Transfer the beef in your slow cooker.
Add the remaining ingredients and cook on low settings for 6 hours.
Serve the dip warm.

Swiss Cheese Fondue

Time: 4 1/4 hours   Servings: 10

Ingredients:

1 garlic cloves   1 cup grated Cheddar
2 cups dry white wine   2 tablespoons cornstarch
2 cups grated Swiss cheese   1 pinch nutmeg

Directions:

Rub the inside of your slow cooker with a garlic clove. Discard the clove once done.
Add the remaining ingredients and cook on low heat for 4 hours.
Serve the fondue warm with vegetable sticks, croutons or pretzels.

SPICY CHICKEN TAQUITOS

Time: 6 1/2 hours   Servings: 8

Ingredients:

4 chicken breasts, cooked and diced
1 cup cream cheese
2 jalapeno peppers, chopped
1/2 cup canned sweet corn, drained

1/2 teaspoon cumin powder
4 garlic cloves, minced
16 taco-sized flour tortillas
2 cups grated Cheddar cheese

Directions:

In a bowl, mix the chicken, cream cheese, garlic, cumin, poblano peppers and corn. Stir in the cheese as well. Place your tortillas on your working surface and top each tortilla with the cheese mixture. Roll the tortillas tightly to form an even roll. Place the rolls in your slow cooker. Cook on low settings for 6 hours. Serve warm.

QUICK LAYERED APPETIZER

Time: 7 1/2 hours   Servings: 10

Ingredients:

4 chicken breasts, cooked and diced
1 teaspoon dried basil
1 teaspoon dried oregano
1 cup cream cheese
1/4 teaspoon chili powder

Salt and pepper to taste
4 tomatoes, sliced
4 large tortillas
2 cups shredded mozzarella

Directions:

Mix the chicken, basil, oregano, cream cheese, chili powder, salt and pepper in a bowl.
Begin layering the chicken mixture, tomatoes, tortillas and mozzarella in your slow cooker.
Cover and cook on low settings for 7 hours. Allow to cool then slice and serve.

ORIENTAL CHICKEN BITES

Time: 7 1/4 hours   Servings: 10

Ingredients:

4 chicken breasts, cubed
2 sweet onions, sliced
1 teaspoon grated ginger
4 garlic cloves, minced
1/2 teaspoon cinnamon powder
1 teaspoon smoked paprika

1 teaspoon cumin powder
1 cup chicken stock
1/2 lemon, juiced
2 tablespoons olive oil
Salt and pepper to taste

Directions:

Combine all the ingredients in your slow cooker.
Add salt and pepper to taste and mix well until the ingredients are evenly distributed.
Cover and cook on low settings for 7 hours.
Serve the chicken bites warm or chilled.

Sweet Corn Jalapeno Dip

Time: 2 1/4 hours   Servings: 10

Ingredients:
4 bacon slices, chopped
3 cans sweet corn, drained
4 jalapenos, seeded and chopped
1 cup sour cream

1 cup grated Cheddar cheese
1/2 cup cream cheese
1 pinch nutmeg
2 tablespoons chopped cilantro

Directions:
Combine the corn, jalapenos, sour cream, Cheddar, cream cheese and nutmeg in a slow cooker.
Cook on high settings for 2 hours.
When done, stir in the cilantro and serve the dip warm.
Store it in an airtight container in the fridge for up to 2 days. Re-heat it when need it.

Pretzel Party Mix

Time: 2 1/4 hours   Servings: 10

Ingredients:
4 cups pretzels
1 cup peanuts
1 cup pecans
1 cup crispy rice cereals

1/4 cup butter, melted
1 teaspoon Worcestershire sauce
1 teaspoon salt
1 teaspoon garlic powder

Directions:
Combine the pretzels, peanuts, pecans and rice cereals in your slow cooker.
Drizzle with melted butter and Worcestershire sauce and mix well then sprinkle with salt and garlic powder.
Cover and cook on high settings for 2 hours, mixing once during cooking.
Allow to cool before serving.

Maple Syrup Glazed Carrots

Time: 6 1/4 hours   Servings: 8

Ingredients:
3 pounds baby carrots
4 tablespoons butter, melted
3 tablespoons maple syrup

1/8 teaspoon pumpkin pie spices
1 teaspoon salt

Directions:
Place the baby carrots in your slow cooker and add the remaining ingredients.
Mix until the carrots are evenly coated.
Cover and cook on low settings for 6 hours.
Serve the carrots warm or chilled.

BALSAMICO **P**ULLED **P**ORK

Time: 8 1/4 hours   Servings: 6

Ingredients:

2 pounds boneless pork shoulder
2 tablespoons honey
1/4 cup balsamic vinegar
1/4 cup hoisin sauce
1 tablespoon Dijon mustard

1/4 cup chicken stock
2 garlic cloves, minced
2 shallots, sliced
2 tablespoons soy sauce

Directions:

Combine the honey, vinegar, hoisin sauce, mustard, stock, garlic, shallots and soy sauce in your slow cooker.
Add the pork shoulder and roll it in the mixture until evenly coated.
Cover the slow cooker and cook on low settings for 8 hours.
When done, shred the meat into fine pieces and serve warm or chilled.

CARNE **A**SADA **N**ACHOS

Time: 10 1/2 hours   Servings: 8

Ingredients:

2 pounds flanks steak
1 teaspoon salt
1 teaspoon smoked paprika
1/2 teaspoon chili powder
2 tablespoons brown sugar
1 teaspoon cumin powder
1 teaspoon garlic powder
2 tablespoons canola oil

1 cup dark beer
8 oz. tortillas chips
1 cup red salsa
1 can sweet corn, drained
2 cups grated Monterey jack cheese
Sour cream for serving
Chopped cilantro for serving

Directions:

Mix the salt, paprika, chili powder, sugar, cumin powder and garlic powder in a bowl. Spread this mix over the steak and rub it well into the meat.
Heat the oil in a skillet and add the steak in the hot oil. Cook on all sides for 4-5 minutes just to sear it.
Transfer the meat in your slow cooker and pour the beer over.
Cook on low settings for 8 hours.
When done, remove from the pot and cut the flank steak into thin slices.
Clean the pot then place the tortilla chips on the bottom.
Cover the tortilla chips with red salsa, followed by flank steak, corn and cheese.
Cook on low settings for 2 additional hours.
Serve right away.

Bacon Black Bean Dip

Time: 6 1/4 hours   Servings: 6

Ingredients:

6 bacon slices
2 cans black beans, drained
2 shallots, sliced
1 garlic cloves, chopped
1 cup red salsa
1/2 cup beef stock

1 tablespoon brown sugar
1 tablespoon molasses
1/2 teaspoon chili powder
1 tablespoon apple cider vinegar
2 tablespoons Bourbon
Salt and pepper to taste

Directions:

Heat a skillet over medium flame and add the bacon. Cook until crisp then transfer the bacon and its fat in your slow cooker. Stir in the remaining ingredients and cook on low settings for 6 hours. When done, partially mash the beans and serve the dip right away.

White Bean Hummus

Time: 8 1/4 hours   Servings: 8

Ingredients:

1 pound dried white beans, rinsed
2 cups water
2 cups chicken stock
1 bay leaf
1 thyme sprig

4 garlic cloves, minced
Salt and pepper to taste
2 tablespoons canola oil
2 large sweet onions, sliced

Directions:

Combine the white beans, water, stock, bay leaf and thyme in your slow cooker. Add salt and pepper to taste and cook the beans on low settings for 8 hours. When done, drain the beans well (but reserve 1/4 cup of the liquid) and discard the bay leaf and thyme. Transfer the bean in a food processor. Add the reserved liquid and pulse until smooth. Season with salt and pepper and transfer in a bowl. Heat the canola oil in a skillet and add the onions. Cook for 10 minutes over medium flame until the onions begin to caramelize. Top the hummus with caramelized onions and serve.

Spicy Monterey Jack Fondue

Time: 4 1/4 hours   Servings: 6

Ingredients:

1 garlic clove
1 cup white wine
2 cups grated Monterey Jack cheese
1/2 cup grated Parmesan
1 red chili, seeded and chopped

1 tablespoon cornstarch
1/2 cup milk
1 pinch nutmeg
1 pinch salt
1 pinch ground black pepper

Directions:

Rub the inside of your slow cooker's pot with a garlic clove just to infuse it with aroma.
Add the white wine into the pot and stir in the cheeses, red chili, cornstarch and milk.

Season with nutmeg, salt and black pepper and cook on low heat for 4 hours.
The fondue is best served warm with bread sticks or vegetables.

Tahini Cheese Dip

Time: 2 1/4 hours   Servings: 8

Ingredients:
1/2 cup tahini paste
1 cup whole milk
1/8 teaspoon garlic powder
1/2 teaspoon cumin powder

1/4 pound grated Gruyere
1/4 cup grated Emmentaler cheese
Salt and pepper to taste
1 pinch nutmeg

Directions:
Combine all the ingredients in your slow cooker.
Add salt and pepper if needed and cover the pot with its lid.
Cook on high settings for 2 hours.
Serve the dip warm.

Tahini Chickpea Dip

Time: 6 1/4 hours   Servings: 6

Ingredients:
2 cups dried chickpeas, rinsed
5 cups water
1 bay leaf
Salt and pepper to taste

1 lemon, juiced
1/4 cup tahini paste
2 tablespoons olive oil
1 pinch red pepper flakes

Directions:
Combine the chickpeas, water, bay leaf, salt and pepper in a slow cooker. Cook on low settings for 6 hours then drain and transfer in a food processor. Stir in the remaining ingredients and pulse until smooth. Spoon into a bowl and serve fresh or store in an airtight container in the fridge.

Roasted Bell Peppers Dip

Time: 2 1/4 hours   Servings: 8

Ingredients:
4 roasted red bell peppers, drained
2 cans chickpeas, drained
1/2 cup water
1 shallot, chopped

4 garlic cloves, minced
Salt and pepper to taste
2 tablespoons lemon juice
2 tablespoons olive oil

Directions:
Combine the bell peppers, chickpeas, water, shallot and garlic in a slow cooker. Add salt and pepper as needed and cook on high settings for 2 hours. When done, puree the dip in a blender, adding the lemon juice and olive oil as well. Serve the dip fresh or store it in the fridge in an airtight container for up to 2 days.

CHARRED TOMATO SALSA

Time: 3 hours   Servings: 8

Ingredients:

4 ripe tomatoes, sliced
2 tablespoons olive oil
1 teaspoon dried basil
1/2 teaspoon dried mint
2 shallots, chopped

1 jalapeno pepper, chopped
1 can black beans, drained
1/4 cup chicken stock
1 bay leaf
Salt and pepper to taste

Directions:

Place the tomato slices in a baking tray and sprinkle with salt, pepper, basil and mint.
Drizzle with olive oil and cook in the preheated oven at 350F for 35-40 minutes until the slices begin to caramelize.
Transfer the tomatoes in a slow cooker and add the remaining ingredients.
Cook on high settings for 2 hours and serve the salsa warm or chilled.

PIMIENTO CHEESE DIP

Time: 2 1/4 hours   Servings: 8

Ingredients:

1/2 pound grated Cheddar
1/4 pound grated pepper Jack cheese
1/2 cup sour cream
1/2 cup green olives, sliced

2 tablespoons diced pimientos
1 teaspoon hot sauce
1/4 teaspoon garlic powder
1/4 teaspoon onion powder

Directions:

Combine all the ingredients in a slow cooker.
Cover the pot with its lid and cook on high settings for 2 hours.
The dip is best served warm with vegetable sticks or bread sticks.

EGGPLANT CAVIAR

Time: 3 1/4 hours   Servings: 6

Ingredients:

2 large eggplants, peeled and cubed
4 tablespoons olive oil
1 teaspoon dried basil
1 teaspoon dried oregano

1 lemon, juiced
2 garlic cloves, minced
Salt and pepper to taste

Directions:

Combine the eggplant cubes, olive oil, basil and oregano in a slow cooker.
Add salt and pepper to taste and cook on high settings for 3 hours.
When done, stir in the lemon juice, garlic, salt and pepper and mash the mix well with a potato masher.
Serve the dip chilled.

Sausage and Pepper Appetizer

Time: 6 1/4 hours   Servings: 8

Ingredients:

6 fresh pork sausages, skins removed
2 tablespoons olive oil
1 can fire roasted tomatoes
4 roasted bell peppers, chopped

1 poblano pepper, chopped
1 shallot, chopped
1 cup grated Provolone cheese
Salt and pepper to taste

Directions:

Heat the oil in a skillet and stir in the sausage meat. Cook for 5 minutes, stirring often.
Transfer the meat in your slow cooker and add the remaining ingredients.
Season with salt and pepper and cook on low settings for 6 hours.
Serve the dish warm or chilled.

Bacon Baked Potatoes

Time: 3 1/4 hours   Servings: 8

Ingredients:

3 pounds new potatoes, halved
8 slices bacon, chopped
1 teaspoon dried rosemary

1/4 cup chicken stock
Salt and pepper to taste

Directions:

Heat a skillet over medium flame and stir in the bacon. Cook until crisp.
Place the potatoes in a slow cooker. Add the bacon bits and its fat, as well as rosemary, salt and pepper and mix until evenly distributed.
Pour in the stock and cook on high heat for 3 hours.
Serve the potatoes warm.

French Onion Dip

Time: 4 1/4 hours   Servings: 10

Ingredients:

4 large onions, chopped
2 tablespoons olive oil
1 tablespoon butter

1 1/2 cups sour cream
1 pinch nutmeg
Salt and pepper to taste

Directions:

Combine the onions, olive oil, butter, salt, pepper and nutmeg in a slow cooker.
Cover and cook on high settings for 4 hours.
When done, allow to cool then stir in the sour cream and adjust the taste with salt and pepper.
Serve the dip right away.

Teriyaki Chicken Wings

Time: 6 1/4 hours

Servings: 6

Ingredients:

2 tablespoons brown sugar
1 tablespoon molasses
1/2 teaspoon garlic powder
1/2 teaspoon ground ginger
1/2 cup soy sauce

1/2 cup pineapple juice
1/4 cup water
2 tablespoons canola oil
3 pounds chicken wings

Directions:

Combine all the ingredients in a slow cooker and mix until evenly coated.
Cover the pot with its lid and cook on low settings for 6 hours.
Serve the chicken wings warm or chilled.

Goat Cheese Stuffed Mushrooms

Time: 4 1/4 hours

Servings: 6

Ingredients:

12 medium size mushrooms
6 oz. goat cheese
1 egg

1/2 cup breadcrumbs
1 poblano pepper, chopped
1 teaspoon dried oregano

Directions:

Mix the goat cheese, egg, breadcrumbs, pepper and oregano in a bowl.
Stuff each mushroom with the goat cheese mixture and place them all in a slow cooker.
Cover the pot and cook on low settings for 4 hours.
Serve the mushrooms warm or chilled.

Pepperoni Pizza Dip

Time: 3 1/4 hours

Servings: 10

Ingredients:

1 1/2 cups pizza sauce
4 peperoni, sliced
2 shallots, chopped
2 red bell peppers, diced

1/2 cup black olives, pitted and chopped
1 cup cream cheese
1 cup shredded mozzarella
1/2 teaspoon dried basil

Directions:

Combine the pizza sauce and the rest of the ingredients in your slow cooker.
Cover the pot with its lid and cook on low settings for 3 hours.
The dip is best served warm with bread sticks or tortilla chips.

CREAMY POTATOES

Time: 6 1/4 hours   Servings: 6

Ingredients:

3 pounds small new potatoes, washed
4 bacon slices, chopped
1 teaspoon dried oregano
1 shallot, chopped
2 tablespoons olive oil

2 garlic cloves, chopped
Salt and pepper to taste
1 cup sour cream
2 green onions, chopped
2 tablespoons chopped parsley

Directions:

Combine the potatoes, bacon, oregano, shallot, olive oil and garlic in a slow cooker. Add salt and pepper and mix until the ingredients are well distributed. Cover the pot with its lid and cook on low settings for 6 hours. When done, mix the cooked potatoes with sour cream, onions and parsley and serve right away.

BEER BBQ MEATBALLS

Time: 7 1/2 hours   Servings: 10

Ingredients:

2 pounds ground pork
1 pound ground beef
1 carrot, grated
2 shallots, chopped
1 egg
1/2 cup breadcrumbs
1/2 teaspoon cumin powder

Salt and pepper to taste
1 cup dark beer
1 cup BBQ sauce
1 bay leaf
1/2 teaspoon chili powder
1 teaspoon apple cider vinegar

Directions:

Mix the ground pork and beef in a bowl. Add the carrot, shallots, egg, breadcrumbs, cumin, salt and pepper and mix well. Form small meatballs and place them on your chopping board. For the beer sauce, combine the beer, BBQ sauce, bay leaf, chili powder and vinegar in a slow cooker. Place the meatballs in the pot and cover with its lid. Cook on low settings for 7 hours. Serve the meatballs warm or chilled.

BABA GANOUSH

Time: 4 1/4 hours   Servings: 4

Ingredients:

1 large eggplant, halved
2 garlic cloves, minced
2 tablespoons olive oil
1 tablespoon tahini paste

1 tablespoon lemon juice
1 tablespoon chopped parsley
Salt and pepper to taste

Directions:

Spread the garlic over each half of eggplant. Season them with salt and pepper and drizzle with olive oil. Place the eggplant halves in your slow cooker and cook on low settings for 4 hours. When done, scoop out the eggplant flesh and place it in a bowl. Mash it with a fork. Stir in the tahini paste, lemon juice and parsley and mix well. Serve the dip fresh.

Beer Cheese Fondue

Time: 2 1/4 hours

Servings: 8

Ingredients:

1 shallot, chopped
1 garlic clove, minced
1 cup grated Gruyere cheese
2 cups grated Cheddar
1 tablespoon cornstarch

1 teaspoon Dijon mustard
1/2 teaspoon cumin seeds
1 cup beer
Salt and pepper to taste

Directions:

Combine the shallot, garlic, cheeses, cornstarch, mustard, cumin seeds and beer in your slow cooker. Add salt and pepper to taste and mix well. Cover the pot with its lid and cook on high settings for 2 hours. Serve the fondue warm.

Mozzarella Stuffed Meatballs

Time: 6 1/2 hours

Servings: 8

Ingredients:

2 pounds ground chicken
1 teaspoon dried basil
1/2 teaspoon dried oregano
1 egg

1/2 cup breadcrumbs
Salt and pepper to taste
Mini-mozzarella balls as needed
1/2 cup chicken stock

Directions:

Mix the ground chicken, basil, oregano, egg, breadcrumbs, salt and pepper in a bowl. Take small pieces of the meat mixture and flatten it in your palm. Place a mozzarella ball in the center and gather the meat around the mozzarella. Shape the meatballs, making sure they are well sealed and place them in a slow cooker. Add the chicken stock and cook on low settings for 6 hours. Serve the meatballs warm or chilled.

Marinara Turkey Meatballs

Time: 6 1/2 hours

Servings: 8

Ingredients:

2 pounds ground turkey
1 carrot, grated
1 potato, grated
1 shallot, chopped
1 tablespoon chopped parsley
1 tablespoon chopped cilantro
4 basil leaves, chopped
1/2 teaspoon dried mint
1 egg

1/4 cup breadcrumbs
Salt and pepper to taste
2 cups marinara sauce

Directions:

Mix the turkey, carrot, potato, shallot, parsley, cilantro, basil, mint, egg and breadcrumbs in a bowl. Add salt and pepper to taste and mix well. Pour the marinara sauce in your slow cooker then form meatballs and drop them in the sauce. Cover the pot with its lid and cook on low settings for 6 hours. Serve the meatballs warm or chilled.

FOUR CHEESE DIP

Time: 4 1/4 hours   Servings: 8

Ingredients:

1/2 pound fresh Italian sausages,
    skins removed
2 tablespoons olive oil
1 cup tomato sauce
1 cup cottage cheese
1 cup shredded mozzarella cheese

1/2 cup grated Parmesan cheese
1 cup grated Cheddar cheese
1/2 teaspoon dried thyme
1/2 teaspoon dried basil
Salt and pepper to taste

Directions:

Heat the oil in a skillet and stir in the sausages. Cook for 5 minutes, stirring often then transfer the sausages in a slow cooker. Add the remaining ingredients and season with salt and pepper. Cook on low settings for 4 hours. The dip is best served warm.

QUICK PARMESAN BREAD

Time: 1 1/4 hours   Servings: 8

Ingredients:

4 cups all-purpose flour
1/2 teaspoon salt
1/2 cup grated Parmesan cheese

1 teaspoon baking soda
2 cups buttermilk
2 tablespoons olive oil

Directions:

Mix the flour, salt, parmesan cheese and baking soda in a bowl. Stir in the buttermilk and olive oil and mix well with a fork. Shape the dough into a loaf and place it in your slow cooker. Cover with its lid and cook on high heat for 1 hour. Serve the bread warm or chilled.

CRANBERRY BAKED BRIE

Time: 2 1/4 hours   Servings: 6

Ingredients:

1 wheel of Brie
1/2 cup cranberry sauce

1/2 teaspoon dried thyme

Directions:

Spoon the cranberry sauce in your slow cooker. Sprinkle with thyme and top with the Brie cheese. Cover with a lid and cook on low settings for 2 hours. The cheese is best served warm with bread sticks or tortilla chips.

CLASSIC BREAD IN A CROCK POT

Time: 1 1/2 hours   Servings: 8

Ingredients:

2 teaspoons active dry yeast
1 teaspoon sugar
1 cup warm water
1/2 cup yogurt

1 egg
2 tablespoons olive oil
3 cups all-purpose flour
1/2 teaspoon salt

Directions:

Mix the yeast, sugar, warm water, yogurt, egg and olive oil in a bowl. Stir in the flour and salt and mix well. Knead the dough for 5-10 minutes until even and non-sticky. Place the dough in your slow cooker and cover with its lid. Cook on high settings for 1 1/4 hours. Serve the bread warm or chilled.

CARAMELIZED ONION AND CRANBERRY DIP

Time: 6 1/4 hours   Servings: 16

Ingredients:

2 tablespoons olive oil
4 red onions, sliced
1 apple, peeled and diced
1 cup frozen cranberries
1/4 cup balsamic vinegar
1/4 cup fresh orange juice

2 tablespoons brown sugar
1 teaspoon orange zest
1 bay leaf
1 thyme sprig
1 teaspoon salt

Directions:

Heat the oil in a skillet and stir in the onions. Cook for 10 minutes until the onions begin to caramelize. Transfer the onions in a slow cooker and stir in the remaining ingredients. Cover with a lid and cook on low settings for 6 hours. Serve the dip chilled.

CHEESEBURGER MEATBALLS

Time: 6 1/4 hours   Servings: 8

Ingredients:

2 pounds ground pork
1 shallot, chopped
2 tablespoons beef stock
1 egg
1/4 cup breadcrumbs

1 teaspoon Cajun seasoning
1/2 teaspoon dried basil
Salt and pepper to taste
2 cups shredded processed cheese

Directions:

Mix the pork, shallot, beef stock, egg, breadcrumbs, Cajun seasoning and basil in a bowl. Add salt and pepper to taste and mix well. Form small meatballs and place them in the slow cooker. Top with shredded cheese and cook on low settings for 6 hours. Serve the meatballs warm.

Bacon Wrapped Dates

Time: 1 3/4 hours

Servings: 8

Ingredients:
16 dates, pitted
16 almonds

16 slices bacon

Directions:
Stuff each date with an almond. Wrap each date in bacon and place the wrapped dates in your slow cooker. Cover with its lid and cook on high settings for 1 1/4 hours. Serve warm or chilled.

Parmesan Zucchini Frittata

Time: 6 1/4 hours

Servings: 8

Ingredients:
2 zucchinis, finely sliced
2 garlic cloves, minced
1 teaspoon dried mint
1 teaspoon dried oregano
6 eggs

2 tablespoons plain yogurt
1 tablespoon chopped parsley
1/2 cup grated Parmesan
Salt and pepper to taste

Directions:
Mix the zucchinis, garlic, dried mint and oregano in a slow cooker. Add salt and pepper to taste. In a bowl, mix the eggs, yogurt, parsley and Parmesan. Pour the egg mixture over the zucchinis and cover the pot with its lid. Cook on low settings for 6 hours. Serve the frittata sliced, warm or chilled.

Hoisin Chicken Wings

Time: 7 1/4 hours

Servings: 8

Ingredients:
4 pounds chicken wings
2/3 cup hoisin sauce
4 garlic cloves, minced
1 teaspoon grated ginger
1 teaspoon sesame oil

1 tablespoon molasses
1 teaspoon hot sauce
1/4 teaspoon ground black pepper
1/2 teaspoon salt

Directions:
Mix the hoisin sauce, garlic, ginger, sesame oil, molasses, hot sauce, black pepper and salt in your slow cooker. Add the chicken wings and toss them around until evenly coated.
Cover with a lid and cook on low settings for 7 hours.
Serve the wings warm or chilled.

RANCH TURKEY BITES

Time: 7 1/4 hours

Servings: 6

Ingredients:

2 pounds turkey breast, cubed
1 carrot, sliced
1/2 teaspoon garlic powder
1 tablespoon Ranch dressing seasoning

1 teaspoon hot sauce
1 cup tomato sauce
Salt and pepper to taste

Directions:

Combine all the ingredients in a slow cooker. Mix well until the ingredients are well distributed and adjust the taste with salt and pepper. Cover with a lid and cook on low settings for 7 hours. Serve the turkey bites warm or chilled.

TURKEY MEATLOAF

Time: 6 1/4 hours

Servings: 8

Ingredients:

1 1/2 pounds ground turkey
1 carrot, grated
1 sweet potato, grated
1 egg

1/4 cup breadcrumbs
1/4 teaspoon chili powder
Salt and pepper to taste
1 cup shredded mozzarella

Directions:

Mix all the ingredients in a bowl and season with salt and pepper as needed. Give it a good mix then transfer the mixture in your slow cooker. Level the mixture well and cover with the pot's lid. Cook on low settings for 6 hours. Serve the meatloaf warm or chilled.

ARTICHOKE BREAD PUDDING

Time: 6 1/2 hours

Servings: 10

Ingredients:

6 cups bread cubes
6 artichoke hearts, drained and chopped
1/2 cup grated Parmesan
4 eggs
1/2 cup sour cream
1 cup milk

4 oz. spinach, chopped
1 tablespoon chopped parsley
2 tablespoons olive oil
Salt and pepper to taste
1/2 teaspoon dried oregano
1/2 teaspoon dried basil

Directions:

Combine the bread cubes, artichoke hearts and Parmesan in your slow cooker. Add the spinach and parsley as well. In a bowl, mix the eggs, sour cream, milk, oregano and basil, as well as salt and pepper. Pour this mixture over the bread and press the bread slightly to make sure it soaks up all the liquid. Cover the pot with its lid and cook on low settings for 6 hours. The bread can be served both warm and chilled.

Bacon Chicken Sliders

Time: 4 1/2 hours

Servings: 8

Ingredients:

2 pounds ground chicken
1 egg
1/2 cup breadcrumbs

1 shallot, chopped
Salt and pepper to taste
8 bacon slices

Directions:

Mix the chicken, egg, breadcrumbs and shallot in a bowl. Add salt and pepper to taste and give it a good mix. Form small sliders then wrap each slider in a bacon slice. Place the sliders in a slow cooker. Cover with its lid and cook on high settings for 4 hours, making sure to flip them over once during cooking. Serve them warm.

Chili Corn Cheese Dip

Time: 2 1/4 hours

Servings: 8

Ingredients:

1 pound ground beef
2 tablespoons olive oil
1 shallot, chopped
1 can sweet corn, drained
1 can kidney beans, drained
1/2 cup beef stock
1 cup diced tomatoes

1/2 cup black olives, pitted and chopped
1 teaspoon dried oregano
1/2 teaspoon chili powder
1/2 teaspoon cumin powder
1/4 teaspoon garlic powder
2 cups grated Cheddar cheese
Tortilla chips for serving

Directions:

Heat the oil in a skillet and stir in the ground beef. Cook for 5-7 minutes, stirring often. Transfer the meat in a slow cooker and add the remaining ingredients. Add salt and pepper to taste and cover with its lid. Cook on high settings for 2 hours. Serve the dip warm with tortilla chips.

Southwestern Nacho Dip

Time: 6 1/4 hours

Servings: 10

Ingredients:

1 pound ground pork
1 cup apple juice
4 garlic cloves, chopped
2 cups BBQ sauce
2 tablespoons brown sugar
Salt and pepper to taste
1 1/2 cups sweet corn

1 can black beans, drained
1 cup diced tomatoes
2 jalapeno peppers, chopped
2 tablespoons chopped cilantro
2 cups grated Cheddar
1 lime, juiced
Nachos for serving

Directions:

Heat a skillet over medium flame and add the pork. Cook for a few minutes, stirring often. Transfer the pork in your slow cooker and add the apple juice, garlic, BBQ sauce, brown sugar, salt and pepper. Cook on high settings for 2 hours. After 2 hours, add the remaining ingredients and continue cooking for 4 hours on low settings. Serve the dip warm with nachos.

Marmalade Glazed Meatballs

Time: 7 1/2 hours   Servings: 8

Ingredients:

2 pounds ground pork
1 shallot, chopped
4 garlic cloves, minced
1 carrot, grated
1 egg
Salt and pepper to taste

1 cup orange marmalade
2 cups BBQ sauce
1 bay leaf
1 teaspoon Worcestershire sauce
Salt and pepper to taste

Directions:

Mix the ground pork, shallot, garlic, carrot, egg, salt and pepper in a bowl.
Form small meatballs and place them on your working surface.
For the sauce, mix the orange marmalade, sauce, bay leaf, Worcestershire sauce, salt and pepper in your slow cooker.
Place the meatballs in the sauce. Cover with its lid and cook on low settings for 7 hours.
Serve the meatballs warm.

Creamy Chicken Dip

Time: 3 1/4 hours   Servings: 6

Ingredients:

1 cup cream cheese
1 1/2 cups cooked and diced chicken
2 cups shredded Monterey Jack cheese
1/4 cup white wine

1 lime, juiced
1/4 teaspoon cumin powder
2 garlic cloves, chopped
Salt and pepper to taste

Directions:

Combine all the ingredients in your slow cooker.
Add salt and pepper to taste and cook on low settings for 3 hours.
The dip is best served warm with tortilla chips or bread sticks.

Soups

BUTTERNUT SQUASH CREAMY SOUP

Time: 4 1/4 hours   Servings: 6

Ingredients:

1 sweet onion, chopped
2 garlic cloves, chopped
2 tablespoons olive oil
2 parsnips, cubed
2 cups butternut squash cubed
1 celery root, peeled and cubed

1 potato, peeled and cubed
3 cups water
2 cups chicken stock
Salt and pepper to taste
1 pinch cayenne pepper
1/4 teaspoon cumin powder

Directions:

Heat the oil in a skillet and stir in the onion and garlic.
Sauté for 2-3 minutes until softened then transfer in your slow cooker.
Add the remaining ingredients then season with salt and pepper.
Cook the soup on low settings for 4 hours.
When done, remove the lid and puree the soup with an immersion blender.
Serve the soup warm.

CAJUN BLACK BEAN SOUP

Time: 6 1/4 hours   Servings: 8

Ingredients:

2 tablespoons olive oil
1 red onion, chopped
1 garlic clove, chopped
1 parsnip, diced
1 celery stalk, sliced
1 red bell pepper, cored and diced
1 green bell pepper, cored and diced
2 jalapenos, chopped
1 teaspoon dried thyme

1/2 teaspoon dried basil
1/2 teaspoon dried oregano
1 teaspoon Cajun seasoning
4 cups chicken stock
1 cup tomato paste
2 cups water
2 cans (15 oz.) black beans, drained
Salt and pepper to taste
2 tablespoons chopped cilantro for serving

Directions:

Heat the oil in a skillet and stir in the onion, garlic, parsnip and bell peppers.
Cook for 5 minutes, stirring often, until softened.
Transfer the mixture in your slow cooker and add the remaining ingredients.
Adjust the taste with salt and pepper as needed and cook on low settings for 6 hours.
When done, stir in the chopped cilantro and serve right away.

CREAMY WHITE BEAN SOUP

Time: 4 1/4 hours   Servings: 6

Ingredients:

1 tablespoon olive oil
1 sweet onion, chopped
2 garlic cloves, chopped
1/2 celery root, peeled and cubed
1 parsnip, diced

1 can (15 oz.) white beans, drained
2 cups chicken stock
3 cups water
1/2 teaspoon dried thyme
Salt and pepper to taste

Directions:

Heat the oil in a skillet and stir in the onion, garlic, celery and parsnip. Cook for 5 minutes until softened then transfer the mix in your slow cooker. Add the rest of the ingredients and cook on low settings for 4 hours. When done, puree the soup with an immersion blender and pulse until smooth and creamy. Serve the soup warm and fresh.

HAM WHITE BEAN SOUP

Time: 2 1/4 hours   Servings: 6

Ingredients:

1 tablespoon olive oil
4 oz. ham, diced
1 sweet onion, chopped
2 garlic cloves, chopped
1 yellow bell pepper, cored and diced
1 red bell pepper, cored and diced

1 carrot, diced
1 cup diced tomatoes
1 can (15 oz.) white beans, drained
2 cups chicken stock
3 cups water
Salt and pepper to taste

Directions:

Heat the oil in a skillet and add the ham. Cook for 2 minutes then stir in the onion and garlic. Sauté for 2 additional minutes. Transfer the mixture in your slow cooker and stir in the remaining ingredients. Adjust the taste with salt and pepper and cook on high settings for 2 hours. Serve the soup warm or chilled.

CREAMY BACON SOUP

Time: 1 3/4 hours   Servings: 6

Ingredients:

1 tablespoon olive oil
6 bacon slices, chopped
1 sweet onion, chopped
1 1/2 pounds potatoes, peeled and cubed
1 parsnip, diced

1/2 celery root, cubed
2 cups chicken stock
3 cups water
Salt and pepper to taste

Directions:

Heat the oil in a skillet and add the bacon. Cook until crisp then remove the bacon on a plate. Pour the fat of the bacon in your slow cooker and add the remaining ingredients. Adjust the taste with salt and pepper and cook on high settings for 1 1/2 hours. When done, puree the soup with an immersion blender until smooth. Pour the soup in a bowl and top with bacon. Serve right away.

$\mathcal{P}$INTO BEAN CHILI SOUP

Time: 4 1/4 hours   Servings: 10

Ingredients:

2 tablespoons olive oil
1 red onion, chopped
2 red bell peppers, cored and diced
1 garlic clove, chopped
1/2 teaspoon chili powder
1/2 teaspoon cumin powder
2 cups butternut squash cubes
2 cups cooked pinto beans

1/2 cup canned sweet corn, drained
2 cups water
4 cups chicken stock
2 tablespoons tomato paste
1 bay leaf
1 thyme sprig
Salt and pepper to taste

Directions:

Heat the oil in a skillet and stir in the onion. Cook for 2 minutes until softened. Transfer the onion in your slow cooker. Add the bell peppers, garlic, chili powder, cumin and butternut squash, as well as pinto beans, corn, water, stock, tomato paste, bay leaf and thyme. Season with salt and pepper and cook the soup on low settings for 4 hours. Serve the soup warm or chilled.

$\mathcal{B}$LACK BEAN SOUP

Time: 7 1/4 hours   Servings: 8

Ingredients:

1/2 pound black beans, rinsed
2 cups chicken stock
5 cups water
1 sweet onion, chopped
2 carrots, diced
1 parsnip, diced
1 celery stalk, diced
1 red bell peppers, cored and diced

2 tomatoes, diced
2 tablespoons tomato paste
1/2 teaspoon cumin powder
1/4 teaspoon chili powder
1 bay leaf
Salt and pepper to taste
2 tablespoons chopped cilantro for serving
1/2 cup sour cream for serving

Directions:

Combine the black beans, chicken stock, water and vegetables in your slow cooker.
Add the cumin powder, chili powder, bay leaf, salt and pepper and cook the soup on low settings for 7 hours.
When done, stir in the cilantro. Pour the soup in bowls and top with sour cream just before serving.

$\mathcal{T}$HREE BEAN SOUP

Time: 4 1/2 hours   Servings: 10

Ingredients:

2 tablespoons olive oil
2 sweet onions, chopped
2 garlic cloves, minced
2 red bell peppers, cored and diced

2 carrots, diced
1 can (15 oz.) black beans, drained
1 can (15 oz.) kidney beans, drained
1 can (15 oz.) pinto beans, drained

2 cups chicken stock
4 cups water
1 cup diced tomatoes
Salt and pepper to taste

1 lime, juiced
1/2 cup sour cream
2 tablespoons chopped parsley

Directions:

Heat the oil in a skillet and stir in the onions, garlic, peppers and carrot. Sauté for 5 minutes. Transfer the mixture in your slow cooker and stir in the beans, stock, water, tomatoes, salt and pepper. Cook on low settings for 4 hours. When done, add the lime juice. Pour the soup in serving bowls and top with sour cream and parsley. The soup is best served warm or cold.

POSOLE SOUP

Time: 6 1/4 hours

Servings: 8

Ingredients:

1 tablespoons canola oil
1 pound pork tenderloin, cubed
1 sweet onion, chopped
2 garlic cloves, chopped
1/2 teaspoon cumin powder
1/2 teaspoon dried oregano
1/2 teaspoon dried basil
1/4 teaspoon chili powder

1 can (15 oz.) black beans, drained
1 can sweet corn, drained
1 cup diced tomatoes
2 jalapeno peppers, chopped
4 cups chicken stock
2 cups water
Salt and pepper to taste
2 limes, juiced

Directions:

Heat the canola oil in a skillet and stir in the tenderloin. Cook for 5 minutes on all sides.
Add the pork in your slow cooker and stir in the remaining ingredients, except the lime juice.
Add salt and pepper to taste and cook on low settings for 6 hours.
When done, stir in the lime juice and serve the soup warm or chilled.

PROVENCAL BEEF SOUP

Time: 7 1/4 hours

Servings: 8

Ingredients:

2 tablespoons olive oil
1 pound beef roast, cubed
1 sweet onion, chopped
1 garlic clove, chopped
2 carrots, sliced
1 celery stalk, sliced
1 can diced tomatoes

1 cup beef stock
1 cup red wine
4 cups water
1/2 teaspoon dried thyme
1 bay leaf
Salt and pepper to taste

Directions:

Heat the oil in a skillet and stir in the beef roast. Cook on all sides for a few minutes then transfer the beef in a slow cooker. Add the remaining ingredients and adjust the taste with salt and pepper. Cook on low settings for 7 hours. Serve the soup warm or chilled.

Sausage Bean Soup

Time: 3 1/4 hours   Servings: 8

Ingredients:

2 bacon slices, chopped
1 sweet onion, chopped
1 garlic clove, chopped
1/2 teaspoon dried rosemary
1/2 teaspoon dried thyme
4 pork sausages, sliced
1 carrot, diced

1 parsnip, diced
1 celery stalk, sliced
1 can diced tomatoes
1 can (15 oz.) white beans, drained
2 cups chicken stock
4 cups water
Salt and pepper to taste

Directions:

Heat a skillet over medium flame and stir in the bacon. Sauté for 2-3 minutes until crisp. Transfer the bacon in your slow cooker. Add the remaining ingredients and season with salt and pepper. Cook the soup on high settings for 3 hours. The soup is best served warm, but it tastes great chilled as well.

Curried Lentil Soup

Time: 4 1/4 hours   Servings: 8

Ingredients:

4 bacon slices, chopped
1 sweet onion, chopped
2 garlic cloves, chopped
1 cup dried lentils, rinsed
1 carrot, diced
1 celery stalk, sliced
1 parsnip, diced
1 cup diced tomatoes

2 cups chicken stock
4 cups water
1 teaspoon curry powder
1/4 teaspoon ground ginger
Salt and pepper to taste
1 lime, juiced
2 tablespoons chopped parsley

Directions:

Heat a skillet over medium flame and stir in the bacon. Cook for a few minutes until crisp. Transfer the bacon in a slow cooker and stir in the onion, garlic, lentils, carrot, celery, parsnip, tomatoes, stock, water, curry powder and ginger. Add salt and pepper to taste and cook on low settings for 4 hours. When done, stir in the lime juice and chopped parsley and serve the soup warm or chilled.

Tuscan Chicken Soup

Time: 6 1/4 hours   Servings: 6

Ingredients:

2 chicken breasts, cubed
2 tablespoons canola oil
1 shallot, chopped
1 carrot, diced
1 parsnip, diced

1 celery stalk, sliced
1 red bell peppers, cored and diced
1 can (15 oz.) cannellini beans, drained
1 can diced tomatoes
2 cups chicken stock

2 cups water
Salt and pepper to taste

1 teaspoon dried Italian herbs
2 oz. Parmesan shavings

Directions:

Heat the canola oil in a skillet and stir in the chicken. Cook for a few minutes on all sides until golden brown. Transfer the chicken in your slow cooker.

Add the shallot, parsnip, celery, bell peppers, beans, tomatoes, stock and water.

Add salt and pepper to taste, as well as the herbs and cook on low settings for 6 hours.

Serve the soup warm or chilled, topped with Parmesan shavings.

Mixed Bean Vegetarian Soup

Time: 4 1/4 hours   Servings: 8

Ingredients:

1 tablespoon olive oil
1 sweet onion, chopped
1 garlic clove, chopped
1 carrot, diced
1 celery stalk, sliced
1 red bell pepper, cored and diced
1/2 teaspoon chili powder
1/2 teaspoon cumin powder
2 cups vegetable stock

1 can (15 oz.) white bean, drained
1 can (15 oz.) cannellini beans, drained
1 cup diced tomatoes
2 cups water
Salt and pepper to taste
2 tablespoons chopped cilantro
1 lime, juiced
1 avocado, peeled and sliced

Directions:

Heat the oil in a skillet and add the onion, carrot, garlic and celery. Cook for 5 minutes until softened.

Transfer in your slow cooker and stir in the remaining ingredients, except the cilantro, lime and avocado.

Adjust the taste with salt and pepper and cook on low settings for 4 hours.

When done, pour the soup into serving bowls and top with cilantro and avocado.

Drizzle with lime juice and serve right away.

Tomato Beef Soup

Time: 8 1/4 hours   Servings: 8

Ingredients:

2 tablespoons olive oil
2 bacon slices, chopped
2 pounds beef roast, cubed
2 sweet onions, chopped
2 tomatoes, peeled and diced
2 cups tomato sauce

1 cup beef stock
3 cups water
Salt and pepper to taste
1 thyme sprig
1 rosemary sprig

Directions:

Heat the oil in a skillet and add the bacon. Cook until crisp and stir in the beef roast. Cook for 5 minutes on all sides. Transfer the beet and bacon in a slow cooker. Add the remaining ingredients and adjust the taste with salt and pepper.

Cook on low settings for 8 hours.

Serve the soup warm or chilled.

Coconut Squash Soup

Time: 2 1/4 hours   Servings: 6

Ingredients:

1 tablespoon olive oil
1 shallot, chopped
1/2 teaspoon grated ginger
2 garlic cloves, minced
1 tablespoon curry paste
1 teaspoon brown sugar
1 teaspoon Worcestershire sauce

3 cups butternut squash cubes
2 cups chicken stock
2 cups water
1 cup coconut milk
1 tablespoon tomato paste
Salt and pepper to taste

Directions:

Heat the oil in a skillet and stir in the shallot, garlic, ginger and curry paste. Sauté for 1 minute then transfer the mixture in your slow cooker. Add the remaining ingredients and season with salt and pepper. Cover with its lid and cook on high settings for 2 hours. When done, puree the soup with an immersion blender until smooth. Pour the soup into serving bowls and serve it warm.

French Onion Soup

Time: 1 3/4 hours   Servings: 6

Ingredients:

4 sweet onions, sliced
2 tablespoons butter
1 tablespoon canola oil
1 teaspoon brown sugar
4 cups beef stock
2 cups water

1 tablespoon red wine vinegar
Salt and pepper to taste
1 thyme sprig
1 rosemary sprig
Toasted bread for serving
Grated Gruyere cheese for serving

Directions:

Heat the butter and oil in a skillet and stir in the onion. Cook for 10-15 minutes until they begin to caramelize, adding the brown sugar half way through the cooking time. This step is compulsory as caramelizing the onions improves their taste. Transfer the onions in your slow cooker and add the stock, water, red wine vinegar, thyme and rosemary. Season with salt and pepper and cook on high settings for 1 1/2 hours. For serving, pour the hot soup into bowls and top right away with a slice of toasted bread and plenty of grated cheese. Serve right away.

Shrimp Soup

Time: 6 1/4 hours   Servings: 6

Ingredients:

2 tablespoons olive oil
1 large sweet onion, chopped
1 fennel bulb, sliced
4 garlic cloves, chopped
1 cup dry white wine

1/2 cup tomato sauce
2 cup water
1 teaspoon dried oregano
1 teaspoon dried basil
1 pinch chili powder

4 medium size tomatoes, peeled and diced
1 bay leaf
1/2 pound cod fillets, cubed

1/2 pound fresh shrimps, peeled and deveined
Salt and pepper to taste
1 lime, juiced

Directions:

Heat the oil in a skillet and stir in the onion, fennel and garlic. Sauté for 5 minutes until softened.

Transfer the mixture in your slow cooker and stir in the wine, tomato sauce, water, oregano, basil, chili powder, tomatoes and bay leaf.

Cook on high settings for 1 hour then add the cod and shrimps, as well as lime juice, salt and pepper and continue cooking on low settings for 5 additional hours.

Serve the soup warm or chilled.

CREAMY POTATO SOUP

Time: 6 1/2 hours

Servings: 6

Ingredients:

6 bacon slices, chopped
1 sweet onion, chopped
1 can condensed chicken soup
6 medium size potatoes, peeled and cubed

2 cups water
Salt and pepper to taste
1 1/2 cups half and half
1 tablespoon chopped parsley

Directions:

Heat a skillet over medium flame and add the bacon. Cook until crisp then transfer the bacon and its fat in your slow cooker.

Add the onion, chicken soup, potatoes, water, salt and pepper and cook on low settings for 4 hours.

Add the half and half and continue cooking for 2 additional hours.

When done, stir in the chopped parsley and serve the soup warm.

ITALIAN BARLEY SOUP

Time: 6 1/4 hours

Servings: 6

Ingredients:

1 pound beef roast, cubed
2 tablespoons olive oil
1 large sweet onion, chopped
1 carrot, sliced
1 parsnip, sliced
2 ripe tomatoes, peeled and diced
2 cups beef stock

3 cups water
1/2 cup uncooked barley
1/2 teaspoon dried oregano
1 teaspoon dried basil
1/2 teaspoon dried thyme
Salt and pepper to taste

Directions:

Heat the oil in a skillet and stir in the beef. Cook for 5-6 minutes on all sides.

Transfer the beef in your slow cooker and stir in the remaining ingredients.

Add salt and pepper to taste and cook the soup on low settings for 6 hours.

The soup is best served warm.

QUICK LENTIL HAM SOUP

Time: 1 3/4 hours   Servings: 6

Ingredients:

1 tablespoon olive oil   1/2 teaspoon dried basil
4 oz. ham, diced   1 cup dried lentils, rinsed
1 carrot, diced   2 cups water
1 celery stalk, sliced   1/2 cup tomato sauce
1 shallot, chopped   1 1/2 cups chicken stock
1/2 teaspoon dried oregano   Salt and pepper to taste

Directions:

Combine the olive oil, ham, carrot, celery, shallot, oregano, basil, lentils, water, tomato sauce and stock.
Add salt and pepper to taste and cook on high settings for 1 1/2 hours.
The soup can be served both warm and chilled.

SPLIT PEA SAUSAGE SOUP

Time: 6 1/4 hours   Servings: 8

Ingredients:

2 cups split peas, rinsed   1 red chili, chopped
8 cups water   1/2 teaspoon dried oregano
4 Italian sausages, sliced   2 tablespoons tomato paste
1 sweet onion, chopped   Salt and pepper to taste
2 carrots, diced   1 lemon, juiced
1 celery stalk, diced   2 tablespoons chopped parsley
1 garlic clove, chopped

Directions:

Combine the split peas, water, sausages, onion, carrots, celery, garlic, red chili, oregano and tomato paste in your slow cooker. Add salt and pepper to taste and cook on low settings for 6 hours. When done, stir in the lemon juice and parsley and serve the soup warm.

ZUCCHINI SOUP

Time: 2 1/4 hours   Servings: 6

Ingredients:

1 pound Italian sausages, sliced   2 cups vegetable stock
2 celery stalks, sliced   1/2 teaspoon dried oregano
2 zucchinis, cubed   1/2 teaspoon dried basil
2 large potatoes, peeled and cubed   1/4 teaspoon garlic powder
2 yellow bell peppers, cored and diced   Salt and pepper to taste
2 carrots, sliced   2 tablespoons chopped parsley
1 shallot, chopped
3 cups water

Directions:

Combine the sausages, celery stalks, zucchinis, potatoes, bell peppers, carrots, shallot, water, stock and seasoning in your slow cooker.

Add salt and pepper to taste and cook on high settings for 2 hours.

When done, stir in the parsley and serve the soup warm.

BEEF TACO SOUP

Time: 7 1/4 hours   Servings: 8

Ingredients:

1 pound beef stock, cubed
1 tablespoon olive oil
1 onion, chopped
1 garlic clove, chopped
1 can (15 oz.) black beans, drained
1 can (15 oz.) cannellini beans, drained
1 cup canned corn, drained
1 cup tomato sauce

1 cup dark beer
2 tablespoons taco seasoning
1 jalapeno pepper, chopped
Salt and pepper to taste
3 cups water
2 cups beef stock
1 avocado, sliced
1/2 cup sour cream

Directions:

Heat the oil in a skillet and add the onion and beef, garlic. Sauté for 2 minutes then transfer in your slow cooker.

Stir in the beans, corn, tomato sauce, beer, taco seasoning and jalapeno.

Add salt and pepper to taste and cook on low settings for 7 hours.

To serve, pour the soup into serving bowls and top with sour cream and avocado slices.

SOUTHWESTERN BEAN SOUP

Time: 6 1/4 hours   Servings: 8

Ingredients:

2 tablespoons olive oil
1 pound ground chicken
2 cans (15 oz.) white beans, drained
1 can diced tomatoes
1 cup sweet corn, drained
1 shallot, chopped
1 jalapeno pepper, chopped
2 garlic cloves, chopped

1/2 teaspoon chili powder
1/2 teaspoon cumin powder
1/2 teaspoon coriander seeds
Salt and pepper to taste
2 cups chicken stock
3 cups water
1 lime, juiced

Directions:

Heat the oil in a skillet. Add the chicken and cook for 5 minutes, stirring all the time. Transfer the chicken in your slow cooker and stir in the beans, tomatoes, corn, shallot, pepper, garlic, chili powder, cumin powder, coriander seeds, salt and pepper to taste. Add the stock and water as well. Cover the pot and cook on low settings for 6 hours. Stir in the lime juice and serve the soup warm.

Spicy Black Bean Soup

Time: 6 1/4 hours   Servings: 6

Ingredients:

1 tablespoon olive oil
1 shallot, chopped
1 carrot, diced
2 jalapeno peppers, chopped
2 cups chicken stock
1 can (15 oz.) black beans, drained

4 cups water
1/2 teaspoon chili powder
1/2 teaspoon cumin powder
1/2 cup diced tomatoes
Salt and pepper to taste
1/2 cup sour cream

Directions:

Combine the olive oil, shallot, carrot, jalapeno peppers, stock, beans, water and spices in your slow cooker. Add salt and pepper to taste and cook on low settings for 6 hours. Cook on low settings for6 hours. Serve the soup warm, topped with sour cream.

Chicken Sausage Soup

Time: 6 1/2 hours   Servings: 8

Ingredients:

1 pound Italian sausages, sliced
1 sweet onion, chopped
2 garlic cloves, chopped
1 red bell pepper, cored and diced
1 carrot, diced
1/2 teaspoon dried oregano
1/2 teaspoon dried basil
1 can diced tomatoes

1 can cannellini beans
1/4 cup dry white wine
2 cups chicken stock
3 cups water
1/2 cup short pasta
Salt and pepper to taste
2 tablespoons chopped parsley

Directions:

Combine the sausages, onion, garlic, bell pepper, carrot, oregano, basil, tomatoes, beans, wine, stock and water in a slow cooker.
Cook on high settings for 1 hour then add the pasta and continue cooking for 5 hours.
Serve the soup warm, topped with freshly chopped parsley.

Beef Cabbage Soup

Time: 7 1/2 hours   Servings: 8

Ingredients:

1 pound beef roast, cubed
2 tablespoons olive oil
1 sweet onion, chopped
1 carrot, grated
1 small cabbage head, shredded
1 can (15 oz.) diced tomatoes

2 cups beef stock
2 cups water
1/2 teaspoon cumin seeds
Salt and pepper to taste

Directions:

Heat the oil in a skillet and add the beef roast. Cook for 5-6 minutes on all sides then transfer the meat in your slow cooker. Add the remaining ingredients and season with salt and pepper. Cook on low settings for 7 hours. Serve the cabbage soup warm.

Beef Vegetable Soup

Time: 7 1/4 hours   Servings: 8

Ingredients:

1 pound beef roast, cubed
2 tablespoons canola oil
1 celery stalk, sliced
1 sweet onion, chopped
1 carrot, sliced
1 garlic clove, chopped
1/2 head cauliflower, cut into florets

2 large potatoes, peeled and cubed
1 cup diced tomatoes
1/2 teaspoon dried basil
2 cups beef stock
4 cups water
Salt and pepper to taste

Directions:

Heat the oil in a skillet and add the beef. Cook on all sides for a few minutes then transfer the beef in your slow cooker. Add the remaining ingredients and season with salt and pepper. Cover and cook on low settings for 7 hours. The soup is delicious either warm or chilled.

Sweet Corn Chowder

Time: 6 1/4 hours   Servings: 8

Ingredients:

2 shallots, chopped
4 medium size potatoes, peeled and cubed
1 celery stalk, sliced
1 can (15 oz.) sweet corn, drained

2 cups chicken stock
2 cups water
Salt and pepper to taste

Directions:

Combine the shallot, potatoes, celery, corn, stock and water in a slow cooker.
Add salt and pepper to taste and cook on low settings for 6 hours.
When done, remove a few tablespoons of corn from the pot then puree the remaining soup in the pot.
Pour the soup into serving bowls and top with the reserved corn.
Serve warm.

Chicken Enchilada Soup

Time: 6 1/2 hours   Servings: 8

Ingredients:

1 tablespoon olive oil
2 shallots, chopped
2 garlic cloves, chopped

1 chicken breast, diced
1 can (15 oz.) diced tomatoes
1 can (15 oz.) sweet corn, drained

1 can (4 oz.) green chile, chopped
2 cups chicken stock
4 cups water
1/2 teaspoon cumin powder

1/2 teaspoon chili powder
1 bay leaf
Salt and pepper to taste

Directions:

Combine the olive oil, shallots, garlic and chicken in a skillet and cook for 5 minutes.
Transfer the chicken in your slow cooker and add the remaining ingredients.
Add salt and pepper to taste and cook on low settings for 6 hours.
Serve the soup warm.

ITALIAN BARLEY SOUP

Time: 6 1/4 hours

Servings: 8

Ingredients:

2 tablespoons olive oil
1 shallot, chopped
1 garlic clove, chopped
1 carrot, diced
1 celery stalk, diced
2 red bell peppers, cored and diced
2 tomatoes, peeled and diced
2 cups vegetable stock

1 teaspoon dried oregano
1 teaspoon dried basil
2/3 cup pearl barley
3 cups water
2 cups fresh spinach, chopped
1 lemon, juiced
Salt and pepper to taste

Directions:

Heat the oil in a skillet and stir in the shallot, garlic, carrot and celery, as well as bell peppers.
Cook for 5 minutes just until softened then transfer in your slow cooker. You can skip this step, but sautéing the vegetables first improves the taste.
Add the remaining ingredients to the pot and season with salt and pepper.
Cook on low settings for 6 hours.
The soup is great served either warm or chilled.

HAM BONE CABBAGE SOUP

Time: 7 1/4 hours

Servings: 8

Ingredients:

1 ham bone
1 sweet onion, chopped
1 mediums size cabbage head, shredded
2 tablespoons tomato paste
1 can diced tomatoes

2 cups beef stock
Salt and pepper to taste
1 bay leaf
1 thyme sprig
1 lemon, juiced

Directions:

Combine the ham bone, onion, cabbage, tomato paste, tomatoes, stock, bay leaf and thyme sprig in your slow cooker.
Add salt and pepper to taste and cook on low settings for 7 hours.
When done, stir in the lemon juice and serve the soup warm.

Lima Bean Soup

Time: 7 1/4 hours   Servings: 8

Ingredients:

2 bacon slices, chopped
4 cups frozen lima beans
2 shallots, chopped
2 carrots, diced
2 potatoes, peeled and cubed
1 celery stalk, sliced

1 can diced tomatoes
2 cups vegetable stock
3 cups water
1 bay leaf
Salt and pepper to taste
1 tablespoon chopped cilantro

Directions:

Combine the bacon, lima beans, shallots, carrots, potatoes, celery and tomatoes in a slow cooker.
Add the remaining ingredients, except cilantro and season with salt and pepper.
Cook on low settings for 7 hours.
When done, stir in the chopped cilantro and serve the soup warm.

Okra Vegetable Soup

Time: 7 1/4 hours   Servings: 8

Ingredients:

1 pound ground beef
2 tablespoons canola oil
2 shallots, chopped
1 carrot, sliced
1 can fire roasted tomatoes, chopped
2 cups chopped okra
1/2 cup green peas

2 potatoes, peeled and cubed
1/2 cup sweet corn, drained
Salt and pepper to taste
2 cups water
2 cups chicken stock
1 lemon, juiced

Directions:

Heat the oil in a skillet and stir in the beef. Cook for a few minutes then transfer the meat in your slow cooker.
Add the shallots, carrot, tomatoes, okra, peas, potatoes, corn, water and stock, as well as lemon juice, salt and pepper.
Cook the soup on low settings for 7 hours.
Serve the soup warm and fresh.

Mexican Beef Soup

Time: 8 1/4 hours   Servings: 6

Ingredients:

1 pound ground beef
2 tablespoons canola oil
2 red bell peppers, cored and diced
1 sweet onion, chopped
2 cups beef stock
1 can (15 oz.) diced tomatoes

1 can (15 oz.) black beans, drained
3 cups water
1/2 cup red salsa
1 chipotle pepper, chopped
Salt and pepper to taste

Directions:

Heat the oil in a skillet and stir in the beef. Cook for 5 minutes, stirring often, then transfer the beef in your slow cooker.

Add the remaining ingredients and adjust the taste with salt and pepper.

Cook on low settings for 8 hours.

Serve the soup warm or chilled.

HUNGARIAN BORSCHT

Time: 8 1/4 hours   Servings: 8

Ingredients:

1 pound beef roast, cubed

2 tablespoons canola oil

4 medium size beets, peeled and cubed

1 can diced tomatoes

2 potatoes, peeled and cubed

1 sweet onion, chopped

2 tablespoons tomato paste

Salt and pepper to taste

4 cups water

1 cup vegetable stock

1/2 teaspoon cumin seeds

1 teaspoon red wine vinegar

1 teaspoon honey

1/2 teaspoon dried dill

1 teaspoon dried parsley

Directions:

Heat the oil in a skillet and stir in the beef. Cook for a few minutes on all sides until golden.

Transfer the meat in your slow cooker and add the beets, tomatoes, potatoes, onion and tomato paste.

Add salt and pepper, as well as the remaining ingredients and cook on low settings for 8 hours.

Serve the soup warm or chilled.

CHICKEN RICE SOUP

Time: 7 1/4 hours   Servings: 8

Ingredients:

2 chicken breasts, cubed

2 tablespoons canola oil

2 carrots, diced

2 red bell peppers, cored and diced

1 celery stalk, sliced

1 sweet onion, chopped

1 parsnip, diced

1 can diced tomatoes

2 cups water

2 cups chicken stock

2/3 cup white rice, rinsed

Salt and pepper to taste

Directions:

Heat the canola oil in a skillet and stir in the chicken. Cook for 5 minutes on all sides until golden.

Transfer the chicken in a slow cooker and stir in the remaining ingredients.

Add salt and pepper to taste and cook on low settings for 7 hours.

Serve the soup warm or re-heat it when needed.

Ham Potato Chowder

Time: 4 1/4 hours   Servings: 8

Ingredients:

1 tablespoon olive oil
1 sweet onion, chopped
1 can condensed chicken soup
2 cups water
4 potatoes, peeled and cubed

1 cup diced ham
1 cup sweet corn, drained
1/2 teaspoon celery seeds
1/2 teaspoon cumin seeds
Salt and pepper to taste

Directions:

Mix the olive oil, onion, chicken soup, water, potatoes, ham and corn in your slow cooker. Add the celery seeds and cumin seeds and season with salt and pepper. Cook on high settings for 4 hours. Serve the soup warm.

Potato Kielbasa Soup

Time: 6 1/4 hours   Servings: 8

Ingredients:

1 pound kielbasa sausages, sliced
1 sweet onion, chopped
2 carrots, diced
1 parsnip, diced
1 garlic clove, chopped
2 red bell peppers, cored and diced

2 large potatoes, peeled and cubed
2 cups chicken stock
3 cups water
1/2 pound fresh spinach, shredded
1 lemon, juiced
Salt and pepper to taste

Directions:

Combine the sausages, onion, carrots, parsnip, garlic, potatoes and bell peppers in your slow cooker.
Stir in the stock, water, spinach and lemon juice then add salt and pepper to taste.
Cook on low settings for 6 hours.
Serve the soup warm or chilled.

Curried Corn Chowder

Time: 8 1/4 hours   Servings: 8

Ingredients:

1 sweet onion, chopped
2 garlic cloves, chopped
2 cups chicken stock
1 can (15 oz.) sweet corn, drained
2 large potatoes, peeled and cubed

1/2 chili pepper, chopped
1 1/2 cups whole milk
Salt and pepper to taste
1/4 teaspoon cumin seeds

Directions:

Combine the onion, garlic, stock, sweet corn, potatoes and chili pepper in your slow cooker.
Add the remaining ingredients and season with salt and pepper. Cook on low settings for 8 hours.
Serve the soup warm and fresh.

Two-Fish Soup

Time: 6 1/4 hours

Servings: 8

Ingredients:

1 tablespoon canola oil
1 sweet onion, chopped
1 red bell pepper, cored and diced
1 chipotle pepper, chopped
1 carrot, diced
1 celery stalk, diced

1 cup diced tomatoes
1 lemon, juiced
3 salmon fillets, cubed
3 cod fillets, cubed
2 tablespoons chopped parsley
Salt and pepper to taste

Directions:

Heat the canola oil in a skillet and add the onion. Sauté for 2 minutes until softened. Transfer the onion in a slow cooker and stir in the remaining ingredients. Add salt and pepper to taste and cook on low settings for 6 hours. Serve the soup warm.

Creamy Cauliflower Soup

Time: 3 1/4 hours

Servings: 6

Ingredients:

1 tablespoon canola oil
1 sweet onion, chopped
2 garlic cloves, chopped
1 head cauliflower, cut into florets
2 medium size potatoes, peeled and cubed

1 can condensed cream of chicken soup
Salt and pepper to taste
1/2 cup water
1/2 cup grated Parmesan cheese

Directions:

Heat the oil in a skillet and add the onion. Cook for 2 minutes then transfer the onion in your slow cooker. Add the remaining ingredients, except the cheese, and season with salt and pepper. Cook on high settings for 3 hours. When done, puree the soup with an immersion blender. Serve the soup warm.

Stroganoff Soup

Time: 8 1/4 hours

Servings: 8

Ingredients:

2 pound beef roast, cubed
2 tablespoons all-purpose flour
2 tablespoons canola oil
1 sweet onion, chopped
1 can condensed cream of mushroom soup

2 cups chicken stock
1 cup water
1/2 cup sour cream
Salt and pepper to taste

Directions:

Season the beef with salt and pepper and sprinkle with flour. Heat the oil in a skillet and stir in the beef. Cook for a few minutes on all sides then transfer the beef in your slow cooker. Add the onion, soup, stock, water and sour cream. Season with salt and pepper and cook on low settings for 8 hours. Serve the soup warm.

Winter Veggie Soup

Time: 6 1/2 hours   Servings: 8

Ingredients:

1 sweet onion, chopped
2 carrots, sliced
1 celery stalk, sliced
1/2 head cabbage, shredded
1 parsnip, sliced
1 celery root, peeled and cubed

Salt and pepper to taste
2 cups vegetable stock
3 cups water
1 cup diced tomatoes
1/4 cup white rice, rinsed
1 lemon, juiced

Directions:

Combine the onion, carrots, celery, cabbage, parsnip, celery, stock, water, tomatoes and rice in your slow cooker.
Add salt and pepper to taste, as well as the rice and cook on low settings for 6 hours.
The soup is best served warm.

Spiced Creamy Pumpkin Soup

Time: 5 1/4 hours   Servings: 6

Ingredients:

1 shallot, chopped
2 carrots, sliced
2 garlic cloves, chopped
2 tablespoons olive oil
1 medium sugar pumpkin, peeled and cubed
2 cups chicken stock
2 cups water

1 thyme sprig
Salt and pepper to taste
1/2 cinnamon stick
1 star anise
1/2 teaspoon cumin powder
1/4 teaspoon chili powder

Directions:

Combine the shallot, carrots, garlic and olive oil in a skillet. Cook for 5 minutes until softened. Transfer in your slow cooker and add the remaining ingredients, including the spices. Cook on low settings for 5 hours then remove the cinnamon, thyme sprig and star anise and puree the soup with an immersion blender. The soup can be served either warm or chilled.

Kielbasa Kale Soup

Time: 6 1/4 hours   Servings: 8

Ingredients:

1 pound kielbasa sausages, sliced
1 sweet onion, chopped
1 carrot, diced
1 parsnip, diced
1 red bell pepper, cored and diced
1 can (15 oz.) white beans, drained
1 cup diced tomatoes

1/2 pound kale, shredded
2 cups chicken stock
2 cups water
1/2 teaspoon dried oregano
1/2 teaspoon dried basil
Salt and pepper to taste

Directions:

Combine the kielbasa sausages, onion, carrot, parsnip, bell pepper, white beans, tomatoes and kale in a slow cooker.

Add the remaining ingredients and season with salt and pepper.

Cook on low settings for 6 hours.

Serve the soup warm or chilled.

LEMONY SALMON SOUP

Time: 4 1/4 hours   Servings: 6

Ingredients:

1 shallot, chopped

1 garlic clove, chopped

1 celery stalk, sliced

1 carrot, sliced

1 parsnip, sliced

1 red bell pepper, cored and diced

1/2 teaspoon dried oregano

1/2 teaspoon dried basil

2 cups milk

2 cups water

1 lemon, juiced

1 teaspoon lemon zest

1 pound salmon fillets, cubed

Salt and pepper to taste

Directions:

Combine the shallot, garlic, celery, carrot, parsnip and bell pepper in your slow cooker.

Add the dried herbs, milk, water, lemon juice and lemon zest and cook for 1 hour on high settings.

Add the fish and season with salt and pepper.

Cook for 3 additional hours on low settings.

Serve the soup warm or chilled.

CREAMY NOODLE SOUP

Time: 8 1/4 hours   Servings: 8

Ingredients:

2 chicken breasts, cubed

2 tablespoons all-purpose flour

2 shallots, chopped

1 celery stalk, sliced

1 can condensed chicken soup

2 cups water

2 cups chicken stock

Salt and pepper to taste

1 cup green peas

6 oz. egg noodles

Directions:

Sprinkle the chicken with salt, pepper and flour and place it in your slow cooker.

Add the remaining ingredients and season with salt and pepper.

Cover and cook on low settings for 8 hours.

This soup is best served warm.

Asparagus Crab Soup

Time: 2 1/4 hours   Servings: 6

Ingredients:

1 tablespoon olive oil
1 shallot, chopped
1 celery stalk, sliced
1 bunch asparagus, trimmed and chopped
1 cup green peas

1 cup chicken stock
2 cups water
Salt and pepper to taste
1 can crab meat, drained

Directions:

Heat the oil in a skillet and add the shallot and celery. Sauté for 2 minutes until softened then transfer in your slow cooker. Add the asparagus, green peas, stock and water and season with salt and pepper. Cook on high settings for 2 hours. When done, puree the soup with an immersion blender until creamy. Pour the soup into serving bowls and top with crab meat. Serve the soup right away.

Orange Sweet Potato Soup

Time: 3 1/2 hours   Servings: 8

Ingredients:

2 tablespoons olive oil
1 shallot, chopped
2 carrots, sliced
1/2 celery stalk
2 large sweet potatoes, peeled and cubed
2 oranges, juiced
1 teaspoon orange zest

2 cups chicken stick
1 bay leaf
1/2 cinnamon stalk
Salt and pepper to taste
1 teaspoon pumpkin seeds oil
2 tablespoons pumpkin seeds

Directions:

Heat the olive oil in a skillet and add the shallot and carrots. Sauté for 5 minutes then transfer in your slow cooker.
Add the celery stalk, potatoes, orange juice, orange zest, stock, bay leaf, cinnamon, salt and pepper.
Cook the soup on high settings for 2 hours then on low settings for 1 additional hour.
When done, remove the bay leaf and cinnamon stick and puree the soup with an immersion blender.
To serve, pour the soup into bowls and top with pumpkin seeds drizzle of pumpkin seed oil. Serve right away.

Cream of Broccoli Soup

Time: 2 1/4 hours   Servings: 6

Ingredients:

2 shallots, chopped
2 garlic cloves, chopped
2 tablespoons olive oil
1 head broccoli, cut into florets
2 potatoes, peeled and cubed
1 cup chicken stock

2 cups water
Salt and pepper to taste
1/2 teaspoon dried basil
1/2 teaspoon dried oregano

Directions:

Heat the oil in a skillet and stir in the shallots and garlic. Sauté for a few minutes until softened then transfer in your slow cooker. Add the broccoli, potatoes, chicken stock and water, as well as dried herbs, salt and pepper. Cook on high settings for 2 hours then puree the soup in a blender until creamy and rich. Pour the soup into bowls in order to serve.

HAM AND WHITE BEAN SOUP

Time: 6 1/4 hours   Servings: 8

Ingredients:

2 tablespoons olive oil
1 sweet onion, chopped
1 garlic clove, chopped
1 yellow bell pepper, cored and diced
1 celery stalk, diced
1 cup diced ham

2 cans (15 oz.) white beans, drained
2 cups chicken stock
3 cups water
Salt and pepper to taste
2 tablespoons chopped parsley

Directions:

Heat the oil in a skillet and stir in the onion, garlic, celery and bell pepper. Sauté for 5 minutes until softened and transfer in your slow cooker. Add the ham, white beans, stock and water and season with salt and pepper. Cook on low settings for 6 hours. To serve, pour the soup into bowls and top with parsley. The soup can be served both warm and chilled.

CHEESY BROCCOLI SOUP

Time: 4 1/4 hours   Servings: 8

Ingredients:

1 shallot, chopped
2 garlic cloves, chopped
2 tablespoons olive oil
1 head broccoli, cut into florets
1 large potato, peeled and cubed

1 can condensed chicken soup
2 cups water
1/2 teaspoon dried oregano
1 cup grated Cheddar soup
Salt and pepper to taste

Directions:

Heat the olive oil in a skillet and stir in the shallot and garlic. Cook for 2 minutes until softened. Transfer the shallot and garlic in your slow cooker and add the remaining ingredients. Cook on low settings for 4 hours then puree the soup with an immersion blender. Serve the soup warm.

CHUNKY POTATO HAM SOUP

Time: 8 1/2 hours   Servings: 8

Ingredients:

2 cups diced ham
1 sweet onion, chopped
1 garlic clove, chopped
1 leek, sliced

1 celery stalk, sliced
2 carrots, sliced
2 pounds potatoes, peeled and cubed
1/2 teaspoon dried oregano

1/2 teaspoon dried basil
2 cups chicken stock

3 cups water
Salt and pepper to taste

Directions:

Combine all the ingredients in your slow cooker. Add salt and pepper to taste and cook on low settings for 8 hours. Serve the soup warm or chilled.

LEEK POTATO SOUP

Time: 6 1/2 hours

Servings: 8

Ingredients:

4 leeks, sliced
1 tablespoon olive oil
4 bacon slices, chopped
1 celery stalk, sliced
4 large potatoes, peeled and cubed
2 cups chicken stock
3 cups water

1 bay leaf
Salt and pepper to taste
1/4 teaspoon cayenne pepper
1/4 teaspoon smoked paprika
1 thyme sprig
1 rosemary sprig

Directions:

Heat the oil in a skillet and add the bacon. Cook until crisp then stir in the leeks. Sauté for 5 minutes until softened then transfer in your slow cooker. Add the remaining ingredients and cook on low settings for about 6 hours. Serve the soup warm.

CREAMY LEEK AND POTATO SOUP

Time: 6 1/4 hours

Servings: 6

Ingredients:

2 tablespoons olive oil
2 leeks, sliced
1 tablespoon all-purpose flour
2 cups chicken stock
2 cups water

4 large potatoes, peeled and cubed
Salt and pepper to taste
1/2 cup heavy cream
1 thyme sprig

Directions:

Heat the oil in a skillet and add the leeks. Sauté for 5 minutes until softened. Add the flour and cook for 1 additional minute. Transfer the mixture in your slow cooker and add the remaining ingredients, except the cream. Cook on low settings for 6 hours. When done, remove the thyme sprig, add the cream and puree the soup with an immersion blender. Serve the soup warm or chilled.

LENTIL SOUP WITH GARLIC TOPPING

Time: 6 1/2 hours   Servings: 8

Ingredients:

Soup:

1/2 cup red lentils, rinsed
1/2 cup green lentils, rinsed
1 shallot, chopped
1 celery stalk, sliced
1 carrot, diced
1 red bell pepper, cored and diced
1/2 cup tomato sauce
1 bay leaf

2 cups water
2 cups chicken stock
Salt and pepper to taste

Topping:

3 garlic cloves, chopped
2 tablespoons chopped parsley
2 tomatoes, peeled and diced
Salt and pepper to taste
1 tablespoon olive oil

Directions:

To make the soup, combine all the ingredients in your slow cooker. Add salt and pepper to taste and cook on low settings for 6 hours. For the topping, mix the garlic, parsley, tomatoes, salt, pepper and olive oil in a bowl. Pour the warm soup into serving bowls and top with the tomato and garlic topping. Serve right away.

MINESTRONE SOUP

Time: 6 1/4 hours   Servings: 8

Ingredients:

4 ripe tomatoes, peeled and diced
2 tablespoons tomato paste
4 sun-dried tomatoes, chopped
2 cups water
4 cups vegetable stock
2 carrots, diced
2 celery stalks, diced
2 garlic cloves, chopped
1 sweet onion, chopped
1 zucchini, cubed

1 cup frozen green peas
1 teaspoon dried oregano
1 thyme sprig
1 bay leaf
1 can red beans, drained
1 cup small pasta
Salt and pepper to taste
2 tablespoons chopped parsley
Grated Parmesan for serving

Directions:

Combine the tomatoes, tomato paste and the remaining ingredients, except chopped parsley, in your slow cooker. Add salt and pepper as needed and cook the soup on low settings for 6 hours.
The soup is best served warm, topped with chopped parsley and grated Parmesan.

Roasted Bell Pepper Quinoa Soup

Time: 6 1/2 hours

Servings: 6

Ingredients:

1 shallot, chopped
1 garlic clove, chopped
4 roasted red bell peppers, chopped
1/2 cup tomato paste
2 cups vegetable stock
1 cup water

1/2 cup red quinoa, rinsed
1/2 teaspoon dried oregano
1/2 teaspoon dried basil
1 pinch cayenne pepper
Salt and pepper to taste

Directions:

Combine the shallot, garlic, bell peppers, tomato paste, stock and water in your slow cooker. Add the quinoa, herbs and spices, as well as salt and pepper to taste and cover with a lid. Cook on low settings for 6 hours. Serve the soup warm or chilled.

Red Chili Quinoa Soup

Time: 3 1/4 hours

Servings: 8

Ingredients:

2 shallots, chopped
1 carrot, diced
1/2 celery root, peeled and diced
1 can diced tomatoes
1/2 cup quinoa, rinsed
1 can (15 oz.) red beans, drained

2 cups water
2 cups chicken stock
Salt and pepper to taste
1/2 teaspoon chili powder
2 tablespoons chopped cilantro for serving
Sour cream for serving

Directions:

Combine the shallots, carrot, celery and diced tomatoes in your slow cooker. Add the quinoa, water, stock and chili powder and season with salt and pepper. Cook on high settings for 3 hours. Serve the soup warm, topped with cilantro and sour cream.

Corn and Red Pepper Chowder

Time: 8 1/4 hours

Servings: 8

Ingredients:

2 tablespoons olive oil
1 shallot, chopped
1 red bell pepper, cored and diced
2 large potatoes, peeled and cubed
2 cups frozen sweet corn
2 cups chicken stock
2 cups water
1/4 teaspoon smoked paprika
1/4 teaspoon cumin powder

Salt and pepper to taste

Directions:

Heat the oil in a skillet and stir in the shallot.

Sauté until softened then transfer in your slow cooker.

Add the remaining ingredients and adjust the taste with salt and pepper.

Cook on low settings for 8 hours.

When done, puree the soup in a blender and serve it warm.

CHUNKY MUSHROOM SOUP

Time: 8 1/2 hours   Servings: 8

Ingredients:

1 sweet onion, chopped
1 garlic clove, chopped
1 yellow bell pepper, cored and diced
2 tablespoons olive oil
1 pound fresh mushrooms, chopped
1 zucchini, cubed
2 large potatoes, peeled and cubed

2 tomatoes, peeled and diced
2 cups vegetable stock
3 cups water
1/2 cup tomato sauce
Salt and pepper to taste
1 lemon, juiced
1 tablespoon chopped dill

Directions:

Heat the oil in a skillet and stir in the onion, garlic and bell pepper. Sauté for 5 minutes until softened then transfer in your slow cooker.

Add the mushrooms, zucchini, potatoes, tomatoes, stock, water and tomato sauce then season with salt and pepper.

Cook on low settings for 8 hours.

When done, add the lemon juice and chopped dill and serve the soup warm or chilled.

CURRIED VEGETABLE SOUP

Time: 6 1/2 hours   Servings: 10

Ingredients:

1 sweet onion, finely chopped
4 garlic cloves, chopped
2 tablespoons olive oil
1 teaspoon grated ginger
1/2 head cauliflower, cut into florets
2 large potatoes, peeled and cubed
1/2 head cabbage, shredded

2 tomatoes, peeled and diced
1 cup green peas
2 tablespoons red curry paste
2 cups vegetable stock
4 cups water
1/2 lemongrass talk, crushed
Salt and pepper to taste

Directions:

Heat the olive oil in a skillet and stir in the onion and garlic. Cook for 2 minutes then add the ginger and curry paste.

Sauté for 2 additional minutes then transfer in your slow cooker.

Add the cauliflower, potatoes, cabbage, tomatoes, green peas, stock and water, as well as the lemongrass stalk.

Season with salt and pepper and cook on low settings for 6 hours.

Serve the soup warm.

Mixed Veggies Coconut Soup

Time: 7 1/2 hours   Servings: 8

Ingredients:

1 sweet onion, chopped
2 garlic cloves, chopped
1 teaspoon grated ginger
2 tablespoons red curry paste
2 tablespoons olive oil
1/2 head cauliflower, cut into florets
2 large sweet potatoes, peeled and cubed

1/2 teaspoon cumin powder
1/4 teaspoon chili powder
1 cup coconut milk
3 cups vegetable stock
Salt and pepper to taste
1/2 lemongrass stalk

Directions:

Heat the oil in a skillet or saucepan and add the onion, garlic, ginger and curry paste. Cook for a few minutes until softened then transfer in your slow cooker. Add the cauliflower, sweet potatoes, cumin powder, chili powder and coconut milk, as well as stock and lemongrass. Season with salt and pepper and cook on low settings for 7 hours. When done, remove the lemongrass stalk and puree the soup in a blender or use an immersion blender instead. Serve the soup warm.

Pumpkin Hearty Soup

Time: 6 1/4 hours   Servings: 10

Ingredients:

2 tablespoons olive oil
2 shallots, chopped
2 garlic cloves, chopped
1 red chili, seeded and chopped
1/4 teaspoon grated ginger
2 tablespoons tomato paste
1 can diced tomatoes
1 can (15 oz.) black beans, drained

2 cups pumpkin cubes
2 cups water
3 cups vegetable stock
1 bay leaf
Salt and pepper to taste
1/2 cinnamon stick
1/4 teaspoon cumin powder

Directions:

Heat the oil in a skillet or saucepan and add the shallots, garlic, red chili and ginger. Cook for 3-4 minutes then transfer in your slow cooker. Add the tomato paste, tomatoes, black beans and pumpkin, as well as the water, stock, bay leaf, cinnamon and cumin. Adjust the taste with salt and cook on low settings for 6 hours. Serve the soup warm and fresh.

Chunky Pumpkin and Kale Soup

Time: 6 1/2 hours   Servings: 6

Ingredients:

1 sweet onion, chopped
1 red bell pepper, cored and diced
1/2 red chili, chopped
2 tablespoons olive oil

2 cups pumpkin cubes
2 cups vegetable stock
2 cups water
1 bunch kale, shredded

1/2 teaspoon cumin seeds   Salt and pepper to taste

Directions:

Combine the onion, bell pepper, chili and olive oil in your slow cooker.

Add the remaining ingredients and adjust the taste with salt and pepper.

Mix gently just to evenly distribute the ingredients then cook on low settings for 6 hours.

Serve the soup warm or chilled.

WHITE CHICKEN CHILI SOUP

Time: 7 1/2 hours   Servings: 8

Ingredients:

1 pound ground chicken   2 cans (15 oz.) white beans, drained
2 tablespoons olive oil   2 cups chicken stock
1 yellow bell pepper, cored and diced   3 cups water
2 carrots, diced   1/2 teaspoon chili powder
1 celery stalk, diced   Salt and pepper to taste
1 parsnip, diced

Directions:

Heat the oil in a skillet and stir in the chicken. Cook for 5 minutes, stirring often, then transfer the meat in your slow cooker. Add the remaining ingredients and season with salt and pepper.

Cover the pot and cook on low settings for 7 hours.

Serve the soup either warm or chilled.

ITALIAN VEGGIE PASTA SOUP

Time: 8 1/2 hours   Servings: 10

Ingredients:

2 tablespoons olive oil   2 cups chicken stock
1 sweet onion, chopped   4 cups water
2 garlic cloves, chopped   1 bay leaf
2 red bell peppers, cored and diced   1/2 teaspoon dried basil
2 zucchinis, sliced   1 teaspoon dried oregano
1 can white beans, drained   1/2 cup fusilli pasta
2 ripe tomatoes, peeled and diced   1/4 cup short pasta of your choice
1 cup tomato sauce   Salt and pepper to taste

Directions:

Heat the oil in a skillet or saucepan and stir in the onion, garlic, bell peppers and zucchinis.

Sauté for 5 minutes, stirring often, then transfer in your slow cooker.

Add the remaining ingredients and season with salt and pepper.

Cook on low settings for 8 hours.

The soup can be served both warm and chilled.

GARAM MASALA CHICKEN SOUP

Time: 8 1/4 hours   Servings: 8

Ingredients:

8 chicken drumsticks
2 tablespoons canola oil
1 sweet onion, chopped
2 garlic cloves, chopped
1 teaspoon garam masala
1 pound potatoes, peeled and cubed
1 cup coconut milk

2 cups chicken stock
2 cups water
1 cup tomato sauce
1 bay leaf
1/2 lemongrass stalk, crushed
1/2 teaspoon cumin seeds
Salt and pepper to taste

Directions:

Heat the canola oil in a skillet and add the chicken drumsticks. Cook on all sides until golden brown and crusty then transfer in your slow cooker. Add the remaining ingredients then season with salt and pepper.
Cook on low settings for 8 hours.
Serve the soup warm or chilled.

ORANGE SALMON SOUP

Time: 2 1/4 hours   Servings: 8

Ingredients:

1 sweet onion, chopped
1 garlic clove, chopped
1 celery stalk, sliced
1 small fennel bulb, sliced
1 cup diced tomatoes
3 salmon fillets, cubed

2 cups vegetable stock
3 cups water
1 lemon, juiced
1 orange, juiced
1/2 teaspoon grated orange zest
Salt and pepper to taste

Directions:

Combine the onion, garlic, celery, fennel bulb, tomatoes, salmon, stock and water in your slow cooker.
Add the remaining ingredients and season with salt and pepper.
Cook on high settings for 2 hours.
Serve the soup warm or chilled.

CREAMY TORTELLINI SOUP

Time: 6 1/4 hours   Servings: 6

Ingredients:

1 shallot, chopped
1 garlic clove, chopped
1/2 pound mushrooms, sliced
1 can condensed cream of mushroom soup
2 cups chicken stock
1 cup water

1/2 teaspoon dried oregano
1/2 teaspoon dried basil
1 cup evaporated milk
7 oz. cheese tortellini
Salt and pepper to taste

Directions:

Combine the shallot, garlic, mushrooms, cream of mushroom soup, stock, water, dried herbs and milk in your slow cooker. Add the cheese tortellini and season with salt and pepper.

Cook on low settings for 6 hours.

Serve the soup warm.

SPICY CHILI SOUP WITH TOMATILLOS

Time: 8 1/2 hours   Servings: 8

Ingredients:

1/2 pound beef roast, cubed
10 oz. canned tomatillos, rinsed, drained and chopped
1 dried ancho chili, seeded and chopped
1 jalapeno pepper, chopped
1 can (15 oz.) black beans, drained
1 can fire roasted tomatoes

1 cup beef stock
4 cups water
Salt and pepper to taste
1 bay leaf
1 thyme sprig
Chopped cilantro and sour cream for serving

Directions:

Combine the beef roast, tomatillos, ancho chili, jalapeno pepper and black beans in your slow cooker.

Add the tomatoes, beef stock, water, salt and pepper, as well as bay leaf and thyme sprig.

Cook on low settings for 8 hours.

The soup is best served warm, topped with chopped cilantro and a dollop of sour cream.

PORTOBELLO MUSHROOM SOUP

Time: 6 1/4 hours   Servings: 6

Ingredients:

4 Portobello mushrooms, sliced
1 shallot, chopped
2 garlic cloves, chopped
1 cup diced tomatoes
1 tablespoon tomato paste
2 cups chicken stock

1 can condensed cream of mushroom soup
Salt and pepper to taste
1/2 teaspoon cumin seeds
1 tablespoon chopped parsley
1 tablespoon chopped cilantro

Directions:

Combine the mushrooms, shallot, garlic, tomatoes, tomato paste, stock and mushroom soup in your slow cooker.

Add the cumin seeds then season with salt and pepper.

Cook on low settings for 6 hours.

When done, stir in the chopped parsley and cilantro.

Serve the soup warm.

Bouillabaisse Soup

Time: 6 1/2 hours   Servings: 8

Ingredients:

1 shallot, chopped
2 garlic cloves, chopped
1 red bell pepper, cored and diced
1 carrot, diced
1 fennel bulb, sliced
1 cup diced tomatoes
2 cups vegetable stock

2 large potatoes, peeled and cubed
1 celery stalk, sliced
1/2 lemon, juiced
1 pound haddock fillets, cubed
Salt and pepper to taste
1 tablespoon chopped parsley

Directions:

Combine the shallot, garlic, bell pepper, carrot, fennel, tomatoes and stock in your slow cooker. Add the potatoes, celery, lemon juice, salt and pepper and cook on high settings for 1 hour. Add the haddock fillets and continue cooking for 5 minutes on low settings. Serve the soup warm, topped with chopped parsley

Pork and Corn Soup

Time: 8 1/4 hours   Servings: 8

Ingredients:

1 pound pork roast, cubed
1 sweet onion, chopped
2 bacon slices, chopped
1 garlic clove, chopped
2 carrots, sliced
1 celery stalk, sliced
2 yellow bell peppers, cored and diced

2 cups frozen sweet corn
1/2 teaspoon cumin seeds
1/2 red chili, sliced
2 cups chicken stock
4 cups water
Salt and pepper to taste
2 tablespoons chopped cilantro

Directions:

Combine the pork roast, sweet onion, bacon and garlic in a skillet and cook for 5 minutes, stirring all the time. Transfer in your slow cooker and add the carrots, celery, bell peppers, sweet corn, cumin seeds, red chili, stock, water, salt and pepper. Cook on low settings for 8 hours. When done, add the chopped cilantro and serve the soup warm.

Creamy Tomato Soup with Flour Dumplings

Time: 8 1/4 hours   Servings: 8

Ingredients:

2 tablespoons olive oil
2 shallots, chopped
2 garlic cloves, chopped
2 pounds ripe tomatoes, peeled and cubed
1 carrot, sliced
1 celery root, peeled and cubed
2 cups chicken stock

2 cups water
1/2 teaspoon dried oregano
1/2 teaspoon dried basil
1/2 red chili, sliced
1 tablespoon brown sugar
1 teaspoon balsamic vinegar
Salt and pepper to taste

1 egg

1 teaspoon canola oil

4 teaspoons all-purpose flour

Directions:

Heat the olive oil in a skillet and stir in the shallots and garlic. Sauté for 2 minutes until softened then transfer in your slow cooker. Add the tomatoes, carrot, celery, stock, water, oregano and basil, as well as chili, brown sugar and balsamic vinegar. Season with salt and pepper to taste and cook on low settings for 6 hours. When done, puree the soup with an immersion blender. In a small bowl, mix the egg, canola oil and flour. Give it a good mix and add salt to taste. Drop small pieces of this dough into the tomato soup and continue cooking for 2 additional hours on low settings. Serve the soup warm or chilled.

CURRIED TURKEY SOUP

Time: 6 1/2 hours

Servings: 8

Ingredients:

2 tablespoons olive oil
1 1/2 pounds turkey breast, cubed
2 carrots, diced
1 sweet onion, chopped
1 celery stalk, sliced
2 garlic cloves, chopped

1 teaspoon grated ginger
1 cup coconut milk
3 cups chicken stock
1 cup water
1 tablespoon curry powder
Salt and pepper to taste

Directions:

Heat the oil in a skillet and stir in the turkey. Cook on all sides for a few minutes until golden then transfer in your slow cooker. Add the carrots, onion, celery, garlic, ginger, coconut milk, stock, water and curry powder. Season with salt and pepper and cook on low settings for 6 hours. Serve the soup warm.

HAM AND SWEET POTATO SOUP

Time: 3 1/2 hours

Servings: 6

Ingredients:

1 1/2 cups diced ham
1 sweet onion, chopped
1 carrot, diced
1 celery stalk, diced
1 parsnip, diced
2 large sweet potatoes, peeled and cubed

2 cups chicken stock
2 cups water
1 bay leaf
1 thyme sprig
Salt and pepper to taste

Directions:

Combine all the ingredients in your slow cooker.
Add salt and pepper to taste and cook on high settings for 3 hours.
Serve the soup warm and fresh.

Indian Cauliflower Creamy Soup

Time: 6 1/2 hours   Servings: 8

Ingredients:

2 tablespoons olive oil
1 sweet onion, chopped
1 celery stalk, sliced
2 garlic cloves, chopped
1 tablespoon red curry paste
1 cauliflower head, cut into florets

2 medium size potatoes, peeled and cubed
2 cups vegetable stock
2 cups water
1/4 teaspoon cumin powder
1 pinch red pepper flakes
Salt and pepper to taste

Directions:

Heat the oil in a skillet and stir in the onion, celery and garlic. Sauté for 2 minutes until softened. Transfer the mix in your slow cooker. Add the remaining ingredients and cook on low settings for 6 hours. When done, puree the soup with an immersion blender and serve it warm.

Moroccan Lentil Soup

Time: 6 1/4 hours   Servings: 6

Ingredients:

1 large sweet onion, chopped
2 garlic cloves, chopped
2 tablespoons olive oil
2 carrots, diced
1 parsnip, diced
1 cup chopped cauliflower
1/2 teaspoon cumin powder
1/4 teaspoon turmeric powder

1/2 teaspoon ground coriander
2 cups water
3 cups chicken stock
1 cup red lentils
2 tablespoons tomato paste
2 tablespoons lemon juice
Salt and pepper to taste

Directions:

Heat the oil in a skillet and stir in the onion, garlic, carrots and parsnip. Cook for 5 minutes then transfer in your slow cooker. Stir in the cauliflower, cumin powder, turmeric and coriander, as well as water, stock, lentils and tomato paste. Add the lemon juice, salt and pepper and cook on low settings for 6 hours. Serve the soup warm or chilled.

Black Bean Mushroom Soup

Time: 6 1/2 hours   Servings: 8

Ingredients:

1 shallot, chopped
2 garlic cloves, chopped
1 can (15 oz.) black beans, drained
1/2 pound mushrooms, sliced
1 can fire roasted tomatoes
2 cups vegetable stock
4 cups water

1/2 teaspoon mustard seeds
1/2 teaspoon cumin seeds
Salt and pepper to taste
2 tablespoons chopped parsley

Directions:

Combine the shallot, garlic and black beans with the mushrooms, tomatoes, stock, water and seeds in your slow cooker. Add salt and pepper to taste and cook on low settings for 6 hours. When done, add the parsley and serve the soup warm.

THREE BEAN QUINOA SOUP

Time: 7 1/2 hours   Servings: 10

Ingredients:

2 tablespoons olive oil
2 sweet onions, chopped
2 garlic cloves, chopped
1 celery stalk, sliced
2 carrots, diced
1/2 cup dried black beans
1/4 cup dried kidney beans
1/4 cup cannellini beans
1/2 teaspoon cumin seeds

1/2 teaspoon chili powder
4 cups chicken stock
4 cups water
1 rosemary sprig
1 thyme sprig
1/4 cup red quinoa, rinsed
1/2 cup tomato sauce
Salt and pepper to taste

Directions:

Heat the oil in a skillet and stir in the onion and garlic. Cook for 2 minutes until softened then transfer in your slow cooker. Add the celery, carrots, beans, cumin seeds, chili powder, stock, water and herbs.
Stir in the quinoa and tomato sauce and season with salt and pepper.
Cook on low settings for 7 hours and serve the soup warm.

GARLICKY CHICKEN SOUP

Time: 6 1/4 hours   Servings: 6

Ingredients:

1 large chicken breast (bone in)
1 cup chicken stock
6 cups water
2 carrots, diced
1 sweet onion, chopped
1 parsnip, diced

1/2 celery root, peeled and diced
Salt and pepper to taste
1 cup sour cream
2 egg yolks
4 garlic cloves, minced
2 tablespoons chopped parsley

Directions:

Combine the chicken breast, stock, water, carrots, onion, parsnip and celery in your slow cooker.
Add salt and pepper to taste and cook on low settings for 6 hours.
When done, remove the chicken breast and place aside.
In a small bowl, mix the sour cream, egg yolks and garlic then pour this mixture over the hot soup. Mix well and stir in the parsley.
Remove the meat off the bone and shred it finely. Add it into the soup.
Serve the soup right away.

Vegetable Chicken Soup

Time: 7 1/2 hours   Servings: 8

Ingredients:

2 chicken breasts, cubed
1 sweet onion, chopped
1 garlic clove, chopped
2 carrots, diced
1 parsnip, diced
1 celery stalk, diced
1 red bell pepper, cored and diced

1 cup diced tomatoes
Salt and pepper to taste
1 cup chicken stock
4 cups water
1 can condensed cream of chicken soup
1 lemon, juiced
1 tablespoon chopped parsley

Directions:

Combine the chicken and the remaining ingredients in your slow cooker.
Add salt and pepper as needed and cook on low settings for 7 hours.
The soup is best served warm, but it can also be re-heated.

Summer Squash Chickpea Soup

Time: 2 1/2 hours   Servings: 6

Ingredients:

1 sweet onion, chopped
1 garlic clove, chopped
1 carrot, diced
1 celery stalk, sliced
2 summer squashes, cubed
1 can (15 oz.) chickpeas, drained
2 cups chicken stock
3 cups water

1 cup diced tomatoes
1 bay leaf
1 thyme sprig
Salt and pepper to taste
1 lemon, juiced
1 tablespoon chopped cilantro
1 tablespoon chopped parsley

Directions:

Combine the onion, garlic, celery, carrot, summer squash, chickpeas, stock and water in your slow cooker.
Add the tomatoes, bay leaf, thyme, salt and pepper and cook on high settings for 2 hours.
When done, stir in the lemon juice, parsley and cilantro and serve the soup warm.

Tomato Fish Soup

Time: 3 1/2 hours   Servings: 6

Ingredients:

1 shallot, chopped
2 garlic cloves, chopped
1 tablespoon olive oil
4 ripe tomatoes, pureed
2 cups vegetable stock
1 cup water

1 bay leaf
1 lemon, juiced
Salt and pepper to taste
1 pound salmon fillets, cubed
2 haddock fillets, cubed

Directions:

Heat the oil in a skillet and stir in the shallot and garlic. Sauté for 2 minutes until softened then transfer in your slow cooker.

Stir in the tomato puree, stock, water, bay leaf and lemon juice and season with salt and pepper.

Cook on high settings for 1 hour then add the fish and continue cooking for 2 additional hours.

Serve the soup warm or chilled.

BEEF MUSHROOM SOUP

Time: 8 1/2 hours   Servings: 8

Ingredients:

1 pound beef roast, cubed
2 tablespoons canola oil
1 sweet onion, chopped
2 garlic cloves, chopped
1 pound mushrooms, sliced
1 can fire roasted tomatoes

2 cups beef stock
5 cups water
1 bay leaf
1 thyme sprig
1/2 teaspoon caraway seeds
Salt and pepper to taste

Directions:

Heat the oil in a skillet and stir in the beef roast. Cook on all sides for a few minutes then transfer in your slow cooker.

Add the onion, garlic, mushrooms, tomatoes, stock and water, as well as bay leaf and thyme sprig, plus the caraway seeds.

Season with salt and pepper and cook on low settings for 8 hours.

The soup is best served warm.

HUNGARIAN GOULASH SOUP

Time: 8 1/2 hours   Servings: 8

Ingredients:

2 sweet onions, chopped
1 pound beef roast, cubed
2 tablespoons canola oil
2 carrots, diced
1/2 celery stalk, diced
2 red bell peppers, cored and diced
1 1/2 pounds potatoes, peeled and cubed

2 tablespoons tomato paste
1 cup diced tomatoes
1/2 cup beef stock
5 cups water
1/2 teaspoon cumin seeds
1/2 teaspoon smoked paprika
Salt and pepper to taste

Directions:

Heat the oil in a skillet and stir in the beef. Cook for 5 minutes on all sides then stir in the onion. Sauté for 2 additional minutes then transfer in your slow cooker.

Add the remaining ingredients and season with salt and pepper.

Cook on low settings for 8 hours.

Serve the soup warm.

MOROCCAN LAMB SOUP

Time: 7 1/2 hours   Servings: 6

Ingredients:

1 pound lamb shoulder
1 teaspoon turmeric powder
1/2 teaspoon cumin powder
1/2 teaspoon chili powder
2 tablespoons canola oil
2 cups chicken stock
3 cups water

1 cup fire roasted tomatoes
1 cup canned chickpeas, drained
1 thyme sprig
1/2 teaspoon dried sage
1/2 teaspoon dried oregano
Salt and pepper to taste
1 lemon, juiced

Directions:

Sprinkle the lamb with salt, pepper, turmeric, cumin powder and chili powder. Heat the oil in a skillet and add the lamb. Cook on all sides for a few minutes then transfer it in a slow cooker. Add the remaining ingredients and season with salt and pepper. Cook the soup on low settings for 7 hours. Serve the soup warm.

SHREDDED BEEF SOUP

Time: 8 1/2 hours   Servings: 8

Ingredients:

1 1/2 pounds beef roast
1 sweet onion, chopped
2 garlic cloves, chopped
2 carrots, sliced
2 celery stalks, sliced
2 red bell peppers, cored and diced
1/2 teaspoon cumin powder
1/2 teaspoon dried oregano

1/2 teaspoon dried basil
1/2 teaspoon chili powder
2 cups chicken stock
5 cups water
2 jalapenos, chopped
1 cup fire roasted tomatoes
Salt and pepper to taste

Directions:

Combine the onion, garlic, carrots, celery, bell peppers, cumin powder, oregano, basil, chili powder, stock and water in your slow cooker. Add the jalapenos and tomatoes, as well as salt and pepper then place the beef in the center of the cooker, making sure it's covered in liquid. Cook on low settings for 8 hours. When done, shred the beef into fine threads and serve the soup warm.

CHICKEN SWEET POTATO SOUP

Time: 6 1/4 hours   Servings: 6

Ingredients:

2 chicken breasts, cubed
2 tablespoons olive oil
2 shallots, chopped
1 celery stalk, sliced

1 can fire roasted tomatoes
1 1/2 pounds sweet potatoes, peeled and
   cubed
1 cup chicken stock

4 cups water
Salt and pepper to taste
1/2 teaspoon cumin seeds

1/4 teaspoon caraway seeds
1 thyme sprig

Directions:

Heat the oil in a skillet and stir in the chicken, shallots and celery. Sauté for a few minutes until softened then transfer in your slow cooker.

Add the remaining ingredients and season with salt and pepper.

Cook on low settings for 6 hours.

The soup is best served warm.

HOT AND SOUR SOUP

Time: 7 1/2 hours

Servings: 8

Ingredients:

2 oz. dried shiitake mushrooms
1 pound fresh mushrooms, sliced
1 can (8 oz.) bamboo shoots, drained
2 carrots, sliced
1 sweet onion, chopped
14 oz. tofu, cubed
1/2 head green cabbage, shredded

1 teaspoon grated ginger
1/2 teaspoon chili flakes
2 cups chicken stock
5 cups water
2 tablespoons soy sauce
2 tablespoons rice vinegar
2 green onions, sliced

Directions:

Place the shiitake mushrooms in a bowl and cover them with boiling water. Allow to rehydrate for 10 minutes then chop and place in your slow cooker.

Add the remaining ingredients, except the green onions and cook on low settings for 7 hours.

When done, stir in the green onions and serve right away.

SWEDISH SPLIT PEA SOUP

Time: 6 1/4 hours

Servings: 8

Ingredients:

2 cups yellow split peas, rinsed
4 cups chicken stock
4 cups water
1 large sweet onion, chopped
2 carrots, diced

1 celery stalk, diced
2 cups diced ham
1/2 teaspoon dried oregano
1/2 teaspoon dried marjoram
Salt and pepper to taste

Directions:

Combine the split peas, stock, water, onion, carrots and celery stalk in your slow cooker.

Add the ham, herbs, salt and pepper and cook on low settings for 6 hours.

Serve the soup warm.

CHICKEN CHICKPEA SOUP

Time: 6 1/4 hours   Servings: 8

Ingredients:

1/4 pound dried chickpeas, rinsed   2 garlic cloves, chopped
2 chicken breasts, cubed   1 leek, sliced
1 chorizo link, sliced   2 cups chicken stock
2 tablespoons canola oil   6 cups water
2 carrots, diced   1/2 teaspoon dried marjoram
1 celery stalk   Salt and pepper to taste
1 pound potatoes, peeled and cubed   2 tablespoons chopped cilantro

Directions:

Heat the oil in a skillet and add the chicken and chorizo. Sauté for 5 minutes on all sides then transfer in your slow cooker. Add the carrots, celery, potatoes, garlic, leek, stock, water and marjoram, as well as salt and pepper. Cook on low settings for 6 hours. When done, stir in the cilantro and serve the soup warm.

QUINOA SOUP WITH PARMESAN TOPPING

Time: 3 1/2 hours   Servings: 6

Ingredients:

2 chicken breasts, cubed   1 garlic clove, chopped
2 tablespoons olive oil   1 cup diced tomatoes
2/3 cup quinoa, rinsed   2 cups chicken stock
1/2 teaspoon dried oregano   4 cups water
1/2 teaspoon dried basil   Salt and pepper to taste
1 sweet onion, chopped   1 cup grated Parmesan for serving

Directions:

Heat the oil in a skillet and add the chicken. Cook on all sides until golden brown then transfer the chicken in your slow cooker. Add the remaining ingredients, except the Parmesan, and cook on high settings for 3 hours.
When done, pour the soup into serving bowls and top with grated Parmesan before serving.

TURKEY TORTELLINI SOUP

Time: 8 1/2 hours   Servings: 8

Ingredients:

1 pound turkey breast, cubed   2 cups chicken stock
2 tablespoons olive oil   6 cups water
2 carrots, sliced   1/2 teaspoon dried oregano
1 celery stalk, sliced   Salt and pepper to taste
1 parsnip, sliced   1 lemon, juiced
1 red bell pepper, cored and diced
2 tomatoes, peeled and diced
10 oz. spinach tortellini

Directions:

Heat the oil in a skillet and add the turkey. Cook on all sides until golden then transfer the meat in your slow cooker.
Add the carrots, celery, parsnip, bell pepper, tomatoes, stock, water and oregano, as well as tortellini and lemon juice.
Season with salt and pepper and cook on low settings for 8 hours.
Serve the soup warm or chilled.

$\mathcal{P}$ORK APPLESAUCE SOUP

Time: 7 1/2 hours   Servings: 6

Ingredients:

1 pound pork roast, cubed
2 bacon slices, chopped
1 shallot, chopped
1 garlic clove, chopped
1 red bell pepper, cored and diced
1 carrot, sliced
1 parsnip, diced
1 green apple, peeled and diced

1 cup applesauce
2 cups chicken stock
2 cups water
1 cup fire roasted tomatoes
1 bay leaf
1 thyme sprig
Salt and pepper to taste
1 teaspoon apple cider vinegar

Directions:

Heat a skillet over medium flame and add the pork and bacon. Cook on all sides until golden then transfer the pork in your slow cooker.
Add the remaining ingredients and season with salt and pepper.
Cook on low settings for 7 hours and serve the soup warm.

$\mathcal{S}$MOKED SAUSAGE LENTIL SOUP

Time: 6 1/4 hours   Servings: 6

Ingredients:

2 links smoked sausages, sliced
1 sweet onion, chopped
2 carrots, diced
1 cup red lentils
1/2 cup green lentils
2 cups chicken stock
2 cups water

1/2 teaspoon smoked paprika
1 bay leaf
1 thyme sprig
1 lemon, juiced
1 cup fire roasted tomatoes
Salt and pepper to taste

Directions:

Combine the sausages with the remaining ingredients in your slow cooker.
Add salt and pepper to taste and cover with a lid.
Cook on low settings for 6 hours.
The soup can be served both warm and chilled.

Salmon Fennel Soup

Time: 5 1/4 hours

Servings: 6

Ingredients:

1 shallot, chopped
1 garlic clove, sliced
1 fennel bulb, sliced
1 carrot, diced
1 celery stalk, sliced

3 salmon fillets, cubed
1 lemon, juiced
1 bay leaf
Salt and pepper to taste

Directions:

Combine the shallot, garlic, fennel, carrot, celery, fish, lemon juice and bay leaf in your slow cooker.
Add salt and pepper to taste and cook on low settings for 5 hours.
Serve the soup warm.

Smoked Sausage Cabbage Soup

Time: 7 1/4 hours

Servings: 8

Ingredients:

4 smoked sausage links, sliced
2 sweet onions, chopped
1 head green cabbage, shredded
1 cup fire roasted tomatoes
1 thyme sprig

2 cups chicken stock
4 cups water
1/4 teaspoon cumin seeds
1/4 teaspoon chili powder
Salt and pepper to taste

Directions:

Combine the sausage links, onions, cabbage, tomatoes, thyme sprig, stock, water, cumin seeds and chili powder in your slow cooker. Add salt and pepper to taste and cook on low settings for 7 hours. Serve the soup warm.

Creamy Edamame Soup

Time: 2 1/4 hours

Servings: 6

Ingredients:

1 tablespoon olive oil
2 shallots, chopped
2 garlic cloves, chopped
1 large potato, peeled and cubed
1 celery root, peeled and cubed
1 pound frozen edamame

Salt and pepper to taste
2 cups chicken stock
1 cup water
1/4 teaspoon dried oregano
1/4 teaspoon dried marjoram

Directions:

Heat the oil in a skillet and stir in the shallots and garlic. Sauté for 2 minutes until softened then transfer in your slow cooker. Add the remaining ingredients and season with salt and pepper. Cook on high settings for 2 hours.
When done, puree the soup with an immersion blender until creamy.
Serve the soup right away.

Pork Edamame Soup

Time: 6 1/4 hours   Servings: 8

Ingredients:

1 pound pork roast, cubed
1 large sweet onion, chopped
1 garlic clove, chopped
2 carrots, sliced
1 parsnip, diced
1 celery root, diced
1 red bell pepper, cored and diced

2 cups edamame
1 large potato, peeled and diced
2 cups chicken stock
4 cups water
Salt and pepper to taste
2 tablespoons chopped parsley

Directions:

Combine the pork, onion, garlic, carrots, parsnip, celery, red bell pepper, edamame, potato, stock and water in a slow cooker.

Add salt and pepper to taste and cook on low settings for 6 hours.

When done, stir in the chopped parsley and serve the soup warm.

Chicken Pearl Barley Soup

Time: 6 1/2 hours   Servings: 8

Ingredients:

3 chicken breasts, cubed
2 tablespoons olive oil
1 teaspoon dried oregano
1/2 teaspoon paprika
1 large sweet onion, chopped
2 carrots, sliced
2 celery stalks, sliced

2 tomatoes, peeled and diced
2 potatoes, peeled and cubed
1/2 cup pearl barley
2 cups chicken stock
4 cups water
Salt and pepper to taste
2 tablespoons chopped parsley

Directions:

Heat the oil in a skillet and add the chicken. Cook on all sides for a few minutes until golden then transfer in your slow cooker. Add the oregano, paprika, onion, carrots, celery, tomatoes, potatoes, pearl barley, water, chicken stock, salt and pepper. Cook on low settings for 6 hours.

When done, stir in the parsley and serve the soup warm.

Roasted Tomato Soup

Time: 5 hours   Servings: 6

Ingredients:

2 pounds heirloom tomatoes, halved
2 red onions, halved
4 garlic cloves
1 teaspoon dried oregano
2 tablespoons olive oil

2 cups vegetable stock
1 cup water
1 carrot, sliced
1/2 celery root, peeled and cubed
Salt and pepper to taste

Directions:

Combine the tomatoes, red onions, garlic and oregano in a baking tray lined with parchment paper. Season with salt and pepper and roast in the preheated oven at 400F for 30 minutes. Transfer the vegetables and juices in your slow cooker. Add the remaining ingredients and cook on low settings for 4 hours. When done, puree the soup with an immersion blender. The soup can be served warm or chilled.

SUMMER VEGETABLE SOUP

Time: 6 1/2 hours   Servings: 8

Ingredients:

1 sweet onion, chopped
1 garlic clove, chopped
2 tablespoons olive oil
1 zucchini, cubed
1 yellow squash, cubed
1/2 head cauliflower, cut into florets
1/2 head broccoli, cut into florets
2 ripe tomatoes, peeled and cubed

1 carrot, sliced
1 celery stalk, sliced
1/2 cup edamame
2 cups chicken stock
5 cups water
Salt and pepper to taste
1 lemon, juiced
1 tablespoon chopped parsley

Directions:

Combine the onion, garlic, olive oil and the rest of the ingredients in your slow cooker. Add salt and pepper to taste and cook on low settings for 6 hours. When done, stir in the lemon juice and parsley and serve the soup warm or chilled.

BEAN MEDLEY SOUP

Time: 8 1/2 hours   Servings: 10

Ingredients:

2 sweet onions, chopped
2 carrots, diced
1 celery stalk, sliced
1 parsnip, diced
2 red bell peppers, cored and diced
1/4 cup dried black beans
1/4 cup dried kidney beans
1/4 cup dried cannellini beans

1/2 cup dried white beans
1/4 cup dried chickpeas
1 can fire roasted tomatoes
2 cups chicken stock
6 cups water
1 bay leaf
Salt and pepper to taste

Directions:

Combine all the ingredients in your slow cooker.
Add salt and pepper to taste and cook on low settings for 8 hours.
Serve the soup warm or chilled.

Spiced Pork Soup

Time: 7 1/4 hours   Servings: **8**

Ingredients:

1 pound pork roast, cubed
1 tablespoon all-purpose flour
1 teaspoon dried oregano
1 teaspoon cumin powder
1/2 teaspoon smoked paprika
1/4 teaspoon cinnamon powder
4 bacon slices, chopped
1 can fire roasted tomatoes

2 carrots, diced
1 celery stalk, sliced
2 red bell peppers, cored and diced
2 large potatoes, peeled and cubed
1 large sweet potatoes, peeled and cubed
2 cups chicken stock
5 cups water
Salt and pepper to taste

Directions:

Season the pork with salt and pepper and sprinkle it with flour, oregano, cumin powder, paprika and cinnamon.
Heat a skillet in a skillet and add the bacon. Cook until crisp then add the pork and cook for a few minutes. Transfer the meat and bacon in your slow cooker.
Add the remaining ingredients and cook on low settings for 7 hours.
Serve the soup warm.

Meatball Soup

Time: 6 1/2 hours   Servings: **8**

Ingredients:

1 pound ground pork
1/4 cup white rice
1/2 teaspoon dried oregano
1/2 teaspoon dried basil
Salt and pepper to taste
1 sweet onion, chopped
2 celery stalk, sliced

1 carrot, sliced
1 fennel bulb, sliced
1 cup diced tomatoes
2 cups chicken stock
4 cups water
Salt and pepper to taste

Directions:

Mix the pork, rice, oregano, basil, salt and pepper in a bowl.
Combine the onion, celery stalk, carrot, fennel, tomatoes, stock and water in your slow cooker.
Adjust the taste with salt and pepper then form small meatballs and place them in the slow cooker.
Cook on low settings for 6 hours.
Serve the soup warm.

CREAMY CARROT LENTIL SOUP

Time: 2 1/4 hours   Servings: 6

Ingredients:

2 tablespoons olive oil
4 carrots, sliced
1 shallot, chopped
1 small fennel bulb, sliced
1/2 cup red lentils
2 cups chicken stock

2 cups water
1/4 teaspoon cumin powder
Salt and pepper to taste
1 thyme sprig
1 rosemary sprig

Directions:

Heat the oil in a skillet and add the shallot and carrots. Sauté for 5 minutes then transfer the mixture in your slow cooker. Add the remaining ingredients and cook on high settings for 2 hours. When done, remove the thyme and rosemary and puree the soup with an immersion blender. Serve the soup warm.

ROASTED CHICKEN STOCK

Time: 9 hours   Servings: 10

Ingredients:

1 whole chicken, cut into smaller pieces
2 carrots, cut in half
1 parsnip
1 celery root, peeled and sliced
2 onions, halved

10 cups water
1 bay leaf
1 rosemary sprig
1 thyme sprig
Salt and pepper to taste

Directions:

Season the chicken with salt and pepper and place it in a baking tray. Roast in the preheated oven at 400F for 40 minutes. Transfer the chicken in your slow cooker and add the remaining ingredients. Season with salt and pepper and cook on low settings for 8 hours. Use the stock right away or store in the fridge or freezer.

FISH SWEET CORN SOUP

Time: 2 1/4 hours   Servings: 6

Ingredients:

2 bacon slices, chopped
1 sweet onion, chopped
2 cups milk
2 cups frozen sweet corn

2 potatoes, peeled and diced
1 pound haddock fillets, cubed
Salt and pepper to taste

Directions:

Cook the bacon in a skillet and transfer in your slow cooker. Add the remaining ingredients and season with salt and pepper. cook on high settings for 2 hours. Serve the soup warm.

CREAMY MEDITERRANEAN SOUP

Time: 4 1/4 hours   Servings: 6

Ingredients:
2 tablespoons olive oil
1 sweet onion, chopped
1 garlic clove, chopped
1/2 head cauliflower, cut into florets
1 head broccoli, cut into florets

1 teaspoon dried oregano
2 cups vegetable stock
2 cups water
2 tablespoons Italian pesto
Salt and pepper to taste

Directions:
Heat the oil in a skillet and add the onion and garlic. Sauté for 2 minutes until softened. Transfer in your slow cooker and add the remaining ingredients. Season with salt and pepper and cook on low settings for 4 hours. When done, puree the soup with an immersion blender and serve the soup warm.

CHICKEN CHICKPEA SOUP

Time: 6 1/2 hours   Servings: 6

Ingredients:
2 chicken breasts, cubed
2 tablespoons olive oil
2 shallots, chopped
1 pound potatoes, peeled and diced
1 can (15 oz.) chickpeas, drained
2 cups chicken stock

4 cups water
2 tablespoons lemon juice
1 teaspoon dried tarragon
Salt and pepper to taste
1 cup buttermilk

Directions:
Heat the oil in a skillet and add the chicken. Cook on all sides until golden then transfer in your slow cooker. Add the remaining ingredients, except the buttermilk, and cook on low settings for 6 hours. When done, add the buttermilk and serve the soup warm.

CURRIED PRAWN SOUP

Time: 6 1/4 hours   Servings: 6

Ingredients:
2 tablespoons olive oil
2 shallots, chopped
1 carrot, sliced
1/2 head cauliflower, cut into florets
2 cups cherry tomatoes, halved
2 cups chicken stock

4 cups water
2 tablespoons lemon juice
1 tablespoon red curry paste
Salt and pepper to taste
1 pound fresh shrimps, peeled and deveined

Directions:
Combine the olive oil, shallots, carrot, cauliflower and tomatoes in your slow cooker. Add the stock, water, curry paste and lemon juice and season with salt and pepper. Place the shrimps on top and cook on high settings for 2 hours. Serve the soup warm.

Three Cheese Broccoli Soup

Time: 2 1/2 hours   Servings: 6

Ingredients:

2 tablespoons butter   10 oz. broccoli florets
1 sweet onion, chopped   Salt and pepper to taste
1 garlic clove, chopped   1 cup grated Cheddar cheese
1 tablespoon all-purpose flour   1 cup grated Monterey Jack
1 1/2 cups evaporated milk   1/2 cup grated Parmesan
4 cups chicken stock

Directions:

Heat the butter in a skillet and stir in the onion and garlic. Sauté for 2 minutes until softened then add the flour and cook 1 additional minute. Transfer the mixture in your slow cooker and add the milk, stock, broccoli and cheeses. Season with salt and pepper if needed and cook on high settings for 2 hours. Serve the soup warm.

Bacon Potato Soup

Time: 6 1/2 hours   Servings: 8

Ingredients:

1 cup diced bacon   2 pounds potatoes, peeled and cubed
1 sweet onion, chopped   2 cups chicken stock
1 garlic clove, chopped   4 cups water
1 carrot, diced   Salt and pepper to taste
1 celery stalk, sliced   1/4 teaspoon cumin seeds

Directions:

Heat a skillet over medium flame and add the bacon. Cook until golden on all sides and transfer in your slow cooker. Add the remaining ingredients and season with salt and pepper. Cook on low settings for 6 hours. Serve the soup warm.

Beef Bacon Barley Soup

Time: 8 1/2 hours   Servings: 8

Ingredients:

4 bacon slices, chopped   4 cups water
1 pound beef steak, cubed   1/2 teaspoon dried basil
1/2 teaspoon smoked paprika   1/2 teaspoon dried oregano
1 medium onion, chopped   Salt and pepper to taste
4 small potatoes, peeled and cubed
1 cup baby carrots, halved
1 cup frozen sweet corn
1 cup fire roasted tomatoes
1/2 cup pearl barley, rinsed
2 cups beef stock

Directions:

Heat a skillet over medium flame and add the bacon. Cook until crisp then stir in the beef. Cook on all sides until golden for about 5 minutes. Transfer in your slow cooker. Add the remaining ingredients and season with salt and pepper. Cook the soup on low settings for 8 hours. Serve the soup warm.

Pesto Chicken Soup

Time: 6 1/4 hours   Servings: 6

Ingredients:

1 chicken breast, cubed
1 shallot, chopped
1 garlic clove, chopped
1 can (15 oz.) white beans, drained
1 parsnip, diced

1 celery stalk, sliced
2 tablespoons Italian pesto
1/2 cup chopped parsley
Salt and pepper to taste

Directions:

Combine the chicken, shallot, garlic, beans, parsnip, celery and pesto in a slow cooker.
Add the parsley and season with salt and pepper.
Cook on low settings for 6 hours and serve the soup warm and fresh.

Herbed Chickpea Soup

Time: 6 1/4 hours   Servings: 6

Ingredients:

1 cup dried chickpeas
1 shallot, chopped
1 carrot, diced
1 red bell pepper, cored and diced
1 celery stalk, sliced
1 small fennel bulb, chopped
2 cups chicken stock

4 cups water
2 tablespoons tomato paste
2 tablespoons chopped parsley
2 tablespoons chopped cilantro
1 tablespoon chopped dill
Salt and pepper to taste

Directions:

Combine the chickpeas, shallot, carrot, bell pepper, celery, fennel, tomato paste, stock and water in your slow cooker.
Add salt and pepper to taste and cook on low settings for 6 hours.
When done, stir in the chopped herbs and serve the soup warm and fresh.

Spicy White Chicken Soup

Time: 6 1/4 hours   Servings: 8

Ingredients:

2 chicken breasts, cubed
2 tablespoons olive oil
1 large onion, chopped
2 garlic cloves, chopped

2 cups chicken stock
1 parsnip, diced
1/2 teaspoon cumin seeds
1/4 teaspoon cayenne pepper

1/2 teaspoon dried oregano
1/2 teaspoon dried basil
2 cans (15 oz.) white beans, drained

5 cups water
1 bay leaf
Salt and pepper to taste

Directions:

Heat the oil in a skillet and add the chicken. Cook on all sides until golden then transfer in your slow cooker.
Add the onion, garlic, stock, parsnip, cumin seeds, cayenne pepper, oregano, basil, beans, water and bay leaf.
Adjust the taste with salt and pepper and cook on low settings for 6 hours.
Serve the soup warm and fresh.

CHICKEN GNOCCHI SOUP

Time: 6 1/4 hours   Servings: 8

Ingredients:

1 sweet onion, chopped
1 garlic clove, chopped
8 chicken thighs, without skin
2 carrots, sliced
1 celery stalk, sliced
1 cup frozen green peas
8 oz. gnocchi

1 can condensed cream of mushroom soup
2 cups chicken stock
3 cups water
1 thyme sprig
1 rosemary sprig
Salt and pepper to taste

Directions:

Combine the onion, garlic, chicken thighs, carrots, celery, peas and gnocchi in your slow cooker.
Add the mushroom soup, stock, water, thyme and rosemary and season with salt and pepper.
Cook on low settings for 6 hours.
The soup is best served warm.

BEEF TORTELLINI SOUP

Time: 8 1/2 hours   Servings: 8

Ingredients:

1 pound beef roast, cubed
2 tablespoons olive oil
1 large onion, chopped
1 carrot, sliced
1 celery stalk, sliced
2 garlic cloves, chopped
1 cup diced tomatoes
1/2 teaspoon dried basil

8 oz. cheese tortellini
1/4 cup dried kidney beans, rinsed
2 cups beef stock
1/2 cup dark beer
4 cups water
1 bay leaf
Salt and pepper to taste

Directions:

Heat the oil in a skillet and add the beef. Cook on all sides until golden brown, for about 5 minutes, then transfer in your slow cooker.
Add the remaining ingredients and season with salt and pepper.
Cook on low settings for 8 hours.
Serve the soup warm.

Chicken Sausage Rice Soup

Time: 6 1/4 hours

Servings: 6

Ingredients:

2 fresh chicken sausages, sliced
1 shallot, chopped
1 carrot, sliced
1 celery stalk, sliced
1 yellow bell pepper, cored and diced
1 cup diced tomatoes

2 large potatoes, peeled and cubed
1/4 cup jasmine rice
2 cups chicken stock
4 cups water
Salt and pepper to taste

Directions:

Combine the chicken, shallot and the rest of the ingredients in your slow cooker.
Add salt and pepper to taste and cook on low settings for 6 hours.
The soup is best served warm.

Spinach Sweet Potato Soup

Time: 3 1/2 hours

Servings: 6

Ingredients:

1 shallot, chopped
1 garlic clove, chopped
1/2 pound ground chicken
2 tablespoons olive oil
2 medium size sweet potatoes, peeled and
  cubed
2 cups chicken stock

4 cups water
Salt and pepper to taste
4 cups fresh spinach, shredded
1/2 teaspoon dried oregano
1/2 teaspoon dried basil
1 tablespoon chopped parsley

Directions:

Heat the oil in a skillet and add the ground chicken, shallot and garlic. Cook for about 5 minutes, stirring often.
Transfer the meat mix in your slow cooker and add the potatoes, stock, water, salt and pepper.
Cook on high settings for 2 hours then stir in the spinach, oregano, basil and parsley and cook one additional hour on high.
Serve the soup warm.

Thick Green Lentil Soup

Time: 6 1/4 hours

Servings: 8

Ingredients:

1 cup dried green lentils, rinsed
1/2 cup red lentils, rinsed
2 cups chicken stock
4 cups water
1/2 teaspoon cumin powder
1/4 teaspoon chili powder

1/2 teaspoon dried oregano
1 celery stalk, chopped
1 shallot, chopped
Salt and pepper to taste
2 tablespoons lemon juice
1 tablespoon chopped parsley

Directions:

Combine the lentils, stock, water, cumin powder, chili, oregano, celery and shallot in your slow cooker.

Add salt and pepper to taste and cook on low settings for 6 hours.

When done, stir in the lemon juice and parsley and serve right away.

Herbed Spinach Lentil Soup

Time: 3 1/4 hours   Servings: 8

Ingredients:

1 cup green lentils, rinsed
1 celery stalk, sliced
1 carrot, sliced
1 sweet onion, chopped
2 sweet potatoes, peeled and cubed
2 cups chicken stock

6 cups water
1 bay leaf
1 thyme sprig
Salt and pepper to taste
4 cups fresh spinach, shredded

Directions:

Combine the lentils, celery, carrot, onion, potatoes, stock and water in your slow cooker.

Add the bay leaf and thyme and season with salt and pepper.

Cook on high settings for 2 hours then add the spinach and cook one more hour.

Serve the soup warm or chilled.

Kale Potato Soup

Time: 2 1/4 hours   Servings: 6

Ingredients:

1 shallot, chopped
1 garlic clove, chopped
1 celery stalk, sliced
2 carrots, sliced
1 1/2 pounds potatoes, peeled and cubed
1/2 cup diced tomatoes

1/4 pound kale, chopped
2 cups chicken stock
4 cups water
Salt and pepper to taste
1/4 teaspoon chili flakes
2 tablespoons lemon juice

Directions:

Combine the shallot, garlic, celery, carrots, potatoes and tomatoes in your slow cooker.

Add the kale, chili flakes, lemon juice, water and stock and season with salt and pepper.

Cook on high settings for 2 hours.

Serve the soup warm.

Chicken Parmesan Soup

Time: 8 1/4 hours   Servings: 8

Ingredients:

8 chicken thighs
1 sweet onion, chopped

1 celery stalk, sliced
1 carrot, sliced

1 celery root, peeled and cubed
2 large potatoes, peeled and cubed
1 can diced tomatoes
2 cups chicken stock

6 cups water
Salt and pepper to taste
2 tablespoons chopped parsley
Parmesan shavings for serving

Directions:

Combine the chicken thighs, onion, celery, carrot, celery root, potatoes and tomatoes in your slow cooker.
Add the stock, water, salt and pepper and cook on low settings for 8 hours.
When done, stir in the chopped parsley.
Serve the soup topped with Parmesan shavings.

Basil Tomato Soup

Time: 6 1/2 hours   Servings: 6

Ingredients:

2 tablespoons olive oil
2 red onions, sliced
1 teaspoon dried basil
1 1/2 pound fresh tomatoes, peeled and cubed
1 celery stalk, sliced

1/2 red chili, seeded and chopped
2 cups vegetable stock
2 cups water
1/2 cup half and half
Salt and pepper to taste

Directions:

Heat the oil in a skillet and add the red onions. Cook on low heat for 10 minutes until softened.
Transfer in your slow cooker and add the remaining ingredients, except the half and half.
Season with salt and pepper and cook on low settings for 6 hours.
When done, puree the soup with an immersion blender, adding the half and half as well.
Serve the soup warm.

Lasagna Soup

Time: 8 1/2 hours   Servings: 8

Ingredients:

1 pound ground beef
2 tablespoons olive oil
1 large sweet onion, chopped
2 garlic cloves, chopped
1 teaspoon dried oregano
1 1/2 cups tomato sauce

1 cup diced tomatoes
2 cups beef stock
6 cups water
1 1/2 cups uncooked pasta shells
Salt and pepper to taste
Grated Cheddar for serving

Directions:

Heat the oil in a skillet and add the ground beef. Cook for 5 minutes then transfer in your slow cooker.
Add the remaining ingredients and season with salt and pepper.
Cook on low settings for 8 hours.
When done, pour into serving bowls and top with cheese.
Serve the soup warm and fresh.

Chicken Tortellini Clear Soup

Time: 8 1/2 hours   Servings: 8

Ingredients:
1 whole chicken, cut into smaller pieces   8 cups water
1 carrot, halved   10 oz. cheese tortellini
1 celery stalk, halved   Salt and pepper to taste
1 parsnip, halved

Directions:
Combine the chicken, carrot, celery, parsnip and water in your slow cooker. Add salt and pepper to taste and cook on low settings for 6 hours. When done, remove and discard the carrot, celery and parsnip then shred the meat off the bone and place it back in the cooker. Add the tortellini and cook on high settings for 2 additional hours. Serve the soup warm and fresh.

Creamy Spinach Tortellini Soup

Time: 6 1/4 hours   Servings: 8

Ingredients:
1 chicken breast, diced   1 can condensed mushroom soup
1 tablespoon olive oil   2 cups sliced mushrooms
2 shallots, chopped   1 cup water
2 garlic cloves, chopped   8 oz. spinach tortellini
2 cups tomato sauce   Salt and pepper to taste
4 cups chicken stock

Directions:
Heat the oil in a skillet and add the chicken. Cook on all sides for 5 minutes then transfer in your slow cooker. Add the remaining ingredients and continue cooking on low settings for 6 hours.
The soup is best served warm, either fresh or re-heated.

Minestrone Soup

Time: 6 1/2 hours   Servings: 6

Ingredients:
1 shallot, chopped   2 potatoes, peeled and diced
1 garlic clove, chopped   1 teaspoon Italian herbs
1 celery stalk, sliced   2 cups chicken stock
1 red bell pepper, cored and diced   4 cups water
1 carrot, diced   1 cup short pasta of your choice
1 cup diced tomatoes   Salt and pepper to taste

Directions:
Combine all the ingredients in your slow cooker.
Add salt and pepper to taste and cook on low settings for 6 hours.
Serve the soup warm or chilled.

BEAN AND BACON SOUP

Time: 6 1/2 hours   Servings: **8**

Ingredients:

1 1/2 cups diced bacon
1 large sweet onion, chopped
2 carrots, diced
1 celery stalk, diced
2 ripe tomatoes, peeled and diced

2 cups dried white beans, rinsed
6 cups water
2 cups chicken stock
1 thyme sprig
Salt and pepper to taste

Directions:

Heat a skillet over medium flame and add the bacon. Cook on all sides until golden then transfer in your slow cooker. Add the remaining ingredients and cook over low settings for 6 hours. Serve the soup warm.

BACON CHEESEBURGER SOUP

Time: 6 1/2 hours   Servings: **8**

Ingredients:

4 bacon slices, chopped
1 pound ground beef
1 large sweet onion, chopped
2 carrots, diced
1 celery stalk, sliced
2 potatoes, peeled and cubed
1 cup diced tomatoes

1/2 teaspoon dried thyme
1/2 teaspoon dried oregano
1 cup cream cheese
2 cups beef stock
5 cups water
Salt and pepper to taste
Processed cheese for serving

Directions:

Heat the bacon in a skillet and cook until crisp. Add the beef and cook for a few minutes, stirring often. Add the remaining ingredients and season with salt and pepper. Cook on low settings for 6 hours. The soup is best served warm, topped with shredded processed cheese.

GRITS POTATO SOUP

Time: 6 1/4 hours   Servings: 6

Ingredients:

4 bacon slices, chopped
1/2 cup grits
2 cups chicken stock
4 cups water
1 1/2 pounds potatoes, peeled and cubed
1/2 celery stalk, sliced

1 carrot, diced
1 parsnip, diced
1 cup diced tomatoes
1/2 teaspoon dried thyme
1/2 teaspoon dried oregano
Salt and pepper to taste

Directions:

Cook the bacon until crisp in a skillet or pan. Transfer in your slow cooker and add the remaining ingredients. Cook the soup on low settings, adjusting the taste with salt and pepper as needed. The soup is done in about 6 hours. Serve warm.

Smoky Sweet Corn Soup

Time: 5 1/2 hours   Servings: 6

Ingredients:

1 shallot, chopped
1 garlic clove, chopped
2 tablespoons olive oil
2 bacon slices, chopped
3 cups frozen corn

2 cups chicken stock
2 cups water
1/4 teaspoon chili powder
Salt and pepper to taste

Directions:

Heat the oil in a skillet and add the garlic, shallot and bacon. Cook on all sides until golden then transfer in your slow cooker. Add the corn, stock, water and chili powder and season with salt and pepper. Cook on low settings for 5 hours. When done, puree the soup with an immersion blender and serve it warm.

Simple Chicken Noodle Soup

Time: 8 1/4 hours   Servings: 8

Ingredients:

1 1/2 pounds chicken breasts, cubed
2 large carrots, sliced
2 celery stalks, sliced
1 onion, chopped
2 cups chicken stock

5 cups water
1 thyme sprig
2 cups dried egg noodles
Salt and pepper to taste

Directions:

Combine all the ingredients in your slow cooker. Add salt and pepper and cook on low settings for 8 hours, mixing once during cooking. Serve the soup warm.

Cream of Chicken Soup

Time: 7 1/2 hours   Servings: 6

Ingredients:

6 chicken thighs
6 cups water
1/4 cup all-purpose flour
1 cup chicken stock

1/4 teaspoon garlic powder
1 pinch chili flakes
Salt and pepper to taste

Directions:

Combine the chicken with water and cook on low settings for 6 hours.
When done, remove the meat from the liquid and shred it off the bone.
Combine the flour with stock and mix well. Add the garlic powder and chili flakes and give it a good mix.
Pour this mixture over the liquid in the crock pot.
Add the meat and cook for 1 additional hour on high settings.
Serve the soup warm and fresh.

Stuffed Bell Pepper Soup

Time: 8 1/2 hours   Servings: 6

Ingredients:

6 medium size red bell peppers, cored
1 pound ground pork
1/2 pound ground beef
2 shallots, chopped
1 carrot, grated
1/4 cup white rice
2 tablespoons chopped parsley
1 teaspoon dried thyme

1/4 teaspoon cumin powder
Salt and pepper to taste
2 cups beef stock
6 cups water
1 can fire roasted tomatoes
1 bay leaf
1 thyme sprig
1 lemon, juiced

Directions:

In a bowl, mix the ground pork, beef, shallots, carrot, rice, chopped parsley, thyme and cumin powder. Add salt and pepper to taste and mix well. Stuff each bell pepper with the meat mixture and place them all in your slow cooker. Add the remaining ingredients and season with salt and pepper. Cook on low settings for 8 hours. Serve the soup warm.

Chicken Wild Rice Soup

Time: 6 1/2 hours   Servings: 6

Ingredients:

3/4 cup wild rice, rinsed
1 pound chicken breasts, cubed
2 celery stalk, sliced
2 carrots, sliced
1 sweet onion, chopped

6 cups chicken stock
1/2 teaspoon dried oregano
1 tablespoon butter
1/2 cup half and half
Salt and pepper to taste

Directions:

Combine all the ingredients in your slow cooker.
Add salt and pepper to taste and cook on low settings for 6 hours.
When done, serve the soup warm and fresh.

Thai Chicken Soup

Time: 6 1/2 hours   Servings: 8

Ingredients:

8 chicken thighs
2 celery stalks, sliced
1 sweet onion, chopped
1 teaspoon grated ginger
1 teaspoon fish sauce
2 tablespoons soy sauce
1 tablespoon brown sugar
1 lime, juiced

2 cups coconut milk
2 cups chicken stock
4 cups water
1 lemongrass stalk, crushed
1 cup green peas
Salt and pepper to taste

Directions:

Combine the chicken, celery, onion, ginger, fish sauce, soy sauce, sugar and lime juice in your slow cooker. Add the remaining ingredients and season with salt and pepper if needed. Cook the soup on low settings for 6 hours. Serve the soup warm and fresh.

Chicken Taco Soup

Time: 6 1/2 hours   Servings: 8

Ingredients:

4 chicken breasts, cut into strips
1 large onion, chopped
2 garlic cloves, chopped
1 can (15 oz.) pinto beans, drained
1 can (15 oz.) black beans, drained
1 cup diced tomatoes
1/2 cup canned corn, drained

1 cup dark beer
1 tablespoon Taco seasoning
2 cups chicken stock
4 cups water
Salt and pepper to taste
Tortilla chips for serving

Directions:

Combine the chicken, onion, garlic, beans and tomatoes in your slow cooker. Add the corn, beer, seasoning, stock and water then season with salt and pepper. Cook the soup on low settings for 6 hours. Serve the soup warm, topped with tortilla chips.

Cheddar Garlic Soup

Time: 2 1/4 hours   Servings: 6

Ingredients:

8 garlic cloves, chopped
2 tablespoons olive oil
1 teaspoon cumin seeds
1 teaspoon mustard seeds
2 tablespoons all-purpose flour

2 cups chicken stock
1/4 cup white wine
4 cups water
3 cups grated Cheddar
Salt and pepper to taste

Directions:

Heat the oil in a skillet and add the garlic. Sauté on low heat for 2 minutes then add the seeds and cook for 1 minute to release flavor. Add the flour and cook for 1 hour then transfer the mix in your slow cooker. Add the remaining ingredients and season with salt and pepper. Cook on high settings for 2 hours. The soup is best served warm.

Meatball Tortellini Soup

Time: 6 1/2 hours   Servings: 6

Ingredients:

1/2 pound ground chicken
1/4 cup white rice
1 garlic clove, chopped
1 tablespoon chopped parsley

2 cups chicken stock
4 cups water
1 celery stalk, sliced
1 carrot, sliced

1 shallot, chopped   Salt and pepper to taste
6 oz. spinach tortellini

Directions:

Mix the chicken, rice, garlic, parsley, salt and pepper in a bowl. Combine the stock, water, celery, carrot, shallot, salt and pepper in your slow cooker. Form small meatballs and drop them in the liquid. Add the tortellini as well and cook on low settings for 6 hours. Serve the soup warm and fresh.

Tuscan Kale and White bean Soup

Time: 8 1/2 hours   Servings: 8

Ingredients:

1 1/2 cups dried white beans, rinsed   6 cups water
1 sweet onion, chopped   1 bay leaf
2 carrots, diced   1 teaspoon dried basil
1 celery stalk, sliced   1 bunch kale, shredded
1 teaspoon dried oregano   Salt and pepper to taste
2 cups chicken stock   1 lemon, juiced

Directions:

Combine the beans, onion, carrots, celery, dried herbs, stock and water in your slow cooker.
Add salt and pepper to taste and throw in the bay leaf as well.
Cook on low settings for 4 hours then add the kale and lemon juice and cook for 4 additional hours.
Serve the soup warm or chilled.

Garlicky Spinach Soup with Herbed Croutons

Time: 2 1/4 hours   Servings: 6

Ingredients:

1 pound fresh spinach, shredded   Salt and pepper to taste
1/2 teaspoon dried oregano   1 lemon, juiced
1 shallot, chopped   1/2 cup half and half
4 garlic cloves, chopped   10 oz. one-day old bread, cubed
1/2 celery stalk, sliced   3 tablespoons olive oil
2 cups water   1 teaspoon dried basil
2 cups chicken stock   1 teaspoon dried marjoram

Directions:

Combine the spinach, oregano, shallot, garlic and celery in your slow cooker.
Add the water, stock and lemon juice, as well as salt and pepper to taste and cook on high settings for 2 hours.
While the soup is cooking, place the bread cubes in a large baking tray and drizzle with olive oil. Sprinkle with salt and pepper and cook in the preheated oven at 375F for 10-12 minutes until crispy and golden.
When the soup is done, puree it with an immersion blender, adding the half and half while doing so.
Serve the soup warm, topped with herbed croutons.

COMFORTING CHICKEN SOUP

Time: 8 1/2 hours   Servings: 8

Ingredients:
1 whole chicken, cut into pieces   6 oz. egg noodles
2 carrots, cut into sticks   2 garlic cloves, chopped
1 celery stalk, sliced   Salt and pepper to taste
4 potatoes, peeled and cubed   1 whole onion
8 cups water   1 bay leaf

Directions:
Combine all the ingredients in your slow cooker. Add salt and pepper to taste and cook on low settings for 8 hours. Serve the soup warm.

TUSCAN WHITE BEAN SOUP

Time: 6 1/2 hours   Servings: 6

Ingredients:
1 cup dried white beans   1 bay leaf
2 cups chicken stock   2 cups spinach, shredded
4 cups water   Salt and pepper to taste
1 carrot, diced   1 teaspoon dried oregano
1 celery stalk, diced   1 teaspoon dried basil
4 garlic cloves, chopped   1/2 lemon, juiced
2 tablespoons tomato paste

Directions:
Combine the beans, stock, water, carrot, celery, garlic and tomato paste in your slow cooker. Add the bay leaf, dried herbs and lemon juice, as well as salt and pepper. Cook on low settings for 4 hours then add the spinach and cook for 2 additional hours on low settings. Serve the soup warm or chilled.

VEGETABLE CHICKPEA SOUP

Time: 6 1/2 hours   Servings: 6

Ingredients:
2/3 cup dried chickpeas, rinsed   2 ripe tomatoes, peeled and diced
2 cups chicken stock   1 red bell pepper, cored and diced
4 cups water   1 potato, peeled and diced
1 celery stalk, sliced   1 tablespoon lemon juice
1 carrot, diced   Salt and pepper to taste
1 shallot, chopped

Directions:
Combine all the ingredients in your slow cooker. Add salt and pepper to taste and cook on low settings for 6 hours. Serve the soup warm and fresh.

Main Dishes

Vegetables

Spinach Bean Casserole

Time: 6 1/2 hours   Servings: 8

Ingredients:

2 bacon slices, chopped
2 sweet onions, chopped
1 carrot, diced
1 celery stalk, sliced
4 garlic cloves, chopped
2 tablespoons tomato paste
1/2 cup tomato sauce

1/2 teaspoon dried sage
1 1/2 cups dried black beans, rinsed
2 cups vegetable stock
2 cups water
4 cups fresh spinach, shredded
1 bay leaf
Salt and pepper to taste

Directions:

Heat a skillet over medium flame and add the bacon. Cook until crisp then stir in the onions and garlic. cook for 2 minutes until softened. Transfer in your slow cooker and add the remaining ingredients.
Season with salt and pepper to taste and cook on low settings for 6 hours.
Serve the stew warm and fresh.

White Bean Spinach Enchiladas

Time: 3 1/4 hours   Servings: 6

Ingredients:

2 tablespoons olive oil
2 shallots, chopped
2 garlic cloves, chopped
1 can (15 oz.) white beans, drained
1 can sweet corn, drained
2 cups spinach, shredded

1 cup vegetable stock
1/2 teaspoon cumin powder
1 cup red salsa
Salt and pepper to taste
Flour tortillas for serving
Grated Cheddar for serving

Directions:

Heat the oil in a skillet and add the shallot. Cook for a few minutes, stirring often, then transfer in your slow cooker.
Add the remaining ingredients and season with salt and pepper.
Cook on high settings for 3 hours.
When done, spoon the mixture into flour tortillas and top with grated cheese.
Serve the enchiladas right away.

Layered Spinach Ricotta Lasagna

Time: 6 1/2 hours   Servings: 10

Ingredients:

16 oz. frozen spinach, thawed
1 cup ricotta cheese
1/2 teaspoon dried marjoram
1/2 teaspoon dried basil
2 garlic cloves, chopped

1/2 cup grated Parmesan
2 1/2 cups tomato sauce
Salt and pepper to taste
6 lasagna noodles
2 cups shredded mozzarella cheese

Directions:

Mix the spinach, ricotta, marjoram, basil, garlic, parmesan, salt and pepper in a bowl.

Begin layering the lasagna noodles, spinach and ricotta filling and the tomato sauce in your slow cooker.

Top with shredded mozzarella and cook on low settings for 6 hours.

Serve the lasagna warm.

Summer Squash Lasagna

Time: 6 1/2 hours   Servings: 8

Ingredients:

2 summer squashes, cut into thin strips
4 tablespoons Italian pesto
4 ripe tomatoes, pureed
1 can chickpeas, drained
1/2 cup red lentils
1 shallot, chopped

1/2 cup chopped parsley
1 lemon, juiced
1/2 teaspoon dried thyme
1 pinch chili flakes
Salt and pepper to taste
1 1/2 cups shredded mozzarella

Directions:

Mix the chickpeas, lentils, parsley, lemon juice, thyme and chili flakes in a bowl. Add salt and pepper to taste and mix well.

Place a few squash slices in your slow cooker. Brush with pesto and top with part of the chickpea mix. Pour a few spoonfuls of tomato puree and continue layering squash slices, pesto, chickpea mix and tomato puree. End with a layer of mozzarella and cook on low settings for 6 hours.

Serve the lasagna warm.

Vegetable medley Stew

Time: 6 1/2 hours   Servings: 10

Ingredients:

2 tablespoons olive oil
1 sweet onion, chopped
4 garlic cloves, chopped
1/2 head cauliflower, cut into florets
2 red bell peppers, cored and diced
1 carrot, sliced
1 parsnip, cubed

1 zucchini, cubed
1 cup cherry tomatoes, halved
1/2 cup tomato sauce
2 cups vegetable stock
1 bay leaf
Salt and pepper to taste

Directions:

Heat the oil in a skillet and add the onion and garlic. Cook for 2 minutes until softened then transfer in your slow cooker.

Add the remaining ingredients and add salt and pepper to taste.

Cook on low settings for 6 hours.

Serve the stew warm and fresh.

Quick Zucchini Stew

Time: 1 3/4 hours

Servings: 4

Ingredients:

1 tablespoon olive oil
1 shallot, chopped
1 garlic clove, chopped
2 large zucchinis, cubed

2 ripe tomatoes, diced
1 bay leaf
1/2 cup Vegetable stock
Salt and pepper to taste

Directions:

Combine all the ingredients in your slow cooker. Add salt and pepper to taste and cook on high settings for 1 1/2 hours. Serve the soup warm and fresh.

Spicy Sweet Potato Chili

Time: 5 1/2 hours

Servings: 8

Ingredients:

2 tablespoons olive oil
2 shallots, chopped
1 garlic clove, chopped
1/4 teaspoon cumin powder
1/2 teaspoon curry powder
1 carrot, diced

1 1/2 pounds sweet potatoes, peeled and cubed
1 can (15 oz.) black beans, drained
1/2 teaspoon chili powder
2 cups vegetable stock
2 tablespoons tomato paste
Salt and pepper to taste

Directions:

Heat the oil in a skillet and add the shallots and garlic. Sauté for 2 minutes then transfer in your slow cooker. Add the remaining ingredients and season with salt and pepper. Cook the chili on low settings for 5 hours. Serve the chili warm.

Sweet Potato Curry

Time: 2 1/2 hours

Servings: 6

Ingredients:

2 tablespoons olive oil
1 shallot, chopped
2 garlic cloves, chopped
2 red bell peppers, cored and diced
1 carrot, diced
1/2 teaspoon cumin powder
1/2 teaspoon curry powder

1 pinch chili powder
2 tablespoons tomato paste
1 pound sweet potatoes, peeled and cubed
1 cup vegetable stock
1/2 cup coconut milk
1 bay leaf
Salt and pepper to taste

Directions:

Heat the oil in a skillet and add the shallot and garlic. Sauté for 2 minutes until softened then transfer in your slow cooker. Add the remaining ingredients and season with salt and pepper. Cook on high settings for 2 hours. Serve the curry warm.

Bean Tomato Stew

Time: 7 1/2 hours   Servings: 8

Ingredients:

2 red onions, chopped
2 garlic cloves, chopped
1 red bell pepper, cored and diced
1 carrot, diced
1 celery stalk, diced
2 tomatoes, peeled and diced
1 cup fire roasted tomatoes

2 tablespoons tomato paste
1 cup dried black beans, rinsed
2 cups vegetable stock
1 cup water
1 bay leaf
1 thyme sprig
Salt and pepper to taste

Directions:

Combine the onions, garlic, bell pepper, carrot and celery in your slow cooker. Add the remaining ingredients and season with salt and pepper. Cook on low settings for 7 hours. The stew is best served warm.

Cocoa Black Bean Chili

Time: 8 1/2 hours   Servings: 10

Ingredients:

2 tablespoons olive oil
2 red onions, chopped
4 garlic cloves, chopped
1/2 teaspoon chili powder
1/2 teaspoon cumin powder
1 red bell pepper, cored and diced
1 large carrot, diced
1 tablespoon cocoa powder

2 tablespoons tomato paste
1/2 cinnamon stick
1 bay leaf
2 cups dried black beans
2 cups vegetable stock
3 cups water
Salt and pepper to taste

Directions:

Heat the oil in a skillet and stir in the onions and garlic. Sauté for 5 minutes until softened then transfer in your slow cooker. Add the spices and the remaining ingredients and season with salt and pepper. Cook on low settings for 8 hours. Serve the chili warm.

Barley Black Bean Stew

Time: 3 1/4 hours   Servings: 6

Ingredients:

1 shallot, chopped
1 garlic clove, chopped
1 can (15 oz.) black beans, drained
1 cup canned corn, drained
1/2 cup pearl barley
1 1/2 cups vegetable stock
1/2 cup diced tomatoes

1/4 teaspoon chili powder
1/4 teaspoon cumin powder
Salt and pepper to taste
2 tablespoons chopped cilantro
1 green onion, chopped

Directions:

Combine the shallot, garlic, black beans, corn, pearl barley and stock in your slow cooker.

Add the stock, tomatoes, chili powder and cumin powder and season with salt and pepper.

Cook on high settings for 3 hours.

When done, stir in the cilantro and green onion.

Serve the soup warm.

Couscous with Vegetables

Time: 2 1/2 hours   Servings: 6

Ingredients:

1 cup couscous
2 cups vegetable stock
2 red bell peppers, cored and diced
2 carrots, diced
1/2 head broccoli, cut into florets

1 lemon, juiced
1/2 cup chopped parsley
2 tablespoons chopped cilantro
Salt and pepper to taste

Directions:

Combine the couscous, stock, peppers, carrots and broccoli in your slow cooker.

Add salt and pepper to taste and cook on high settings for 2 hours.

When done, stir in the remaining ingredients and serve fresh.

Zucchini Bean Stew

Time: 2 1/4 hours   Servings: 6

Ingredients:

1 can (15 oz.) white beans, drained
1 red bell pepper, cored and diced
1 zucchini, cubed
1 celery stalk, diced
1 can diced tomatoes

2 garlic cloves, chopped
1 teaspoon dried Italian herbs
Salt and pepper to taste
1 cup vegetable stock
1 bay leaf

Directions:

Combine the beans, bell pepper and zucchini in your slow cooker.

Add the remaining ingredients and adjust the taste with salt and pepper.

Cook on high settings for 2 hours.

The stew is best served warm.

Three Bean Chili

Time: 8 1/2 hours   Servings: 8

Ingredients:

1/2 cup dried white beans, rinsed
1/2 cup cannellini beans, rinsed
1/2 cup kidney beans, rinsed

2 carrots, diced
1 celery stalk, diced
1 onion, chopped

2 garlic cloves, chopped
2 tablespoons tomato paste
1/2 cup diced tomatoes
1 bay leaf
1/2 red chili, sliced

1/2 teaspoon cumin powder
2 cups vegetable stock
1 cup water
Salt and pepper to taste

Directions:

Combine the beans, carrots, celery, onion and garlic in your slow cooker.

Add the remaining ingredients and season with salt and pepper.

Cook the chili on low settings for 8 hours.

The dish is best served warm.

Rice Bean Stew

Time: 6 1/4 hours   Servings: 6

Ingredients:

1/2 cup wild rice
1 can black beans, drained
1 celery stalk, diced
2 tomatoes, peeled and diced
2 tablespoons pine nuts

2 cups vegetable stock
Salt and pepper to taste
2 tablespoons chopped parsley
1/2 lemon, juiced

Directions:

Combine the rice, beans, celery stalk and tomatoes in your slow cooker.

Add the remaining ingredients, except the parsley and lemon juice, and season with salt and pepper.

Cook on low settings for 6 hours.

When done, stir in the lemon juice and chopped parsley and serve the stew warm or chilled.

Cuban Beans

Time: 8 1/4 hours   Servings: 6

Ingredients:

1 cup dried black beans, rinsed
2 cups vegetable stock
2 cups water
1 cup chopped onion
2 red bell peppers, cored and diced
1 green bell pepper, cored and diced
1 teaspoon fennel seeds

1/2 teaspoon cumin seeds
1/2 teaspoon ground coriander
1 teaspoon sherry wine vinegar
1 can fire roasted tomatoes
1 green chile, chopped
Salt and pepper to taste

Directions:

Combine the beans and the remaining ingredients in your slow cooker.

Add salt and pepper as needed and cook on low settings for 8 hours.

Serve the beans warm in tortillas or over cooked rice.

Tofu Chickpea Curry

Time: 6 1/2 hours   Servings: 6

Ingredients:

12 oz. firm tofu, cubed
2 tablespoons olive oil
1 teaspoon curry powder
1 large onion, chopped
2 garlic cloves, chopped
2 cups cauliflower florets
1 large sweet potato, peeled and cubed

1 can (15 oz.) chickpeas, drained
1 cup diced tomatoes
1 cup coconut milk
1 cup vegetable stock
1 kaffir lime leaf
1 teaspoon grated ginger
Salt and pepper to taste

Directions:

Heat the oil in a skillet and add the tofu. Cook on all sides until golden and crusty.
Sprinkle with curry powder and fry just 1 additional minute. Transfer in your slow cooker.
Add the remaining ingredients and season well.
Cook on low settings for 6 hours.
Serve the curry warm.

Curried Coconut Chickpeas

Time: 2 1/4 hours   Servings: 6

Ingredients:

2 cans (15 oz.can) chickpeas, drained
2 shallots, chopped
2 garlic cloves, chopped
1 can diced tomatoes
1 cup coconut milk

1/2 cup vegetable stock
1 teaspoon curry powder
Salt and pepper to taste
2 tablespoons chopped cilantro

Directions:

Combine the chickpeas, shallots, garlic, tomatoes, coconut milk, stock and curry powder in your slow cooker.
Add salt and pepper to taste and cook on high settings for 2 hours.
When done, stir in the chopped cilantro and serve the dish warm.

White Bean Artichoke Ragout

Time: 6 1/2 hours   Servings: 8

Ingredients:

2 tablespoons olive oil
2 leeks, sliced
1 carrot, sliced
4 garlic cloves, chopped
2 cans (15 oz.) cannellini beans, drained
2 potatoes, peeled and cubed
6 artichoke hearts, drained and chopped

1 small fennel bulb, sliced
1/2 teaspoon dried basil
1 cup vegetable stock
Salt and pepper to taste

Directions:

Heat the oil in a skillet and add the leeks. Cook for 5 minutes until softened and transfer in your slow cooker.

Add the remaining ingredients and season with salt and pepper.

Cook on low settings for 6 hours.

The ragout is best served warm.

MARINARA SAUCE

Time: 6 1/2 hours   Servings: 8

Ingredients:

3 tablespoons olive oil
2 large onions, chopped
2 carrots, grated
1 celery stalk, diced
4 garlic cloves, minced
1/2 teaspoon dried oregano
1/4 teaspoon red pepper flakes

2 tablespoons tomato paste
2 pounds fresh tomatoes, peeled and pureed
Salt and pepper to taste
1 teaspoon honey
1 teaspoon red wine vinegar
1 bay leaf
1/2 cup vegetable stock

Directions:

Heat the oil in a skillet or saucepan and add the onions and garlic. Sauté for 5 minutes until softened then transfer in your slow cooker.

Add the remaining ingredients and season with salt and pepper.

Cook on low settings for 6 hours.

Serve the marinara sauce right away with pasta or store it in an airtight container in the freezer until needed.

PINTO BEAN CHILI WITH BUTTERNUT SQUASH

Time: 6 1/4 hours   Servings: 8

Ingredients:

3 cups butternut squash cubes
2 cans (15 oz.) pinto beans, drained
1 cup canned corn, drained
1 large onion, chopped
2 garlic cloves, chopped
2 tablespoons tomato paste
1/2 cup tomato sauce

1 cup vegetable stock
1/2 teaspoon chili powder
1 bay leaf
1 thyme sprig
Salt and pepper to taste
1 lime, sliced

Directions:

Combine the butternut squash, pinto beans, canned corn, onion, garlic and tomato paste in your slow cooker.

Add the remaining ingredients and season with salt and pepper.

Cook on low settings for 6 hours.

Serve the chili warm, drizzled with lime juice.

Veggie Chickpea Curry

Time: 6 1/4 hours

Servings: 6

Ingredients:

1 cup dried chickpeas, rinsed
1 large onion, chopped
1 carrot, sliced
1 teaspoon curry
1 teaspoon grated ginger
2 garlic cloves, chopped
2 potatoes, peeled and diced

1 red bell pepper, cored and diced
1 poblano pepper, chopped
1 cup fire roasted tomatoes
2 cups vegetable stock
Salt and pepper to taste
1 bay leaf
Chopped cilantro for serving

Directions:

Combine all the ingredients in your slow cooker.
Add salt and pepper to taste and cook the curry on low settings for 6 hours.
The curry is best served warm, topped with chopped cilantro.

White Bean Casoulet

Time: 6 1/2 hours

Servings: 6

Ingredients:

2 tablespoons olive oil
1 large onion, chopped
2 carrots, diced
1 parsnip, diced
2 garlic cloves, chopped
2 cans white beans, drained

1 cup vegetable stock
1 thyme sprig
1 1/2 cups diced tomatoes
1 bay leaf
Salt and pepper to taste

Directions:

Heat the oil in a skillet and add the onion, carrot and garlic. Sauté for 2 minutes until softened and translucent then transfer in your slow cooker.
Add the remaining ingredients and cook on low settings for 6 hours.
Serve the cassoulet warm.

Saucy Tomato White Bean Stew

Time: 6 1/2 hours

Servings: 8

Ingredients:

1 red onion, chopped
2 garlic cloves, chopped
1 can (28 oz.) diced tomatoes
1 teaspoon Worcestershire sauce
1 1/2 cups white beans, rinsed
3 cups vegetable stock
1 bay leaf

1 thyme sprig
1 rosemary sprig
Salt and pepper to taste

Directions:

Combine the beans and the remaining ingredients in your slow cooker.

Add salt and pepper and cover with a lid. Cook on low settings for 6 hours until the beans are tender and saucy.

Serve the stew warm and fresh.

Kidney Bean Chili with Crunchy Corn Chip Topping

Time: 2 3/4 hours   Servings: 6

Ingredients:

2 cans kidney beans, drained
1 red onion, chopped
1/2 red chili, chopped
2 garlic cloves, chopped
1 carrot, sliced
1 red bell pepper, cored and diced
1 cup diced tomatoes

1/2 teaspoon cumin powder
1 cup vegetable stock
1 bay leaf
Salt and pepper to taste
2 cups corn chips
2 tablespoons olive oil
1 teaspoon smoked paprika

Directions:

Combine the kidney beans, onion, red chili, garlic, carrot, bell pepper, tomatoes, cumin powder, stock and bay leaf in your slow cooker.

Add salt and pepper and cook on high settings for 2 1/2 hours.

For the topping, spread the corn chips in a baking tray and drizzle with olive oil. Sprinkle with paprika and bake in the preheated oven at 400F for 7-8 minutes until golden.

Serve the chili warm, topped with crunchy corn chips.

White Bean Chili over Creamy Grits

Time: 6 3/4 hours   Servings: 8

Ingredients:

2 cups dried white beans, rinsed
2 cups vegetable stock
2 cups water
1 onion, chopped
2 garlic cloves, chopped
1 carrot, diced
1 celery stalk, diced
1 red chili, chopped

1/2 teaspoon cumin powder
1 cup fire roasted tomatoes
1 bay leaf
2 cups spinach, shredded
Salt and pepper to taste
1 cup grits
2 cups whole milk
1 cup grated Cheddar

Directions:

Combine the beans, stock, water, onion, garlic, carrot, celery, red chili, tomatoes, cumin powder and bay leaf in your slow cooker. Top with shredded spinach.

Add salt and pepper to taste and cook on low settings for 6 1/2 hours.

To make the creamy grits, pour the milk in a saucepan. Bring to a boil and add the grits. Cook on low heat until creamy then remove from heat and add the cheese.

Spoon the grits into the serving bowls and top with white bean stew.

ROASTED BELL PEPPER STEW

Time: 2 1/2 hours   Servings: 6

Ingredients:

2 tablespoons olive oil
1 large onion, chopped
3 garlic cloves, minced
1 carrot, grated
1 parsnip, grated
1 large jar roasted red bell pepper, chopped
2 tablespoons tomato paste

1 cup tomato sauce
1/2 cup vegetable stock
1/4 teaspoon cumin powder
1/4 teaspoon dried oregano
1 bay leaf
1 thyme sprig
Salt and pepper to taste

Directions:

Heat the oil in a skillet and add the onion, garlic and carrot. Cook for 5 minutes until softened.
Transfer in your slow cooker and add the remaining ingredients.
Season with salt and pepper and cook on high settings for 2 hours.
Serve the stew warm and fresh.

QUINOA BLACK BEAN CHILI

Time: 6 1/2 hours   Servings: 6

Ingredients:

2 tablespoons olive oil
1 shallot, chopped
2 garlic cloves, chopped
1 can (15 oz.) black beans, drained
2 poblano peppers, chopped
1/2 cup quinoa, rinsed

2 cups vegetable stock
1 cup diced tomatoes
1 tablespoon tomato paste
1/4 teaspoon cumin powder
Salt and pepper to taste
Chopped cilantro for serving

Directions:

Heat the oil in a skillet and stir in the shallot and garlic. Sauté for 2 minutes until softened then transfer in your slow cooker.
Add the remaining ingredients and season with salt and pepper.
Cover with a lid and cook on low settings for 6 hours.
Serve the chili warm and fresh, topped with chopped cilantro.

PARSNIP BUTTERNUT SQUASH STEW

Time: 4 1/2 hours   Servings: 6

Ingredients:

2 tablespoons olive oil
1 sweet onion, chopped
3 parsnips, diced
4 cups butternut squash cubes
1 green apple, peeled and diced

1 cup diced tomatoes
1/2 teaspoon cumin powder
1/2 teaspoon ground coriander
1/2 teaspoon fennel seeds
1 pinch chili powder

1 thyme sprig
Salt and pepper to taste

Plain yogurt for serving

Directions:

Heat the oil in a skillet and add the onion and parsnips. Cook for 5 minutes until softened then transfer in your slow cooker.

Add the remaining ingredients and cook on low settings for 4 hours, adjusting the taste with salt and pepper as needed.

Serve the stew warm, topped with plain yogurt if you want.

Quick Lentil Stew

Time: 2 1/4 hours

Servings: 6

Ingredients:

1 cup red lentils, rinsed
1/2 cup green lentils, rinsed
1 cup diced tomatoes
1 large onion, chopped
2 garlic cloves, chopped
1 carrot, diced
1 celery stalk, diced

1 jalapeno, chopped
1/4 teaspoon cumin powder
1/4 teaspoon garam masala
2 cups vegetable stock
Salt and pepper to taste
1 bay leaf

Directions:

Combine the lentils, tomatoes, onion, garlic, carrot, celery, jalapeno, cumin powder, garam masala and stock in your slow cooker.

Add the bay leaf, salt and pepper and cook on high settings for 2 hours.

Serve the stew warm and fresh.

Chipotle Lentil Chili

Time: 6 1/2 hours

Servings: 8

Ingredients:

2 tablespoons olive oil
2 shallots, chopped
4 garlic cloves, chopped
2 carrots, diced
1 chipotle pepper, seeded and chopped
1 can (15 oz.) black beans, drained
2/3 cup brown lentils

1 cup diced tomatoes
2 cups vegetable stock
1/4 teaspoon chili powder
1/4 teaspoon cumin powder
Salt and pepper to taste
1 bay leaf

Directions:

Heat the oil in a skillet and add the shallots and garlic. Cook for 2 minutes until softened then transfer the mixture in your slow cooker.

Add the remaining ingredients and season with salt and pepper.

Cook on low settings for 6 hours.

Serve the chili warm.

CAULIFLOWER LENTIL STEW

Time: 6 1/4 hours

Servings: 6

Ingredients:

1 shallot, chopped
2 garlic cloves, chopped
1 celery stalk, sliced
1 carrot, sliced
1 small head cauliflower, cut into florets
1/2 cup red lentils, rinsed

2 cups vegetable stock
1 cup diced tomatoes
1 bay leaf
1/4 teaspoon cumin powder
1 pinch cayenne pepper
Salt and pepper to taste

Directions:

Combine all the ingredients in your slow cooker.
Add salt and pepper to taste and cook on low settings for 6 hours.
When done, serve the stew warm and fresh.

LEEK POTATO STEW

Time: 4 1/2 hours

Servings: 6

Ingredients:

2 tablespoons olive oil
2 leeks, sliced
2 celery stalks, sliced
2 carrots, diced
1 1/2 pounds potatoes, peeled and cubed

2 tablespoons tomato paste
1/2 cup diced tomatoes
1 bay leaf
1 thyme sprig
Salt and pepper to taste

Directions:

Heat the oil in your slow cooker and add the leeks. Cook for 5 minutes until softened then transfer the mix in your slow cooker.
Add the remaining ingredients and season with salt and pepper.
Cook on low settings for 4 hours.
The stew is best served warm.

MADRAS LENTILS

Time: 4 1/4 hours

Servings: 6

Ingredients:

1 cup dried red lentils, rinsed
1/2 cup brown lentils, rinsed
1 cup tomato sauce
2 cups vegetable stock
1 large potato, peeled and cubed
1 shallot, chopped
3 garlic cloves, chopped
1/2 teaspoon cumin powder

1/2 teaspoon dried oregano
Salt and pepper to taste
1/2 cup coconut milk

Directions:

Mix the lentils, tomato sauce, stock, potato, shallot, garlic, cumin powder, oregano and coconut milk in your slow cooker.

Add salt and pepper to taste and cook over low settings for 4 hours.

Serve the lentils warm or store them in an airtight container in the freezer until needed.

VEGETARIAN GUMBO

Time: 8 1/2 hours   Servings: 6

Ingredients:

2 tablespoons olive oil
1 sweet onion, chopped
1 celery stalk, sliced
2 garlic cloves, chopped
1 red bell pepper, cored and diced
2 tablespoons all-purpose flour
2 cups vegetable stock
1 cup diced tomatoes

1 can (15 oz.) kidney beans, drained
2 cups sliced mushrooms
1 summer squash, cubed
1 cup chopped okra
1 teaspoon Cajun seasoning
1/2 cup coconut milk
Salt and pepper to taste

Directions:

Heat the oil in a skillet and add the onion, celery, garlic and bell pepper and cook for 5 minutes until softened. Add the flour and cook for 1 additional minute then transfer the mixture in your slow cooker.

Add the remaining ingredients and season with salt and pepper.

Cook on low settings for 8 hours.

Serve the gumbo warm.

BUTTERNUT SQUASH CURRY

Time: 6 1/2 hours   Servings: 6

Ingredients:

2 shallots, chopped
4 garlic cloves, chopped
4 cups butternut squash
1 can (15 oz.) chickpeas, drained
1 cup diced tomatoes
1 cup coconut milk

1 cup vegetable stock
2 tablespoons red curry paste
Salt and pepper to taste
2 cups fresh spinach
2 tablespoons chopped parsley

Directions:

Combine the shallots, garlic, butternut squash, chickpeas, tomatoes, coconut milk and stock in your slow cooker.

Add the rest of the ingredients and season with salt and pepper.

Cook on low settings for 6 hours.

Serve the squash warm and fresh.

Vegetarian Fajitas

Time: 6 1/4 hours

Servings: 8

Ingredients:

4 heirloom tomatoes, peeled and diced
4 oz. green chilies, chopped
2 red bell peppers, cored and diced
1 small onion, chopped
1 teaspoon cumin powder
1/4 teaspoon chili powder

1/2 teaspoon dried oregano
1/2 cup vegetable stock
1 can (15 oz.) kidney beans, drained
Salt and pepper to taste
Flour tortillas for serving

Directions:

Combine the tomatoes, green chilies, bell peppers, onion, cumin powder, chili powder, oregano, stock and beans in your slow cooker.

Add salt and pepper to taste and cook on low settings for 6 hours.

Serve the dish warm, wrapped in flour tortillas.

Sweet and Spicy Vegetable Curry

Time: 3 1/4 hours

Servings: 6

Ingredients:

2 tablespoons olive oil
2 shallots, chopped
4 garlic cloves, chopped
2 carrots, sliced
1 parsnip, diced
1 red bell pepper, cored and diced
2 celery stalks, sliced
1/2 head green cabbage, shredded
1 green apple, peeled and diced
1 cup canned chickpeas, drained

2 cups cauliflower florets
1 cup tomato sauce
1 cup vegetable stock
1/2 teaspoon chili powder
1/2 teaspoon cumin powder
1 teaspoon curry powder
1 tablespoon brown sugar
1/2 cup coconut milk
Salt and pepper to taste

Directions:

Heat the oil in your slow cooker and add the shallots, garlic, carrots, parsnip, bell pepper and celery. Cook for 5 minutes until softened then transfer in your slow cooker.

Add the remaining ingredients and season with salt and pepper.

Cook on high settings for 3 hours.

The curry is best served warm.

BBQ Tofu

Time: 2 1/4 hours   Servings: 4

Ingredients:

4 thick slices firm tofu
1 shallot, sliced
2 garlic cloves, minced
1 cup BBQ sauce

1 teaspoon Worcestershire sauce
1/4 teaspoon cumin powder
1 pinch cayenne pepper
1 thyme sprig

Directions:

Combine the shallot, garlic, BBQ sauce, Worcestershire sauce, cumin powder, cayenne pepper and thyme in your slow cooker. Add the tofu and coat it well.
Cover the pot with its lid and cook on high settings for 2 hours.
Serve the tofu warm with your favorite side dish.

Hoisin Braised Tofu

Time: 2 1/4 hours   Servings: 4

Ingredients:

4 slices firm tofu
1/2 cup hoisin sauce
1 tablespoon soy sauce
1 teaspoon grated ginger

1 teaspoon rice vinegar
1/2 teaspoon sesame oil
2 garlic cloves, minced
1 teaspoon molasses

Directions:

Mix the hoisin sauce, ginger, vinegar, sesame oil, garlic and molasses in your slow cooker.
Add the tofu and coat it well then cover the pot with its lid and cook on high settings for 2 hours.
Serve the tofu warm with your favorite side dish.

Mushroom Stroganoff

Time: 6 1/4 hours   Servings: 6

Ingredients:

1 1/2 pounds mushrooms, sliced
2 tablespoons all-purpose flour
1 onion, chopped
4 garlic cloves, chopped
2 tablespoons olive oil

1/2 teaspoon smoked paprika
1 cup half and half
1/2 cup vegetable stock
Salt and pepper to taste

Directions:

Heat the oil in a skillet. Add the onion and garlic and cook for 2 minutes then transfer in your slow cooker.
Sprinkle the mushrooms with flour and coat them well. Place in your slow cooker.
Add the remaining ingredients and season with salt and pepper.
Cook on low settings for 6 hours.
Serve the stroganoff warm.

Greek Rice Stew

Time: 6 1/4 hours

Servings: 6

Ingredients:

2 tablespoons olive oil
2 garlic cloves, chopped
1 shallot, chopped
1/2 teaspoon dried oregano
1/2 teaspoon dried basil
1/2 teaspoon dried marjoram
1 1/2 cups white rice

3 cups vegetable stock
1/2 cup green peas
1 zucchini, cubed
1/2 cup Kalamata olives, pitted and s iced
Salt and pepper to taste
1/2 lemon, juiced
2 tablespoons chopped parsley

Directions:

Heat the oil in a skillet and stir in the garlic and shallot. Sauté for 2 minutes then transfer in your slow cooker. Add the oregano, basil marjoram, rice, stock, green peas, zucchini, olives, salt and pepper and cook on low settings for 6 hours. When done, stir in the lemon juice and parsley and serve the rice warm.

Coconut Bean Curry

Time: 6 1/2 hours

Servings: 6

Ingredients:

2 cans pinto beans, drained
1 tablespoon olive oil
1 shallot, chopped
2 garlic cloves, chopped
1 teaspoon grated ginger
1/2 teaspoon chili powder
1/2 teaspoon cumin powder

1 teaspoon curry powder
1 cup coconut milk
1 cup vegetable stock
2 tablespoons tomato paste
1 bay leaf
1 teaspoon brown sugar
Salt and pepper to taste

Directions:

Combine the beans and the remaining ingredients in your slow cooker. Season with salt and pepper. Cook on low settings for 6 hours. Serve the bean curry warm.

Wild Rice Veggie Stew

Time: 6 1/2 hours

Servings: 6

Ingredients:

1 cup wild rice
3 cups vegetable stock
2 carrots, diced
2 celery stalks, diced

1 shallot, chopped
1 oz. dried porcini, crushed
1 cup sliced mushrooms
Salt and pepper to taste

Directions:

Combine all the ingredients in your slow cooker. Add salt and pepper to taste and cook on low settings for 6 hours. Serve the stew warm and fresh.

CAULIFLOWER MASHED POTATOES

Time: 4 1/2 hours   Servings: 4

Ingredients:
1 pound potatoes, peeled and cubed   2 tablespoons coconut oil
2 cups cauliflower florets   1/4 cup coconut milk
1/4 cup vegetable stock   Salt and pepper to taste

Directions:
Combine the potatoes, cauliflower, stock, coconut oil and coconut milk in your slow cooker.
Add salt and pepper to taste and cook on low settings for 4 hours.
When done, mash with a potato masher and serve right away.

SPRING MASHED POTATOES

Time: 2 1/2 hours   Servings: 4

Ingredients:
1 1/2 pounds potatoes, peeled and cubed
1 cup water   1 green onion, chopped
Salt and pepper to taste   1 garlic clove, minced
1/4 cup coconut milk

Directions:
Combine the potatoes and water in your slow cooker. Add salt and pepper and cook on high settings for 2 hours.
When done, puree the potatoes with a masher and stir in the coconut milk, onion and garlic.
Serve the mashed potatoes warm.

LEMONY ARTICHOKES

Time: 6 1/2 hours   Servings: 4

Ingredients:
4 large artichokes   3/4 cup vegetable stock
1 lemon, juiced   Salt and pepper to taste
2 garlic cloves, minced   1 rosemary sprig

Directions:
Peel the artichokes and clean them well.
Place them in your slow cooker and add the remaining ingredients.
Cook on low settings for 6 hours and serve the artichokes warm.

LENTIL STUFFED BELL PEPPERS

Time: 6 1/2 hours   Servings: 6

Ingredients:

6 red bell peppers, cored
3 cups cooked red lentils
1/2 cup red rice
2 carrots, grated
1 large onion, chopped
2 tablespoons tomato paste
1 celery stalk, diced

1/2 teaspoon dried oregano
1/2 teaspoon dried basil
1 pinch nutmeg
Salt and pepper to taste
1 cup tomato sauce
2 cups vegetable stock

Directions:

Combine the lentils, rice, carrots, onion, tomato paste, celery, oregano, basil and nutmeg in a bowl. Season with salt and pepper. Stuff the bell peppers with the lentil mixture and place each pepper in your slow cooker. Add the tomato sauce and stock and cook on low settings for 6 hours. Serve the bell peppers warm.

GREEK STUFFED ZUCCHINI BOATS

Time: 2 1/2 hours   Servings: 4

Ingredients:

2 zucchinis
1 shallot, chopped
2 garlic cloves, chopped
1 carrot, grated
1 small eggplant, peeled and diced

2 tablespoons tomato paste
Salt and pepper to taste
1 cup tomato sauce
1 thyme sprig
1 bay leaf

Directions:

Pour the tomato sauce in your slow cooker. Add the thyme and bay leaf.
Cut the zucchinis in half and scoop out part of the flesh, leaving the skins intact. Chop the flesh well.
Mix the zucchini flesh with shallot, garlic, eggplant, tomato paste, salt and pepper in a bowl.
Fill each zucchini half with this mixture and place in your slow cooker.
Cover the pot and cook on high settings for 2 hours.
Serve the zucchini boats warm.

ROASTED BELL PEPPER CANNELLINI STEW

Time: 6 1/4 hours   Servings: 6

Ingredients:

1 can (15 oz.) cannellini beans, drained
4 roasted red bell peppers, chopped
2 garlic cloves, chopped
1 shallot, chopped
2 ripe tomatoes, peeled and diced
1/2 cup tomato sauce

1 cup vegetable stock
1/2 teaspoon dried basil
Salt and pepper to taste
1 pinch cumin powder
2 tablespoons chopped parsley

Directions:

Combine the beans, bell peppers, garlic, shallot, tomatoes, tomato sauce, stock, basil and cumin in your slow cooker.

Add salt and pepper to taste and cook on low settings for 6 hours.

When done, stir in the parsley and serve the stew warm or chilled.

Vegetarian Jambalaya

Time: 6 1/2 hours   Servings: 6

Ingredients:

1 tablespoon olive oil
2 shallots, chopped
2 garlic cloves, chopped
8 oz. seaman, cubed
1 red bell pepper, cored and diced
1 celery stalk, sliced

2 cups vegetable stock
1 teaspoon miso paste
1 teaspoon Cajun seasoning
1 cup white rice
1/2 teaspoon turmeric powder
Salt and pepper to taste

Directions:

Heat the oil in a skillet and add the shallots and garlic. Sauté for 2 minutes until softened then transfer in your slow cooker.

Add the remaining ingredients and season with salt and pepper as needed. Cook on low settings for 6 hours and serve the dish warm and fresh.

Pearl Barley Mushroom Stew

Time: 6 1/4 hours   Servings: 6

Ingredients:

1 pound mushrooms, sliced
1 shallot, chopped
2 garlic cloves, chopped
1 celery stalk, sliced
1/2 cup dried red lentils

1/2 cup pearl barley, rinsed
2 cups vegetable stock
Salt and pepper to taste
1 bay leaf
1 cup diced tomatoes

Directions:

Combine all the ingredients in your slow cooker.

Adjust the taste with salt and pepper and cook on low settings for 6 hours.

The dish is best served warm.

Spicy Vegetarian Chili

Time: 6 1/2 hours   Servings: 8

Ingredients:

2 tablespoons olive oil
2 shallots, chopped
4 garlic cloves, chopped
2 cups cauliflower florets

1 zucchini, cubed
1 can (15 oz.) chickpeas, drained
1 can (15 oz.) black beans, drained
1 can fire toasted tomatoes

1 cup canned corn, drained
2 red bell peppers, cored and diced
1 celery stalk, diced
1 teaspoon chili powder
1 cup tomato sauce

2 cups vegetable stock
1 bay leaf
Salt and pepper to taste
Sour cream for serving

Directions:

Heat the oil in a skillet and add the shallots and garlic. Cook for a few minutes until softened then transfer in your slow cooker. Add the remaining ingredients and adjust the taste with salt and pepper.
Cook on low settings for 6 hours.
Serve the chili warm, topped with sour cream.

MEDITERRANEAN STEW

Time: 6 1/2 hours

Servings: 8

Ingredients:

2 tablespoons olive oil
1 large onion, chopped
4 garlic cloves, minced
1 large eggplant, peeled and cubed
4 roasted red bell peppers, chopped
2 zucchinis, cubed
2 cups okra
1 carrot, sliced
1 tomato, diced

1 cup tomato sauce
1 cup vegetable stock
1/4 cup golden raisins
1/2 teaspoon cumin powder
1/2 teaspoon turmeric powder
1 pinch red pepper flakes
1/2 teaspoon dried oregano
1/2 teaspoon dried basil
Salt and pepper to taste

Directions:

Heat the oil in a skillet and add the onion and garlic. Cook for 2 minutes until softened.
Transfer in your slow cooker and add the remaining ingredients. Season with salt and pepper.
Cook on low settings for 6 hours.
Serve the stew warm.

TOMATO CHICKPEA STEW

Time: 6 1/2 hours

Servings: 6

Ingredients:

1 1/2 cups dried chickpeas, rinsed
1 large onion, chopped
2 red bell peppers, cored and diced
1 zucchini, sliced
2 ripe tomatoes, peeled and diced

1 1/2 cups tomato sauce
1 1/2 cups vegetable stock
1 pinch chili powder
1/2 teaspoon cumin powder
Salt and pepper to taste

Directions:

Combine the chickpeas, onion, bell peppers, zucchini, tomatoes, tomato sauce, stock, chili powder and cumin powder in your slow cooker. Add salt and pepper to taste and cook on low settings for 6 hours.
Serve the stew warm.

*A*UTUMNAL STEW

Time: 6 1/4 hours   Servings: 6

Ingredients:

4 cups butternut squash cubes
1 shallot, chopped
2 garlic cloves, chopped
2 red apples, peeled and diced
1 celery stalk, sliced
1 carrot, sliced

2 ripe tomatoes, peeled and diced
1/4 teaspoon cumin powder
1 pinch chili powder
1/2 cup tomato sauce
1/2 cup vegetable stock
Salt and pepper to taste

Directions:

Combine all the ingredients in your slow cooker.
Add salt and pepper to taste and cook on low settings for 6 hours.
Serve the stew warm and fresh.

*V*EGETARIAN COCONUT CURRY

Time: 7 1/2 hours   Servings: 8

Ingredients:

1 1/2 pounds potatoes, peeled and cubed
2 carrots, sliced
1 cup green peas
1 teaspoon curry powder
1/2 teaspoon chili powder

1/2 teaspoon red pepper flakes
2 red bell peppers, cored and diced
1 1/2 cups coconut milk
1/2 cup vegetable stock
Salt and pepper to taste

Directions:

Combine the potatoes, carrots, green peas, curry powder, chili powder, red pepper flakes, bell peppers, coconut milk
and stock in your slow cooker.
Add salt and pepper to taste and cook on low settings for 7 hours.
Serve the curry warm.

*M*ARINATED MUSHROOMS

Time: 8 1/4 hours   Servings: 8

Ingredients:

24 oz. fresh mushrooms, sliced
1/2 cup butter
1 cup water

1 cup soy sauce
1/4 teaspoon chili powder
1 teaspoon rice vinegar

Directions:

Combine all the ingredients in your slow cooker.
Cook on low settings for 8 hours.
Serve the mushrooms warm or chilled.

Hearty Vegan Chili

Time: 7 1/2 hours   Servings: **8**

Ingredients:

2 tablespoons olive oil
1 red bell pepper, cored and diced
1 green bell pepper, cored and diced
1 yellow bell pepper, cored and diced
1 zucchini, cubed
1 carrot, sliced
1 shallot, chopped
4 garlic cloves, chopped
1 large potato, peeled and cubed

2 tablespoons tomato paste
1/2 cup diced tomatoes
1 can (15 oz.) cannellini beans, drained
4 cups spinach, shredded
1 cup vegetable stock
1/2 teaspoon chili powder
1 thyme sprig
Salt and pepper to taste

Directions:

Heat the oil in a skillet and stir in the shallot, garlic and bell peppers. Cook for 5 minutes until softened then transfer in your slow cooker. Add the remaining ingredients and season with salt and pepper. Cook on low settings for 7 hours. Serve the chili warm.

Pumpkin Spinach Stew

Time: 6 1/2 hours   Servings: **8**

Ingredients:

2 tablespoons olive oil
2 sweet onions, chopped
4 garlic cloves, chopped
1 small pumpkin, peeled and cubed
1 cup diced tomatoes
1 tablespoon tomato paste

1/2 teaspoon cumin seeds
1 pinch cayenne pepper
1 cup vegetable stock
Salt and pepper to taste
2 cups fresh spinach

Directions:

Heat the oil in your skillet and add the onions and garlic. Sauté for 2 minutes until softened then transfer in your slow cooker. Add the remaining ingredients and season with salt and pepper. Cook on low settings for 6 hours. The stew is best served warm and fresh.

Quick Okra Stew

Time: 2 1/4 hours   Servings: **6**

Ingredients:

1 shallot, chopped
2 garlic cloves, chopped
1/2 teaspoon cumin seeds
1/2 teaspoon mustard seeds
1/4 teaspoon smoked paprika
1 pound fresh okra, trimmed

1 cup fire roasted tomatoes
1/2 cup vegetable stock
Salt and pepper to taste

Directions:

Combine all the ingredients in your slow cooker. Add salt and pepper to taste and cover with a lid. Cook on high settings for 2 hours. Serve the stew warm and fresh.

SOUTHWESTERN STYLE ONE POT MEAL

Time: 6 1/2 hours   Servings: 6

Ingredients:

1 cup dried black eyed peas, soaked overnight
1 red bell pepper, cored and diced
1 shallot, chopped
2 garlic cloves, chopped
1 can (10 oz.) sweet corn, drained
1 can diced tomatoes

1/4 teaspoon chili powder
1/2 teaspoon cumin powder
1/2 cup wild rice
4 cups vegetable stock
Salt and pepper to taste

Directions:

Combine the black eyes peas with the remaining ingredients in your slow cooker.
Add salt and pepper to taste and cook on low settings for 6 hours.
Serve the meal warm and fresh.

CREAMY MUSHROOM STEW

Time: 6 1/4 hours   Servings: 6

Ingredients:

1 pound cremini mushrooms, sliced
2 tablespoons all-purpose flour
2 tablespoons olive oil
2 shallots, chopped
1/4 cup vegetable stock

4 garlic cloves, chopped
1 cup whole milk
1/2 cup cream cheese
Salt and pepper to taste

Directions:

Sprinkle the mushrooms with flour. Heat the oil in a skillet and add the mushrooms. Sauté on each side until golden then transfer the mushrooms in your slow cooker. Add the remaining ingredients and adjust the taste with salt and pepper. Cook on low settings for 6 hours. Serve the stew warm.

EGGPLANT CASSEROLE

Time: 5 1/2 hours   Servings: 6

Ingredients:

2 large eggplants, peeled and cubed
1 sweet onion, chopped
2 garlic cloves, chopped
1/2 teaspoon dried thyme
1/2 teaspoon dried oregano
1 cup fire roasted tomatoes

1 1/2 cups vegetable stock
1/2 cup short pasta of your choice
Salt and pepper to taste

Directions:

Combine the eggplants and the remaining ingredients in your slow cooker.

Add salt and pepper to taste and cook on low settings for 5 hours.

Serve the casserole warm and fresh.

Slow Cooker Ratatouille

Time: 6 1/2 hours   Servings: 8

Ingredients:

1 large onion, chopped
1 tablespoon olive oil
4 garlic cloves, finely chopped
1 large zucchini, cubed
1 large eggplant, peeled and cubed
2 cups sliced mushrooms

3 ripe tomatoes, peeled and diced
2 red bell peppers, cored and diced
1/2 cup vegetable stock
1 thyme sprig
Salt and pepper to taste

Directions:

Combine all the ingredients in your slow cooker, adding salt and pepper as needed.

Cook on low settings for 6 hours.

The ratatouille can be served either warm or chilled.

Kitchen Sink Stew

Time: 7 1/2 hours   Servings: 8

Ingredients:

1 onion, chopped
2 garlic cloves, chopped
1/2 teaspoon smoked paprika
1 cup canned corn, drained
2 cups sliced mushrooms
2 cups chopped okra
1 cup frozen green peas

1 zucchini, cubed
2 tablespoons tomato paste
1 cup diced tomatoes
1 can (15 oz.) black beans, drained
1/2 teaspoon dried oregano
Salt and pepper to taste

Directions:

Combine all the ingredients in your crock pot.

Add salt and pepper to taste and cook on low settings for 7 hours.

The stew is best served warm, but you can also re-heat it or freeze it into individual portions for later.

Chickpea Curry

Time: 4 1/4 hours   Servings: 6

Ingredients:

2 tablespoons coconut oil
1 sweet onion, chopped
2 garlic cloves, chopped

1/2 teaspoon grated ginger
1/2 teaspoon cumin powder
1/4 teaspoon ground coriander

1/2 teaspoon turmeric powder
1/4 teaspoon curry powder
4 cups cooked chickpeas, drained
1 can diced tomatoes

1/2 cup vegetable stock
1/2 cup coconut milk
Salt and pepper to taste

Directions:

Heat the coconut oil in a skillet and add the onion and garlic. Cook for 2 minutes until softened then add the spices and cook for 30 seconds just to release flavor.

Transfer in your slow cooker and add the remaining ingredients.

Adjust the taste with salt and pepper and cook on low settings for 4 hours.

Serve the curry warm.

Layered Vegetable Stew

Time: 7 1/2 hours   Servings: 8

Ingredients:

2 tablespoons olive oil
2 large onions, sliced
1 zucchini, sliced
2 carrots, sliced
1 large eggplant, peeled and sliced
2 potatoes, peeled and sliced

4 ripe tomatoes, sliced
1 1/2 cups tomato sauce
1/4 teaspoon garlic powder
1/2 teaspoon dried oregano
1/2 teaspoon dried marjoram
Salt and pepper to taste

Directions:

Drizzle the oil at the bottom of your slow cooker.

Add the onions and layer the remaining vegetables in the exact order as they appear on the list above.

Mix the tomato sauce, garlic powder, oregano, marjoram, salt and pepper in a bowl. Season properly and pour over the vegetables. Cook on low settings for 7 hours.

Serve the stew warm and fresh or chilled.

Mexican Vegetable Casserole

Time: 6 1/4 hours   Servings: 6

Ingredients:

1 can (15 oz.) black beans, drained
1 can (10 oz.) sweet corn, drained
2 jalapeno peppers, chopped
1 can fire roasted tomatoes
Salt and pepper to taste

1/2 cup all-purpose flour
1/4 cup butter, chilled and cubed
1/4 teaspoon cumin powder
1/2 teaspoon baking powder
1/2 cup chilled buttermilk

Directions:

Combine the beans, corn, jalapeno peppers and tomatoes in your slow cooker. Add salt and pepper to taste.

In a bowl, mix the flour, cumin and butter and rub the mixture well until sandy.

Stir in the chilled buttermilk and mix quickly with a fork.

Drop spoonfuls of batter over the vegetables and cover the pot with its lid.

Cook on low settings for 6 hours.

Serve the casserole warm.

Cheesy Potato Casserole

Time: 6 1/2 hours   Servings: 6

Ingredients:

2 1/2 pounds potatoes, peeled and sliced
2 large onions, sliced
2 tomatoes, sliced
4 garlic cloves, minced
1 1/2 cups tomato sauce

1/2 teaspoon dried oregano
1/2 teaspoon dried thyme
1/2 cup vegetable stock
Salt and pepper to taste
1 1/2 cups grated Cheddar

Directions:

Layer the potatoes and onions in your crock pot. Finish the layering with tomatoes. Mix the garlic, tomato sauce, oregano, thyme and stock in a bowl. Add salt and pepper to taste then pour this mixture over the potatoes. Top with cheese and cook on low settings for 6 hours. Serve the casserole warm and fresh.

Barley and Bean Tacos

Time: 6 1/4 hours   Servings: 10

Ingredients:

1 red onion, chopped
1 cup frozen corn
1 can (15 oz.) black beans, drained
1 cup fire roasted tomatoes
1 cup pearl barley
2 cups vegetable stock

1/2 teaspoon cumin powder
1/2 teaspoon chili powder
Salt and pepper to taste
10-14 taco shells
1/2 cup chopped cilantro for serving
2 limes for serving

Directions:

Combine the onion, corn, black beans, tomatoes, pearl barley, stock, cumin powder and chili powder in your crock pot. Add salt and pepper to taste and cook on low settings for 6 hours. When done, spoon the mixture into taco shells and top with chopped cilantro. Drizzle with lime juice and serve fresh.

Wild Rice Stuffed Bell Peppers

Time: 6 1/2 hours   Servings: 6

Ingredients:

6 red bell peppers, cored
1/2 cup tomato sauce
1 can (15 oz.) black beans, drained
2 cups cooked wild rice
1 shallot, chopped

1 carrot, grated
Salt and pepper to taste
1 1/2 cups vegetable stock
1 thyme sprig

Directions:

Mix the tomato sauce, black beans, shallot, carrot, salt and pepper in a bowl. Stuff each bell pepper with this mixture and place them all in your slow cooker. Add the stock and thyme in the pot as well and cook on low settings for 6 hours. Serve the bell peppers warm and fresh.

RED LENTIL DAL

Time: 6 1/4 hours   Servings: 10

Ingredients:

2 cups red lentils, rinsed
4 cups water
1 can diced tomatoes
1 sweet onion, chopped
2 garlic cloves, chopped
1 teaspoon grated ginger
1 teaspoon turmeric powder
1/4 teaspoon ground cardamom

1 bay leaf
1/2 teaspoon cumin powder
1/2 teaspoon fenugreek seeds
1/2 teaspoon mustard seeds
1 teaspoon fennel seeds
Salt and pepper to taste
1 lemon, juiced for serving
Cooked rice for serving

Directions:

Combine the seeds in a skillet and cook for 1 minute just until their flavor is released. Place aside. Combine the rest of the ingredients in your slow cooker. Add the seeds as well and cook on low settings for 6 hours. To serve, spoon the dal over cooked rice and finish with a drizzle of lemon juice.

SPICY RED LENTIL CURRY

Time: 6 1/4 hours   Servings: 6

Ingredients:

1 shallot, chopped
3 garlic cloves, chopped
1 cup dried red lentils, rinsed
2 cups cauliflower florets
2 carrots, sliced
1 teaspoon grated ginger
1/2 teaspoon cumin powder

1 teaspoon curry powder
1 cup diced tomatoes
1 tablespoon tomato paste
2 cups vegetable stock
1 teaspoon brown sugar
Salt and pepper to taste
2 cups fresh spinach

Directions:

Combine the shallot, garlic, lentils, cauliflower, carrots, ginger, cumin, curry powder, tomatoes, tomato paste, stock and brown sugar in your slow cooker. Add salt and pepper to taste and top with spinach. Cook on low settings for 6 hours. Serve the curry warm and fresh.

FENNEL TOMATO PASTA SAUCE

Time: 8 1/4 hours   Servings: 10

Ingredients:

2 tablespoons olive oil
2 onions, chopped
4 garlic cloves, chopped
1 large fennel bulb, chopped
1 can (28 oz.) diced tomatoes
2 tablespoons tomato paste

1 cup tomato sauce
1 cup vegetable stock
1 bay leaf
1 thyme sprig
Salt and pepper to taste

Directions:

Heat the oil in a skillet and add the onions and garlic. Cook for 5 minutes until softened and caramelized slightly. Transfer in your slow cooker.

Add the remaining ingredients, as well as salt and pepper.

Cook on low settings for 8 hours.

The sauce can be served warm or can be frozen into individual portions and used when needed. You can also leave it chunkier or puree it into a fine sauce.

AFRICAN SWEET POTATO STEW

Time: 6 1/2 hours   Servings: 6

Ingredients:

1 onion, chopped
2 garlic cloves, chopped
1 1/2 pounds sweet potatoes, peeled and
  cubed
1 can diced tomatoes
1 cup vegetable stock

2 tablespoons peanut butter
1 teaspoon grated ginger
1 pinch chili powder
4 cups fresh spinach
Salt and pepper to taste
Chopped peanuts for serving

Directions:

Mix the onion, garlic, potatoes, tomatoes, stock and peanut butter in your crock pot.

Add the remaining ingredients and season with salt and pepper as needed.

Cook on low settings for 6 hours.

The stew is best served warm, topped with chopped peanuts.

CHIPOTLE BEAN AND QUINOA ONE POT STEW

Time: 8 1/4 hours   Servings: 10

Ingredients:

1 pound dried black beans, rinsed and soaked
  in water overnight
2/3 cup quinoa, rinsed
2 shallots, chopped
3 garlic cloves, chopped
2 red bell peppers, cored and diced
1/2 teaspoon cumin powder
1/2 teaspoon coriander powder

1/2 teaspoon mustard seeds
1 cinnamon stick
1 dried chipotle pepper
2 cups vegetable stock
5 cups water
1 cup diced tomatoes
Salt and pepper to taste

Directions:

Combine the beans, quinoa, shallots, garlic, bell peppers, cumin powder, coriander seeds, mustard seeds, cinnamon stick, chipotle pepper, stock, water and tomatoes in your slow cooker.

Add salt and pepper to taste and cook on low settings for 8 hours.

When done, remove and discard the cinnamon stick and chipotle pepper as they tend to go bitter the longer they stay in the stew.

The stew is best served warm.

Butternut Squash Chili

Time: 6 1/4 hours   Servings: 8

Ingredients:

1 shallot, chopped
1 celery stalk, sliced
2 carrots, diced
1 red apple, cored and diced
4 garlic cloves, chopped
1 can (15 oz.) black beans, drained
6 cups butternut squash cubes
1 teaspoon chili powder

1/2 teaspoon cumin powder
2 cups vegetable stock
1 cup coconut milk
2 tablespoons tomato paste
1 bay leaf
Salt and pepper to taste
Cooked rice and chopped cilantro for serving

Directions:

Combine the shallot, celery, carrots, red apple, garlic and black beans in your slow cooker. Add the remaining ingredients and season with salt and pepper. Cook the chili on low settings for 6 hours. Serve the chili over cooked rice and top with chopped cilantro. Serve right away.

Bulgur Chili

Time: 8 1/4 hours   Servings: 8

Ingredients:

1 cup bulgur wheat
1 large onion, chopped
2 cups sliced mushrooms
1 red bell pepper, cored and diced
2 garlic cloves, chopped
2 cups vegetable stock
1 cup diced tomatoes
1 can (15 oz.) black beans, drained

1 can (15 oz.) kidney beans, drained
1 tablespoon brown sugar
1 teaspoon apple cider vinegar
1 teaspoon chili powder
Salt and pepper to taste
1 bay leaf
1 thyme sprig

Directions:

Combine the bulgur and the remaining ingredients in your crock pot.
Add salt and pepper to taste and cook on low settings for 8 hours, mixing a few times during the cooking time to make sure it's cooked evenly.
Serve the chili warm.

Buffalo Cauliflower

Time: 6 1/4 hours   Servings: 6

Ingredients:

1 head cauliflower, cut into florets
1 onion, chopped
1 can diced tomatoes
1 can fire roasted green chilies, chopped

1 teaspoon hot sauce
1/2 cup tomato sauce
1 teaspoon cumin powder
1 can (15 oz.) cannellini beans, drained

Salt and pepper to taste   Grated Cheddar for serving

Directions:
Combine the cauliflower and the rest of the ingredients in your slow cooker.
Add salt and pepper to taste and cook on low settings for 6 hours.
Serve the dish warm.

Cauliflower Mashed Sweet Potato

Time: 6 1/4 hours   Servings: 6

Ingredients:
1 head cauliflower, cut into florets   2 garlic cloves, chopped
1 pound sweet potatoes, peeled and cubed   1 cup vegetable stock
1 shallot, chopped   Salt and pepper to taste

Directions:
Combine all the ingredients in your slow cooker.
Add salt and pepper to taste and cook on low settings for 6 hours.
When done, mash the mix with a potato masher and serve warm.

Roasted Slow Cooker Chili

Time: 8 hours   Servings: 8

Ingredients:
1 pound heirloom tomatoes, halved   1 teaspoon chili powder
2 red onions, sliced   1/2 teaspoon cumin powder
2 red bell peppers, cored and sliced   1/2 teaspoon ground coriander
2 tablespoons olive oil   1 cup vegetable stock
1 teaspoon dried thyme   Salt and pepper to taste
2 cans (15 oz. each) black beans, drained

Directions:
Mix the tomatoes, red onions, bell peppers, olive oil and thyme in a baking tray.
Add salt and pepper to taste.
Cook in the preheated oven at 400F for 30 minutes then transfer the veggies in your crock pot.
Add the remaining ingredients and adjust the taste with salt and pepper.
Cook on low settings for 7 hours.
Serve the chili warm and fresh.

Curried Potato Stew

Time: 4 1/2 hours   Servings: 6

Ingredients:
2 pounds potatoes, peeled and cubed   2 garlic cloves, chopped
1 shallot, chopped   2 red bell peppers, cored and diced

1/2 celery stalk, diced
1 tablespoon red curry paste
1 tablespoon tomato paste
1 cup diced tomatoes
1 cup vegetable stock

1 bay leaf
1/2 lemongrass stalk, crushed
Salt and pepper to taste
Chopped cilantro for serving

Directions:

Combine the potatoes, shallot, garlic, bell peppers, celery, curry paste, tomato paste, stock, lemongrass stalk and bay leaf in your slow cooker.

Add salt and pepper to taste and cook on low settings for 4 hours.

Serve the stew warm, topped with chopped cilantro.

Indian Spiced Lentils

Time: 6 1/4 hours   Servings: 6

Ingredients:

2 garlic cloves, chopped
1 sweet onion, chopped
2 tablespoons olive oil
1 cup red lentils, rinsed
1 sweet potato, peeled and cubed
1/2 teaspoon cumin powder
1/4 teaspoon chili powder

1/2 teaspoon turmeric powder
1/2 teaspoon garam masala
1 cup tomato sauce
2 cups vegetable stock
1/2 teaspoon grated ginger
Salt and pepper to taste

Directions:

Combine the lentils and the remaining ingredients in your slow cooker.

Add salt and pepper to taste and cook on low settings for 6 hours.

Serve the lentils warm.

BBQ Lentils

Time: 2 1/4 hours   Servings: 6

Ingredients:

2 shallots, chopped
1 carrot, diced
1 red bell pepper, cored and diced
3 garlic cloves, chopped
1 tablespoon apple cider vinegar
1/2 teaspoon mustard seeds

1/2 teaspoon cumin seeds
1 cup red lentils
1/4 cup brown lentils
1 cup BBQ sauce
1 1/2 cups vegetable stock
Salt and pepper to taste

Directions:

Combine the shallots, carrot, bell pepper, garlic, vinegar, mustard seeds and cumin seeds in your slow cooker.

Add the remaining ingredients and season with salt and pepper to taste.

Cook on high settings for 2 hours.

Serve the lentils warm.

Bourbon Baked Beans

Time: 10 1/4 hours   Servings: 8

Ingredients:

1 pound dried black beans, rinsed
1 cup bourbon
1/4 cup maple syrup
1 cup BBQ sauce
2 cups vegetable stock
1/2 cup ketchup

1 teaspoon mustard seeds
1 tablespoon molasses
1 tablespoon apple cider vinegar
1 teaspoon Worcestershire sauce
Salt and pepper to taste

Directions:

Combine the black beans, bourbon, maple syrup, BBQ sauce, stock, ketchup, seeds, molasses, Worcestershire sauce and vinegar in your crock pot.
Add salt and pepper to taste and cook on low settings for 10 hours.
Serve the beans warm or chilled.

Creamy Butternut Squash Coconut Chili

Time: 6 1/2 hours   Servings: 6

Ingredients:

2 tablespoons olive oil
2 shallots, sliced
2 garlic cloves, chopped
1 celery stalk, sliced
1 carrot, sliced
2 ripe tomatoes, peeled and cubed
4 cups butternut squash cubes

1 cup tomato sauce
1 cup coconut milk
1/4 teaspoon fennel seeds
1/2 teaspoon cumin seeds
1 thyme sprig
Salt and pepper to taste

Directions:

Heat the oil in a skillet and add the shallots and garlic. Cook for 2 minutes until softened then transfer in your slow cooker. Add the remaining ingredients and season with salt and pepper.
Cook on low settings for 6 hours.

Spinach Lentil Stew

Time: 6 1/4 hours   Servings: 6

Ingredients:

1 shallot, chopped
4 garlic cloves, chopped
2 tablespoon tomato paste
1/2 teaspoon cumin powder
1/2 teaspoon coriander seeds
1/2 teaspoon turmeric powder
1/4 teaspoon chili powder

1/4 teaspoon garam masala
1 cup red lentils, rinsed
1 cup diced tomatoes
1 1/2 cups vegetable stock
1/2 cup coconut cream
1 thyme sprig
Salt and pepper to taste

Directions:

Combine the shallot, garlic, tomato paste, spices, lentils, tomatoes, stock, coconut cream and thyme in your slow cooker. Add salt and pepper to taste and cook on low settings for 6 hours.

The stew is best served warm.

Mashed Sweet Potato with Lentils

Time: 6 1/4 hours   Servings: 6

Ingredients:

1 pound sweet potatoes, peeled and cubed
2/3 cup red lentils, rinsed
1 shallot, chopped
1 garlic clove, chopped

2 cups vegetable stock
Salt and pepper to taste
1/4 teaspoon cumin seeds
1 pinch chili powder

Directions:

Combine the sweet potatoes, lentils, shallot, garlic, stock, cumin seeds, chili powder, salt and pepper in your slow cooker.

Cook on low settings for 6 hours.

When done, puree the mixture with a potato masher.

Serve warm.

Quinoa Black Bean Chili

Time: 6 1/4 hours   Servings: 6

Ingredients:

1/2 cup quinoa, rinsed
1 can (15 oz.) black beans, drained
1 can fire roasted tomatoes
1 sweet onion, chopped
2 garlic cloves, chopped

1 1/2 cups vegetable stock
1/4 teaspoon chili powder
1/4 teaspoon cumin powder
Salt and pepper to taste

Directions:

Combine the quinoa, black beans, tomatoes, onion, garlic and stock, as well as chili powder and cumin powder.

Season with salt and pepper and cook on low settings for 6 hours.

Serve the chili warm.

Spinach Potato Stew

Time: 4 1/4 hours   Servings: 6

Ingredients:

2 pounds potatoes, peeled and cubed
2 tablespoons olive oil
1 shallot, chopped
2 garlic cloves, chopped
1/4 teaspoon cumin powder

1/4 teaspoon coriander powder
1/4 teaspoon fennel seeds
4 cups spinach
1 cup vegetable stock
Salt and pepper to taste

Directions:

Heat the oil in a skillet and add the shallot and garlic. Cook for 2 minutes until softened then add the spices and sauté just for 30 seconds to release flavors.

Transfer in your slow cooker and add the remaining ingredients.

Season with salt and pepper and cook on low settings for 4 hours.

Serve the stew warm.

PUTTANESCA PIZZA

Time: 2 1/2 hours   Servings: 6

Ingredients:

Dough:

2 cups all-purpose flour
1 teaspoon active dry yeast
1 cup warm water
1/4 teaspoon salt
2 tablespoons olive oil

Topping:

1/2 cup crushed fire roasted tomatoes
1/4 cup Kalamata olives, pitted and sliced
1/4 cup green olives, sliced
1 tablespoon capers, chopped
1/2 teaspoon dried basil
1/2 teaspoon dried oregano

Directions:

To make the dough, combine all the ingredients in a bowl and knead for a few minutes in a bowl.

Roll the dough into a round that fits in your slow cooker.

Top with tomatoes, olives, capers and dried herbs.

Cook on high settings for 1 1/2 hours.

Serve the pizza warm.

VEGETABLE POT PIE

Time: 6 1/2 hours   Servings: 6

Ingredients:

1 celery stalk, diced
1 carrot, diced
1 red bell pepper, cored and diced
1 onion, chopped
1/2 teaspoon dried oregano
1 tablespoon all-purpose flour

1 cup green peas
1 cup chopped green beans
1 cup vegetable stock
Salt and pepper to taste
6 oz. biscuit dough

Directions:

Combine the celery, carrot, bell pepper, onion, oregano and flour in a bowl and mix well.

Transfer the mix in your slow cooker and add the green peas, beans and stock, as well as salt and pepper.

Top with biscuit dough and cook on low settings for 6 hours.

Serve the pot pie warm.

Tofu Eggplant Stew

Time: 6 1/2 hours   Servings: 6

Ingredients:

2 tablespoons olive oil
6 oz. firm tofu, cubed
1 sweet onion, chopped
3 garlic cloves, chopped
1 large eggplant, peeled and cubed
2 red bell peppers, cored and diced

1 cup fire roasted tomatoes
1 tablespoon tomato paste
1 1/4 cups vegetable stock
1 thyme sprig
Salt and pepper to taste

Directions:

Heat the oil in a skillet and add the tofu. Cook on all sides until golden brown then transfer in your slow cooker.
Add the remaining ingredients and season with salt and pepper. Cook on low settings for 6 hours.
Serve the stew warm and fresh.

Teriyaki Tofu

Time: 2 1/4 hours   Servings: 6

Ingredients:

1 1/2 pounds firm tofu, cubed
1 cup pineapple juice
1/2 cup vegetable stock
1 tablespoon tamarind paste
1 tablespoon mirin
2 tablespoons brown sugar

1 teaspoon sesame oil
1 teaspoon grated ginger
1/2 teaspoon garlic powder
2 tablespoons soy sauce
Cooked rice for serving

Directions:

Combine all the ingredients in your slow cooker.
Cook on high settings for 2 hours.
Serve the tofu over cooked white rice.

Mushroom Barley Risotto

Time: 4 1/4 hours   Servings: 6

Ingredients:

2 tablespoons olive oil
2 cups sliced mushrooms
1 shallot, chopped
1 garlic clove, chopped
3/4 cup risotto rice

1/4 cup white wine
1 1/2 cups vegetable stock
1 bay leaf
Salt and pepper to taste

Directions:

Combine all the ingredients in your slow cooker. Add salt and pepper to taste and cook on low settings for 4 hours.
Serve the risotto warm.

WILD MUSHROOM BARLEY RISOTTO

Time: 6 1/4 hours

Servings: 6

Ingredients:

2 tablespoons olive oil
1 shallot, chopped
1 celery stalk, diced
1 garlic clove, minced
1 carrot, diced

1 cup pearl barley
2 cups vegetable stock
1/4 cup grated Parmesan
Salt and pepper to taste
1 thyme sprig

Directions:

Heat the oil in a skillet and add the shallot, celery, garlic and carrot. Cook for 2 minutes until softened. Transfer in your slow cooker.

Add the remaining ingredients, except the Parmesan, and season with salt and pepper.

Cook on low settings for 6 hours.

When done, add the cheese and mix well.

Serve the risotto warm.

CREAMED SWEET CORN

Time: 3 1/4 hours

Servings: 6

Ingredients:

2 cans (15 oz.) sweet corn, drained
1 cup cream cheese
1 cup grated Cheddar cheese

1/2 cup heavy cream
Salt and pepper to taste
1 pinch nutmeg

Directions:

Combine the corn, cream cheese, Cheddar and cream in your slow cooker.

Add the nutmeg, salt and pepper and cook on low settings for 3 hours.

Serve the creamed corn warm.

SPRING VEGETABLE FARRO

Time: 5 1/4 hours

Servings: 6

Ingredients:

2 tablespoons olive oil
1 small onion, chopped
1 celery stalk, sliced
1 cup farro
2 cups vegetable stock

1 bunch asparagus, trimmed and chopped
1 cup green peas
Salt and pepper to taste
1/2 lemon, juiced

Directions:

Combine the olive oil, onion, celery, farro, stock, asparagus and green peas in your slow cooker.

Add salt and pepper to taste and cook on low settings for 5 hours.

When done, stir in the lemon juice and serve the dish fresh.

WHOLE ROASTED CAULIFLOWER

Time: 6 1/4 hours   Servings: 4

Ingredients:

1 head cauliflower
1 cup tomato sauce
1/4 teaspoon garlic powder
1/4 teaspoon onion powder

1/2 teaspoon dried thyme
1/4 teaspoon salt
1 pinch cayenne pepper
1/2 cup vegetable stock

Directions:

Place the cauliflower in your slow cooker. Combine the remaining ingredients in a bowl and pour this mixture over the cauliflower. Cover with a lid and cook on low settings for 6 hours. Serve the cauliflower warm and fresh.

FAVA BEAN STEW

Time: 7 1/4 hours   Servings: 8

Ingredients:

1 pound frozen fava beans
2 leeks, sliced
1 shallot, chopped
1 garlic clove, chopped
1 celery stalk, sliced
1 carrot, sliced

1 can diced tomatoes
1 bay leaf
1 cup vegetable stock
1 thyme sprig
1/4 teaspoon cumin seeds
Salt and pepper to taste

Directions:

Combine all the ingredients in your slow cooker, adding salt and pepper to taste.
Cook on low settings for 7 hours.
The stew is best served warm and fresh.

GARLICKY LENTIL STEW

Time: 4 1/4 hours   Servings: 6

Ingredients:

1 cup red lentils
6 garlic cloves, chopped
1 onion, chopped
1/2 teaspoon grated ginger
1/2 teaspoon garam masala
1 teaspoon brown sugar
2 tablespoons tomato paste

1 cup vegetable stock
1 cup diced tomatoes
1 cup coconut milk
1 bay leaf
1 thyme sprig
Salt and pepper to taste

Directions:

Combine the lentils, garlic, onion, garam masala and the remaining ingredients in your slow cooker.
Add salt and pepper to taste and cook on low settings for 4 hours.
The stew is best served warm and fresh.

ORZO ENCHILADA SAUCE

Time: 8 1/4 hours   Servings: 8

Ingredients:

2 tablespoons olive oil
1 large onion, chopped
2 carrots, diced
1 celery stalk, diced
1 cup orzo
1 cup diced tomatoes

2 cups vegetable stock
2 tablespoons tomato paste
1 can (15 oz.) black beans, drained
Salt and pepper to taste
2 tablespoons chopped cilantro for serving
Flour tortillas for serving

Directions:

Heat the oil in a skillet and add the onion, carrots and celery. Cook for 2 minutes until softened then transfer in your slow cooker.

Add the remaining ingredients and season with salt and pepper.

Cook on low settings for 8 hours.

When done, serve the sauce warm in tortillas, topped with chopped cilantro.

ORIENTAL CHICKPEA STEW

Time: 8 1/2 hours   Servings: 8

Ingredients:

2 tablespoons olive oil
2 large onions, chopped
4 garlic cloves, chopped
1 celery stalk, sliced
1 carrot, diced
1/4 teaspoon cumin seeds
1/2 teaspoon fennel seeds
1/2 teaspoon ground ginger

1 pinch cinnamon powder
2 cups dried chickpeas, rinsed
1 head cauliflower, cut into florets
1 can diced tomatoes
3 cups vegetable stock
1 bay leaf
1 thyme sprig
Salt and pepper to taste

Directions:

Heat the oil in a skillet and add the onions, garlic, celery and carrot. Cook for 5 minutes until softened then transfer in your slow cooker.

Add the remaining ingredients and season with enough salt and pepper.

Cook on low settings for 8 hours.

Serve the stew warm and fresh.

CURRIED TOFU LENTILS

Time: 6 1/4 hours   Servings: 6

Ingredients:

8 oz. firm tofu, cubed
2 tablespoons canola oil
2 tablespoons red curry paste

1 cup red lentils
2 cups vegetable stock
2 cups cauliflower florets

2 tablespoons tomato paste
1 bay leaf
1/2 lemongrass stalk, crushed

1/2 teaspoon grated ginger
Salt and pepper to taste

Directions:

Heat the oil in a skillet and add the tofu. Cook on all sides until golden brown and crusty then transfer in your slow cooker.

Add the remaining ingredients and season with salt and pepper.

Cook on low settings for 6 hours.

Serve the dish warm and fresh.

QUINOA TOFU VEGGIE STEW

Time: 6 1/4 hours

Servings: 6

Ingredients:

6 oz. firm tofu, cubed
1/2 cup quinoa, rinsed
1 celery stalk, sliced
1 parsnip, diced
1 carrot, diced
1/2 cup green peas

1 cup cauliflower florets
1 cup broccoli florets
1 tablespoon Pesto sauce
2 tablespoons green lentils
1 cup vegetable stock
Salt and pepper to taste

Directions:

Combine all the ingredients in your crock pot.

Add salt and pepper to taste and cook on low settings for 6 hours.

Serve the stew warm and fresh.

ZUCCHINI ROLLS IN TOMATO SAUCE

Time: 7 hours

Servings: 8

Ingredients:

2 large zucchinis
2 carrots, cut into match sticks
2 parsnips, cut into matchsticks
1 large eggplant, cut into sticks
1 cup tomato sauce

1 cup vegetable stock
1 bay leaf
1 teaspoon dried thyme
1/2 teaspoon dried oregano
Salt and pepper to taste

Directions:

Using a vegetable peeler, cut thin ribbons of zucchini and lay them flat on your chopping board.

Place a few sticks of parsnip, carrot and eggplant at one end of each zucchini ribbon then tightly roll.

Arrange the rolls in your slow cooker and add the remaining ingredients.

Season with salt and pepper and cook on low settings for 6 hours.

Serve warm.

Summer Lasagna

Time: 6 1/2 hours

Servings: 8

Ingredients:

1 large zucchini
1 large eggplant
1 can diced tomatoes
1 cup white rice
1 celery stalk, diced

1/2 teaspoon dried oregano
2 tablespoons chopped parsley
2 cups vegetable stock
Salt and pepper to taste
1 1/2 cups shredded mozzarella

Directions:

Cut the zucchini and eggplant into thin ribbons using a vegetable peeler. Mix the tomatoes, white rice, celery, oregano, parsley, salt and pepper. Layer the zucchini, eggplant and rice mixture in your slow cooker. Add the stock and top with cheese. Cook on low settings for 6 hours. Serve the lasagna warm.

Tofu Broccoli Rice

Time: 4 1/4 hours

Servings: 8

Ingredients:

2 tablespoons olive oil
1 large head broccoli, cut into small florets
8 oz. firm tofu, cubed
1 cup white rice
1/4 cup white wine
2 cups vegetable stock

1 tablespoon lemon juice
1/4 teaspoon garlic powder
1/4 teaspoon onion powder
1/2 teaspoon dried oregano
Salt and pepper to taste

Directions:

Heat the oil in a skillet and add the firm tofu. Cook on all sides until golden. Transfer in your slow cooker and add the remaining ingredients. Season with salt and pepper and cook on low settings for 6 hours.
Serve the dish warm and fresh.

Oat Sweet Potato Chili

Time: 6 1/4 hours

Servings: 6

Ingredients:

2 large sweet potatoes, peeled and cubed
1 tablespoon olive oil
1 can pinto beans, drained
1 shallot, chopped
2 garlic cloves, chopped

1/4 teaspoon chipotle powder
1/2 teaspoon dried oregano
1/4 cup oat groats
2 cups vegetable stock
Salt and pepper to taste

Directions:

Combine the sweet potatoes and the remaining ingredients in your crock pot.
Add salt and pepper to taste and cook on low settings for 6 hours.
Serve the chili warm and fresh.

Tofu Korma

Time: 8 1/4 hours   Servings: 6

Ingredients:

8 oz. firm tofu, cubed
2 tablespoons olive oil
2 red bell peppers, cored and diced
1 carrot, diced
1/2 celery stalk, diced
2 cups cauliflower florets
1 cup diced tomatoes

1/2 teaspoon grated ginger
1/2 teaspoon turmeric powder
1/4 teaspoon chili powder
1/2 teaspoon curry powder
1 cup vegetable stock
1/2 cup coconut milk
Salt and pepper to taste

Directions:

Heat the oil in a skillet and add the tofu. Cook on all sides until golden brown then transfer in your slow cooker. Add the remaining ingredients in your crock pot and season with salt and pepper. Cook on low settings for 8 hours. Serve the korma warm and fresh.

Vegetarian Bolognese Sauce

Time: 8 1/4 hours   Servings: 10

Ingredients:

12 oz. firm tofu, crumbled
2 tablespoons olive oil
2 large onions, chopped
6 garlic cloves, minced
2 celery stalks, diced
2 carrots, grated
1 parsnip, grated
1 teaspoon dried basil

1 teaspoon dried oregano
2 tablespoons tomato paste
1 can (15 oz.) diced tomatoes
1 cup vegetable stock
Salt and pepper to taste
1 bay leaf
2 tablespoons lemon juice

Directions:

Heat the oil in a skillet and add the tofu. Cook for a few minutes until golden then transfer in your slow cooker. Add the remaining ingredients and adjust the taste with salt and pepper. Cook on low settings for 8 hours. Serve the Bolognese sauce fresh or freeze it in individual portions in airtight containers.

Black Eyed Peas Stew

Time: 8 1/4 hours   Servings: 8

Ingredients:

2 cups dried black eyed peas, rinsed
2 carrots, diced
2 red bell peppers, cored and diced
1/2 teaspoon grated ginger
2 cups water
2 cups vegetable stock

2 garlic cloves, minced
2 tablespoons tomato paste
1 cup diced tomato
2 cups baby spinach
Salt and pepper to taste

Directions:

Combine the peas, carrots, bell peppers, ginger, water, stock, garlic, tomato paste, diced tomatoes and spinach in your crock pot. Add salt and pepper to taste and cook on low settings for 8 hours. Serve the stew warm and fresh.

Mango Tofu Curry

Time: 3 1/4 hours   Servings: 6

Ingredients:

8 oz. firm tofu, cubed
2 tablespoons olive oil
2 shallots, chopped
2 garlic cloves, minced
1/4 teaspoon cayenne pepper
1/4 teaspoon garam masala
1/4 teaspoon ground ginger

1/4 teaspoon cumin powder
1 bay leaf
1 cup coconut milk
1 ripe mango, peeled and cubed
2 tablespoons tomato paste
1 cup vegetable stock
Salt and pepper to taste

Directions:

Heat the oil in a skillet and add the tofu. Cook on all sides until golden brown then transfer in your slow cooker. Add the remaining ingredients and adjust the taste with salt and pepper. Cook on high settings for 3 hours. Serve the curry warm and fresh.

Eggplant Tapenade

Time: 4 1/4 hours   Servings: 6

Ingredients:

1 large eggplant, peeled and diced
1 tablespoon olive oil
1 cup green olives, pitted and sliced
1/2 cup black olives, pitted and sliced
1 can fire roasted tomatoes

2 artichoke hearts, diced
1 cup vegetable stock
Salt and pepper to taste
1/4 teaspoon dried basil
1/4 teaspoon dried oregano

Directions:

Combine the eggplant, olive oil, olives, tomatoes, stock and herbs in your slow cooker.
Add salt and pepper to taste and cook on low settings for 2 hours then on high for 2 additional hours.
Serve the tapenade warm or chilled.

Asian Eggplant Stew

Time: 2 1/4 hours   Servings: 4

Ingredients:

1 large eggplant, peeled and cubed
3 tablespoons coconut oil
1/4 cup hoisin sauce
1 tablespoon soy sauce
1/2 cup coconut milk

1 teaspoon rice vinegar
1/2 teaspoon grated ginger
1 pinch cayenne pepper

Directions:

Heat the oil in a skillet and add the eggplant. Cook on all sides until golden then transfer in your slow cooker.
Add the remaining ingredients and cook on high settings for 4 hours.
Serve the stew chilled.

CITRUS BLACK BEAN STEW

Time: 6 3/4 hours   Servings: 6

Ingredients:

1 cup dried black beans, rinsed
2 cups vegetable stock
1 orange, zested and juiced
1 tablespoon lemon juice
1 teaspoon lemon zest
2 large onions, chopped
2 garlic cloves, minced

1 red bell pepper, cored and diced
1 red chili, chopped
1 teaspoon cumin seeds
1 teaspoon dried oregano
1 teaspoon dried thyme
Salt and pepper to taste

Directions:

Combine the beans, stock, orange zest and juice, lemon juice, lemon zest, onions, garlic, bell pepper, red chili, and spices in your crock pot.
Add salt and pepper as needed and cook on low settings for 6 1/2 hours
Serve the stew warm or chilled.

SPICY CHICKPEA STEW

Time: 8 1/4 hours   Servings: 6

Ingredients:

1 1/2 cups dried chickpeas, rinsed
2 shallots, chopped
1 celery stalk, diced
1 can fire roasted tomatoes
1 teaspoon dried oregano

2 cups vegetable stock
1 bay leaf
1/2 teaspoon garlic powder
1/4 teaspoon chili powder
Salt and pepper to taste

Directions:

Combine the chickpeas, shallots, celery, tomatoes, oregano, stock and spices in your crock pot.
Add salt and pepper as needed and cook on low settings for 7 hours.
Serve the chickpea chili warm and fresh or store it in individual containers in the freezer.

MEDITERRANEAN CHICKPEAS

Time: 2 1/4 hours   Servings: 6

Ingredients:

2 cans chickpeas, drained
2 shallots, chopped
1 red bell pepper, cored and diced

1/2 celery stalk, diced
3 garlic cloves, minced
1 cup diced tomatoes

1 cup tomato sauce
1 bay leaf
1 tablespoon lemon juice

Salt and pepper to taste
1 tablespoon chopped parsley

Directions:

Combine the chickpeas, shallots, bell pepper, celery, tomatoes, tomato sauce, bay leaf, lemon juice, salt and pepper in your crock pot.
Cook on high settings for 2 hours, until thickened and rich.
Serve the chickpeas warm.

COLLARD GREENS STEW

Time: 6 1/4 hours

Servings: 6

Ingredients:

1 tablespoon olive oil
2 garlic cloves, chopped
1 cup dried black beans, rinsed
1/2 cup tomato sauce

2 cups vegetable stock
1 bunch collard greens, shredded
Salt and pepper to taste
1 tablespoon chopped cilantro for serving

Directions:

Combine all the ingredients in your crock pot, adding salt and pepper as needed.
Cook on low settings for 6 hours.
Serve the stew warm and fresh or chilled.

RED WINE VEGETABLE STEW

Time: 6 1/2 hours

Servings: 8

Ingredients:

2 tablespoons olive oil
1 large onion, chopped
2 garlic cloves, minced
2 large carrots, sliced
2 parsnips, diced
2 sweet potatoes, peeled and cubed
2 red potatoes, peeled and cubed

1 cup diced tomatoes
4 Portobello mushrooms, sliced
1/2 cup red wine
1 1/2 cups vegetable stock
1 bay leaf
1 thyme sprig
Salt and pepper to taste

Directions:

Heat the oil in a skillet and add the onion and garlic. Cook for 2 minutes until softened then transfer in your slow cooker.
Add the remaining ingredients and season with salt and pepper.
Cook on low settings for 6 hours.
Serve the stew warm and fresh.

JAMAICAN RED BEAN STEW

Time: 8 1/4 hours   Servings: 6

Ingredients:

1 cup dried red beans, rinsed
1 large red onion, chopped
3 garlic cloves, minced
2 large sweet potatoes, peeled and cubed
1/2 teaspoon cumin powder
1/4 teaspoon cayenne pepper
1/2 teaspoon dried thyme

1 teaspoon jerk seasoning
2 tablespoons tomato paste
1 cup diced tomatoes
2 cups vegetable stock
Salt and pepper to taste
2 tablespoons chopped cilantro

Directions:

Combine the beans, onion, garlic and potatoes in your slow cooker.
Add the spices, tomato paste, tomatoes, stock, salt and pepper and cook on low settings for 8 hours.
When done, add the cilantro and serve the stew warm and fresh.

NOODLE STROGANOFF

Time: 6 1/2 hours   Servings: 6

Ingredients:

2 large Portobello mushrooms, sliced
1 oz. dried wild mushrooms, chopped
1 teaspoon Worcestershire sauce
1 large onion, chopped
1 can condensed cream of mushroom soup

1 cup tofu cream
1 1/2 cup vegetable stock
1/2 cup short pasta of your choice
Salt and pepper to taste

Directions:

Combine the mushrooms, Worcestershire sauce, onion, mushroom soup, tofu cream, stock and short pasta in your crock pot. Season with salt and pepper and cook on low settings for 6 hours. Serve the stroganoff warm or chilled.

PUMPKIN APPLE STEW

Time: 6 1/2 hours   Servings: 6

Ingredients:

4 cups pumpkin cubes
2 red apples, peeled and cubed
1/2 cinnamon stick
2 tablespoons olive oil
2 shallots, chopped
2 garlic cloves, chopped

2 ripe tomatoes, peeled and diced
1/4 cup red wine
1 cup vegetable stock
Salt and pepper to taste
1 bay leaf
1 thyme sprig

Directions:

Combine the pumpkin cubes, apples, cinnamon stick, olive oil, shallots, garlic and the remaining ingredients.
Season with salt and pepper to taste and cook on low settings for 6 hours.
Serve the stew warm and fresh or chilled.

Indian Chickpea Curry

Time: 8 1/4 hours   Servings: 8

Ingredients:

1 1/2 cups dried chickpeas
2 cups butternut squash cubes
1/2 teaspoon chili powder
1 teaspoon curry powder
1/2 teaspoon garam masala
2 tablespoons tomato paste
1/2 cup tomato sauce
1/2 teaspoon cumin powder
1/2 teaspoon dried oregano

2 cups vegetable stock
1 cup coconut milk
1 stalk lemongrass, crushed
1 bay leaf
2 kaffir lime leaves
Salt and pepper to taste
1 lime, juiced
2 tablespoons chopped cilantro

Directions:

Combine all the ingredients in a crock pot. Add salt and pepper to taste and cook on low settings for 8 hours. Serve the curry warm, topped with chopped cilantro and lime juice.

Spiced Lentil Stew

Time: 3 1/4 hours   Servings: 6

Ingredients:

2 tablespoons olive oil
1 large onion, chopped
2 garlic cloves, chopped
1/2 teaspoon cumin powder
1/4 teaspoon chili powder
1/2 teaspoon grated ginger
1/2 teaspoon coriander seeds

1/2 teaspoon turmeric powder
1 cup red lentils
2 cups vegetable stock
1/2 cup tomato sauce
Salt and pepper to taste
Chopped cilantro for serving

Directions:

Heat the oil in a skillet and stir in the onion and garlic. Cook for 2 minutes until softened then add the spices and sauté for 30 seconds just until the flavors are released. Transfer the mixture in your slow cooker and add the remaining ingredients. Season with salt and pepper and cook on high settings for 3 hours. Serve the stew warm and fresh, topped with chopped cilantro.

Thai Style Butternut Squash Tofu Stew

Time: 6 1/2 hours   Servings: 6

Ingredients:

8 oz. firm tofu, cubed
2 tablespoons olive oil
2 carrots, sliced
2 cups butternut squash cubes
1 pinch chili powder

1/2 teaspoon grated ginger
1 lemongrass stalk, crushed
1/4 teaspoon cumin seeds
1/2 teaspoon turmeric powder
Salt and pepper to taste

Directions:

Heat the oil in a skillet and add the tofu. Cook on all sides until golden brown. Transfer in your slow cooker and add the remaining ingredients. Cook the stew on low settings for 6 hours. The stew is best served warm.

Creamy Lentil Stew

Time: 7 1/4 hours   Servings: 8

Ingredients:

1 cup red lentils
1 large sweet potato, peeled and diced
1 carrot, diced
2 ripe tomatoes, peeled and diced
2 cups vegetable stock

1/2 teaspoon cumin seeds
1/2 red chili, chopped
Salt and pepper to taste
1 bay leaf

Directions:

Combine all the ingredients in your crock pot.
Add salt and pepper to taste and cook on low settings for 7 hours.
Serve the stew warm and fresh.

Green Pea Tomato Stew

Time: 2 1/4 hours   Servings: 6

Ingredients:

2 shallots, chopped
2 garlic cloves, chopped
2 tablespoons olive oil
1 celery stalk, sliced
1 red bell pepper, cored and diced

1 carrot, diced
1 pound frozen green peas
1 cup diced tomatoes
1 bay leaf
Salt and pepper to taste

Directions:

Heat the oil in a skillet and stir in the shallots and garlic. Cook for 2 minutes until softened then transfer in your slow cooker. Add the remaining ingredients and season with salt and pepper. Cook on high for 2 hours. Serve the stew warm or chilled.

Slow Cooker Steamed Rice

Time: 4 hours   Servings: 8

Ingredients:

2 cups white rice
4 cups water

1 bay leaf
Salt and pepper to taste

Directions:

Combine all the ingredients in your crock pot.
Add salt and pepper as needed and cook on low settings for 4 hours. If possible, stir once during the cooking process.
Serve the rice warm or chilled, as a side dish to your favorite veggie main dish.

SPINACH CASSEROLE

Time: 6 1/4 hours   Servings: 6

Ingredients:

16 oz. frozen spinach   4 eggs
1 cup green peas   1/4 cup all-purpose flour
2 cups cottage cheese   1/2 teaspoon baking powder
2 tablespoons butter   Salt and pepper to taste

Directions:

Combine all the ingredients in a bowl and season with salt and pepper. Mix well.
Pour the mixture in your crock pot and cook on low settings for 6 hours.
Serve the casserole warm.

QUINOA BUTTERNUT SQUASH CASSEROLE

Time: 6 1/2 hours   Servings: 6

Ingredients:

1 1/2 cups cooked quinoa   2 cups bread cubes
2 cups butternut squash cubes   1 can (15 oz.) black beans, drained
1 shallot, chopped   4 eggs, beaten
2 garlic cloves, chopped   Salt and pepper to taste

Directions:

Combine all the ingredients in your slow cooker, adding salt and pepper to taste.
Cook on low settings for 6 hours.
Serve the casserole warm.

MUNG BEAN STEW

Time: 6 1/4 hours   Servings: 6

Ingredients:

1 cup mung beans, rinsed   1/2 teaspoon dried oregano
1/2 cup brown rice   1/2 teaspoon dried basil
3 cups vegetable stock   1/4 teaspoon cumin seeds
1 celery stalk, sliced   1/4 teaspoon smoked paprika
1 carrot, diced   Salt and pepper to taste
2 ripe tomatoes, peeled and diced

Directions:

Combine the beans, brown rice, stock, celery, carrot, tomatoes, oregano and basil in your crock pot.
Add salt and pepper to taste and cook on low settings for 6 hours.
The stew is best served warm.

VEGETABLE SHEPHERD'S PIE

Time: 7 1/2 hours   Servings: 6

Ingredients:
1 cup frozen green peas
1 cup frozen corn
2 large carrots, diced
2 cups sliced mushrooms
1 tablespoon cornstarch

Salt and pepper to taste
1 1/2 cups vegetable stock
1/2 teaspoon dried oregano
1 1/2 pounds potatoes, peeled and cubed

Directions:
Begin by cooking the potatoes. Once cooked, mash them with a potato masher, adding part of the cooking liquid to obtain a smooth puree.

Combine the vegetables with cornstarch, salt and pepper in a bowl.

Transfer in your slow cooker and add the stock.

Top with the mashed potatoes and cook on low settings for 7 hours.

Serve the pie warm or chilled. It can also be re-heated.

HERBED BARLEY CASSEROLE

Time: 6 1/2 hours   Servings: 6

Ingredients:
2 tablespoons olive oil
1 small onion, chopped
2 garlic cloves, chopped
3 cups cooked barley
1/2 teaspoon dried oregano
1/2 teaspoon dried sage

1/2 cup tomato sauce
2 cups sliced mushrooms
1/2 cup sweet corn
2 tablespoons pine nuts
Salt and pepper to taste

Directions:
Heat the oil in a skillet and add the onion and garlic. Cook for 2 minutes until softened then transfer in your slow cooker. Add the remaining ingredients and season with salt and pepper.

Cook on low settings for 6 hours.

Serve the casserole warm and fresh.

CHICKPEA TIKKA MASALA

Time: 6 1/2 hours   Servings: 6

Ingredients:
2 tablespoons olive oil
1 large onion, chopped
4 garlic cloves, chopped
1 teaspoon grated ginger
1 teaspoon garam masala
1/2 teaspoon turmeric powder

1/2 teaspoon red chili, sliced
2 cans (15 oz. each) chickpeas, drained
1 can diced tomatoes
1 cup coconut milk
Salt and pepper to taste
Chopped cilantro for serving

Directions:

Heat the oil in a skillet and stir in the onion and garlic. Cook for 2 minutes until softened and translucent then transfer in your crock pot.

Add the remaining ingredients and season well with salt and pepper.

Cover and cook on low settings for 6 hours.

The chickpea tikka masala is best served warm.

INDIAN STYLE TOFU STEW

Time: 2 1/4 hours   Servings: 6

Ingredients:

2 tablespoons olive oil
8 oz. firm tofu, cubed
1 teaspoon cumin powder
1/2 teaspoon chili powder
1/4 teaspoon ground coriander
1/2 teaspoon turmeric powder

1 1/2 cups coconut milk
1 head cauliflower, cut into florets
1 bay leaf
1/2 lemongrass stalk, crushed
Salt and pepper to taste

Directions:

Season the tofu with cumin, chili, coriander and turmeric powder.

Heat the oil in a skillet and add the tofu. Cook on all sides until golden and fragrant.

Transfer in your slow cooker and add the remaining ingredients.

Cook on high settings for 2 hours.

Serve the stew warm or chilled.

ROOT VEGETABLE RISOTTO

Time: 6 1/4 hours   Servings: 6

Ingredients:

1 cup white rice
2 tablespoons olive oil
1 parsnip, diced
1 carrot, diced
1 parsley root, diced
1 sweet potato, peeled and diced

1/2 teaspoon dried sage
Salt and pepper to taste
1/4 cup white wine
1 3/4 cups vegetable stock
2 tablespoons grated Parmesan

Directions:

Combine the rice, oil, parsnip, carrot, parsley root, potato, sage, white wine and stock in your slow cooker.

Season with salt and pepper as needed and cook on low settings for 6 hours.

When done, stir in the grated cheese and serve the risotto warm and fresh.

Red Wine Braised Tempeh

Time: 8 1/4 hours   Servings: 6

Ingredients:

16 oz. tempeh, cubed
2 red onions, sliced
1/4 cup dried figs, chopped
2 tablespoons olive oil

1 cup red wine
1 cup tomato sauce
1 bay leaf
Salt and pepper to taste

Directions:

Combine the tempeh, onions, figs, olive oil, red wine, tomato sauce and bay leaf in your slow cooker.
Add salt and pepper as needed and cook on low settings for 8 hours.
The tempeh is best served warm.

Tofu Ratatouille

Time: 3 1/2 hours   Servings: 6

Ingredients:

10 oz. firm tofu, cubed
2 tablespoons olive oil
1 teaspoon cumin powder
1 small eggplant, peeled and cubed
1 red onion, chopped
2 ripe tomatoes, peeled and diced

1 carrot, diced
2 red bell peppers, cored and diced
1 zucchini, cubed
1/2 teaspoon dried oregano
Salt and pepper to taste

Directions:

Season the tofu with cumin powder, salt and pepper if needed.
Heat the oil in a skillet and add the tofu. Cook on all sides until golden then transfer in your crock pot.
Add the rest of the ingredients and cook on high settings for 3 hours.
Serve the dish warm when it's done.

Mexican Quinoa

Time: 6 1/4 hours   Servings: 6

Ingredients:

1/2 cup red quinoa, rinsed
2 red bell peppers, cored and diced
2 jalapenos, chopped
1 shallot, chopped
2 garlic cloves, chopped

2 ripe tomatoes, peeled and diced
1 can (15 oz.) black beans, drained
1/2 cup frozen sweet corn
1 1/2 cups vegetable stock
Salt and pepper to taste

Directions:

Combine the quinoa and the remaining ingredients in your slow cooker.
Add salt and pepper to taste and cook on low settings for 6 hours.
The dish is best served warm, although it can become a cold salad the next day as well.

INDIAN SPICED QUINOA STEW

Time: 7 1/4 hours   Servings: 6

Ingredients:

2 tablespoons olive oil
2 shallots, chopped
2 garlic cloves, chopped
1/2 cup red quinoa, rinsed
1/2 cup red lentils, rinsed
1 large sweet potato, peeled and cubed

1 turnip, peeled and cubed
1/2 teaspoon turmeric powder
1/2 teaspoon garam masala
Salt and pepper to taste
3 cups vegetable stock

Directions:

Combine all the ingredients in your crock pot. Add salt and pepper as needed and cook on low settings for 7 hours.
Serve the stew warm or chilled.

CROCK POT JAMBALAYA

Time: 6 1/2 hours   Servings: 8

Ingredients:

2 tablespoons olive oil
8 oz. firm tofu, cubed
1 large onion, chopped
2 red bell peppers, cored and diced
2 garlic cloves, chopped
1/2 teaspoon Cajun seasoning

2 ripe tomatoes, peeled and diced
1/2 head cauliflower, cut into florets
1 large sweet potato, peeled and cubed
1 tablespoon tomato paste
1 1/4 cups vegetable stock
Salt and pepper to taste

Directions:

Heat the oil in a skillet and add the tofu. Cook on low settings for a few minutes until golden brown.
Transfer in your slow cooker and add the rest of the ingredients, adjusting the taste with salt and pepper.
Cook on low settings for 6 hours. Serve the jambalaya warm and fresh.

BUTTERNUT SQUASH BALLS

Time: 2 1/2 hours   Servings: 6

Ingredients:

1 small butternut squash
1 cup cooked quinoa
1 garlic clove, chopped
1 shallot, chopped
1/2 teaspoon dried cumin powder

1/2 teaspoon dried oregano
Salt and pepper to taste
1 can diced tomatoes
1 cup vegetable stock

Directions:

Combine the tomatoes and stock in your crock pot. Peel the squash and grate it on the fine grater if possible. Add the remaining ingredients and mix well. Form small balls and drop them in the cooking liquid. Serve the dish warm, with cooked rice or potato mash if you like.

Chinese Hot Pot

Time: 2 1/4 hours   Servings: 6

Ingredients:

1 tablespoon canola oil
2 garlic cloves, chopped
1 teaspoon grated ginger
1 shallot, chopped
1 carrot, cut into sticks
1 celery stalk, cut into sticks
1 cup chopped chestnuts
1 cup vegetable stock

10 oz. firm tofu, cubed
4 oz. shiitake mushrooms, chopped
2 red bell peppers, cored and sliced
1/4 teaspoon chili flakes
1 teaspoon tamarind paste
2 tablespoons soy sauce
1/2 teaspoon sesame oil

Directions:

Heat the oil in a skillet and add the garlic, ginger, shallot, carrot and celery. Cook for 2 minutes then transfer in your slow cooker.

Add the remaining ingredients and cook on high settings for 2 hours.

Serve the dish warm.

Stuffed Onions

Time: 8 1/4 hours   Servings: 4

Ingredients:

4 large onions
1 pound ground pork
1 carrot, grated
2 garlic cloves, minced
1/2 teaspoon dried oregano

1/2 cup breadcrumbs
Salt and pepper to taste
1 cup vegetable stock
1 bay leaf
1 thyme sprig

Directions:

Carefully hollow out the onions leaving the outer layers intact.

In a bowl, mix the pork, carrot, garlic, oregano and breadcrumbs in a bowl. Season with salt and pepper and mix well.

Stuff the onions with the mixture and place them in your slow cooker.

Add the stock, bay leaf and thyme and cook on low settings for 8 hours.

Serve the onions warm and fresh.

Boston Baked Beans

Time: 6 1/4 hours   Servings: 8

Ingredients:

1 pound dried kidney beans
2 tablespoons molasses
1 teaspoon mustard seeds
1 teaspoon Worcestershire sauce
2 tablespoons brown sugar

1 large onion, chopped
2 cups vegetable stock
1/2 teaspoon celery seeds
1/2 teaspoon cumin seeds
1 cup water

1 bay leaf   Salt and pepper to taste

Directions:

Combine the kidney beans, molasses, mustard seeds, Worcestershire sauce, brown sugar, onion and stock in your slow cooker.

Season with salt and pepper and add the celery seeds, cumin seeds, water and bay leaf.

Cook on low settings for 6 hours.

Serve the beans warm and fresh.

FENNEL RISOTTO

Time: 4 1/4 hours   Servings: 6

Ingredients:

1 small fennel bulb, sliced   1 cup white rice
2 tablespoons olive oil   1/4 cup white wine
2 garlic cloves, chopped   2 cups vegetable stock
1 shallot, chopped   Salt and pepper to taste

Directions:

Heat the oil in a skillet and add the garlic and shallot. Cook for 2 minutes until softened then stir in the fennel. Cook for another 2 minutes then transfer in your slow cooker.

Add the remaining ingredients and season with salt and pepper.

Cook on low settings for 4 hours.

Serve the risotto warm and fresh.

ASPARAGUS BARLEY STEW

Time: 6 1/4 hours   Servings: 6

Ingredients:

1 bunch asparagus, trimmed and chopped   1 cup pearl barley
1 shallot, chopped   2 cups vegetable stock
1 garlic clove, chopped   Salt and pepper to taste
1/2 teaspoon fennel seeds   1/2 cup grated Parmesan

Directions:

Combine the asparagus, shallot, garlic, fennel seeds, pearl barley and stock in your slow cooker.

Add salt and pepper to taste and cook on low settings for 6 hours.

When done, stir in the Parmesan and serve the stew warm and fresh.

BLACK BEAN PORTOBELLO CHILI

Time: 8 1/2 hours   Servings: 8

Ingredients:

2 tablespoons olive oil   4 garlic cloves, chopped
2 shallots, chopped   1/2 pound dried black beans

1/2 teaspoon mustard seeds
1/2 teaspoon chili powder
1/4 teaspoon cardamom powder
4 Portobello mushrooms, sliced
1 cup diced tomatoes
2 cups vegetable stock

2 cups water
1 bay leaf
1 thyme sprig
Salt and pepper to taste
1 lime for serving

Directions:

Heat the oil in a skillet and stir in the shallots and garlic. Cook for 2 minutes until softened then transfer in your slow cooker.

Add the rest of the ingredients and season with salt and pepper.

Cook on low settings for 8 hours.

Serve the chili warm and fresh, drizzled with lime juice.

CREAMY CHICKPEA STEW

Time: 6 1/2 hours   Servings: 6

Ingredients:

1 cup dried chickpeas, rinsed
2 cups grated butternut squash
1/2 teaspoon cumin seeds
1/4 teaspoon mustard seeds

2 cups vegetable stock
1 cup diced tomatoes
1 bay leaf
Salt and pepper to taste

Directions:

Combine the chickpeas, butternut squash, cumin seeds, mustard seeds, stock, tomatoes and bay leaf.

Season with salt and pepper and cook on low settings for 6 hours.

Serve the stew warm and fresh.

ASIAN MARINATED EGGPLANTS

Time: 2 1/4 hours   Servings: 6

Ingredients:

2 medium size eggplants, peeled and cubed
2 tablespoons olive oil
2 garlic cloves, chopped
1 large onion, sliced
1/2 teaspoon cumin seeds
1/4 teaspoon chili powder

1 oz. dried porcini mushrooms, rehydrated and chopped
1/2 teaspoon dried oregano
1/4 cup soy sauce
1 teaspoon hot sauce

Directions:

Combine all the ingredients in your crock pot.

Cook the eggplants on high settings for 2 hours.

Serve the eggplants chilled.

CHEESY THREE BEAN CHILI

Time: 8 1/2 hours

Servings: 8

Ingredients:

2 tablespoons olive oil
2 sweet onions, chopped
4 garlic cloves, chopped
1 celery stalk, sliced
1 carrot, diced
1 cup dried black beans
1 cup kidney beans

1/2 cup red beans
1 can fire roasted tomatoes
2 bay leaves
2 cups vegetable stock
2 cups water
Salt and pepper to taste
1 cup grated Cheddar for serving

Directions:

Heat the oil in a skillet and stir in the onions, garlic, celery and carrot. Cook on low settings for 5 minutes until softened then transfer in your crock pot. Add the remaining ingredients and season with salt and pepper. Cook on low settings for 8 hours and serve the chili warm, topped with grated Cheddar.

HERBED RISOTTO

Time: 4 1/4 hours

Servings: 6

Ingredients:

2 tablespoons olive oil
1 shallot, chopped
1 cup white rice
2 cups spinach, shredded
2 tablespoons chopped cilantro

2 tablespoons chopped parsley
4 basil leaves, chopped
2 cups vegetable stock
Salt and pepper to taste
1/2 cup grated Parmesan

Directions:

Combine the olive oil, shallot, rice, spinach, cilantro, parsley, basil, stock, salt and pepper in your slow cooker. Cook on low settings for 4 hours. When done, add the Parmesan and serve the risotto warm and fresh.

SUMMER SQUASH CASSEROLE

Time: 4 1/4 hours

Servings: 6

Ingredients:

3 summer squashes, sliced
2 tablespoons olive oil
2 garlic cloves, minced
1 sweet onion, chopped
2 green bell peppers, cored and diced

2 cups cherry tomatoes, halved
2 cups cooked rice
4 eggs, beaten
Salt and pepper to taste
1 cup shredded mozzarella

Directions:

Combine the summer squash, olive oil, garlic, onion, bell peppers, tomatoes and rice in your slow cooker. Add salt and pepper to taste then pour the eggs over and top with cheese. Cook on low settings for 4 hours. Serve the casserole warm and fresh.

Tomato Crouton Stew

Time: 6 1/4 hours   Servings: 6

Ingredients:

4 ripe heirloom tomatoes, peeled and cubed
2 sweet onions, chopped
2 tablespoons olive oil
2 garlic cloves, chopped
2 red bell peppers, cored and diced
2 tablespoons tomato paste

1 1/2 cups vegetable stock
4 cups bread croutons
Salt and pepper to taste
1/2 teaspoon dried thyme
1/2 teaspoon dried oregano

Directions:

Heat the oil in a skillet and add the onions and garlic. Cook on low settings for 2 minutes until softened then transfer in your slow cooker.
Add the remaining ingredients and season with salt and pepper.
Cook on low settings for 6 hours.
Serve the stew warm and fresh.

Pinto Bean Sloppy Joes

Time: 8 1/4 hours   Servings: 6

Ingredients:

2 tablespoons olive oil
2 carrots, sliced
1 shallot, chopped
4 garlic cloves, minced
1/2 teaspoon chili powder
1 cup dried pinto beans
2 red bell peppers, cored and diced
1 tablespoon balsamic vinegar

2 tablespoons tomato paste
1 cup diced tomatoes
2 cups water
1 small head green cabbage, shredded
1 cup frozen corn
1/2 teaspoon mustard seeds
Salt and pepper to taste

Directions:

Heat the oil in a skillet and add the carrots, shallot and garlic and cook on low settings for 5 minutes.
Transfer in your crock pot and add the remaining ingredients.
Season with salt and pepper and cook on low settings for 8 hours.
Serve the dish warm or chilled.

White Bean Chard Stew

Time: 6 1/4 hours   Servings: 6

Ingredients:

2 cans (15 oz. each) white beans, drained
1 bunch green chard, shredded
1 shallot, chopped
2 garlic cloves, minced

1 leek, sliced
1 fennel bulb, sliced
1 red bell pepper, cored and sliced
1/2 cup vegetable stock

1 cup diced tomatoes
1/2 teaspoon dried oregano

1/2 teaspoon dried basil
Salt and pepper to taste

Directions:

Combine the white beans and the remaining ingredients in your crock pot.

Add enough salt and pepper and cook on low settings for 6 hours.

Serve the stew warm and fresh or freeze it in individual portions for as long as needed.

DRIED TOMATO STEW

Time: 2 1/4 hours

Servings: 6

Ingredients:

2 tablespoons olive oil
1 shallot, chopped
2 garlic cloves, minced
1 fennel bulb, sliced
1 zucchini, cubed

1 yellow bell pepper, cored and diced
1/2 cup sun-dried tomatoes, chopped
1 tablespoon lemon juice
1 cup vegetable stock
Salt and pepper to taste

Directions:

Heat the oil in a skillet and add the shallot, garlic and fennel. Cook for 2 minutes until softened then transfer in your crock pot.

Add the remaining ingredients and season with salt and pepper.

Cook the stew on high settings for 2 hours.

Serve the stew warm and fresh.

MEDITERRANEAN CROCK POT STEW

Time: 6 1/2 hours

Servings: 6

Ingredients:

2 tablespoons olive oil
1 large onion, chopped
2 carrots, sliced
2 red bell peppers, cored and diced
2 ripe tomatoes, peeled and diced
4 sun-dried tomatoes, chopped
2 zucchinis, cubed

1/2 cup pitted black olives
2 tablespoons tomato paste
1 tablespoon lemon juice
1 1/2 cups vegetable stock
Salt and pepper to taste
2 tablespoons pesto sauce for serving

Directions:

Heat the oil in a skillet and stir in the onion, carrots and bell peppers and cook for 5 minutes.

Transfer in your slow cooker and add the remaining ingredients, seasoning with salt and pepper to taste.

Cook on low settings for 6 hours.

Serve the stew warm and fresh.

Tofu Vegetable Hot Pot

Time: 6 1/4 hours   Servings: 8

Ingredients:

1 large onion, chopped
2 cups baby carrots
1 turnip, cubed
1 parsnip, diced
2 carrots, sliced
2 cups chopped green beans
4 garlic cloves, chopped
1 star anise

1/2 cinnamon stick
4 oz. shiitake mushrooms, chopped
1 tablespoon balsamic vinegar
12 oz. firm tofu, cubed
2 tablespoons soy sauce
1 tablespoon brown sugar
Salt and pepper to taste

Directions:

Combine all the vegetables and tofu in your crock pot. Season well with salt and pepper and cook on low settings for 6 hours. The stew is best served warm, although it can also be frozen into individual portions.

Pineapple Slow Cooked Tofu

Time: 6 1/4 hours   Servings: 6

Ingredients:

18 oz. firm tofu, cubed
1 can crushed pineapple
1 shallot, chopped
4 garlic cloves, minced
1 teaspoon grated ginger
1 tablespoon date syrup

1 chipotle pepper, chopped
2 tablespoons soy sauce
2 tablespoons tomato paste
1 lime, juiced
1/2 teaspoon sesame oil
Salt and pepper to taste

Directions:

Combine all the ingredients in your crock pot. Add salt and pepper as needed and cook on low settings for 6 hours. Serve the dish fresh or chilled.

Three Bean Cornbread Casserole

Time: 6 1/2 hours   Servings: 8

Ingredients:

1 can (15 oz.) black beans, drained
1 can (15 oz.) red beans, drained
1 can (15 oz.) white beans, drained
1 cup fire roasted tomatoes
2 red bell peppers, cored and diced
2 tablespoons tomato sauce
1 cup frozen corn
1 jalapeno pepper, chopped
1 cup vegetable stock

1/2 teaspoon dried thyme
1/2 cup yellow cornmeal
1/2 cup all-purpose flour
1 teaspoon baking powder
1/2 cup buttermilk
1/2 cup whole milk
1/4 teaspoon cumin seeds
Salt and pepper to taste

Directions:

Combine the beans, tomatoes, bell peppers, tomato sauce, corn, jalapeno pepper, stock and thyme in your slow cooker. Add salt and pepper to taste.

In a bowl, mix the cornmeal, flour, baking powder, buttermilk, milk, salt and pepper. Give it a quick mix.

Spoon the batter over the vegetable mix and cook on low settings for 6 hours.

Serve the dish warm.

SPICY FRIED BEANS

Time: 2 1/2 hours   Servings: 6

Ingredients:

2 cans (15 oz. each) white beans, drained
2 red bell peppers, cored and diced
1 can fire roasted tomatoes
1 teaspoon chili powder
1/2 teaspoon cumin powder

2 tablespoons tomato paste
1 cup vegetable stock
Salt and pepper to taste
1 chipotle pepper, chopped

Directions:

Combine all the ingredients in your slow cooker, adding salt and pepper to taste.

Cook on high settings for 2 hours.

The beans are best served warm.

TOMATO SAUCE BEANS OVER MILKY GRITS

Time: 2 1/2 hours   Servings: 6

Ingredients:

2 cans (15 oz. each) white beans, drained
1/4 cup sun-dried tomatoes, chopped
1 can fire roasted tomatoes
1 thyme sprig
1 bay leaf

Salt and pepper to taste
1 1/2 cups whole milk
2/3 cup corn grits
1 tablespoon butter
1/2 cup grated Cheddar

Directions:

Combine the beans, tomatoes, thyme, bay leaf, salt and pepper in your slow cooker.

Cook on high settings for 2 hours.

In the meantime, bring the milk to a boil and add the grits. Cook in a saucepan over low heat until the liquid is absorbed.

Serve the beans over cooked grits.

TEMPEH BUTTERNUT SQUASH STEW

Time: 6 1/4 hours   Servings: 8

Ingredients:

10 oz. tempeh, cubed
2 tablespoons olive oil

2 shallots, chopped
3 garlic cloves, chopped

1/2 teaspoon cumin seeds
1/2 teaspoon mustard seeds
1/4 teaspoon all-spice powder
1 dried ancho chile, chopped
4 cups butternut squash cubes

1 can fire roasted tomatoes
Salt and pepper to taste
1 bay leaf
1 thyme sprig

Directions:

Heat the oil in a skillet and add the tempeh. Cook until golden then transfer in your slow cooker.

Add the rest of the ingredients and season with salt and pepper as needed.

Cook on low settings for 6 hours.

Serve the stew warm or chilled.

Paste Veggie Stew

Time: 6 1/4 hours   Servings: 8

Ingredients:

1 large onion, chopped
1 celery stalk, sliced
2 garlic cloves, chopped
1/2 head cauliflower, cut into florets
1 cup diced tomatoes
1 cup green peas

2 cups chopped green beans
1/2 teaspoon dried oregano
1/2 teaspoon dried basil
1 cup short pasta of your choice
2 cups vegetable stock
Salt and pepper to taste

Directions:

Combine the onion, celery, cauliflower and the remaining ingredients in your crock pot.

Add salt and pepper to taste and cook on low settings for 6 hours.

Serve the stew warm and fresh.

Tempeh Quinoa Stew

Time: 6 1/4 hours   Servings: 6

Ingredients:

8 oz. tempeh, crumbled
1 celery stalk, sliced
1 carrot, diced
1 garlic clove, minced
2 red bell peppers, cored and diced
1 cup diced tomatoes

3/4 cup red quinoa, rinsed
2 cups vegetable stock
1/2 teaspoon dried oregano
1/2 teaspoon dried basil
Salt and pepper to taste

Directions:

Combine the tempeh, celery, garlic, bell peppers, tomatoes, quinoa, stock and herbs in your crock pot.

Add salt and pepper to taste and cook on low settings for 6 hours.

Serve the stew warm and fresh.

QUINOA CORN STEW

Time: 3 1/4 hours   Servings: 6

Ingredients:

2 cups frozen corn
1/2 cup quinoa, rinsed
1 tablespoon olive oil
1 large shallot, chopped
2 garlic cloves, mined
1 jalapeno pepper, chopped

1 celery stalk, diced
1/4 teaspoon cumin powder
1/4 teaspoon fennel seeds
1/4 teaspoon chili powder
Salt and pepper to taste
1 1/2 cups vegetable stock

Directions:

Combine all the ingredients in your crock pot. Add salt and pepper to taste and cook on high settings for 2 hours then 1 additional hour on low settings. Serve the stew warm and fresh.

LIME BEAN STEW

Time: 6 1/4 hours   Servings: 8

Ingredients:

2 cups dried lime beans
2 carrots, sliced
2 celery stalks, sliced
1 head cauliflower, cut into florets
1 teaspoon grated ginger
1 cup diced tomatoes

1 cup tomato sauce
2 cups vegetable stock
1 bay leaf
1 thyme sprig
Salt and pepper to taste

Directions:

Combine the beans, carrots, celery, cauliflower, ginger, tomatoes, tomato sauce, stock, salt and pepper, as well as bay leaf and thyme in your crock pot. Season with salt and pepper as needed and cook on low settings for 6 hours. The stew is best served warm.

JAMAICAN RED BEAN STEW

Time: 8 1/4 hours   Servings: 10

Ingredients:

1 pound dried red beans, rinsed
4 garlic cloves, chopped
2 large red onions, finely chopped
1 can (15 oz.) fire roasted tomatoes
1 teaspoon curry powder
1/4 teaspoon chili powder
4 cups vegetable stock

2 cups baby carrots
2 sweet potatoes, peeled and cubed
1 bay leaf
1/2 cup coconut milk
1/4 teaspoon all-spice powder
Salt and pepper to taste

Directions:

Combine all the ingredients in your crock pot. Add salt and pepper to taste and cook on low settings for 8 hours. Serve the stew warm and fresh.

Herbed Vegetable Meatloaf

Time: 6 1/4 hours   Servings: **8**

Ingredients:

2 tablespoons olive oil
1 large onion, finely chopped
4 garlic cloves, minced
1 teaspoon dried thyme
1 teaspoon dried oregano
2 cups cooked quinoa

1 can (15 oz.) cannellini beans, drained
2 tablespoons chopped cilantro
1/4 cup chopped parsley
2 eggs
1/4 cup breadcrumbs
Salt and pepper to taste

Directions:

Combine the oil, onion, garlic, thyme, oregano, quinoa, beans, cilantro, parsley, eggs, salt and pepper in a bowl.
Add the breadcrumbs, salt and pepper and spoon the mixture in your crock pot.
Cook on low settings for 6 hours. Serve the meatloaf warm or chilled.

Mixed Lentil Spicy Stew

Time: 6 1/4 hours   Servings: **8**

Ingredients:

1/2 cup red lentils
1/2 cup brown lentils
1/2 cup green lentils
1 large onion, finely chopped
2 carrots, diced
1 celery stalk, diced
2 cups cauliflower florets
1/2 teaspoon cumin seeds

1/2 teaspoon mustard seeds
1/2 teaspoon fennel seeds
1 bay leaf
1 thyme sprig
1/4 teaspoon chili powder
1/2 teaspoon ground ginger
Salt and pepper to taste

Directions:

Combine the lentils, onion, carrots, celery, cauliflower florets, seeds, spices, salt and pepper in your crock pot.
Cook on low settings for 6 hours and serve the stew warm and fresh.

Pineapple Baked Beans

Time: 2 1/4 hours   Servings: **6**

Ingredients:

1 can (15 oz.) black beans, drained
1 can fire roasted tomatoes
1 cup crushed pineapple
1 shallot, chopped
2 garlic cloves, chopped

1/2 cup BBQ sauce
1 tablespoon maple syrup
1/2 teaspoon cumin powder
1/2 teaspoon ground ginger
Salt and pepper to taste

Directions:

Combine all the ingredients in your crock pot. Season with salt and pepper and cook on high settings for 2 hours.
Serve the beans warm.

BROCCOLI RICE PILAF

Time: 2 1/4 hours   Servings: 4

Ingredients:
1 head broccoli, cut into florets
1 shallot, chopped
2/3 cup white rice
1 cup vegetable stock

1 cup water
Salt and pepper to taste
1/2 teaspoon dried oregano

Directions:
Combine all the ingredients in your crock pot.
Add salt and pepper to taste and cook the pilaf on high settings for 2 hours.
The pilaf is best served warm and fresh.

CREAMY POTATOES

Time: 5 1/2 hours   Servings: 8

Ingredients:
2 pounds Yukon gold potatoes, peeled and
    finely sliced
2 garlic cloves, minced
1 teaspoon dried oregano

1 cup cream cheese
1 cup whole milk
1 pinch nutmeg
Salt and pepper to taste

Directions:
Season the potatoes with salt and pepper and layer them in your crock pot.
Mix the garlic, oregano, cream cheese, milk and nutmeg in a bowl. Pour this mixture over the potatoes and cook on low settings for 5 hours.
Serve the potatoes warm or chilled.

VEGGIE REFRIED BEANS

Time: 6 1/4 hours   Servings: 6

Ingredients:
2 cans (15 oz. each) black beans, drained
1 cup vegetable stock
2 tablespoons tomato paste
1 chipotle pepper, chopped

4 garlic cloves, minced
1 tablespoon adobo sauce from chipotle
Salt and pepper to taste

Directions:
Combine all the ingredients in your crock pot.
Add salt and pepper as needed and cook on low settings for 6 hours.
Serve the beans warm or chilled.

Layered Sweet Potatoes

Time: 6 1/2 hours   Servings: 8

Ingredients:

2 tablespoons olive oil
2 large sweet potatoes, peeled and finely sliced
2 onions, finely sliced
1 pinch nutmeg
2 cups whole milk

1/2 cup cream cheese
2 eggs, beaten
1/2 teaspoon garlic powder
Salt and pepper to taste

Directions:

Grease your slow cooker then layer the potatoes and onions in your slow cooker. Mix the nutmeg, milk, eggs and garlic powder in a bowl. Add salt and pepper to taste then pour over the veggies. Cook on low settings for 6 hours. Serve the dish warm.

Stuffed Butternut Squash

Time: 6 1/2 hours   Servings: 6

Ingredients:

1 large butternut squash, halved
2 cups cooked lentils
1 shallot, chopped
2 garlic cloves, minced

1/2 teaspoon cumin powder
1/4 teaspoon chili powder
Salt and pepper to taste
1/2 cup vegetable stock

Directions:

Place the butternut squash in your crock pot. Mix the lentils, shallot, garlic, cumin powder and chili powder in a bowl. Add salt and pepper to taste then spoon the mixture into the butternut squash halves. Add the stock in the crock pot as well and cook on low settings for 6 hours. Serve the butternut squash warm and fresh.

Vegetarian Fajitas

Time: 6 1/4 hours   Servings: 6

Ingredients:

2 tablespoons olive oil
2 red bell peppers, cored and sliced
1 yellow bell pepper, cored and sliced
1 shallot, sliced
4 garlic cloves, chopped
1/4 teaspoon chili powder
1/4 teaspoon cumin powder

1 tablespoon soy sauce
12 oz. seitan, crumbled
1/2 cup vegetable stock
1/2 cup tomato sauce
Salt and pepper to taste
Flour tortillas for serving

Directions:

Heat the oil in a skillet and add the seitan. Cook until golden then transfer in your slow cooker. Add the remaining ingredients and season with salt and pepper. Cook on low settings for 6 hours. Serve the fajitas warm, wrapped in tortillas.

Spinach Cottage Cheese Casserole

Time: 6 1/4 hours   Servings: 6

Ingredients:
2 bags frozen spinach, thawed
1 1/2 cups cottage cheese
2 tablespoons all-purpose flour
1/2 teaspoon dried oregano

1/2 teaspoon dried basil
4 eggs, beaten
Salt and pepper to taste

Directions:
Combine all the ingredients in a bowl. Mix well and season with salt and pepper.
Pour the mixture in your crock pot.
Cook on low settings for 6 hours.
Serve the casserole warm or chilled.

Green Bean Casserole

Time: 6 1/4 hours   Servings: 6

Ingredients:
1 pound green beans, trimmed and chopped
1/2 pound fresh spinach, shredded
1/2 cup cream cheese
1 shallot, chopped
1 cup whole milk

4 eggs, beaten
1/2 cup breadcrumbs
Salt and pepper to taste

Directions:
Combine all the ingredients in your slow cooker.
Add salt and pepper to taste and cook on low settings for 6 hours.
Serve the casserole warm or chilled.

Seitan Chow Mein

Time: 2 1/4 hours   Servings: 6

Ingredients:
1/2 pound seitan, diced
2 celery stalks, sliced
2 carrots, sliced
2 green onions, chopped
2 tablespoons soy sauce
1/2 cup vegetable stock

1 pinch chili flakes
1 cup green peas
1 cup water chestnuts, chopped
1 tablespoon cornstarch
1/4 cup cold water

Directions:
Combine the seitan, celery, carrots, green onions, soy sauce, stock, chili flakes, green peas and water chestnuts in your crock pot. Cook on high settings for 1 hour then add the cornstarch and water and cook for 1 additional hour.
Serve the dish warm and fresh.

Chinese Tofu Kung Pao

Time: 6 1/4 hours

Servings: 6

Ingredients:

1 pound firm tofu, cubed
1 tablespoon canola oil
1 tablespoon lime juice
1 tablespoon soy sauce
1 tablespoon tahini paste
1 teaspoon grated ginger
1 onion, sliced

1/4 teaspoon red pepper flakes
2 red bell peppers, cored and sliced
2 cups sliced mushrooms
1 small bok choy, shredded
Salt and pepper to taste
1/2 cup peanuts, chopped

Directions:

Mix the tofu, lime juice, soy sauce and tahini paste in a bowl. Heat the oil in a skillet and add the tofu. Cook for a few minutes on all sides then transfer in your crock pot. Add the remaining ingredients and season with salt and pepper. Cook on low settings for 6 hours. Serve the dish warm and fresh.

Five Spice Marinated Tofu

Time: 8 1/4 hours

Servings: 6

Ingredients:

18 oz. firm tofu, cubed
1/4 cup soy sauce
1 teaspoon sesame oil
2 garlic cloves, minced

1 teaspoon grated ginger
1 teaspoon five spices powder
1 cup vegetable stock

Directions:

Combine all the ingredients in your crock pot.
Cover and cook on low settings for 8 hours.
Serve the tofu warm or chilled.

Bok Choy Shiitake Crock Pot Fry Up

Time: 2 1/4 hours

Servings: 6

Ingredients:

2 garlic cloves, minced
1 teaspoon grated ginger
1 sweet onion, sliced
2 tablespoons canola oil
1 cup chopped shiitake mushrooms

2 cups sliced button mushrooms
2 tablespoons bok choy
2 green onions, chopped
1 teaspoon sesame oil
1/4 teaspoon chili powder

Directions:

Heat the oil in a skillet and stir in the garlic, ginger and onion. Cook for 1 minute until fragrant then transfer in your crock pot. Add the remaining ingredients and cook on high settings for 2 hours.
Serve the fry up warm.

INDIAN MIXED VEGGIE CURRY

Time: 8 1/2 hours   Servings: 8

Ingredients:

2 tablespoons canola oil
1 head cauliflower, cut into florets
4 potatoes, peeled and cubed
1 cup green peas
1 cup snap peas
2 sweet potatoes, peeled and cubed
1 zucchini, cubed
2 heirloom tomatoes, peeled and diced

1/4 teaspoon chili powder
1/2 teaspoon cumin powder
1 teaspoon curry powder
1/2 teaspoon turmeric powder
2 tablespoons tomato paste
3 cups vegetable stock
Salt and pepper to taste

Directions:

Combine the oil and the rest of the ingredients in your crock pot.
Season with salt and pepper and cook on low settings for 8 hours.
Serve the curry warm and fresh.

SEITAN RICE PILAF

Time: 8 1/4 hours   Servings: 8

Ingredients:

1 pound seitan, cubed
1 large onion, chopped
1 celery stalk, diced
1 large carrot, diced

1/2 cup green peas
1 cup white rice
2 cups vegetable stock
Salt and pepper to taste

Directions:

Combine all the ingredients in your crock pot.
Add salt and pepper to taste and cook on low settings for 8 hours.
Serve the pilaf warm and fresh.

SAVORY SWEET POTATO APPLE CASSEROLE

Time: 6 1/4 hours   Servings: 6

Ingredients:

1 1/2 pounds sweet potatoes, peeled and
   cubed
4 red apples, peeled, cored and diced
2 shallots, chopped
2 garlic cloves, minced

1 tablespoon brown sugar
1 pinch nutmeg
1 cup vegetable stock
Salt and pepper to taste

Directions:

Combine all the ingredients in your crock pot and season with salt and pepper.
Cook on low settings for 6 hours. Serve the casserole warm or chilled.

SPANISH RICE PILAF

Time: 6 1/4 hours   Servings: 6

Ingredients:

1 cup white rice
1 onion, chopped
1 green bell pepper, cored and diced
1 red bell pepper, cored and diced
1 cup red salsa

1 cup frozen corn
1 cup green peas
2 cups vegetable stock
1/4 teaspoon chili powder
Salt and pepper to taste

Directions:

Combine all the ingredients in your slow cooker then add salt and pepper as needed.
Cook on low settings for 6 hours.
Serve the pilaf warm and fresh.

TEMPEH CARNITAS

Time: 6 1/2 hours   Servings: 6

Ingredients:

1 pound tempeh, cut into thin strips
2 tablespoons canola oil
4 garlic cloves, minced
1 large onion, finely chopped

1/2 teaspoon dried oregano
1/2 teaspoon dried basil
1 cup vegetable stock
Salt and pepper to taste

Directions:

Heat the oil in a skillet and add the tempeh. Cook on all sides until golden then transfer in your slow cooker.
Add the remaining ingredients and cook on low settings for 6 hours.
Serve the dish warm.

CURRIED RICE AND LENTILS

Time: 6 1/4 hours   Servings: 6

Ingredients:

1 cup white rice
1/2 cup red lentils
1 cup diced tomatoes
3 cups vegetable stock

2 tablespoons tomato paste
1/4 teaspoon garlic powder
1 shallot, chopped
Salt and pepper to taste

Directions:

Combine all the ingredients in your crock pot.
Add salt and pepper to taste and cook on low settings for 6 hours.
Serve the dish warm and fresh.

*H*ERBED BARLEY CASSEROLE

Time: 7 1/4 hours   Servings: 8

Ingredients:

1 cup pearl barley
1 large onion, finely chopped
4 garlic cloves, chopped
1 teaspoon dried oregano
1 teaspoon dried basil
1/2 teaspoon dried thyme
1 cup diced tomatoes
1 zucchini, diced

2 red bell peppers, cored and diced
2 cups sliced mushrooms
2 cups vegetable stock
2 tablespoons pine nuts
2 tablespoons chopped parsley
1 tablespoon chopped cilantro
Salt and pepper to taste

Directions:

Combine the pearl barley and the remaining ingredients in your crock pot.
Add salt and pepper to taste and cook on low settings for 7 hours.
The casserole is best served warm.

*E*GGPLANT PARMIGIANA

Time: 8 1/4 hours   Servings: 6

Ingredients:

4 medium eggplants, peeled and finely sliced
1/4 cup all-purpose flour
4 cups marinara sauce

1 cup grated Parmesan
Salt and pepper to taste

Directions:

Season the eggplants with salt and pepper and sprinkle with flour.
Layer the eggplant slices and marinara sauce in your crock pot.
Top with the grated cheese and cook on low settings for 8 hours.
Serve the parmigiana warm or chilled.

*A*SPARAGUS CASSEROLE

Time: 6 1/2 hours   Servings: 6

Ingredients:

1 bunch asparagus, trimmed and chopped
1 can condensed cream of mushroom soup
2 hard-boiled eggs, peeled and cubed

1 cup grated Cheddar
2 cups bread croutons
Salt and pepper to taste

Directions:

Combine the asparagus, mushroom soup, hard-boiled eggs, cheese and bread croutons in your slow cooker.
Add salt and pepper to taste and cook on low settings for 6 hours.
Serve the casserole warm and fresh.

Ravioli Stew

Time: 6 1/4 hours   Servings: 6

Ingredients:

1 celery stalk, sliced   1 cup diced tomatoes
2 carrots, sliced   10 oz. spinach ravioli
2 garlic cloves, chopped   1 cup vegetable stock
1 can (15 oz.) cannellini beans, drained   Salt and pepper to taste
1 shallot, chopped   Grated Parmesan for serving
1/2 teaspoon dried basil

Directions:

Combine all the ingredients in your slow cooker and season with salt and pepper.
Cook the stew on low settings for 6 hours.
Serve the stew warm, topped with grated Parmesan cheese.

Vegetarian Hungarian Goulash

Time: 8 1/2 hours   Servings: 8

Ingredients:

2 tablespoons olive oil   1 can fire roasted tomatoes
2 large onions, finely chopped   1 teaspoon smoked paprika
4 garlic cloves, chopped   2 tablespoons tomato paste
2 carrots, diced   2 pounds potatoes, peeled and cubed
1 celery stalk, diced   2 bay leaves
1 can (15 oz.) white beans, drained   2 cups vegetable stock
4 roasted red bell peppers, chopped   Salt and pepper to taste

Directions:

Heat the oil in a skillet and add the onions. Cook for 5 minutes until softened then transfer in your crock pot,
Add the remaining ingredients and adjust the taste with salt and pepper. Cook on low settings for 8 hours.
Serve the stew warm and fresh.

Ginger Glazed Tofu

Time: 2 1/4 hours   Servings: 6

Ingredients:

12 oz. firm tofu, cubed   2 tablespoons soy sauce
1 tablespoon hot sauce   1/2 cup vegetable stock
1 teaspoon grated ginger

Directions:

Season the tofu with hot sauce, ginger and soy sauce. Place the tofu in your crock pot.
Add the stock and cook on high settings for 2 hours.
Serve the tofu warm with your favorite side dish.

Artichoke Black Olive Tagine

Time: 4 1/4 hours

Servings: 6

Ingredients:

12 oz. artichoke hearts, chopped
1 shallot, chopped
1 can (15 oz.) chickpeas, drained
2 garlic cloves, chopped
1/2 teaspoon smoked paprika
1/2 teaspoon cumin powder

1 teaspoon turmeric powder
1 lime, juiced
1/2 cup pitted black olives
1/2 teaspoon dried oregano
1 cup diced tomatoes
Salt and pepper to taste

Directions:

Combine the artichokes, shallot, chickpeas and the remaining ingredients in your crock pot.
Add salt and pepper to taste and cook on low settings for 4 hours.
Serve the tagine warm or chilled.

Beans Bourginon

Time: 8 1/4 hours

Servings: 10

Ingredients:

2 tablespoons olive oil
2 large onions, chopped
2 leeks, sliced
4 garlic cloves, chopped
1 teaspoon dried thyme
2 cups kidney beans, rinsed

2 cups sliced mushrooms
2 carrots, sliced
1/2 cup dry red wine
4 cups vegetable stock or water
2 bay leaves
Salt and pepper to taste

Directions:

Heat the oil in a skillet and add the onions, leeks and garlic. cook for 10 minutes until softened then transfer in your slow cooker. Add the remaining ingredients and cook on low settings for 8 hours.
The dish is best served warm.

Tofu Dumpling Stew

Time: 6 1/2 hours

Servings: 6

Ingredients:

12 oz. firm tofu, cubed
2 tablespoons olive oil
1 large onion, chopped
4 garlic cloves, minced
2 tablespoons soy sauce
2 large carrots, sliced
2 celery stalks, sliced
2 cups sliced mushrooms
1/2 cup tomato sauce

1/2 teaspoon dried sage
1 cup vegetable stock
Salt and pepper to taste
1 cup all-purpose flour
1/2 teaspoon baking soda
1/4 cup butter, chilled and cubed
2 eggs
1/4 cup whole milk

Directions:

Heat the oil in a skillet and add the tofu. Cook on all sides until golden and crusty then add the transfer in your slow cooker.

Add the onion, garlic, soy sauce, carrots, celery, mushrooms, tomato sauce, sage, stock, salt and pepper.

For the dumplings, mix the flour, baking soda and butter, as well as a pinch of salt in a bowl and rub the ingredients well until sandy.

Add the milk and give it a quick mix. Spoon the mixture over the vegetables.

Cover and cook on low settings for 6 hours.

Serve the dish warm and fresh.

Hearty Sweet Potato Stew

Time: 2 1/4 hours   Servings: 4

Ingredients:

2 tablespoons olive oil
2 large carrots, sliced
2 large sweet potatoes, peeled and cubed
1/2 cup red lentils
2 ripe tomatoes, peeled and diced
1 1/2 cups vegetable stock or water

1 bay leaf
1/4 teaspoon cumin seeds
1/4 teaspoon fennel seeds
1/4 teaspoon garlic powder
1/4 teaspoon onion powder
Salt and pepper to taste

Directions:

Combine the ingredients in your crock pot.

Add salt and pepper to taste and cook the stew on high settings for 2 hours.

Serve the stew warm and fresh.

Hominy Casserole

Time: 2 1/4 hours   Servings: 6

Ingredients:

16 oz. canned hominy, drained
1 can condensed cream of chicken soup
1/2 cup breadcrumbs
1 can fire roasted tomatoes
1 can green chilies, chopped
1 onion, chopped

1/2 cup pitted black olives
1/4 teaspoon cayenne pepper
1/4 teaspoon cumin powder
Salt and pepper to taste
1 1/2 cups grated Cheddar

Directions:

Combine the hominy, chicken soup, breadcrumbs, tomatoes, chilies, onion, black olives, spices, salt and pepper in your slow cooker.

Top with grated cheese and cook on high settings for 2 hours.

Serve the casserole warm and fresh.

Garden Crock Pot Chili

Time: 8 1/2 hours   Servings: 8

Ingredients:

2 shallots, chopped
4 garlic cloves, chopped
1 can (15 oz.) kidney beans, drained
1 cup frozen corn
1 head broccoli, cut into florets
1/2 head cauliflower, cut into florets
2 jalapeno peppers, chopped
2 red bell peppers, cored and diced

1 large carrot, sliced
1 can fire roasted tomatoes
1 cup vegetable stock
2 potatoes, peeled and cubed
1 teaspoon chili powder
1/2 teaspoon dried oregano
Salt and pepper to taste

Directions:

Combine the shallots, garlic, kidney beans, corn, broccoli, cauliflower, jalapeno pepper, bell peppers, carrot, tomatoes and stock in your slow cooker. Add the potatoes and chili powder, as well as oregano and season with salt and pepper. Cook on low settings for 8 hours. Serve the chili warm and fresh.

Mexican Tortilla Chip Casserole

Time: 2 1/2 hours   Servings: 6

Ingredients:

1 1/2 cups frozen corn
1 can fire roasted tomatoes
1 cup red salsa
1/2 teaspoon cumin powder
1/2 teaspoon chili powder

2 potatoes, peeled and cubed
1 cup water
Salt and pepper to taste
6 oz. tortilla chips
1 1/2 cups grated Cheddar

Directions:

Combine the corn with tomatoes, red salsa, cumin powder, chili powder, potatoes, salt and pepper in your crock pot. Add the water and mix then top with tortilla chips and cheese.
Cook on high settings for 2 hours.
Serve the casserole warm and fresh.

No Fuss Vegetarian Chili

Time: 8 1/4 hours   Servings: 8

Ingredients:

10 oz. firm tofu, cubed
1 can fire roasted tomatoes
2 red bell peppers, cored and diced
1 yellow bell pepper, cored and diced
4 garlic cloves, chopped
2 sweet onions, chopped
2 cups dried kidney beans

4 cups water
1/2 teaspoon chili powder
1/2 teaspoon cumin powder
1/4 teaspoon chili flakes
Salt and pepper to taste
Chopped cilantro for serving

Directions:

Combine the tofu, tomatoes, bell peppers, garlic, onions, kidney beans, water, chili powder, cumin powder and chili flakes in your crock pot.

Add salt and pepper to taste and cook on low settings for 8 hours.

Serve the chili warm and fresh, topped with chopped cilantro.

Ricotta Veggie Lasagna

Time: 6 1/2 hours

Servings: 8

Ingredients:

2 large zucchinis, finely sliced
2 cups ricotta cheese
10 oz. frozen spinach, thawed and drained
2 cups chopped cauliflower florets

2 cups tomato sauce
2 cups shredded mozzarellas
Salt and pepper to taste

Directions:

Mix the ricotta, spinach and cauliflower florets in your slow cooker. Add salt and pepper to taste.

Layer the zucchinis, ricotta filling and tomato sauce in your crock pot.

Top with mozzarella cheese and cook on low settings for 6 hours.

Serve the lasagna warm and fresh.

Bean and Spinach Enchilada Sauce

Time: 6 1/4 hours

Servings: 8

Ingredients:

1 can (15 oz.) black beans, drained
10 oz. frozen spinach, thawed and drained
1 cup frozen corn
1/2 teaspoon cumin powder
1/2 teaspoon chili powder

1 cup tomato sauce
1 can fire roasted tomatoes
1/2 lime, juiced
Salt and pepper to taste

Directions:

Combine all the ingredients in your crock pot, adding salt and pepper as needed.

Cook on low settings for 6 hours.

Serve the enchilada sauce warm or keep cooking it after wrapping it in flour tortillas. The sauce can also be frozen into individual portions to serve later.

Parmesan Biscuit Pot Pie

Time: 7 1/2 hours

Servings: 8

Ingredients:

2 tablespoons olive oil
2 garlic cloves, chopped
1 large onion, finely chopped
2 carrots, diced

1 parsnip, diced
1 turnip, diced
2 cups sliced mushrooms
1 cup green peas

Salt and pepper to taste
1/2 cup all-purpose flour
1/2 teaspoon baking powder

1 cup grated Parmesan
1/4 cup butter, chilled and cubed
1/2 cup buttermilk

Directions:

Combine the oil, garlic, onion, carrots, parsnip, turnip, mushrooms, green peas, salt and pepper in your slow cooker.
Combine the flour, baking powder and Parmesan in your crock pot. Mix until sandy then stir in the buttermilk.
Spoon the batter over the vegetables and cook on low settings for 7 hours.
Serve the pot pie warm or chilled.

HEARTY BLACK BEAN QUINOA CHILI

Time: 8 1/4 hours

Servings: 8

Ingredients:

2 cups dried black beans
4 cups vegetable stock
1 can fire roasted tomatoes
2 chipotle peppers, chopped
4 garlic cloves, chopped
1 celery stalk, diced

2 red bell peppers, cored and diced
1/2 teaspoon cumin powder
1/4 cup red quinoa, rinsed
1/4 teaspoon chili powder
Salt and pepper to taste
2 tablespoons chopped parsley for serving

Directions:

Combine the beans, stock, tomatoes, chipotle peppers, garlic, celery, bell peppers, cumin powder, quinoa and chili powder in your slow cooker.
Add salt and pepper to taste and cook on low settings for 8 hours.
Serve the chili warm, topped with chopped parsley just before serving.

FARRO PUMPKIN STEW

Time: 6 1/4 hours

Servings: 6

Ingredients:

2 tablespoons butter
1 cup farro, rinsed
2 cups pumpkin cubes
1 shallot, chopped
1 garlic clove, minced
1/4 teaspoon cumin seeds

1/4 teaspoon fennel seeds
1/4 cup white wine
2 1/2 cups vegetable stock
Salt and pepper to taste
1/2 cup grated Parmesan cheese

Directions:

Combine the butter, faro, pumpkin, shallot, garlic, cumin seeds, fennel seeds, wine and stock in your crock pot.
Add salt and pepper to taste and cook on low settings for 6 hours.
Serve the stew warm or chilled.

Madras Vegetable Curry

Time: 3 1/4 hours   Servings: 6

Ingredients:

2 shallots, chopped
4 garlic cloves, chopped
1 small head cauliflower, cut into florets
2 red bell peppers, cored and diced
1 pound potatoes, peeled and cubed
1 can (15 oz.) chickpeas, drained
2 tablespoons red curry paste

1 cup diced tomatoes
1 cup vegetable stock
1/2 cup coconut cream
1 lemongrass stalk, crushed
1 lime, juiced
Salt and pepper to taste
Cooked jasmine rice for serving

Directions:

Combine the garlic, shallots, cauliflower, bell peppers, potatoes, chickpeas, curry paste, stock, coconut cream, lemongrass and lime juice in your slow cooker.

Add salt and pepper to taste and cook the curry on high settings for 3 hours until thickened and rich.

The curry is best served warm, topped over cooked jasmine rice.

Simple Potato Stew

Time: 6 1/2 hours   Servings: 8

Ingredients:

1 large onion, chopped
2 garlic cloves, chopped
2 red bell peppers, cored and diced
2 carrots, sliced
1 celery root, peeled and cubed
2 pounds potatoes, peeled and cubed

2 ripe tomatoes, peeled and diced
2 cups vegetable stock
Salt and pepper to taste
2 bay leaves
2 tablespoons chopped parsley for serving

Directions:

Combine all the ingredients in your crock pot.

Add salt and pepper as needed and cook on low settings for 6 hours.

Serve the stew warm, topped with chopped parsley.

Meatless Pasta Sauce

Time: 4 1/4 hours   Servings: 8

Ingredients:

1 large onion, finely chopped
4 garlic cloves, minced
2 tablespoons olive oil
1 head cauliflower, cut into florets
2 carrots, sliced
2 celery stalks, sliced
1 cup tomato puree

2 ripe tomatoes, peeled and diced
1 cup vegetable stock
1 bay leaf
Salt and pepper to taste

Directions:

Heat the oil in a skillet and add the garlic and onion. Cook for 2 minutes until softened.

In the meantime, place the cauliflower, carrots and celery in a food processor and pulse until grainy.

Combine the cooked onion and garlic with the cauliflower mix in your crock pot and add the remaining ingredients, including salt and pepper.

Cook on low settings for 4 hours.

Serve the sauce warm or freeze it in individual portions for later use.

Balsamic Vegetable Sauce

Time: 6 1/2 hours   Servings: 8

Ingredients:

1 large onion, chopped
4 garlic cloves, chopped
2 red bell peppers, cored and diced
2 cans (15 oz. each) diced tomatoes
10 oz. soy crumbles

2 cups vegetable stock
2 tablespoons balsamic vinegar
1/2 teaspoon dried basil
1/2 teaspoon dried oregano
Salt and pepper to taste

Directions:

Combine all the ingredients in your crock pot.

Season with salt and pepper as needed and cook on low settings for 6 hours.

Serve the sauce warm and fresh or freeze it into individual portions for later.

Couscous Cauliflower Stew

Time: 4 1/4 hours   Servings: 6

Ingredients:

1/2 cup couscous
1 large onion, sliced
1 head cauliflower, cut into florets
2 cups diced tomatoes
2 cups vegetable stock

1 teaspoon dried Italian herbs
1/4 teaspoon chili powder
Salt and pepper to taste
Lemon juice for serving

Directions:

Layer the couscous, onion and cauliflower in your crock pot.

Mix the tomatoes, stock, herbs and chili powder, as well as salt and pepper to taste in a bowl.

Pour this mixture over the vegetables and couscous and cook on low settings for 4 hours.

Serve the dish warm or chilled, drizzled with lemon juice.

Mediterranean Chickpea Feta Stew

Time: 8 1/4 hours   Servings: 8

Ingredients:

2 cups dried chickpeas, rinsed
1 large onion, chopped

2 carrots, diced
1 celery stalk, diced

1 teaspoon dried oregano
1 teaspoon dried basil
1 pinch chili powder
2 heirloom tomatoes, peeled and diced

2 cups vegetable stock
Salt and pepper to taste
8 oz. feta cheese for servings

Directions:

Combine the chickpeas, onion, carrots, celery, oregano, basil, chili powder, tomatoes, salt and pepper, as well as stock in your crock pot.

Cover and cook on low settings for 8 hours.

Serve the stew warm, topped with crumbled feta cheese.

Eggplant Caponata

Time: 6 1/2 hours

Servings: 6

Ingredients:

2 tablespoons olive oil
2 ripe tomatoes, peeled and cubed
2 eggplants, peeled and cubed
1 zucchini, cubed
1 celery stalk, sliced
1 sweet onion, chopped

1/2 cup tomato puree
1 cup vegetable stock
1 tablespoon balsamic vinegar
1/2 teaspoon dried oregano
Salt and pepper to taste
Chopped parsley for serving

Directions:

Combine the olive oil, tomatoes, eggplants, zucchini, celery, onion, tomato puree, stock, vinegar, oregano, salt and pepper in your crock pot.

Cover and cook on low settings for 6 hours.

Serve the caponata fresh, topped with chopped parsley.

Provence Summer Veggie Stew

Time: 6 1/2 hours

Servings: 8

Ingredients:

1 cup frozen pearl onions
3 large carrots, sliced
1 cup frozen corn
1 cup frozen green peas
1 cup vegetable stock
2 zucchinis, cubed

2 ripe tomatoes, peeled and cubed
1 teaspoon herbs de Provence
1 can (15 oz.) chickpeas, drained
Salt and pepper to taste
Cooked white rice for serving

Directions:

Combine the onions, carrots, corn, green peas, stock, zucchinis, tomatoes, herbs, chickpeas, salt and pepper in your crock pot.

Add salt and pepper to taste and cook on low settings for 6 hours.

Serve the stew fresh over cooked white rice or simple.

Asiago Chickpea Stew

Time: 2 1/4 hours   Servings: 4

Ingredients:

2 cans (15 oz. each) chickpeas, drained
2 ripe tomatoes, peeled and diced
1/2 cup vegetable stock
1/2 cup light cream

Salt and pepper to taste
1/2 teaspoon dried oregano
1 cup grated Asiago cheese

Directions:

Combine the chickpeas, tomatoes, stock, cream, salt, pepper and oregano in your crock pot.
Top with grated cheese and cook on high settings for 2 hours.
Serve the stew warm and fresh.

Enchilada Orzo

Time: 3 1/4 hours   Servings: 6

Ingredients:

1 cup orzo
1 can fire roasted tomatoes
1 cup tomato sauce
1 cup vegetable stock
1 cup frozen corn

1 cup frozen green peas
1 can (15 oz.) black beans, drained
Salt and pepper to taste
1 thyme sprig
1 cup grated Cheddar for serving

Directions:

Combine the orzo, tomatoes, tomato sauce, stock, corn, green peas, black beans, thyme, salt and pepper in your slow cooker.
Cook on high settings for 3 hours.
To serve, top the orzo with grated cheese.

Broccoli with Peanuts

Time: 2 1/4 hours   Servings: 6

Ingredients:

2 heads broccoli, cut into florets
1 cup raw peanuts, chopped
4 garlic cloves, chopped
1 shallot, sliced

2 tablespoons olive oil
1 lemon, juiced
1 tablespoons soy sauce
Salt and pepper to taste

Directions:

Combine the broccoli, peanuts, garlic, shallot, olive oil, lemon juice and soy sauce in your slow cooker.
Add salt and pepper to taste and cook the dish on high settings for 2 hours.
Serve the dish warm and fresh.

Layered Eggplant Parmesan Bake

Time: 4 1/4 hours   Servings: 6

Ingredients:

2 large eggplants, peeled and sliced
2 cups tomato sauce
1/2 teaspoon chili powder

1 teaspoon dried basil
2 cups grated Parmesan
Salt and pepper to taste

Directions:

Mix the tomato sauce with chili powder and basil.
Layer the eggplants, tomato sauce and Parmesan in your slow cooker, adding salt and pepper as needed.
Cover and cook on low settings for 4 hours.
Serve the bake warm and fresh.

Ginger Teriyaki Eggplant

Time: 2 1/4 hours   Servings: 4

Ingredients:

1 large eggplant, peeled and cubed
6 oz. firm tofu, cubed
2 tablespoons olive oil
4 garlic cloves, minced
1 teaspoon grated ginger
2 shallots, sliced

1 teaspoon Worcestershire sauce
1 tablespoon soy sauce
1/2 teaspoon cumin seeds
1/4 teaspoon fennel seeds
Salt and pepper to taste

Directions:

Heat the oil in a skillet and add the tofu. Cook on all sides until golden and crusty. Transfer in your slow cooker.
Add the eggplant and the remaining ingredients and season with salt and pepper.
Cook on high settings for 2 hours.
Serve the eggplant warm and fresh.

Honey Orange Glazed Tofu

Time: 4 1/4 hours   Servings: 4

Ingredients:

12 oz. firm tofu, cubed
1 tablespoon grated ginger
1 garlic clove, minced
1 orange, zested and juiced

2 tablespoons soy sauce
1 teaspoon Worcestershire sauce
1/4 cup vegetable stock

Directions:

Combine all the ingredients in your slow cooker.
Cover and cook on low settings for 4 hours.
The tofu is best served warm with your favorite side dish.

CHUNKY PASTA SAUCE

Time: 8 1/4 hours   Servings: 8

Ingredients:
1 can (15 oz.) black beans, drained
1 can (15 oz.) kidney beans
2 cups tomato sauce
1 cup fire roasted tomatoes
1 cup frozen corn
1 cup green peas

1 celery stalk, sliced
1 teaspoon cumin powder
1 teaspoon dried oregano
1 cup vegetable stock
Salt and pepper to taste

Directions:
Combine all the ingredients in your crock pot.
Add salt and pepper to taste and cook on low settings for 8 hours.
Serve the sauce right away or freeze it into individual portions for later serving.

PARMESAN ARTICHOKES

Time: 4 1/4 hours   Servings: 2

Ingredients:
2 large artichokes
1/4 cup breadcrumbs

1/2 cup grated Parmesan
1/2 cup vegetable stock

Directions:
Cut and clean the artichokes.
Mix the breadcrumbs and cheese in a bowl.
Top each artichoke with this mixture and rub it well to make sure it sticks to the artichoke.
Place the artichokes in a crock pot and add the stock.
Cook on low settings for 4 hours.
Serve the artichokes warm.

GLAZED BEETS

Time: 6 1/4 hours   Servings: 6

Ingredients:
6 medium beets, peeled and sliced
2 tablespoons olive oil
1 tablespoon brown sugar
1 teaspoon orange zest
1/2 cup fresh orange juice

1/2 teaspoon cumin seeds
1/4 teaspoon fennel seeds
1/2 teaspoon salt
2 tablespoons balsamic vinegar

Directions:
Combine all the ingredients in your crock pot.
Cook on low settings for 6 hours.
The beets are best served warm or chilled.

Hoisin Tofu

Time: 6 1/4 hours   Servings: 6

Ingredients:
12 oz. firm tofu, sliced
1/4 cup smooth peanut butter
1/4 cup soy sauce
2 tablespoons canola oil

2 garlic cloves
1/4 teaspoon chili powder
1/4 teaspoon cumin powder
1/2 cup water

Directions:
Combine the peanut butter, soy sauce, canola oil, garlic, chili powder, cumin powder and water in your blender. Pulse until smooth.
Mix the tofu and sauce in your crock pot.
Cover and cook on low settings for 6 hours.
Serve the tofu warm with your favorite side dish.

Bacon Brussels Sprouts

Time: 6 1/4 hours   Servings: 6

Ingredients:
2 pounds Brussels sprouts, halved
6 bacon slices, chopped

1/2 cup vegetable stock
Salt and pepper to taste

Directions:
Cook the bacon in a skillet until crisp.
Combine all the ingredients in your crock pot, adding salt and pepper to taste.
Cook on low settings for 6 hours.
Serve the sprouts warm or chilled.

Balsamic Roasted Root Vegetables

Time: 3 1/4 hours   Servings: 4

Ingredients:
1/2 pound baby carrots
2 sweet potatoes, peeled and cubed
2 parsnips, sliced
1 turnip, peeled and sliced
1 large red onion, sliced

2 tablespoons olive oil
1 tablespoon brown sugar
2 tablespoons balsamic vinegar
1/4 cup vegetable stock
Salt and pepper to taste

Directions:
Combine all the ingredients in your crock pot.
Add salt and pepper to taste and cook on high settings for 3 hours.
Serve the vegetables warm and fresh.

CRANBERRY SAUCE

Time: 6 1/4 hours

Servings: 8

Ingredients:

1 pound fresh or frozen cranberries
1/2 cup brown sugar
1 cup fresh orange juice
1 teaspoon grated ginger
1/2 teaspoon cumin powder

1 teaspoon orange zest
1/4 cup red wine
1 red onion, chopped
Salt and pepper to taste

Directions:

Combine all the ingredients in your slow cooker, adding salt and pepper to taste.
Cook the sauce on low settings for 6 hours.
Serve the sauce fresh or freeze it into individual portions.

ALFREDO GREEN BEAN CASSEROLE

Time: 3 1/4 hours

Servings: 6

Ingredients:

1 pound green beans, trimmed and chopped
1 cup Alfredo sauce
1 cup water chestnuts, chopped
2 cups sliced mushrooms

1/2 cup grated Parmesan cheese
1 shallot, sliced
1/2 cup vegetable stock
Salt and pepper to taste

Directions:

Combine all the ingredients in a crock pot. Add salt and pepper to taste.
Cook on high settings for 3 hours.
Serve the casserole warm and fresh.

PEPPERCORN ARTICHOKE CASSEROLE

Time: 6 1/4 hours

Servings: 6

Ingredients:

1 jar artichoke hearts, drained and chopped
4 peppercorns, chopped
1 tablespoon lemon juice
2 celery stalks, sliced

1 cup vegetable stock
1 cup Alfredo sauce
Salt and pepper to taste

Directions:

Combine all the ingredients in your crock pot.
Add salt and pepper to taste and cook on low settings for 6 hours.
The dish is best served warm, but it can also be re-heated.

Spicy Salsa Red Beans

Time: 6 1/4 hours

Servings: 8

Ingredients:

1 pound dried black beans, rinsed
2 cups spicy red salsa
1/2 teaspoon cumin seeds
1/4 teaspoon fennel seeds

2 tablespoons tomato paste
2 cups vegetable stock
Salt and pepper to taste

Directions:

Combine all the ingredients in your crock pot.
Add salt and pepper and cover with a lid.
Cook on low settings for 6 hours.
Serve the beans warm or chilled.

All Green Asparagus Casserole

Time: 4 1/4 hours

Servings: 6

Ingredients:

1 bunch asparagus, trimmed and chopped
1 can cream of celery soup
1 cup green peas
2 cups fresh spinach

2 celery stalks, sliced
Salt and pepper to taste
1/2 cup breadcrumbs
1 cup grated Cheddar

Directions:

Combine the asparagus, celery soup, green peas, spinach and celery in your slow cooker.
Add salt and pepper as needed.
Top with breadcrumbs and cheese and cook on low settings for 4 hours.
Serve the casserole warm and fresh.

Mustard Baked Potatoes

Time: 4 1/4 hours

Servings: 6

Ingredients:

3 pounds potatoes, peeled and cubed
1 tablespoon Dijon mustard
1/4 cup vegetable stock

1/2 teaspoon cumin seeds
4 garlic cloves, minced
1/2 teaspoon salt

Directions:

Combine all the ingredients in your slow cooker. Mix well until evenly coated.
Cover with a lid and cook on low settings for 4 hours.
Serve the potatoes warm.

Molasses Baked Beans

Time: 6 1/4 hours   Servings: 6

Ingredients:
1 pound dried white beans, rinsed
4 cups water
2 tablespoons molasses
1 tablespoon brown sugar

2 tablespoons tomato paste
1 cup diced tomatoes
1 teaspoon mustard seeds
Salt and pepper to taste

Directions:
Combine all the ingredients in your crock pot. Season with salt and pepper to taste.
Cover with a lid and cook on low settings for 6 hours.
Serve the beans warm and fresh.

Bacon Baked Beans

Time: 8 1/4 hours   Servings: 6

Ingredients:
6 bacon slices, chopped
1 tablespoon olive oil
1 pound black beans, rinsed
1 large onion, chopped
1 celery stalk, diced
1 carrot, diced

1 cup tomato sauce
1 cup fire roasted tomatoes
1/4 teaspoon cumin seeds
1/4 teaspoon chili powder
Salt and pepper to taste

Directions:
Heat the oil in a skillet and add the bacon. Cook until crisp then transfer in your slow cooker.
Add the remaining ingredients and adjust the taste with salt and pepper.
Cook on low settings for 8 hours.
Serve the beans warm.

Ketchup Bean Stew

Time: 4 1/4 hours   Servings: 6

Ingredients:
2 cans (15 oz. each) white beans, drained
1 tablespoon brown sugar
1 cup ketchup
1 teaspoon Dijon mustard

1/2 cup vegetable stock
Salt and pepper to taste

Directions:
Combine all the ingredients in your slow cooker.
Add salt and pepper to taste and cover. Cook on low settings for 4 hours.
Serve the stew warm and fresh.

BLACK EYED PEAS AND OKRA STEW

Time: 6 1/4 hours

Servings: 8

Ingredients:

2 cups dried black eyes peas, rinsed
2 cups water
1 cup tomato sauce
2 large onions, chopped
2 cups chopped okra

2 red bell peppers, cored and diced
1 celery stalk, sliced
1 jalapeno peppers, chopped
Salt and pepper to taste

Directions:

Combine all the ingredients in your crock pot.
Add salt and pepper to taste and cook on low settings for 6 hours.
Serve the dish warm and fresh.

GREEN ONION BARLEY RISOTTO

Time: 2 1/4 hours

Servings: 6

Ingredients:

1 cup pearl barley
2 cups vegetable stock
2 cups sliced mushrooms

4 green onions, chopped
Salt and pepper to taste
1/2 cup grated Parmesan

Directions:

Combine the barley, stock, mushrooms and green onions in your crock pot.
Add salt and pepper and cover with a lid.
Cook on high settings for 2 hours.
When done, stir in the cheese and serve the risotto warm and fresh.

CUMIN RED CABBAGE

Time: 6 1/4 hours

Servings: 6

Ingredients:

1 large head red cabbage, shredded
1 red onion, sliced
2 red apples, cored and diced
2 tablespoons olive oil

1/2 cup red wine
1/4 cup vegetable stock
1 teaspoon cumin seeds
Salt and pepper to taste

Directions:

Combine all the ingredients in your crock pot.
Add salt and pepper to taste and cook on low settings for 6 hours.
Serve the cabbage warm or fresh.

BUTTERED BROCCOLI

Time: 1 1/2 hours   Servings: 4

Ingredients:

2 heads broccoli, cut into florets   4 tablespoons butter
1 shallot, sliced   Salt and pepper to taste
2 garlic cloves, chopped

Directions:

Combine all the ingredients in your slow cooker.
Add enough salt and pepper and cook the broccoli on high settings for 1 1/4 hours.
Serve the broccoli warm and fresh.

HERBED BROCCOLI SOUFFLÉ

Time: 2 1/4 hours   Servings: 6

Ingredients:

1 1/2 pounds fresh or frozen broccoli   2 eggs, beaten
1 can cream of celery soup   1 cup grated Cheddar
1 cup mayonnaise   Salt and pepper to taste
1/2 teaspoon onion powder   1 cup crushed crackers
1/2 teaspoon garlic powder

Directions:

Cook the broccoli in a pot of hot water for 10 minutes. Drain and place in a food processor. Pulse until ground.
Stir in the celery soup, mayonnaise, onion powder, garlic powder and eggs.
Pour the mixture in your greased crock pot.
Top with crackers and cheese and cook on high settings for 2 hours.
Serve the soufflé right away.

LAYERED CARROT PUDDING

Time: 6 1/4 hours   Servings: 6

Ingredients:

6 large carrots, finely sliced   1 cup whole milk
2 sweet onions, sliced   Salt and pepper to taste
1 pinch nutmeg   1 cup grated Cheddar
4 eggs, beaten

Directions:

Layer the carrots and onions in your crock pot.
Season with salt, pepper and nutmeg.
Mix the eggs with milk and pour over the carrots.
Top with grated cheese and cook on low settings for 6 hours.
Serve the pudding warm and fresh, although it tastes great chilled as well.

*O*RANGE MARMALADE GLAZED CARROTS

Time: 4 1/4 hours   Servings: 4

Ingredients:

20 oz. baby carrots
1/4 cup orange marmalade
1/4 teaspoon chili powder
1 pinch nutmeg

2 tablespoons water
1/4 teaspoon cumin powder
Salt and pepper to taste

Directions:

Combine the carrots and the remaining ingredients in your slow cooker.
Add salt and pepper and cover with a lid.
Cook on low settings for 4 hours.
Serve the glazed carrots warm or chilled.

*B*UTTER SPRING VEGETABLES

Time: 4 1/4 hours   Servings: 6

Ingredients:

2 carrots, sliced
2 cups snap peas
1/2 pound green beans, trimmed and chopped
1 sweet onion, sliced
1 celery stalk, sliced

1 cup green peas

3 tablespoons butter
Salt and pepper to taste

Directions:

Combine the carrots, snap peas, green peas, green beans, onion and celery.
Add the butter and season with salt and pepper.
Cook on low settings for 4 hours.
Serve the vegetables warm.

*C*ARROT SPINACH WHITE BEAN STEW

Time: 2 1/4 hours   Servings: 6

Ingredients:

2 large carrots, sliced
1 can (15 oz.) white beans, drained
4 cups fresh spinach, shredded
1/4 teaspoon cumin seeds
1/4 teaspoon chili powder

1 pound potatoes, peeled and cubed
1 ripe heirloom tomato, peeled and diced
1/2 cup vegetable stock
Salt and pepper to taste

Directions:

Combine all the ingredients in your slow cooker, adding salt and pepper to fit your taste.
Cover the pot with a lid and cook on high settings for 2 hours.
Serve the stew warm or chilled.

Chicken Recipes

Chicken Layered Potato Casserole

Time: 6 1/2 hours   Servings: 8

Ingredients:

2 pounds potatoes, peeled and sliced
2 chicken breasts, cut into thin strips
1/4 teaspoon chili powder
1/4 teaspoon cumin powder
1/2 teaspoon garlic powder

1/4 teaspoon onion powder
1 cup heavy cream
1 1/2 cups whole milk
Salt and pepper to taste

Directions:

Combine the cream, milk, chili powder, cumin powder, garlic powder and onion powder. Layer the potatoes and chicken in your slow cooker. Pour the milk mix over the potatoes and chicken, seasoning with salt and pepper. Cook on low settings for 6 hours. Serve the casserole warm or chilled.

Creamy Chicken Stew

Time: 6 1/4 hours   Servings: 6

Ingredients:

3 chicken breasts, cubed
2 tablespoons olive oil
1 can condensed cream of chicken soup
1 celery stalk, sliced
1 shallot, sliced

1/2 head cauliflower, cut into florets
2 potatoes, peeled and cubed
1 cup vegetable stock
Salt and pepper to taste

Directions:

Heat the oil in a skillet and add the chicken. Cook for a few minutes until golden on all sides. Transfer the chicken in your crock pot. Add the remaining ingredients and season with salt and pepper. Cook the stew on low settings for 6 hours. Serve the stew warm and fresh.

Orange Glazed Chicken

Time: 6 1/4 hours   Servings: 6

Ingredients:

6 chicken thighs
1 orange, zested and juiced
2 tablespoons olive oil
2 sweet onions, sliced
1 cup vegetable stock

1 tablespoon cornstarch
1 tablespoon balsamic vinegar
1/2 teaspoon Worcestershire sauce
1/4 teaspoon cumin powder
Salt and pepper to taste

Directions:

Combine the chicken, orange zest, orange juice, olive oil, onions, stock, cornstarch, balsamic vinegar, Worcestershire sauce and cumin powder in your crock pot.
Add salt and pepper to taste and cook the chicken on low settings for 6 hours.
Serve the chicken warm and fresh.

Spiced Chicken over Wild Rice

Time: 7 1/4 hours   Servings: 6

Ingredients:

6 chicken thighs
1 teaspoon cumin powder
1/2 teaspoon chili powder
Salt and pepper to taste
1 cup wild rice

2 celery stalk, diced
1 carrot, diced
2 cups sliced mushrooms
2 cups vegetable stock

Directions:

Season the chicken with cumin powder, chili, salt and pepper. Combine the rice, celery, carrot, mushrooms, stock, salt and pepper in your crock pot. Place the chicken on top and cook on low settings for 7 hours. Serve the chicken and rice warm or chilled.

Chicken Garbanzo Curry

Time: 3 1/4 hours   Servings: 6

Ingredients:

2 chicken breasts, cubed
2 tablespoons olive oil
1 sweet onion, chopped
1 celery stalk, sliced
1 carrot, sliced
1/2 head cauliflower, cut into florets

1 can (15 oz.) garbanzo beans, drained
1 cup vegetable stock
1/2 cup coconut milk
1 teaspoon curry powder
1/4 teaspoon chili powder
Salt and pepper to taste

Directions:

Heat the oil in a skillet and add the chicken. Cook for a few minutes on all sides until golden brown. Transfer the chicken in your slow cooker then add the rest of the ingredients. Season with salt and pepper and cook on high settings for 3 hours. Serve the curry warm and fresh.

Chicken Barley Squash Salad

Time: 6 1/4 hours   Servings: 8

Ingredients:

1 pound ground chicken
2 tablespoons olive oil
1 sweet onion, chopped
2 garlic cloves, chopped
1 cup pearl barley
1 cup green peas

2 cups butternut squash cubes
2 cups vegetable stock
Salt and pepper to taste
2 tablespoons chopped parsley
Lemon juice for serving

Directions:

Heat the oil in a skillet and add the chicken. Cook for a few minutes then transfer in your crock pot.
Stir in the remaining ingredients, adjusting the taste with salt and pepper.

Cook on low settings for 6 hours.
Serve the dish warm and fresh, drizzled with lemon juice.

CHICKEN CAULIFLOWER GRATIN

Time: 6 1/4 hours   Servings: 6

Ingredients:

1 head cauliflower, cut into florets
2 chicken breasts, cubed
1/2 teaspoon garlic powder
1 pinch cayenne pepper

1 can condensed cream of chicken soup
Salt and pepper to taste
1 1/2 cups grated Cheddar

Directions:

Combine the cauliflower, chicken, garlic powder, cayenne pepper, chicken soup, salt and pepper in your crock pot.
Top with grated cheese and cook on low settings for 6 hours. Serve the gratin warm and fresh.

VEGETABLE BRAISED CHICKEN

Time: 7 1/2 hours   Servings: 8

Ingredients:

4 chicken breasts, cut into smaller pieces
2 carrots, sliced
2 celery stalks, sliced
1 parsnip, sliced
2 large potatoes, peeled and cubed

2 cups vegetable stock
Salt and pepper to taste
1 thyme sprig
1 rosemary sprig

Directions:

Combine all the ingredients in your slow cooker.
Add salt and pepper and cover with a lid.
Cook on low settings for 7 hours.
Serve the chicken warm and fresh.

PARMESAN CHICKEN

Time: 6 1/4 hours   Servings: 4

Ingredients:

4 chicken breasts
1/2 teaspoon cumin powder
1/4 teaspoon chili powder
1 teaspoon dried thyme

Salt and pepper to taste
1/2 cup chicken stock
1 1/2 cups grated Parmesan

Directions:

Season the chicken with salt, pepper, cumin powder, chili powder and thyme and place it in your crock pot.
Add the stock in the pot as well and top the chicken with grated cheese.
Cook on low settings for 6 hours. Serve the chicken warm.

Thai Chicken Vegetable Medley

Time: 4 1/4 hours   Servings: 6

Ingredients:

2 chicken breasts, cut into strips
2 zucchinis, sliced
2 red bell peppers, cored and sliced
2 heirloom tomatoes, peeled and diced
2 cups button mushrooms
4 garlic cloves, minced

1 leek, sliced
1 tablespoon red Thai curry paste
1 cup coconut milk
1/2 cup vegetable stock
Salt and pepper to taste

Directions:

Combine all the ingredients in your crock pot. Add salt and pepper to taste and cover with a lid. Cook on low settings for 4 hours. Serve the dish warm or chilled.

Cider Braised Chicken

Time: 8 1/4 hours   Servings: 8

Ingredients:

1 whole chicken, cut into smaller pieces
Salt and pepper to taste
1 teaspoon dried thyme
1 teaspoon dried oregano

1 teaspoon cumin powder
Salt to taste
1 1/2 cups apple cider

Directions:

Season the chicken with salt, thyme, oregano and cumin powder and place it in your crock pot.
Add the apple cider and cook on low settings for 8 hours.
Serve the chicken warm with your favorite side dish.

Multigrain Chicken Pilaf

Time: 6 1/2 hours   Servings: 8

Ingredients:

2 chicken breasts, cubed
1/2 cup wild rice
1/2 cup pearl barley
1 leek, sliced
2 garlic cloves, chopped
1 cup frozen edamame
1 cup green peas

1 sweet potato, peeled and cubed
2 cups vegetable stock
Salt and pepper to taste
1/2 teaspoon dried sage
1/2 teaspoon dried oregano
1 tablespoon chopped parsley for serving

Directions:

Combine the chicken, wild rice, pearl barley, leek, garlic, edamame, green peas, sweet potatoes, stock, sage and oregano in your crock pot. Add salt and pepper to taste and cook on low settings for 6 hours.
When done, stir in the parsley and serve the pilaf warm and fresh.

CHICKEN SWEET POTATO STEW

Time: 3 1/4 hours   Servings: 6

Ingredients:
2 chicken breasts, cubed
2 tablespoons butter
2 shallots, chopped
2 pounds sweet potatoes, peeled and cubed
1/2 teaspoon cumin powder

1/2 teaspoon garlic powder
1 pinch cinnamon powder
1 1/2 cups vegetable stock
Salt and pepper to taste

Directions:
Combine the chicken, butter and shallots in your crock pot. Cook for 5 minutes then transfer in your crock pot.
Add the sweet potatoes, cumin powder, garlic and cinnamon, as well as stock, salt and pepper.
Cook on high settings for 3 hours.
Serve the stew warm or chilled.

CREAM CHEESE CHICKEN

Time: 4 1/4 hours   Servings: 4

Ingredients:
4 chicken breasts
1 teaspoon dried Italian herbs
2 tablespoons butter
1 sweet onion, chopped
4 garlic cloves, minced

1 can cream of chicken soup
1 cup cream cheese
1/2 cup chicken stock
Salt and pepper to taste

Directions:
Season the chicken with salt, pepper and Italian herbs. Melt the butter in a skillet and add the chicken. Cook on each side until golden then transfer the chicken in your crock pot.
Add the remaining ingredients and adjust the taste with salt and pepper.
Cook on low settings for 4 hours.
Serve the chicken warm.

PULLED CHICKEN

Time: 8 1/4 hours   Servings: 8

Ingredients:
4 chicken breasts
2 large sweet onions, sliced
1 teaspoon grated ginger

1 cup apple cider
1 cup BBQ sauce
Salt and pepper to taste

Directions:
Combine all the ingredients in your crock pot, adjusting the taste with salt and pepper as needed.
Cook on low settings for 8 hours. When done, shred the chicken into fine threads using two forks.
Serve the chicken warm.

Cheesy Chicken

Time: 2 1/4 hours   Servings: 2

Ingredients:

2 chicken breasts
1 cup cream of chicken soup
1 cup grated Cheddar

1/4 teaspoon garlic powder
Salt and pepper to taste

Directions:

Combine all the ingredients in your crock pot.
Add salt and pepper to taste and cover with a lid.
Cook on high settings for 2 hours.
Serve the chicken warm, topped with plenty of cheesy sauce.

Garden Chicken Stew

Time: 8 1/2 hours   Servings: 8

Ingredients:

3 chicken breasts, cubed
2 tablespoons canola oil
1 onion, chopped
2 carrots, sliced
2 celery stalks, sliced
2 ripe tomatoes, peeled and diced
1 can (15 oz.) white beans, drained

2 cups chicken stock
1 teaspoon dried oregano
1/2 teaspoon dried basil
1 cup tomato sauce
4 large potatoes, peeled and cubed
Salt and pepper to taste

Directions:

Combine all the ingredients in your crock pot. Adjust the taste with salt and pepper and cook the stew on low settings for 8 hours until the chicken and veggies are tender.
Serve the stew warm and fresh.

Swiss Cheese Saucy Chicken

Time: 3 1/4 hours   Servings: 4

Ingredients:

4 boneless chicken breasts
1 celery stalk, sliced
1 shallot, sliced
Salt and pepper to taste

1 can cream of mushrooms soup
1/2 cup chicken stock
1 cup grated Swiss cheese

Directions:

Season the chicken with salt and pepper.
Place the chicken in your crock pot and add the remaining ingredients.
Cook the dish on high settings for 3 hours.
Serve the chicken warm with your favorite side dish.

GARLICKY BUTTER ROASTED CHICKEN

Time: 8 1/4 hours   Servings: 8

Ingredients:
1 whole chicken
1/4 cup butter, softened
6 garlic cloves, minced
2 tablespoons chopped parsley

1 teaspoon dried sage
Salt and pepper to taste
1/2 cup chicken stock

Directions:
Mix the butter, garlic, parsley, sage, salt and pepper in your crock pot. Place the chicken on your working board and carefully lift up the skin on its breast and thighs, stuffing that space with the butter mixture. Place the chicken in your crock pot. Add the stock and cook on low settings for 8 hours. Serve the chicken fresh with your favorite side dish.

BROWN SUGAR GLAZED CHICKEN

Time: 6 1/4 hours   Servings: 4

Ingredients:
4 chicken thighs
2 tablespoons brown sugar
1 teaspoon cumin powder
1/2 teaspoon chili powder

1/2 teaspoon garlic powder
2 tablespoons balsamic vinegar
1 tablespoon soy sauce
1/2 cup chicken stock

Directions:
Mix the brown sugar, cumin powder, chili, balsamic vinegar and soy sauce in a bowl. Spread this mixture over the chicken and rub it well into the skin. Place the chicken in your crock pot. Add the stock in the pot and cook on low settings for 6 hours. Serve the chicken warm.

CHICKEN TIKKA MASALA

Time: 2 1/2 hours   Servings: 4

Ingredients:
4 chicken thighs
2 tablespoons canola oil
2 shallots, chopped
4 garlic cloves, minced
2 tablespoons tomato paste
1 tablespoon garam masala
1 cup diced tomatoes

1 lime, juiced
1 cup coconut milk
1/2 cup chicken stock
Salt and pepper to taste
Cooked rice for serving
Chopped cilantro for serving

Directions:
Heat the oil in a skillet and add the chicken. Cook on all sides until golden then transfer the chicken in your slow cooker. Add the rest of the ingredients and season with salt and pepper. Cook on high settings for 2 hours. Serve the tikka masala warm, topped with chopped cilantro, over cooked rice.

Green Pea Chicken with Biscuit Topping

Time: 6 1/2 hours   Servings: 6

Ingredients:

1 shallot, chopped
1 leek, sliced
2 garlic cloves, chopped
2 chicken breasts, cubed
1 1/2 cups green peas
1/2 pound baby carrots
1 tablespoon cornstarch

1 cup vegetables tock
1/4 cup white wine
1 cup all-purpose flour
1/2 cup butter, chilled and cubed
1/2 cup buttermilk, chilled
Salt and pepper to taste

Directions:

Combine the shallot, leek, garlic, chicken, green peas, baby carrots, cornstarch, stock and wine in your crock pot. Season with salt and pepper.

For the topping, mix the flour, butter, buttermilk, salt and pepper in your food processor.

Pulse just until mixed then spoon the mixture over the vegetables in the crock pot.

Cover and cook on low settings for 6 hours. Serve the dish warm.

Creamy Chicken and Mushroom Pot Pie

Time: 6 1/4 hours   Servings: 6

Ingredients:

4 cups sliced cremini mushrooms
4 carrots, sliced
2 chicken breasts, cubed
1 large onion, chopped
1 cup frozen peas

1 cup vegetable stock
Salt and pepper to taste
1/2 teaspoon dried thyme
1 sheet puff pastry

Directions:

Combine the mushrooms, carrots, chicken, onion, peas, stock and thyme in your crock pot.

Add salt and pepper to taste then top with the puff pastry.

Cover with a lid and cook on low settings for 6 hours.

Serve the pot pie warm and fresh.

Curry Braised Chicken

Time: 8 1/4 hours   Servings: 6

Ingredients:

6 chicken thighs
1 tablespoon grated ginger
1 teaspoon curry powder
1 teaspoon garlic powder
1/2 teaspoon onion powder
1/2 teaspoon cumin powder

1/4 teaspoon chili powder
1/2 cup plain yogurt
1 cup chicken stock
Salt and pepper to taste
Cooked white rice for serving

Directions:

Season the chicken with ginger, curry powder, garlic powder, onion, cumin and chili powder.
Place the chicken in your crock pot then add the yogurt and stock.
Adjust the taste with salt and pepper and cook on low settings for 8 hours.
Serve the chicken warm over cooked white rice.

Bacon Chicken Stew

Time: 6 1/2 hours   Servings: 6

Ingredients:

6 chicken thighs
6 bacon slices, chopped
1 sweet onion, chopped
2 garlic cloves, chopped
2 large carrots, sliced
2 celery stalk, sliced
1 cup green peas

2 cups sliced mushrooms
1/4 cup dry white wine
1 cup vegetable stock
1/2 cup heavy cream
Salt and pepper to taste
1 thyme sprig
1 rosemary sprig

Directions:

Heat a skillet over medium flame. Add the bacon and cook until crisp.
Transfer the bacon in your crock pot and add the remaining ingredients.
Season with salt and pepper and cook on low settings for 6 hours.
Serve the chicken warm.

Soy Braised Chicken

Time: 3 1/4 hours   Servings: 6

Ingredients:

6 chicken thighs
2 shallots, sliced
2 garlic cloves, chopped
1/4 cup apple cider
1/4 cup soy sauce

1 bay leaf
1 tablespoon brown sugar
1/2 teaspoon cayenne pepper
Salt and pepper to taste
Cooked white rice for serving

Directions:

Combine the chicken, shallots, garlic cloves, apple cider, soy sauce, leaf, brown sugar and cayenne pepper in your crock pot.
Adjust the taste with salt and pepper if needed and cook on high settings for 3 hours.
Serve the chicken warm.

*F*ENNEL BRAISED CHICKEN

Time: 6 1/4 hours

Servings: 4

Ingredients:

4 chicken breasts
1 fennel bulb, sliced
1 sweet onion, sliced
2 carrots, sliced

2 oranges, juiced
1 bay leaf
1 1/2 cups chicken stock
Salt and pepper to taste

Directions:

Combine all the ingredients in your crock pot.
Add salt and pepper to taste and cook on low settings for 6 hours.
Serve the chicken warm.

*S*ESAME GLAZED CHICKEN

Time: 3 1/4 hours

Servings: 6

Ingredients:

6 chicken thighs
1 tablespoon sesame oil
2 tablespoon soy sauce
1 tablespoon brown sugar
2 tablespoons fresh orange juice

2 tablespoons hoisin sauce
1 teaspoon grated ginger
1 tablespoon cornstarch
2 tablespoons water
1 tablespoon sesame seeds

Directions:

Combine all the ingredients in your crock pot.
Cook the chicken on high settings for 3 hours.
Serve the chicken warm with your favorite side dish.

*S*WEET GLAZED CHICKEN DRUMSTICKS

Time: 5 1/4 hours

Servings: 4

Ingredients:

2 pounds chicken drumsticks
1 teaspoon grated ginger
1 cup pineapple juice
2 tablespoons soy sauce
2 tablespoons brown sugar

1/4 teaspoon chili powder
2 green onions, chopped
1/4 cup chicken stock
White rice for serving

Directions:

Combine the drumsticks, ginger, pineapple juice, soy sauce, brown sugar, chili, stock and green onions in your crock pot.
Add salt and pepper to taste and cook on low settings for 5 hours.
Serve the dish warm, over cooked white rice.

CHICKEN SHRIMP JAMBALAYA

Time: 8 1/4 hours

Servings: 8

Ingredients:

2 tablespoons olive oil
1 1/2 pounds skinless chicken breasts, cubed
2 large onions, chopped
2 red bell peppers, cored and diced
1 celery stalk, sliced
2 garlic cloves, chopped

1/2 teaspoon dried oregano
1 cup diced tomato
1 1/2 cups chicken stock
Salt and pepper to taste
1 pound fresh shrimps, peeled and cleaned
Cooked white rice for serving

Directions:

Heat the oil in a skillet and add the chicken. Cook for 5 minutes until golden then transfer in your crock pot.
Add the onions, bell peppers, celery, garlic, oregano, tomato and stock.
Add salt and pepper to taste and cook on low settings for 6 hours.
At this point, add the shrimps and cook for 2 more hours.
Serve the jambalaya warm and fresh.

CHICKEN BLACK OLIVE STEW

Time: 6 1/4 hours

Servings: 6

Ingredients:

6 chicken thighs
2 tablespoons olive oil
4 garlic cloves, minced
1 shallot, chopped
1/4 cup dry white wine
2 tablespoons tomato paste

1/2 cup tomato sauce
1/4 teaspoon chili powder
1 can (28 oz.) diced tomatoes
1/2 cup pitted black olives
1/2 cup pitted Kalamata olives
Salt and pepper to taste

Directions:

Combine all the ingredients in your crock pot, adding salt and pepper to taste.
Cook on low settings for 6 hours.
The dish is best served warm.

CHICKEN STROGANOFF

Time: 6 1/4 hours

Servings: 6

Ingredients:

3 chicken breasts, cubed
2 tablespoons butter
2 celery stalks, sliced
2 shallots, chopped
2 garlic cloves, chopped
1 teaspoon dried Italian herbs
1 cup cream cheese

2 cups sliced mushrooms
1 cup vegetable stock
Salt and pepper to taste
Cooked pasta of your choice for serving

Directions:

Melt the butter in a skillet and add the chicken. Cook on all sides until golden then transfer in your crock pot.
Add the remaining ingredients and season with salt and pepper. Cook on low settings for 6 hours.
The stroganoff tastes better warm over cooked pasta of your choice.

Adobo Chicken with Bok Choy

Time: 6 1/2 hours   Servings: 4

Ingredients:

4 chicken breasts
4 garlic cloves, minced
1 sweet onion, chopped
2 tablespoons soy sauce

1 tablespoon brown sugar
1 teaspoon paprika
1 cup chicken stock
1 head bok choy, shredded

Directions:

Mix the chicken, garlic, onion, soy sauce, brown sugar, paprika and stock in your crock pot.
Cook on low settings for 4 hours then add the bok choy and continue cooking for 2 additional hours.
Serve the chicken and bok choy warm.

Creole Chicken

Time: 8 1/4 hours   Servings: 6

Ingredients:

4 chicken breasts, cubed
2 tablespoons creole seasoning
1 can fire roasted tomatoes
1 celery stalk, sliced
2 large onions, chopped

4 garlic cloves, chopped
1 jalapeno pepper, chopped
Salt and pepper to taste
1/2 cup chicken stock

Directions:

Combine all the ingredients in your slow cooker, adjusting the taste with salt and pepper.
Cook the chicken on low settings for 8 hours. Serve the chicken warm with your favorite side dish.

Lemon Garlic Roasted Chicken

Time: 6 1/4 hours   Servings: 6

Ingredients:

6 chicken thighs
1 lemon, sliced
6 garlic cloves, chopped
2 tablespoons butter

1/2 cup chicken stock
1 thyme sprig
1 rosemary sprig

Directions:

Place the chicken in your crock pot and season it with salt and pepper. Top the chicken with lemon slices, garlic, butter, stock, thyme sprig and rosemary sprig. Cook on low settings for 6 hours. Serve the chicken warm and fresh.

PAPRIKA CHICKEN WINGS

Time: 3 1/4 hours

Servings: 4

Ingredients:

2 pounds chicken wings
1 1/2 teaspoons smoked paprika
1/2 teaspoon sweet paprika

1 tablespoon honey
Salt and pepper to taste
1/2 cup chicken stock

Directions:

Combine the chicken wings, paprika, honey, salt and pepper in your crock pot.
Add the stock then cover and cook on high settings for 3 hours.
Serve the chicken warm and fresh with your favorite side dish.

SPINACH CHICKEN

Time: 6 1/2 hours

Servings: 6

Ingredients:

6 chicken thighs, boneless
2 tablespoons canola oil
1/4 cup chopped cilantro
1/4 cup chopped parsley
3 cups fresh spinach, shredded
2 potatoes, peeled and cubed

1 cup vegetable stock
Salt and pepper to taste
1/4 teaspoon cumin powder
1/4 teaspoon chili powder
1/4 teaspoon all-spice powder

Directions:

Combine the chicken and canola oil in a skillet and fry the chicken on all sides until golden.
Transfer the chicken in your crock pot and add the remaining ingredients, including the spices, salt and pepper.
Cook on low settings for 6 hours.
Serve the chicken warm and fresh, although it tastes great chilled as well.

SPICED BUTTER CHICKEN

Time: 6 3/4 hours

Servings: 6

Ingredients:

6 chicken thighs
2 tablespoons butter
1 large onion, chopped
4 garlic cloves, chopped
1 teaspoon curry powder
1 teaspoon garam masala

1/2 teaspoon cumin powder
1/4 teaspoon chili powder
1 1/2 cups coconut milk
Salt and pepper to taste
1/2 cup plain yogurt for serving

Directions:

Heat the butter in your slow cooker. Add the chicken and cook on all sides until golden brown.
Transfer the chicken in your slow cooker and add the remaining ingredients.
Cook on low settings for 6 hours. Serve the chicken warm and fresh.

CORDON BLEU CHICKEN

Time: 6 1/4 hours   Servings: 4

Ingredients:
4 chicken breasts, boneless and skinless
Salt and pepper to taste   4 slices Cheddar cheese
1 teaspoon dried thyme   1/2 cup vegetable stock
4 thick slices ham

Directions:
Season the chicken with salt and pepper and thyme and place it in your crock pot.
Top with a slice of ham and cheese and pour the stock in.
Cook on low settings for 6 hours.
Serve the chicken warm and fresh.

RED WINE CHICKEN AND MUSHROOM STEW

Time: 6 1/2 hours   Servings: 6

Ingredients:
6 chicken thighs   1 cup chicken stock
1 large onion, chopped   1 bay leaf
4 garlic cloves, minced   1 thyme sprig
4 cups sliced mushrooms   Salt and pepper to taste
1/2 cup red wine

Directions:
Combine the chicken, onion, garlic, mushrooms, red wine, stock, bay leaf and thyme in your crock pot.
Add salt and pepper to taste and cook on low settings for 6 hours.
Serve the stew warm and fresh.

TOMATO SOY GLAZED CHICKEN

Time: 8 1/4 hours   Servings: 8

Ingredients:
8 chicken thighs   1 teaspoon chili powder
1/2 cup soy sauce   1/2 cup tomato sauce
2 tablespoons brown sugar

Directions:
Combine all the ingredients in your crock pot.
Cook the chicken on low settings for 8 hours.
Serve the chicken warm and fresh.

MEDLEY VEGETABLE CHICKEN STEW

Time: 8 1/4 hours   Servings: 8

Ingredients:

2 carrots, sliced
1 celery stalk, sliced
1 onion, chopped
4 garlic cloves, chopped
2 sweet potatoes, peeled and cubed
1 can (15 oz.) chickpeas, drained
1/2 teaspoon cumin powder

1/2 teaspoon chili powder
1/2 teaspoon dried oregano
1 can fire roasted tomatoes
8 chicken drumsticks
1 cup vegetable stock
Salt and pepper to taste

Directions:

Combine all the vegetables, spices, chicken and stock in your crock pot.
Season with enough salt and pepper and cook on low settings for 8 hours.
Serve the stew warm and fresh.

BBQ CHICKEN

Time: 8 1/4 hours   Servings: 8

Ingredients:

4 chicken breasts, boneless and skinless,
    halved
1 cup BBQ sauce
1 teaspoon mustard seeds
2 tablespoons lemon juice
1/2 teaspoon garlic powder

2 tablespoons maple syrup
1/2 teaspoon chili powder
1 teaspoon Worcestershire sauce
1/2 cup vegetable stock
Salt and pepper to taste

Directions:

Combine all the ingredients in your crock pot.
Add salt and pepper to taste and cook on low settings for 8 hours.
Serve the chicken warm with your favorite side dish.

SPICY HOT CHICKEN THIGHS

Time: 8 1/4 hours   Servings: 8

Ingredients:

8 chicken thighs
1/4 cup hot sauce
2 tablespoons butter
1/2 teaspoon garlic powder

1/2 cup tomato sauce
1/2 cup vegetable stock
1/2 teaspoon cumin powder
Salt and pepper to taste

Directions:

Combine the chicken thighs with the rest of the ingredients, including salt and pepper in your crock pot.
Cover with a lid and cook on low settings for 8 hours. Serve the chicken thighs warm and fresh.

CREAM CHEESE BUTTON MUSHROOM CHICKEN STEW

Time: 6 1/4 hours   Servings: 6

Ingredients:

2 chicken breasts, cubed
2 tablespoons canola oil
2 garlic cloves, minced
1 shallot, chopped
4 cups button mushrooms

1 cup cream cheese
1 cup vegetable stock
1 thyme sprig
Salt and pepper to taste

Directions:

Heat the oil in a skillet and add the chicken. Cook on medium flame until golden brown, about 5 minutes.
Transfer in your slow cooker and add the remaining ingredients.
Adjust the taste with salt and pepper and cook on low settings for 6 hours.
Serve the chicken stew warm and fresh.

THAI STYLE CHICKEN

Time: 2 1/4 hours   Servings: 4

Ingredients:

2 chicken breasts, cut into thin strips
2 tablespoons soy sauce
1 tablespoon hot sauce

1/4 cup smooth peanut butter
1 tablespoon lime juice
1 teaspoon honey

Directions:

Combine all the ingredients in your crock pot.
Cook the chicken on high settings for 2 hours.
Serve the chicken warm and fresh.

CHICKEN TACO FILLING

Time: 6 1/4 hours   Servings: 8

Ingredients:

4 chicken breasts, halved
1 tablespoon taco seasoning
1 cup chicken stock

1/2 teaspoon celery seeds
1/2 teaspoon cumin powder
1/4 teaspoon chili powder

Directions:

Combine all the ingredients in your crock pot.
Add enough salt and pepper then cover the pot. Cook on low settings for 6 hours.
When done, shred the meat into fine threads and serve it in taco shells.

CHICKEN MOLE

Time: 5 1/4 hours   Servings: 6

Ingredients:

1 onion, finely chopped
1/2 cup golden raisins
4 garlic cloves, chopped
1 chipotle pepper, chopped
2 tablespoons smooth peanut butter

1 can fire roasted tomatoes
1 teaspoon honey
2 pounds chicken drumsticks
Salt and pepper to taste

Directions:

Combine all the ingredients in your slow cooker.
Add salt and pepper and cover with a lid.
Cook on low settings for 5 hours.
Serve the chicken warm and fresh with your favorite side dish.

WHITE CHICKEN CASSOULET

Time: 6 1/4 hours   Servings: 8

Ingredients:

4 chicken breasts, cubed
2 tablespoons canola oil
2 cans (15 oz. each) white beans, drained
2 celery stalks, sliced
2 carrots, sliced

1 large onion, chopped
2 garlic cloves, chopped
1/4 cup dry white wine
1 cup chicken stock
Salt and pepper to taste

Directions:

Heat the oil in a skillet and add the chicken. Cook on all sides for a few minutes until golden then transfer the chicken in your slow cooker. Add the rest of the ingredients in your crock pot and adjust the taste with salt and pepper.
Cook on low settings for 6 hours.
Serve the cassoulet warm and fresh.

LEMON PEPPER CHICKEN

Time: 3 1/4 hours   Servings: 6

Ingredients:

2 pounds chicken drumsticks
2 tablespoons butter
1 lemon, juiced
2 garlic cloves, chopped

1 thyme sprig
1 cup vegetable stock
Salt and pepper to taste

Directions:

Combine all the ingredients in your crock pot.
Add salt and pepper as needed and cook the chicken on high settings for 3 hours.
Serve the chicken warm with your favorite side dish.

Honey Garlic Chicken Thighs with Snap Peas

Time: 6 1/4 hours   Servings: 6

Ingredients:

6 chicken thighs
3 tablespoons honey
1/2 teaspoon cumin powder
1/2 teaspoon smoked paprika

1/2 teaspoon fennel seeds
2 tablespoons soy sauce
1 pound snap peas
1/4 cup vegetable stock

Directions:

Combine the chicken, honey, cumin powder, paprika, fennel seeds and soy sauce in a bowl and mix well until evenly coated.

Mix the snap peas and stock in your crock pot. Place the chicken over the snap peas and cover with a lid.

Cook on low settings for 6 hours.

Serve the chicken and snap peas warm.

Mexican Chicken Stew

Time: 8 1/4 hours   Servings: 8

Ingredients:

4 chicken breasts, cubed
1 can (15 oz.) diced tomatoes
1 cup red salsa
1 can (15 oz.) black beans, drained
1 can (10 oz.) sweet corn, drained

1 teaspoon taco seasoning
1/2 teaspoon chili powder
1 cup chicken stock
1/2 cup cream cheese
Salt and pepper to taste

Directions:

Combine the chicken, tomatoes, red salsa, beans, corn, taco seasoning, chili powder, stock and cream cheese in your slow cooker. Add salt and pepper to taste and cook on low settings for 8 hours.

Serve the stew warm and fresh.

Whole Orange Glazed Chicken

Time: 2 3/4 hours   Servings: 4

Ingredients:

4 chicken thighs
1 large orange, cut into segments
1/2 cup chicken stock
2 tablespoons soy sauce
Cooked white rice for serving

1 tablespoon honey
1 teaspoon hot sauce
1/2 teaspoon sesame seeds

Directions:

Combine all the ingredients in your crock pot.

Cover the pot and cook on high settings for 2 1/2 hours.

Serve the chicken warm over cooked white rice.

Red Salsa Chicken

Time: 8 1/4 hours   Servings: 8

Ingredients:

8 chicken thighs
2 cups red salsa
1/2 cup chicken stock

1 cup grated Cheddar cheese
Salt and pepper to taste

Directions:

Combine the chicken with the salsa and stock in your slow cooker. Add the cheese and cook on low settings for 8 hours. Serve the chicken warm with your favorite side dish.

Arroz Con Pollo

Time: 6 1/4 hours   Servings: 8

Ingredients:

1 cup wild rice
1 cup green peas
2 celery stalks, sliced
1 onion, chopped
1 red chili, chopped
2 ripe tomatoes, peeled and diced

1 cup sliced mushrooms
2 cups vegetable stock
4 chicken breasts, halved
Salt and pepper to taste
1 thyme sprig
1 rosemary sprig

Directions:

Combine the rice, green peas, celery, onion, red chili, tomatoes, mushrooms, stock and chicken in your crock pot. Add the thyme sprig, rosemary, salt and pepper and cook the dish on low settings for 6 hours.
Serve the dish warm and fresh.

Cheesy Chicken Chili

Time: 8 1/4 hours   Servings: 10

Ingredients:

2 pounds boneless, skinless chicken breasts, cubed
2 tablespoons canola oil
4 bacon slices, chopped
2 cups red salsa
1 can (15 oz.) black beans, drained
1 can (15 oz.) kidney beans, drained
1 can (15 oz.) sweet corn, drained
2 celery stalks, sliced

2 large red onions, chopped
1 cup tomato sauce
1 teaspoon chili powder
1 teaspoon cumin powder
1 teaspoon garlic powder
1 1/2 cups chicken stock
Salt and pepper to taste
Grated Cheddar cheese for serving

Directions:

Heat the oil in a skillet and add the bacon. Cook until crisp then stir in the chicken and cook for a few minutes on all sides until golden. Transfer the chicken in your slow cooker and add the remaining ingredients. Season with salt and pepper and cook on low settings for 8 hours. Serve the chili warm, topped with grated cheese.

HOISIN CHICKEN

Time: 2 1/2 hours   Servings: 6

Ingredients:

3 chicken breasts, sliced
1/4 cup hoisin sauce
1/4 cup chicken stock
1 teaspoon sesame oil
2 tablespoons sesame seeds

1 tablespoon soy sauce
2 carrots, sliced
2 garlic cloves, minced
2 green onions, chopped

Directions:

Combine the chicken, hoisin sauce, chicken stock, sesame oil, sesame seeds, soy sauce, carrots and garlic in your crock pot.
Cover and cook on high settings for 2 1/4 hours.
Serve the chicken warm, topped with green onions.

TERIYAKI CHICKEN

Time: 5 1/2 hours   Servings: 6

Ingredients:

2 pounds chicken pieces (drumsticks, wings, thighs)
1/4 cup reduced sodium soy sauce
1/4 cup dry sherry
1/4 cup chicken stock

1 teaspoon sesame oil
1 teaspoon grated ginger
1 teaspoon rice vinegar
2 garlic cloves, minced
2 tablespoons sesame seeds

Directions:

Combine all the ingredients in your crock pot.
Cover and cook on low settings for 5 hours.
Serve the chicken warm and fresh.

JAMAICAN JERK CHICKEN

Time: 7 1/2 hours   Servings: 4

Ingredients:

4 chicken breasts
2 tablespoons jerk seasoning
2 tablespoons olive oil
1/2 cup chicken stock

1/4 cup brewed coffee
1 jalapeno pepper, chopped
Salt and pepper to taste

Directions:

Season the chicken with salt, pepper and jerk seasoning.
Combine the seasoned chicken, stock and coffee, as well as jalapeno pepper in your slow cooker.
Cover with a lid and cook on low settings for 7 hours.
Serve the chicken warm and fresh.

Greek Orzo Chicken

Time: 6 1/2 hours   Servings: 6

Ingredients:

1 cup orzo, rinsed
2 chicken breasts, cubed
1 celery stalk, diced
2 ripe tomatoes, peeled and diced
1 teaspoon dried oregano
1/2 teaspoon dried basil

1/2 teaspoon dried parsley
1/4 cup pitted Kalamata olives
2 cups chicken stock
Salt and pepper to taste
Feta cheese for serving

Directions:

Combine the orzo and the remaining ingredients in your crock pot.
Add salt and pepper to taste and cook on low settings for 6 hours.
Serve the chicken warm and fresh, topped with feta cheese.

Mango Chicken Sauté

Time: 2 3/4 hours   Servings: 6

Ingredients:

2 chicken breasts, cut into thin strips
2 tablespoons canola oil
1 large sweet onion, sliced
4 garlic cloves, chopped
1 large mango, peeled and cubed
1 chipotle pepper, chopped

1/2 teaspoon cumin powder
1/4 teaspoon grated ginger
1 can fire roasted tomatoes
1 cup chicken stock
Salt and pepper to taste

Directions:

Heat the canola oil in your crock pot and add the chicken. Cook on all sides for a few minutes until golden brown.
Transfer the chicken in your crock pot. Add the rest of the ingredients and cover the pot with a lid. Cook the chicken
sauté on high settings for 2 1/2 hours. Serve the dish warm and fresh.

Artichoke Chicken Casserole

Time: 6 1/2 hours   Servings: 6

Ingredients:

2 chicken breasts, cubed
1 jar artichoke hearts, chopped
1 shallot, chopped
2 garlic cloves, chopped
2 red bell peppers, cored and sliced

1 can fire roasted tomatoes
1 teaspoon dried rosemary
1/2 cup chicken stock
2 tablespoons lemon juice
Salt and pepper to taste

Directions:

Combine all the ingredients in your crock pot. Season with salt and pepper according to your taste and cook on low
settings for 6 hours. Serve the casserole warm and fresh.

*I*TALIAN FENNEL BRAISED CHICKEN

Time: 6 1/2 hours   Servings: **8**

Ingredients:

8 chicken thighs
1 large fennel bulb, sliced
1 large onion, sliced
2 garlic cloves, chopped
2 ripe tomatoes, peeled and diced
1 can (15 oz.) cannellini beans, drained

2 yellow bell peppers, cored and sliced
1 teaspoon dried basil
1 rosemary sprig
Salt and pepper to taste
1 cup chicken stock

Directions:

Combine the chicken, fennel and the remaining ingredients in your crock pot.
Add salt and pepper to taste and cook on low settings for 6 hours.
The chicken is best served warm.

*B*UFFALO CHICKEN DRUMSTICKS

Time: 7 1/4 hours   Servings: **8**

Ingredients:

4 pounds chicken drumsticks
2 cups hot BBQ sauce
2 tablespoons tomato sauce
1 tablespoon cider vinegar

1 teaspoon Worcestershire sauce
1 cup cream cheese
Salt and pepper to taste

Directions:

Combine the chicken and the remaining ingredients in your crock pot.
Add salt and pepper to taste and cook on low settings for 7 hours.
Serve the chicken warm and fresh.

*B*LUE CHEESE CHICKEN

Time: 2 1/4 hours   Servings: **4**

Ingredients:

4 chicken breasts
1 teaspoon dried oregano
Salt and pepper to taste

1/2 cup crumbled blue cheese
1/2 cup chicken stock

Directions:

Season the chicken with salt and pepper and place it in your crock pot.
Add the stock then top each piece of chicken with crumbled feta cheese.
Cook on high settings for 2 hours.
Serve the chicken warm.

CASHEW CHICKEN

Time: 4 1/4 hours   Servings: 6

Ingredients:

3 chicken breasts, cut into strips   1 cup cashew nuts, soaked overnight
1 shallot, sliced   1/2 teaspoon ginger powder
1 celery stalk, sliced   1 cup chicken stock
1 head broccoli, cut into florets   Salt and pepper to taste

Directions:

Combine the chicken, shallot, celery and broccoli in your crock pot. Mix the cashew nuts, ginger and stock in a blender. Pulse until smooth then pour this mixture over the chicken in the pot. Season with salt and pepper. Cook on low settings for 4 hours. Serve the chicken warm and fresh.

TURMERIC CHICKEN STEW

Time: 6 1/2 hours   Servings: 6

Ingredients:

2 chicken breasts, cubed   1 cup tomato sauce
1 teaspoon turmeric powder   1 cup coconut milk
2 tablespoons canola oil   1 cup chicken stock
1/2 head cauliflower, cut into florets   2 cups fresh spinach, shredded
1 can (15 oz.) chickpeas, drained   Salt and pepper to taste
2 red bell peppers, cored and diced

Directions:

Season the chicken with salt, pepper and turmeric powder. Heat the canola oil in a skillet and add the chicken. Cook for a few minutes on all sides until golden. Transfer in your slow cooker then add the remaining ingredients. Season with salt and pepper and cook on low settings for 6 hours. Serve the dish warm and fresh.

PEANUT BRAISED CHICKEN

Time: 7 1/4 hours   Servings: 8

Ingredients:

1 large onion, chopped   1 1/2 cups chicken stock
2 large carrots, sliced   1 tablespoon soy sauce
2 red bell peppers, cored and diced   1 lime, juiced
4 pounds skinless chicken thighs   1 teaspoon grated ginger
4 tablespoons smooth peanut butter   Salt and pepper to taste

Directions:

Combine all the ingredients in your crock pot.
Add salt and pepper to taste and cover the pot with its lid.
Cook on low settings for 7 hours.
Serve the chicken warm with your favorite side dish.

ALFREDO CHICKEN

Time: 6 1/4 hours   Servings: 6

Ingredients:

2 pounds chicken drumsticks
2 cups sliced mushrooms
1 can fire roasted tomatoes
1 cup Alfredo pasta sauce
2 tablespoons dry sherry

1/2 teaspoon cumin powder
Salt and pepper to taste
1/2 cup chicken stock
Grated Parmesan cheese for serving

Directions:

Combine the chicken drumsticks, mushrooms, tomatoes, Alfredo sauce, dry sherry and cumin powder, as well as salt and pepper in a crock pot.
Cover and cook on low settings for 6 hours.
Serve the chicken warm, topped with grated cheese.

HERBED CHICKEN AND MUSHROOMS

Time: 5 1/2 hours   Servings: 8

Ingredients:

8 chicken drumsticks
4 cups sliced Champignon mushrooms
1 cup chopped wild mushrooms
2 tablespoons olive oil
1 red onion, sliced
2 red bell peppers, cored and sliced
2 carrots, sliced

2 tomatoes, peeled and diced
1 1/2 cups chicken stock
2 tablespoons tomato paste
1 thyme sprig
1 bay leaf
1 teaspoon dried sage
1 rosemary sprig

Directions:

Combine the chicken, mushrooms, olive oil, red onion, bell peppers, carrots, tomatoes, stock, tomato paste, thyme, bay leaf, sage and rosemary in your crock pot.
Add salt and pepper to taste and cook on low settings for 5 hours.
Serve the chicken and mushrooms warm.

CARAMELIZED ONIONS CHICKEN STEW

Time: 6 1/2 hours   Servings: 6

Ingredients:

2 chicken breasts, cubed
2 tablespoons canola oil
4 bacon slices, chopped
3 large onions, sliced
1 celery stalk, sliced
2 red bell peppers, cored and sliced
1/4 cup dry white wine

1 can fire roasted tomatoes
1/2 teaspoon dried thyme
Salt and pepper to taste

Directions:

Heat the oil in a skillet and add the bacon. Cook until crisp then stir in the onions.

Cook for 10 minutes until the onions are soft and begin to caramelize.

Transfer in your slow cooker. Add the remaining ingredients and season with salt and pepper.

Cook on low settings for 6 hours.

Serve the stew warm and fresh.

Coq au Vin

Time: 8 1/2 hours   Servings: 8

Ingredients:

1 whole chicken, cut into smaller pieces
2 tablespoons canola oil
1 cup miniature onions
4 carrots, sliced
1 pound button mushrooms
1/2 cup red wine

1 cup tomato sauce
2 ripe tomatoes, peeled and diced
2 bay leaves
Salt and pepper to taste
1 thyme sprig
1 rosemary sprig

Directions:

Heat the canola oil in a skillet and add the chicken. Fry on all sides for a few minutes until golden then transfer the chicken in your crock pot.

Add the remaining ingredients and season with salt and pepper.

Cook the coq au vin on low settings for 8 hours.

Serve the dish warm, simple as it is.

Cacciatore Chicken

Time: 7 1/4 hours   Servings: 8

Ingredients:

2 pounds chicken drumsticks
2 tablespoons canola oil
2 celery stalks, sliced
2 cups sliced mushrooms
2 carrots, sliced
1 large onion, sliced
2 garlic cloves, minced
1 red bell pepper, cored and sliced
1 yellow bell pepper, cored and sliced

1/4 cup dry white wine
2 tablespoons tomato paste
1 cup chicken stock
1 tablespoon cornstarch
1/2 teaspoon dried oregano
1 teaspoon dried basil
1 bay leaf
Salt and pepper to taste

Directions:

Heat the canola oil in a skillet or frying pan. Add the chicken and cook on all sides until golden.

Transfer the chicken in your crock pot and add the remaining ingredients.

Season with salt and pepper and cook on low settings for 7 hours.

Serve the chicken warm and fresh.

PEAR ROASTED CHICKEN

Time: 8 1/4 hours

Servings: 6

Ingredients:
6 chicken thighs
2 ripe pears, cored and sliced
1 fennel bulb, sliced
2 shallots, sliced

1 cup apple cider
1 bay leaf
1 thyme sprig
Salt and pepper to taste

Directions:
Combine the chicken with the remaining ingredients in your crock pot.
Add salt and pepper to taste and cook on low settings for 8 hours.
Serve the chicken warm and fresh.

DEVILED CHICKEN

Time: 6 1/4 hours

Servings: 4

Ingredients:
4 chicken breasts
1 cup tomato sauce
1/2 cup hot sauce

2 tablespoons butter
4 garlic cloves, minced
Salt and pepper to taste

Directions:
Combine all the ingredients in your crock pot.
Add salt and pepper and cover with a lid.
Cook on low settings for 6 hours.
Serve the chicken warm and fresh.

GREEK STYLE CHICKEN RAGOUT

Time: 8 1/4 hours

Servings: 8

Ingredients:
4 chicken breasts, halved
1 pound new potatoes, washed
1 pound baby carrots
1 zucchini, cubed
4 garlic cloves, chopped
1 sweet onion, sliced

4 artichoke hearts, chopped
1 lemon, juiced
1 teaspoon dried oregano
Salt and pepper to taste
1 1/2 cups chicken stock

Directions:
Combine the chicken, potatoes, carrots, zucchini, garlic, onion, artichoke hearts, lemon juice, oregano and stock in your slow cooker.
Add salt and pepper to taste and cover with a lid.
Cook on low settings for 8 hours.
Serve the chicken and veggies warm.

Chicken and Sweet Potato Spiced Stew

Time: 4 1/4 hours   Servings: 4

Ingredients:

1 chicken breast, cut into strips
2 tablespoons olive oil
2 large sweet potatoes, peeled and cubed
1 cup coconut milk
1/2 cup chicken stock

1 star anise
1/2 cinnamon stick
1/4 teaspoon cumin seeds
1 rosemary sprig
Salt and pepper to taste

Directions:

Combine all the ingredients listed above in a slow cooker. Adjust the taste with enough salt and pepper and cook on low settings for 4 hours. The stew is best served warm and fresh.

Rich Chicken Rice Stew

Time: 6 1/2 hours   Servings: 8

Ingredients:

3 chicken breasts, cubed
2 tablespoons butter
1 cup white rice
1/2 pound button mushrooms
1 shallot, chopped
1 garlic clove, chopped

1 cup green peas
2 carrots, sliced
2 cups vegetable stock
1/2 cup cream cheese
1 thyme sprig
Salt and pepper to taste

Directions:

Melt the butter in a skillet and add the chicken. Cook on all sides until golden then transfer in your slow cooker. Add the rest of the ingredients and season with salt and pepper. Cook on low settings for 6 hours. The stew is best served warm.

Stout Carrot Chicken Stew

Time: 8 1/4 hours   Servings: 8

Ingredients:

8 chicken thighs
4 bacon slices, chopped
2 tablespoons canola oil
4 garlic cloves, chopped
1 large onion, chopped
1 pound baby carrots
1/2 pound button mushrooms

1 cup tomato sauce
2 tablespoons tomato paste
1 1/2 cups stout beer
1 tablespoon lemon juice
2 bay leaves
1 rosemary sprig
Salt and pepper to taste

Directions:

Heat the canola oil in a crock pot and add the bacon. Cook until crisp then stir in the chicken. Cook on all sides until golden brown then transfer in your crock pot. Add the remaining ingredients and season well with salt and pepper. Cook on low settings for 8 hours. Serve the dish warm and fresh.

African Inspired Chicken Stew

Time: 5 1/4 hours   Servings: 8

Ingredients:

1 1/2 cups red lentils
2 pounds skinless chicken drumsticks
1 tablespoon butter
2 large red onions, chopped
4 garlic cloves, minced
1 teaspoon grated ginger

1/2 teaspoon chili powder
1 teaspoon coriander powder
1/4 teaspoon all-spice powder
1/4 teaspoon ground cloves
1 cup coconut milk
1 cup vegetable stock

Directions:

Combine the lentils, chicken, butter, spices, coconut milk and stock in your slow cooker.
Add enough salt and pepper and cook on low settings for 5 hours.
Serve the stew warm and fresh.

Honey Orange Glazed Chicken Drumsticks

Time: 6 1/4 hours   Servings: 6

Ingredients:

2 pounds chicken drumsticks
1 tablespoon grated zest
2 garlic cloves, minced
2 tablespoons soy sauce
1/4 cup fresh orange juice

1 teaspoon rice vinegar
1/4 teaspoon chili powder
1/4 cup chicken stock
2 tablespoons sesame seeds

Directions:

Combine all the ingredients in your crock pot.
Cover with a lid and cook on low settings for 6 hours.
Serve the chicken warm with your favorite side dish.

Chicken Ravioli In Tomato Sauce

Time: 2 3/4 hours   Servings: 6

Ingredients:

16 oz. chicken ravioli
1 shallot, chopped
4 garlic cloves, minced
1 can fire roasted tomatoes
1 cup vegetables stock

1/4 teaspoon coriander powder
1 pinch cumin powder
2 cups fresh spinach, shredded
Salt and pepper to taste

Directions:

Combine the ravioli, shallot, garlic, tomatoes, stock, coriander powder, cumin and spinach in your slow cooker.
Add salt and pepper and cook on high settings for 2 1/2 hours.
Serve the dish warm and fresh.

Bourbon Braised Chicken

Time: 8 1/4 hours   Servings: 8

Ingredients:
1 large whole chicken
4 red onions, sliced
1 tablespoon dried thyme
2 cups sliced cremini mushrooms

1/2 cup Bourbon
1 cup chicken stock
Salt and pepper to taste

Directions:
Mix the red onions, thyme, mushrooms, Bourbon and stock in your slow cooker.

Add salt and pepper then place the chicken over the veggies.

Cook on low settings for 8 hours. From time to time, spoon the juices in the pan over the chicken.

Serve the chicken warm with your favorite side dish.

Mexican Shredded Chicken

Time: 8 1/4 hours   Servings: 8

Ingredients:
4 chicken breasts
1 can fire roasted tomatoes
1 red onion, sliced
2 chipotle peppers, chopped
2 red bell peppers, cored and sliced

1 can (10 oz.) sweet corn, drained
1 teaspoon taco seasoning
1 cup chicken stock
Salt and pepper to taste

Directions:
Combine the chicken and the rest of the ingredients in your crock pot, adding enough salt and pepper.

Cover and cook on low settings for 8 hours.

When done, shred the chicken finely and serve it warm or chilled.

Cheesy Chicken Burrito Filling

Time: 6 1/4 hours   Servings: 6

Ingredients:
1 1/2 pounds ground chicken
2 tablespoons canola oil
1 can (15 oz.) diced tomatoes
2 cups chicken stock
1 teaspoon chili powder

1 cup brown rice
1 can (15 oz.) black beans, drained
1 can (10 oz.) sweet corn, drained
Salt and pepper to taste
1 1/2 cups grated Cheddar

Directions:
Heat the canola oil in a skillet and add the chicken. Cook for a few minutes, stirring often, then transfer in your crock pot. Add the rest of the ingredients, finishing with grated cheese.

Season with salt and pepper as needed and cook on low settings for 6 hours.

Serve the dish warm and fresh.

Coconut Ginger Chicken

Time: 7 1/4 hours

Servings: 8

Ingredients:
4 chicken breasts, halved
2 teaspoons grated ginger
4 garlic cloves, chopped
1 shallot, chopped
2 tablespoons butter
1 1/2 cups coconut milk
1/2 cup chicken stock

1 can baby corn, drained
1 cup green peas
1/2 cup green beans, chopped
1 pound new potatoes
1 bay leaf
Salt and pepper to taste
1 lemongrass stalk, crushed

Directions:
Melt the butter in a skillet and add the chicken. Cook for a few minutes on all sides then transfer in your crock pot. Add the rest of the ingredients and adjust the taste with salt and pepper. Cook on low settings for 7 hours. Serve the chicken warm.

Banana Chicken Curry

Time: 7 1/4 hours

Servings: 6

Ingredients:
2 pounds chicken drumsticks
1 jalapeno pepper, chopped
1 banana, sliced
1 1/2 cups diced tomatoes
1 large onion, chopped
4 garlic cloves, chopped
1 teaspoon cumin powder

1 teaspoon curry powder
1/4 cup dry white wine
1 bay leaf
1 lemongrass stalk, crushed
1 cup coconut milk
Salt and pepper to taste

Directions:
Combine the chicken, jalapeno, banana, tomatoes, onion, garlic, spices, wine, bay leaf, lemongrass and coconut milk in a slow cooker. Add salt and pepper to taste and cook on low settings for 7 hours. Serve the curry warm or chilled.

Lemon Garlic Whole Roasted Chicken

Time: 8 1/4 hours

Servings: 8

Ingredients:
1 large whole chicken
1 lemon, sliced
8 garlic cloves, crushed
1 rosemary sprig

1 thyme sprig
Salt and pepper to taste
1/2 cup vegetable stock

Directions:
Place half of the lemon slices and garlic in your crock pot. Season the chicken with salt and pepper and place it over the lemon. Top with the remaining lemon and rosemary and thyme sprig. Add the stock as well. Cover and cook on low settings for 8 hours. Serve the chicken warm or chilled.

TARRAGON CHICKEN

Time: 6 1/4 hours

Servings: 6

Ingredients:

3 pounds chicken drumsticks
2 tablespoons Dijon mustard
1/2 cup chicken stock
4 garlic cloves, minced
1 teaspoon dried tarragon

1/2 cup heavy cream
1 tablespoon cornstarch
1 teaspoon lemon zest
Salt and pepper to taste
2 tablespoons chopped parsley for serving

Directions:

Combine the chicken, mustard, chicken stock, garlic, tarragon, cream, cornstarch and lemon zest in your crock pot.
Add salt and pepper to taste and cook on low settings for 6 hours.
Serve the chicken warm and fresh.

BALSAMIC BRAISED CHICKEN WITH SWISS CHARD

Time: 8 1/4 hours

Servings: 8

Ingredients:

2 tablespoons olive oil
1 large onion, sliced
4 garlic cloves, chopped
1 teaspoon dried thyme
2 anchovy fillets
1 teaspoon red pepper flakes
1/4 cup balsamic vinegar

1 can (15 oz.) diced tomatoes
2 bay leaves
8 chicken thighs
1 cup chicken stock
Salt and pepper to taste
1 bunch Swiss chard, shredded

Directions:

Heat the oil in a skillet and add the onion and garlic. sauté for 2 minutes until softened.
Add the rest of the ingredients and season with salt and pepper.
Cook on low settings for 8 hours.
Serve the chicken warm and fresh.

LEMONADE CHICKEN

Time: 7 1/4 hours

Servings: 6

Ingredients:

6 chicken thighs
1 cup lemonade
1/2 cup ketchup

1 tablespoon cornstarch
1/4 teaspoon chili powder
Salt and pepper to taste

Directions:

Combine all the ingredients in a crock pot.
Add salt and pepper to taste and cook on low settings for 7 hours.
Serve the chicken warm and fresh.

Spice Rub Chicken

Time: 8 1/4 hours   Servings: 8

Ingredients:

1 large whole chicken
1 teaspoon cumin powder
1 teaspoon chili powder
1 teaspoon smoked paprika
1/4 teaspoon cayenne pepper

1/4 teaspoon cumin powder
1 teaspoon dried thyme
1 teaspoon dried basil
Salt and pepper to taste
1/2 cup chicken stock

Directions:

Mix the spices in a bowl. Spread the mix over the chicken and rub it well into the skin. Place the chicken in a crock pot and add the stock. Cover and cook on low settings for 8 hours. Serve the chicken warm and fresh.

Chicken Pasta Bake

Time: 4 1/4 hours   Servings: 6

Ingredients:

2 chicken breasts, cubed
2 tablespoons canola oil
1 bunch asparagus, trimmed and chopped
1 cup green peas
1 shallot, chopped
2 garlic cloves, chopped

6 oz. short pasta of your choice
2 cups chicken stock
1/2 cup heavy cream
Salt and pepper to taste
1/2 teaspoon dried basil
1/2 teaspoon dried oregano

Directions:

Heat the oil in a skillet or frying pan and add the chicken. Cook on all sides until golden then transfer the chicken in your crock pot. Add the rest of the ingredients and season with salt and pepper. Cook on low settings for 4 hours. Serve the bake warm and fresh or chilled.

Lime Cilantro Chicken

Time: 6 1/4 hours   Servings: 4

Ingredients:

4 chicken breasts
1 bunch cilantro
1 lime, zested and juiced
1/2 cup chicken stock

1 tablespoon Italian pesto
Salt and pepper to taste
1/2 cup grated Parmesan

Directions:

Combine the cilantro, lime zest and lime juice, as well as stock and pesto in a blender. Pulse until smooth.
Mix the chicken with the cilantro mix in a crock pot.
Top with grated cheese and cook on low settings for 6 hours.
Serve the chicken warm with your favorite side dish.

Fiesta Chicken Stew

Time: 8 1/2 hours   Servings: 8

Ingredients:
3 chicken breasts, cubed
2 tablespoons canola oil
2 red bell peppers, cored and diced
1 yellow bell pepper, cored and diced
1 sweet onion, chopped
4 garlic cloves, minced
1 celery stalk, sliced
1 can (15 oz.) red beans, drained
1 can (15 oz.) cannellini beans, drained

1 cup frozen sweet corn
1 teaspoon chili powder
1 teaspoon dried oregano
1 teaspoon dried thyme
1 teaspoon Cajun seasoning
Salt and pepper to taste
1 can fire roasted tomatoes
1 cup chicken stock

Directions:
Heat the oil in a skillet and add the chicken. Cook on all sides until golden then transfer in your slow cooker. Add the rest of the ingredients and season with salt and pepper. Cover with a lid and cook on low settings for 8 hours. Serve the stew warm and fresh.

Honey Sesame Glazed Chicken

Time: 6 1/4 hours   Servings: 4

Ingredients:
4 chicken breasts
3 tablespoons honey
1/2 teaspoon red pepper flakes
2 garlic cloves, minced
1 teaspoon grated ginger

2 tablespoons soy sauce
1/4 cup ketchup
1/4 cup chicken stock
2 tablespoons sesame seeds
1 teaspoon sesame oil

Directions:
Combine the chicken and the remaining ingredients in your crock pot.
Cover with a lid and cook on low settings for 6 hours.
Serve the chicken warm with your favorite side dish.

Veggie Medley Chicken Meatloaf

Time: 6 1/4 hours   Servings: 8

Ingredients:
2 pounds ground chicken
1 cup cauliflower florets, chopped
4 garlic cloves, chopped
1 shallot, chopped
1/4 cup chopped cilantro
1 carrot, grated
1 zucchini, grated

1 teaspoon dried oregano
1 teaspoon dried basil
1/2 teaspoon cumin powder
1/4 teaspoon cayenne pepper
2 eggs
1/2 cup almond flour
Salt and pepper to taste

Combine the chicken, cauliflower, garlic, shallot, cilantro, carrot, zucchini, herbs, cumin, cayenne pepper, eggs and almond flour in a bowl. Mix well and add salt and pepper. Transfer the mixture in your crock pot and cook on low settings for 6 hours. Serve the meatloaf warm or chilled.

CREAMY SALSA VERDE CHICKEN

Time: 4 1/4 hours   Servings: 6

Ingredients:

2 pounds chicken breast, cubed
1 jar salsa verde
1 cup cream cheese
2 tablespoons chopped cilantro

1/4 cup chicken stock
Salt and pepper to taste
1 ripe avocado for serving
1 lime for serving

Directions:

Combine the chicken, salsa verde, cream cheese, cilantro, stock, salt and pepper in a crock pot.
Cover with a lid and cook on low settings for 4 hours.
Serve the chicken warm, topped with sliced or cubed avocado and a drizzle of lime juice.

CHEESY CHICKEN PASTA

Time: 6 1/4 hours   Servings: 6

Ingredients:

2 cups fusilli pasta
2 chicken breasts, diced
2 cups chicken stock
2 celery stalks, sliced

1 cup cream cheese
1 cup grated Cheddar
1/2 cup grated Parmesan
Salt and pepper to taste

Directions:

Combine all the ingredients in your crock pot. Season with salt and pepper if needed and cook on low settings for 6 hours. Serve the pasta warm.

KOREAN BBQ CHICKEN

Time: 3 1/4 hours   Servings: 4

Ingredients:

4 boneless and skinless chicken breasts
2 tablespoons brown sugar
1/4 cup soy sauce
1/2 cup chicken stock
1 teaspoon chili paste

1 teaspoon grated ginger
1 tablespoon rice vinegar
6 garlic cloves, minced
1 green onion, chopped

Directions:

Mix the chicken and the remaining ingredients in your crock pot. Cover with a lid and cook on high settings for 3 hours. Serve the chicken warm and fresh.

Pork Recipes

RED SALSA PORK TENDERLOIN

Time: 8 1/2 hours   Servings: 8

Ingredients:

4 pounds pork tenderloin
1 teaspoon cumin powder
1 teaspoon ground coriander seeds
1 teaspoon smoked paprika
1 teaspoon garlic powder

2 tablespoons brown sugar
2 cups red salsa
2 red onions, sliced
1/4 cup red wine
Salt and pepper to taste

Directions:

Mix the cumin, coriander seeds, paprika, garlic, brown sugar, salt and pepper in a bowl. Spread this mix over the meat and rub it well into the meat. Combine the red salsa, onions and red wine in your crock pot. Place the pork tenderloin over the salsa and cook on low settings for 8 hours. Serve the pork tenderloin fresh with your favorite side dish.

SWEET AND SPICY PULLED PORK

Time: 9 1/4 hours   Servings: 8

Ingredients:

4 pounds pork shoulder
1 tablespoon cumin powder
1 teaspoon chili powder
1/4 cup brown sugar
1 teaspoon dry mustard
2 chipotle peppers, chopped

6 garlic cloves, minced
1/4 teaspoon ground cloves
1 1/2 teaspoons salt
1 cup pineapple juice
1 cup chickens tock

Directions:

Mix the brown sugar, cumin powder, chili powder, dry mustard, chipotle peppers, garlic and ground cloves, as well as salt in a bowl. Spread this mix over the meat and rub it well. Place the meat in your slow cooker and add the pineapple juice and stock. Cover and cook on low settings for 9 hours. When done, shred the meat into fine threads using 2 forks. It's best served warm.

BRAZILIAN PORK STEW

Time: 7 1/4 hours   Servings: 6

Ingredients:

1/2 pound dried black beans
1 1/2 pounds pork shoulder, cubed
2 sweet onions, chopped
4 bacon slices, chopped
4 garlic cloves, chopped
1 teaspoon cumin seeds

1/2 teaspoon ground coriander
2 bay leaves
1 teaspoon white wine vinegar
2 cups chicken stock
Salt and pepper to taste

Directions:

Combine the beans and pork with the rest of the ingredients in your crock pot. Add salt and pepper to taste and cover with a lid. Cook on low settings for 7 hours. Serve the stew warm and fresh.

*B*BQ Pork Ribs

Time: 11 1/4 hours   Servings: 8

Ingredients:
5 pounds pork short ribs
2 cups BBQ sauce
1 large onion, sliced
1 celery stalk, sliced
1 tablespoon Dijon mustard

1 teaspoon chili powder
1 tablespoon brown sugar
4 garlic cloves, minced
1/4 cup chicken stock
Salt and pepper to taste

Directions:
Combine the pork short ribs, BBQ sauce, onion, celery and mustard, as well as chili, sugar, garlic and stock in your slow cooker. Season with salt and pepper and cook on low settings for 11 hours.
Serve the pork ribs warm and fresh.

*A*PPLE BOURBON PORK CHOPS

Time: 8 1/4 hours   Servings: 6

Ingredients:
6 pork chops
4 red apples, cored and sliced
1/2 cup applesauce
1/4 cup bourbon

1/2 cup chicken stock
1 thyme sprig
1 rosemary sprig
Salt and pepper to taste

Directions:
Season the pork chops with salt and pepper.
Combine the apples, applesauce, bourbon, stock, thyme and rosemary in your slow cooker.
Place the pork chops on top and cook on low settings for 8 hours.
Serve the pork chops with the sauce found in the pot.

*R*ED WINE BRAISED PORK RIBS

Time: 8 1/4 hours   Servings: 8

Ingredients:
5 pounds pork short ribs
4 tablespoons brown sugar
1 tablespoon molasses
2 tablespoons olive oil
1 teaspoon chili powder

1 teaspoon cumin powder
1 teaspoon dried thyme
1 teaspoon salt
1 cup BBQ sauce
1 cup red wine

Directions:
Mix the brown sugar, molasses, olive oil, chili powder, cumin powder, thyme and salt in a bowl.
Spread this mixture over the pork ribs and rub the meat well with the spice. Place in your crock pot.
Add the BBQ sauce and red wine and cook on low settings for 8 hours.
Serve the pork ribs warm.

Onion Pork Tenderloin

Time: 8 1/4 hours   Servings: 6

Ingredients:

3 large sweet onions, sliced
2 tablespoons canola oil
2 pounds pork tenderloin
6 bacon slices

1 thyme sprig
1/2 cup white wine
1/2 cup chicken stock
Salt and pepper to taste

Directions:

Heat the oil in a skillet and add the onions. Cook for 10 minutes on all sides until softened and slightly caramelized.
Transfer the onions in your crock pot and add the rest of the ingredients.
Season with salt and pepper and cook on low settings for 8 hours.

Fennel Infused Pork Ham

Time: 6 1/4 hours   Servings: 8

Ingredients:

4-5 pounds piece of pork ham
2 fennel bulbs, sliced
1 orange, zested and juiced
1/2 cup white wine

1 cup chicken stock
2 bay leaves
1 thyme sprig
Salt and pepper to taste

Directions:

Combine the fennel, orange zest, orange juice, white wine, chicken stock, bay leaves and thyme in your crock pot.
Add salt and pepper and place the ham on top.
Cook on low settings for 6 hours.
Slice and serve the ham warm.

Country Style Pork Ribs

Time: 6 1/4 hours   Servings: 4

Ingredients:

3 pounds short pork ribs
1 teaspoon salt
1 teaspoon garlic powder

1 tablespoon brown sugar
1 teaspoon dried thyme
1 cup pineapple juice

Directions:

Season the pork ribs with salt, garlic powder, brown sugar and thyme and place in your slow cooker.
Add the pineapple juice and cook on low settings for 6 hours.
Serve the pork ribs warm and fresh.

CHILI VERDE

Time: 7 1/4 hours

Servings: 8

Ingredients:

2 pounds pork shoulder, cubed
2 tablespoons canola oil
2 pounds tomatillos, peeled and chopped
1 large onion, chopped
4 garlic cloves, chopped
1 teaspoon dried oregano
1 teaspoon cumin powder

1/2 teaspoon smoked paprika
1/4 teaspoon chili powder
1 bunch cilantro, chopped
2 green chilis, chopped
1 1/2 cups chicken stock
Salt and pepper to taste

Directions:

Heat the oil in a skillet and add the pork shoulder. Cook for a few minutes on all sides until golden then transfer in your slow cooker. Add the rest of the ingredients in your pot as well and season with salt and pepper. Cook on low settings for 7 hours. Serve the chili warm.

MEXICAN PORK ROAST

Time: 8 1/4 hours

Servings: 6

Ingredients:

2 pounds pork shoulder, cubed
1 can fire roasted tomatoes
2 carrots, sliced
2 celery stalks, sliced
1 large onion, chopped

1 teaspoon smoked paprika
1/2 teaspoon cumin powder
1 bay leaf
1 cup chicken stock
Salt and pepper to taste

Directions:

Combine the pork shoulder, tomatoes, carrots, celery, onion, paprika, cumin powder, bay leaf, stock, salt and pepper and cook on low settings for 8 hours. Serve the pork roast warm and fresh.

BALSAMIC ROASTED PORK

Time: 6 1/4 hours

Servings: 8

Ingredients:

4 pounds pork shoulder, cubed
2 tablespoons brown sugar
1 teaspoon five-spice powder
1 teaspoon garlic powder

2 tablespoons honey
1 teaspoon hot sauce
1/4 cup balsamic vinegar
Salt and pepper to taste

Directions:

Mix the sugar, five-spice powder, honey and hot sauce in a bowl. Spread the mix over the pork and rub it well.
Place the pork in your crock pot and add the vinegar.
Season with salt and pepper and cook on low settings for 6 hours.
Serve the pork warm and fresh with your favorite side dish.

Pineapple Cranberry Pork Ham

Time: 7 1/4 hours

Servings: 6

Ingredients:

2-3 pounds piece of smoked ham
1 cup cranberry sauce
1 cup pineapple juice
1/2 teaspoon chili powder
1/2 teaspoon cumin powder

1 cinnamon stick
1 star anise
1 bay leaf
Salt and pepper to taste

Directions:

Mix the cranberry sauce, pineapple juice, chili powder, cumin powder, cinnamon, star anise and bay leaf in your crock pot. Place the ham in the pot and season with salt and pepper if needed. Cook on low settings for 7 hours. Serve the ham and sauce warm with your favorite side dish.

Italian Style Pork Shoulder

Time: 7 1/4 hours

Servings: 6

Ingredients:

2 pounds pork shoulder
1 large onion, sliced
4 garlic cloves, chopped
2 celery stalks, sliced
2 ripe tomatoes, peeled and diced

1/4 cup white wine
1 teaspoon dried thyme
1 teaspoon dried basil
1 thyme sprig
Salt and pepper to taste

Directions:

Combine all the ingredients in your crock pot, adjusting the taste with enough salt and pepper.
Cover with a lid and cook on low settings for 7 hours.
Serve the pork shoulder warm and fresh with your favorite side dish.

Apple Butter Short Ribs

Time: 8 1/4 hours

Servings: 8

Ingredients:

4 pounds pork short ribs
1 cup apple butter
2 tablespoons brown sugar
1 teaspoon garlic powder
1 teaspoon onion powder

1/2 teaspoon chili powder
1/2 cup BBQ sauce
1 cup vegetable stock
Salt and pepper to taste

Directions:

Mix the apple butter, sugar, garlic powder, onion powder, chili powder, BBQ sauce and stock in your slow cooker.
Add the ribs and coat them well then season with salt and pepper.
Cover with a lid and cook on low settings for 8 hours.
Serve the short ribs warm and fresh.

Ginger Beer Pork Ribs

Time: 6 3/4 hours   Servings: 6

Ingredients:

2-3 pounds pork short ribs
1 cup ginger beer
1/2 cup ketchup
1 tablespoon Worcestershire sauce

1 tablespoon Dijon mustard
1/2 teaspoon smoked paprika
1 tablespoon brown sugar
Salt and pepper to taste

Directions:

Combine all the ingredients in your crock pot.
Add enough salt and pepper and cook on low settings for 6 1/2 hours.
Serve the ribs warm and fresh, simple or with your favorite side dish.

Teriyaki Pork Tenderloin

Time: 7 1/4 hours   Servings: 6

Ingredients:

2 pounds pork tenderloin
1/4 cup soy sauce
1/4 cup ketchup
1 onion, chopped
1 tablespoon smooth peanut butter

1 tablespoon brown sugar
1 tablespoon hot sauce
4 garlic cloves, minced
1/4 cup chicken stock or water

Directions:

Combine the soy sauce, ketchup, onion, peanut butter, sugar, hot sauce, garlic and stock in your crock pot.
Add the pork tenderloin and cook on low settings for 7 hours.
Serve the dish warm with your favorite side dish.

Sauerkraut Cumin Pork

Time: 6 1/4 hours   Servings: 6

Ingredients:

1 1/2 pounds pork shoulder, cubed
1 1/2 pounds sauerkraut, shredded
1 large onion, chopped
2 carrots, grated
1 1/2 teaspoons cumin seeds

1/4 teaspoon red pepper flakes
1 cup chicken stock
1 bay leaf
Salt and pepper to taste

Directions:

Combine all the ingredients in your crock pot.
Add enough salt and pepper and cook on low settings for 6 hours.
Serve the pork and sauerkraut warm and fresh.

HERBED ROASTED PORK

Time: 6 1/4 hours

Servings: 6

Ingredients:

2 pounds pork tenderloin
1 cup chopped parsley
1/2 cup chopped cilantro
4 basil leaves
1/4 cup pine nuts

1/2 cup chicken stock
1/2 cup grated Parmesan
Salt and pepper to taste
1 lemon, juiced

Directions:

Mix the parsley, cilantro, basil, pine nuts, stock, cheese, lemon juice, salt and pepper in a blender and pulse until smooth.

Combine the pork tenderloin with the herbed mixture and cook on low settings for 6 hours.

Serve the pork with your favorite side dish.

CHILI BBQ RIBS

Time: 8 1/2 hours

Servings: 8

Ingredients:

6 pounds pork short ribs
2 cups BBQ sauce
1 1/2 teaspoons chili powder
1 teaspoon cumin powder

2 tablespoons brown sugar
2 tablespoons red wine vinegar
1 teaspoon Worcestershire sauce
Salt and pepper to taste

Directions:

Mix the BBQ sauce, chili powder, sugar, vinegar, Worcestershire sauce, salt and pepper in a slow cooker.

Add the short ribs and mix until well coated.

Cover with a lid and cook on low settings for 8 1/4 hours.

Serve the ribs warm and fresh.

LEMON ROASTED PORK TENDERLOIN

Time: 7 1/4 hours

Servings: 6

Ingredients:

2 pounds pork tenderloin
1 lemon, sliced
1 teaspoon black pepper kernels

1 cup canola oil
1 cup vegetable stock
Salt and pepper to taste

Directions:

Combine all the ingredients in your slow cooker.

Add enough salt and pepper and cook on low settings for 7 hours.

Slice the pork and serve it warm.

Sour Cream Pork Chops

Time: 6 1/4 hours

Servings: 6

Ingredients:

6 pork chops, bone in
1 cup sour cream
1/2 cup chicken stock

2 green onions, chopped
2 tablespoons chopped parsley
Salt and pepper to taste

Directions:

Combine the pork chops, sour cream, stock, onions and parsley in your crock pot.
Add salt and pepper to taste and cook on low settings for 6 hours.
Serve the pork chops warm and fresh, topped with plenty of sauce.

Hawaiian Pork Roast

Time: 8 1/4 hours

Servings: 8

Ingredients:

4 pounds pork roast
1 mango, peeled and cubed
1 cup pineapple juice
1 cup frozen cranberries

2 tablespoons red wine vinegar
1 bay leaf
1 rosemary sprig
Salt and pepper to taste

Directions:

Combine the pork roast, mango cubes, pineapple juice, cranberries, vinegar, bay leaf and rosemary sprig in your slow cooker.
Add salt and pepper to taste and cook on low settings for 8 hours.
Serve the pork roast warm and fresh.

Black Bean Pork Stew

Time: 9 1/4 hours

Servings: 10

Ingredients:

2 red onions, chopped
4 garlic cloves, chopped
1 pound dried black beans
1 can fire roasted tomatoes
2 cups chicken stock
2 chipotle peppers, chopped

1 teaspoon dried oregano
1 teaspoon dried basil
1 teaspoon cumin powder
1 teaspoon chili powder
3 pounds pork roast, cubed
Salt and pepper to taste

Directions:

Combine the onions, garlic, black beans, tomatoes, stock, chipotle peppers, oregano, basil, cumin powder, chili powder and pork roast in a slow cooker.
Add salt and pepper to taste and cook on low settings for 9 hours.
Serve the stew warm and fresh or chilled.

Honey Glazed Pork Ribs

Time: 8 1/4 hours   Servings: 6

Ingredients:

4 pounds pork ribs
2 tablespoons honey mustard
2 tablespoons honey
1 tablespoon maple syrup
1 star anise

1/4 cup BBQ sauce
1 cup chicken stock
1 teaspoon salt
1/2 teaspoon cayenne pepper

Directions:

Combine the mustard, honey, maple syrup, star anise, BBQ sauce, stock, salt and cayenne pepper in your slow cooker.
Add the pork ribs and coat them well with the mix. Cover the pot with a lid and cook on low settings for 8 hours.
Serve the pork ribs warm.

Mango Flavored Pulled Pork

Time: 7 1/4 hours   Servings: 8

Ingredients:

4 pounds pork roast, cut into large pieces
1 ripe mango, peeled and diced
1/4 cup bourbon
1 cup chicken stock

1 chipotle pepper, chopped
1 tablespoon balsamic vinegar
1 cup BBQ sauce
Salt and pepper to taste

Directions:

Combine all the ingredients in your crock pot.
Add salt and pepper to taste and cook on low settings for 7 hours.
When done, shred the meat into fine threads and serve it warm or chilled.

Maple Glazed Pork Tenderloin

Time: 4 1/4 hours   Servings: 6

Ingredients:

2 pounds pork tenderloin
2 tablespoons maple syrup
1 tablespoon soy sauce
1 teaspoon hot sauce
1 teaspoon garlic powder

1/2 teaspoon cinnamon powder
1/4 teaspoon all spice powder
1/2 teaspoon ground ginger
1 teaspoon salt
1 can condensed cream of chicken soup

Directions:

Mix the maple syrup, soy sauce, hot sauce, garlic powder, cinnamon, all spice powder, ginger and salt in a bowl.
Spread this mixture over the pork and rub it well.
Pour the soup in your crock pot and place the pork tenderloin over the soup.
Cover and cook on high settings for 4 hours.
Serve the pork warm and fresh.

Pork Sausage Stew

Time: 6 1/4 hours

Servings: 8

Ingredients:

1 pound fresh pork sausages, sliced
1 large onion, finely chopped
2 carrots, diced
1 celery stalk, diced
2 garlic cloves, chopped
1 cup red lentils
2/3 cup brown lentils

1 cup diced tomatoes
1 tablespoon tomato paste
3 cups chicken stock
1 bay leaf
1 chipotle pepper, chopped
Salt and pepper to taste
2 tablespoons chopped parsley for serving

Directions:

Combine the pork sausages, onion, carrots, celery, garlic, lentils, tomatoes, tomato paste, stock, bay leaf and chipotle pepper in your slow cooker. Add salt and pepper to taste and cook on low settings for 6 hours. Serve the stew warm, topped with chopped parsley.

Harvest Pork Stew

Time: 6 1/2 hours

Servings: 8

Ingredients:

2 tablespoons canola oil
2 pounds pork shoulder, cubed
4 garlic cloves, chopped
1 large onion, chopped
3 cups butternut squash cubes
2 red apples, peeled and cubed
1 carrots, sliced

1 1/2 pounds potatoes, peeled and cubed
2 ripe tomatoes, peeled and cubed
1 teaspoon dried rosemary
1 teaspoon dried thyme
2 bay leaves
Salt and pepper to taste
1 cup chicken stock

Directions:

Heat the oil in a skillet and add the pork. Cook on all sides until golden then transfer in your slow cooker. Add the rest of the ingredients and season with salt and pepper. Cover with a lid and cook on low settings for 6 hours. Serve the stew warm and fresh.

Sweet Potato Pork Stew

Time: 6 1/4 hours

Servings: 6

Ingredients:

1 1/2 pounds pork tenderloin, cubed
3 large sweet potatoes, peeled and cubed
2 shallots, chopped
2 red apples, peeled and cubed
1 pinch nutmeg

1 teaspoon Dijon mustard
2 tablespoons tomato paste
2 cups chicken stock
Salt and pepper to taste

Directions:

Combine the pork, sweet potatoes, shallots, apples, nutmeg, mustard, tomato paste and stock in your slow cooker. Add enough salt and pepper and cook on low settings for 6 hours. Serve the pork stew warm or re-heated.

ROASTED BELL PEPPER PORK STEW

Time: 5 1/4 hours   Servings: 6

Ingredients:

2 pounds pork tenderloin, cubed
2 tablespoons canola oil
1 jar roasted bell pepper, drained and chopped
4 garlic cloves, chopped
1 large onion, chopped

1/2 teaspoon red pepper flakes
1 cup chicken stock
1 cup tomato sauce
Salt and pepper to taste

Directions:

Heat the oil in a skillet and add the pork. Cook for a few minutes on all sides until golden. Transfer in your slow cooker.
Add the rest of the ingredients and adjust the taste with salt and pepper.
Cover the pot with its lid and cook on low settings for 5 hours.
Serve the stew warm or chilled.

RED CHILE PULLED PORK

Time: 7 1/4 hours   Servings: 8

Ingredients:

4 pounds pork roast
1 cup tomato sauce
2 red chilis, seeded and chopped

1 large onion, chopped
1 cup red salsa
Salt and pepper to taste

Directions:

Combine all the ingredients in your slow cooker.
Add salt and pepper to fit your taste and cook under the lid on low settings for 7 hours.
When done, shred the pork into fine threads using two forks.
Serve the pork warm and fresh or re-heat it later.

BLACKBERRY PORK TENDERLOIN

Time: 7 1/4 hours   Servings: 6

Ingredients:

2 pounds pork tenderloin
2 cups fresh blackberries
2 red onions, sliced
1/2 teaspoon dried sage
1/2 teaspoon dried oregano

2 tablespoons honey
1 tablespoon balsamic vinegar
1/2 cup chicken stock
Salt and pepper to taste

Directions:

Combine all the ingredients in your crock pot.
Add salt and pepper to taste and cover with a lid.
Cook on low settings for 7 hours.
When done, slice the pork and serve it warm, topped with the sauce that's formed in the pot.

Havana Style Pork Roast

Time: 6 1/4 hours

Servings: 6

Ingredients:

2 pounds pork roast
1 onion, sliced
1 celery stalk, sliced
4 garlic cloves, chopped
1/2 cup fresh orange juice

1 lemon, zested and juiced
1 teaspoon cumin powder
1/4 teaspoon chili powder
1 bay leaf
Salt and pepper to taste

Directions:

Mix all the ingredients in your slow cooker.
Add salt and pepper to taste and cook on low settings for 6 hours.
Serve the pork roast warm and fresh.

Creamy Dijon Pork Shoulder

Time: 7 1/4 hours

Servings: 8

Ingredients:

2 tablespoons canola oil
4 pounds pork tenderloin
4 garlic cloves, chopped
1 large onion, chopped

2 cups sliced mushrooms
2 tablespoons Dijon mustard
1 can condensed cream of mushroom soup
Salt and pepper to taste

Directions:

Heat the canola oil in a skillet. Season the pork with salt and pepper and place it in the hot oil. Fry on each side until golden brown and crusty. Transfer the meat in your slow cooker. Add the rest of the ingredients and season with salt and pepper. Cook on low settings for 7 hours. Serve the pork warm, topped with the creamy sauce found in the pot.

Marsala Pork Chops

Time: 6 1/4 hours

Servings: 6

Ingredients:

6 pork chops
2 tablespoons all-purpose flour
1 teaspoon garlic powder
1 onion, sliced
4 garlic cloves, chopped

2 cups sliced mushrooms
1/2 cup Marsala wine
1 can condensed cream of mushroom soup
Salt and pepper to taste

Directions:

Season the pork chopped with salt and pepper then sprinkle them with flour.
Place the pork chops in your slow cooker and add the rest of the ingredients.
Season with salt and pepper and cook on low settings for 6 hours.
Serve the pork chops and the sauce formed in the pot warm and fresh.

CHIPOTLE PORK CHILI

Time: 8 1/2 hours   Servings: 8

Ingredients:

2 tablespoons canola oil
2 pounds pork shoulder, cubed
2 shallots, chopped
4 garlic cloves, chopped
3 chipotle peppers, chopped
2 cans (15 oz. each) black beans, drained
1 can fire roasted tomatoes
1 teaspoon cumin powder

1/2 teaspoon ground coriander
1 cup tomato sauce
1 cup chicken stock
2 tablespoons tomato paste
2 bay leaves
Salt and pepper to taste
1 lime for serving

Directions:

Heat the oil in a skillet and add the pork shoulder. Cook on all sides until golden then transfer in your crock pot. Add the rest of the ingredients, including salt and pepper. Cook on low settings for 8 hours. Serve the chili warm and fresh.

SLOW COOKED PORK IN TOMATO SAUCE

Time: 8 1/4 hours   Servings: 8

Ingredients:

4 pounds pork tenderloin
2 cups tomato sauce
2 tablespoons tomato paste
1 teaspoon cumin seeds
1 teaspoon fennel seeds

1 teaspoon celery seeds
1 teaspoon garlic powder
2 bay leaves
Salt and pepper to taste

Directions:

Combine all the ingredients in your slow cooker. Add salt and pepper to taste and cook the pork on low settings for 8 hours. When done, slice and serve the pork warm with your favorite side dish.

PORK SAUSAGE RAGU

Time: 6 1/4 hours   Servings: 6

Ingredients:

1 pound fresh pork sausages, casings removed
2 tablespoons olive oil
2 celery stalks, chopped
2 carrots, diced
1/2 teaspoon dried oregano
4 garlic cloves, minced

1 can fire roasted tomatoes
1 cup chickens tock
1 bay leaf
1/2 teaspoon red pepper flakes
1/4 cup dry red wine
Salt and pepper to taste

Directions:

Heat the oil in a skillet and add the pork sausages. Cook for a few minutes, stirring often then transfer in your crock pot. Add the rest of the ingredients and season with salt and pepper. Cook on low settings for 6 hours. Serve the ragu warm or freeze it into individual servings for later use.

Sweet and Sour Pork Chops

Time: 3 1/4 hours   Servings: 6

Ingredients:

6 pork chops
1 large onion, sliced
2 garlic cloves, chopped
1 celery stalk, sliced
2 tablespoons balsamic vinegar

2 tablespoons honey
1 cup apple cider
1 bay leaf
1/4 teaspoon cumin seeds
Salt and pepper to taste

Directions:

Combine the onion, garlic, celery, vinegar, honey, cider, cumin seeds and bay leaf in your crock pot. Season the pork chops with salt and pepper and place them in the pot. Cook on high settings for 3 hours. Serve the chops warm and fresh.

Pork Potato Stew

Time: 6 1/2 hours   Servings: 8

Ingredients:

1 tablespoon canola oil
6 bacon slices, chopped
2 pounds pork shoulder, cubed
1 chorizo, sliced
1 large onion, finely chopped
2 garlic cloves, chopped
2 red bell peppers, cored and diced

2 pounds potatoes, peeled and cubed
2 ripe tomatoes, peeled and diced
1 tablespoon tomato paste
2 cups chicken stock
2 bay leaves
1/4 teaspoon cayenne pepper
Salt and pepper to taste

Directions:

Heat the oil in a skillet and add the bacon. Cook until crisp then add the pork. Continue cooking for a few more minutes until golden then transfer in your crock pot. Add the rest of the ingredients and season with salt and pepper. Cook on low settings for 6 hours. Serve the stew warm and fresh.

Tomato Sauce Pork Roast

Time: 3 1/4 hours   Servings: 4

Ingredients:

2 pounds pork roast, cubed
2 tablespoons canola oil
1/2 cup tomato sauce
1/2 cup chicken stock

2 tablespoons tomato paste
1/4 teaspoon cayenne pepper
Salt and pepper to taste

Directions:

Combine all the ingredients in your slow cooker.
Add salt and pepper to taste and cook on high settings for 3 hours.
Serve the pork roast warm and fresh with your favorite side dish.

Bacon Potato Stew

Time: 6 1/2 hours   Servings: 6

Ingredients:

1 cup diced bacon
1 large onion, chopped
2 carrots, diced
1 celery stalk, diced
2 red bell peppers, cored and diced
2 sweet potatoes, peeled and cubed

1 pound Yukon gold potatoes, peeled and
cubed
1/2 teaspoon cumin seeds
1/2 teaspoon chili powder
1 cup diced tomatoes
Salt and pepper to taste
2 cups chicken stock

Directions:

Heat a skillet and add the bacon. Cook until crisp then transfer in your slow cooker. Add the rest of the ingredients and adjust the taste with salt and pepper. Cook on low settings for 6 hours. Serve the stew warm and fresh.

Miso Braised Pork

Time: 7 1/4 hours   Servings: 8

Ingredients:

4 pounds pork shoulder
6 garlic cloves, minced
1 tablespoon grated ginger
2 tablespoons canola oil

2 tablespoons miso paste
1 cup vegetable stock
1 lemongrass stalk, crushed

Directions:

Mix the garlic, ginger, canola oil, miso paste, stock and lemongrass in your crock pot. Place the pork shoulder in the pot as well and cover with a lid. Cook on low settings for 7 hours. Serve the pork warm with your favorite side dish.

Red Bean Pork Stew

Time: 3 1/4 hours   Servings: 6

Ingredients:

1/2 pound dried red beans, rinsed
1 1/2 pounds pork roast, cubed
1 chorizo link, sliced
4 bacon slices, chopped
4 garlic cloves, chopped
1 red onion, chopped

1 teaspoon hot sauce
1 can fire roasted tomatoes
2 cups vegetable stock
Salt and pepper to taste
1 bay leaf

Directions:

Combine the beans, pork roast, chorizo, bacon, garlic, onion and hot sauce in your slow cooker.
Add the tomatoes, stock, bay leaf, salt and pepper and cook on high settings for 3 hours.
Serve the stew warm. You can also freeze it into smaller portions for later serving.

Smoked Ham and Lima Bean Stew

Time: 6 1/4 hours

Servings: 6

Ingredients:

2 cups diced smoked ham
1 pound dried lima beans
2 cups water
1 cup chicken stock
1 cup diced tomatoes

1 teaspoon Cajun seasoning
1/4 teaspoon garlic powder
1/4 teaspoon onion powder
1/4 teaspoon cayenne pepper
Salt and pepper to taste

Directions:

Mix the ham, beans, water, stock, tomatoes, Cajun seasoning, garlic powder, onion powder, cayenne pepper, salt and pepper in your slow cooker. Cook on low settings for 6 hours. Serve the dish warm.

Spiced Plum Pork Chops

Time: 7 1/4 hours

Servings: 6

Ingredients:

6 pork chops
6 plums, pitted and chopped
1/2 cup apple cider
1/2 cup chicken stock
1 tablespoon balsamic vinegar
2 tablespoons brown sugar

1 star anise
1 cinnamon stick
1 bay leaf
2 whole cloves
Salt and pepper to taste

Directions:

Mix the plums, apple cider, stock, vinegar, brown sugar, star anise, cinnamon, bay leaf and cloves in your crock pot.
Add the pork chops and season with salt and pepper.
Cook on low settings for 7 hours.
Serve the pork chops and the sauce formed in the pot warm, simple or with your favorite side dish.

Green Enchilada Pork Roast

Time: 8 1/4 hours

Servings: 8

Ingredients:

4 pounds pork roast
2 cups green enchilada sauce
1/2 cup chopped cilantro

2 chipotle peppers, chopped
1/2 cup vegetable stock
Salt and pepper to taste

Directions:

Combine the enchilada sauce, cilantro, chipotle peppers and stock in your slow cooker.
Add the pork roast and season with salt and pepper.
Cook on low settings for 8 hours.
Serve the pork warm with your favorite side dish.

Navy Bean Stew

Time: 10 1/4 hours

Servings: 10

Ingredients:

4 pounds pork shoulder, cubed
1/2 cup diced bacon
2 celery stalks, sliced
2 carrots, sliced
2 large onions, chopped
1 pound dried navy beans, rinsed

1 cup dried red beans, rinsed
1 can fire roasted tomatoes
2 chipotle peppers, chopped
1 cup chicken stock
Salt and pepper to taste

Directions:

Combine the pork shoulder, celery, bacon, carrots, onions, navy beans, red beans, tomatoes, chipotle peppers and stock in your crock pot.
Add salt and pepper according to your taste and cook on low settings for 10 hours.
Serve the stew warm and fresh.

Ham Scalloped Potatoes

Time: 6 1/2 hours

Servings: 8

Ingredients:

2 pounds potatoes, peeled and finely sliced
1/2 pound smoked ham, finely sliced
1 large onion, sliced
2 cups whole milk

1 tablespoon all-purpose flour
1 cup heavy cream
Salt and pepper to taste
2 cups grated Cheddar cheese

Directions:

Layer the potatoes, ham and onion in your slow cooker.
Mix the milk, flour and cream in a bowl. Add salt and pepper to taste then pour this mixture over the potatoes.
Cover the pot and cook on low settings for 6 hours.
Serve the scalloped potatoes warm.

Ginger Slow Roasted Pork

Time: 7 1/4 hours

Servings: 8

Ingredients:

4 pounds pork shoulder
2 teaspoons grated ginger
1 tablespoon soy sauce

1 tablespoon honey
1 1/2 cups vegetables stock
Salt and pepper to taste

Directions:

Season the pork with salt and pepper, as well as ginger, soy sauce and honey.
Place the pork in your slow cooker and add the stock.
Cover and cook on low settings for 7 hours.
Serve the pork warm with your favorite side dish.

PROVENCAL PORK STEW

Time: 6 1/4 hours

Servings: 6

Ingredients:

2 pounds pork tenderloin, cubed
1 tablespoon canola oil
6 garlic cloves, minced
2 shallots, chopped
2 carrots, sliced
1 parsnip, diced
1 pound porcini mushrooms, chopped
1/2 cup vegetable stock

1/2 cup red wine
1 cup tomato sauce
1/2 cup pitted black olives, sliced
1 celery stalk, sliced
1 fire roasted tomatoes
2 bay leaves
1 thyme sprig
Salt and pepper to taste

Directions:

Heat the oil in a skillet and add the pork. Cook on all sides until golden. Transfer in your slow cooker. Add the rest of the ingredients and season with salt and pepper. Cover with a lid and cook on low settings for 6 hours. Serve the stew warm and fresh.

SMOKY PORK CHILI

Time: 6 1/4 hours

Servings: 8

Ingredients:

1 tablespoon canola oil
6 bacon slices, chopped
1 pound ground pork
2 onions, chopped
4 garlic cloves, chopped
2 tablespoon tomato paste
1 cup dark beer
1 1/2 teaspoons smoked paprika

1 teaspoon cumin powder
1 pound dried black beans, rinsed
2 1/2 cups vegetable stock
1 cup diced tomatoes
2 bay leaves
1 thyme sprig
Salt and pepper to taste

Directions:

Heat the oil in a skillet and add the bacon. Cook until crisp then stir in the pork. Sauté for a few additional minutes then transfer in your slow cooker. Add the rest of the ingredients and adjust the taste with salt and pepper. Cook on low settings for 6 hours. Serve the chili warm and fresh.

PORK CANNELLINI BEAN STEW

Time: 3 3/4 hours

Servings: 6

Ingredients:

1 pound pork tenderloin, cubed
2 tablespoons canola oil
2 celery stalks, sliced
2 carrots, sliced
1/2 teaspoon dried basil
1/2 teaspoon dried oregano

2 red bell peppers, cored and diced
1 1/2 cups dried cannellini beans, rinsed
3 cups chicken stock
1 rosemary sprig
Salt and pepper to taste

Directions:

Heat the oil in a skillet and add the pork. Cook for a few minutes until golden. Transfer the pork in your slow cooker. Add the rest of the ingredients and season with salt and pepper as needed. Cook the stew on high settings for 3 1/2 hours. Serve the stew warm and fresh.

Curried Roasted Pork

Time: 6 1/4 hours   Servings: 6

Ingredients:

2 pounds pork roast
1 1/2 teaspoons curry powder
1/2 teaspoon chili powder
4 garlic cloves, minced

1 teaspoon dried mint
1 teaspoon dried basil
Salt and pepper to taste
1 cup coconut milk

Directions:

Season the pork roast with salt, pepper, curry powder, chili powder, garlic, mint, basil, salt and pepper to taste. Place the meat in your crock pot and add the coconut milk. Cover and cook on low settings for 6 hours. Serve the pork warm and fresh.

Asian Style Pot Roast

Time: 6 1/4 hours   Servings: 8

Ingredients:

4 pounds boneless chuck roast, trimmed and
   halved
1/4 cup low sodium soy sauce
4 garlic cloves, minced
2 shallots, sliced
1 cup chicken stock

2 tablespoons tomato paste
1 tablespoon hot sauce
1 pound baby carrots
4 potatoes, peeled and halved
Salt and pepper to taste
1/2 lemongrass stalk, crushed

Directions:

Mix the chuck roast, soy sauce, garlic, shallots, chicken stock, tomato paste, hot sauce, carrots, potatoes and lemongrass stalk in your crock pot. Add salt and pepper to taste and cook on low settings for 6 hours. Serve the pork and veggies warm and fresh.

French Onion Roasted Pork Chop

Time: 6 1/4 hours   Servings: 6

Ingredients:

6 pork chops
1/4 cup white wine
1 can condensed onion soup

1 teaspoon garlic powder
Salt and pepper to taste

Directions:

Combine all the ingredients in your slow cooker. Add salt and pepper to taste and cover with a lid. Cook on low settings for 6 hours. Serve the pork chops warm.

Cuban Pork Chops

Time: 6 1/4 hours   Servings: 6

Ingredients:

6 pork chops
2 large onions, sliced
1 teaspoon grated ginger
1 teaspoon cumin seeds
4 garlic cloves, chopped

1 teaspoon chili powder
1 lemon, juiced
1 bay leaf
Salt and pepper to taste
1 cup chicken stock

Directions:

Mix all the ingredients in your slow cooker, adjusting the taste with salt and pepper. Cover and cook on low settings for 6 hours. Serve the pork chops warm.

Red Beans Rice

Time: 3 1/4 hours   Servings: 6

Ingredients:

1 pounds ground pork
1 chorizo link, chopped
1 tablespoon canola oil
1 can (15 oz.) red beans, drained
1 red onion, chopped
1 cup green peas

1/2 cup frozen sweet corn
1/2 cup wild rice
1 1/2 cups chicken stock
Salt and pepper to taste
1 lemon for serving

Directions:

Heat the canola oil in a skillet and add the pork. Cook for 1 few minutes, stirring often then transfer in your crock pot. Add the rest of the ingredients and season with salt and pepper. Cook on high settings for 3 hours until the rice absorbs all the liquid. Before serving, drizzle in the lemon juice and mix well. The dish is best served warm.

Thyme Flavored White Bean Pork Cassoulet

Time: 4 1/4 hours   Servings: 4

Ingredients:

1 pound pork tenderloin, cubed
2 tablespoons canola oil
1 can (15 oz.) white beans, drained
1 celery stalk, sliced
1 shallot, chopped

1 garlic clove, chopped
1 cup diced tomatoes
2 thyme sprigs
1 cup chicken stock
Salt and pepper to taste

Directions:

Heat the oil in a skillet and add the pork. Cook for a few minutes on all sides until golden brown then transfer in your slow cooker. Add the rest of the ingredients in a slow cooker and add salt and pepper to taste. Cook the cassoulet on low settings for 4 hours and serve it warm or chilled.

APRICOT GLAZED GAMMON

Time: 6 1/4 hours

Servings: 6-8

Ingredients:

3-4 pounds piece of gammon joint
1/2 cup apricot preserve
1 teaspoon cumin powder

1/4 teaspoon chili powder
1 cup vegetable stock
Salt and pepper to taste

Directions:

Mix the apricot preserve with cumin powder and chili powder then spread this mixture over the gammon. Place the meat in your slow cooker and add the stock. Cook on low settings for 6 hours. Serve the gammon with your favorite side dish, warm or chilled.

PORK CHICKPEA STEW

Time: 2 1/4 hours

Servings: 6

Ingredients:

1 pound pork roast, cubed
2 tablespoons canola oil
2 celery stalks, sliced
2 carrots, sliced
2 red bell peppers, cored and diced
1 can fire roasted tomatoes

1 can (15 oz.) chickpeas, drained
1 cup chicken stock
1 bay leaf
1 thyme sprig
Salt and pepper to taste

Directions:

Heat the oil in a skillet and add the pork. Cook on all sides until golden then transfer in your crock pot. Add the rest of the ingredients and adjust the taste with salt and pepper. Cook on high settings for 2 hours. Serve the stew warm and fresh, although it tastes great chilled as well.

SPICED PORK BELLY

Time: 7 1/4 hours

Servings: 6

Ingredients:

3 pounds piece of pork belly
1 tablespoon cumin powder
1 tablespoon brown sugar
1 teaspoon chili powder
1 teaspoon grated ginger

1 tablespoon molasses
2 garlic cloves, minced
1 tablespoon soy sauce
1/2 cup white wine

Directions:

Mix the cumin powder, sugar, chili powder, ginger, molasses, garlic and soy sauce in a bowl. Spread this mixture over the pork belly and rub it well into the skin and meat. Place the belly in your crock pot and add the wine. Cook on low settings for 7 hours. Serve the belly warm with your favorite side dish.

VEGGIE MEDLEY ROASTED PORK TENDERLOIN

Time: 7 1/4 hours   Servings: 6

Ingredients:

2 1/2 pounds pork tenderloin   4 garlic cloves
2 ripe heirloom tomatoes, peeled   1 cup cauliflower florets
2 carrots, sliced   1 cup chicken stock
1 shallot   Salt and pepper to taste

Directions:

Combine the tomatoes, carrots, shallot, garlic, cauliflower, stock, salt and pepper in your blender. Pulse until smooth then combine it with the pork tenderloin in your crock pot. Cover with a lid and cook on low settings for 7 hours. When done, slice and serve the pork tenderloin warm.

PEANUT BUTTER PORK BELLY

Time: 6 1/4 hours   Servings: 6

Ingredients:

3 pounds pork belly   4 garlic cloves
1/4 cup smooth peanut butter   1 teaspoon grated ginger
2 tablespoons soy sauce   1 tablespoon honey
1 tablespoon hot sauce   1 chipotle pepper, chopped
1/2 cup vegetable stock

Directions:

Mix the peanut butter, soy sauce, hot sauce, stock, garlic, ginger, honey and chipotle pepper in a crock pot. Add the pork belly and coat it well with the mix. Cover and cook on low settings for 6 hours. Serve the pork belly warm.

LEMON VEGETABLE PORK ROAST

Time: 8 1/4 hours   Servings: 8

Ingredients:

1 large onion, sliced   1/4 cup red wine vinegar
4 pounds pork roast, cut into quarters   2 tablespoons soy sauce
1/2 pounds baby carrots   2 tablespoon ketchup
2 cups snap peas   1 teaspoon garlic powder
2 parsnips, sliced   1/4 teaspoon cayenne pepper
2 large potatoes, peeled and cubed   Salt and pepper to taste
1 cup vegetable stock   1 lemon, sliced
1 tablespoon molasses

Directions:

Combine the onion, pork roast, baby carrots, snap peas, parsnips, potatoes, stock, molasses, vinegar, soy sauce, ketchup, garlic powder and cayenne pepper in your slow cooker. Add salt and pepper to taste and cover with lemon slices. Cover the pot with its lid. Cook on low settings for 8 hours. Serve the roast warm and fresh.

Ham and Green Pea Stew

Time: 2 3/4 hours   Servings: 6

Ingredients:

1 pound pork roast, cubed
2 tablespoons canola oil
1 large onion, finely chopped
4 garlic cloves, chopped
1/4 teaspoon grated ginger
1 pound green peas

1 teaspoon dried mint
1/2 teaspoon dried oregano
1 1/2 cups chicken stock
Salt and pepper to taste
1 bay leaf
1 tablespoon cornstarch

Directions:

Heat the oil in a skillet and add the pork roast. Cook on all sides until golden then transfer in your slow cooker. Add the rest of the ingredients and adjust the taste with salt and pepper. Cook the stew on high settings for 2 1/2 hours. Serve the stew warm and fresh.

Hearty BBQ Pork Belly

Time: 7 1/4 hours   Servings: 8

Ingredients:

4 pounds pork belly, trimmed
2 cups BBQ sauce
2 chipotle peppers, chopped
2 red onions, sliced

6 garlic cloves, chopped
1 teaspoon salt
1 thyme sprig

Directions:

Combine all the ingredients in your slow cooker. Cover and cook on low settings for 7 hours. Serve the pork belly warm with your favorite side dish.

Pork Taco Filling

Time: 6 1/2 hours   Servings: 8

Ingredients:

2 pounds ground pork
2 tablespoons canola oil
2 shallots, chopped
4 garlic cloves, chopped
2 chipotle peppers, chopped
1 cup ginger beer
1 cup pineapple juice

1/2 cup chopped cilantro
1 pound tomatillos, chopped
1 cup frozen corn
Salt and pepper to taste
1 lime, juiced
Flour tortillas or taco shells for serving

Directions:

Heat the oil in a frying pan and add the pork. Cook for a few minutes then transfer in your slow cooker. Add the shallots, garlic, ginger beer, chipotle peppers, pineapple juice, cilantro, tomatillos, corn and lime juice, as well as salt and pepper. Cover with its lid and cook on low settings for 6 hours. Serve the dish warm, wrapped in flour tortillas or taco shells.

Pork Belly over Smoky Sauerkraut

Time: 8 1/2 hours   Servings: 8

Ingredients:
1 pound sauerkraut, chopped
6 bacon slices, chopped
1 teaspoon smoked paprika
1 teaspoon cumin seeds

1/2 teaspoon dried thyme
1 cup chicken stock
4 pounds pork belly
Salt and pepper to taste

Directions:
Mix the sauerkraut, bacon, paprika, cumin seeds, thyme and stock in your crock pot.
Season the pork belly with salt and pepper and place it over the sauerkraut.
Cover and cook on low settings for 8 hours.
Serve the pork belly and sauerkraut warm.

Red Cabbage Pork Stew

Time: 4 1/4 hours   Servings: 6

Ingredients:
1 head red cabbage, shredded
1 1/2 pounds pork roast, cubed
2 tablespoons canola oil
1 large onion, chopped
4 garlic cloves, minced

1 tablespoon maple syrup
1 teaspoon chili powder
1/4 cup apple cider vinegar
Salt and pepper to taste

Directions:
Combine all the ingredients in your crock pot.
Add salt and pepper to taste and cook the dish on low settings for 4 hours.
Serve the stew warm and fresh.

Cheddar Pork Casserole

Time: 5 1/2 hours   Servings: 6

Ingredients:
2 tablespoons canola oil
2 large onions, sliced
1 1/2 pounds ground pork
1 carrot, grated

1 cup finely chopped mushrooms
1/2 cup hot ketchup
Salt and pepper to taste
2 cups grated Cheddar

Directions:
Heat the canola oil in a frying pan and add the onions. Cook on low heat for 10 minutes until they begin to caramelize.
Transfer the onions in your slow cooker. Add the pork, carrot, mushrooms and ketchup and mix well, adjusting the taste with salt and pepper.
Top with Cheddar cheese and cook on low settings for 5 hours.
Serve the casserole preferably warm.

Vietnamese Style Pork

Time: 7 1/4 hours   Servings: 6

Ingredients:
2 pounds pork shoulder
1 teaspoon grated ginger
6 garlic cloves, minced
1/2 cup soy sauce

1/4 cup brown sugar
2 tablespoons white wine vinegar
1 hot red pepper, chopped
1/2 cup vegetable stock or just plain water

Directions:
Combine all the ingredients in your crock pot.
Cover with a lid and cook on low settings for 7 hours.
When done, either slice and serve or shred into fine threads to serve as pulsed pork.

Mushroom Pork Stew

Time: 5 1/4 hours   Servings: 6

Ingredients:
1 pound pork roast, cubed
2 tablespoons canola oil
1 pound button mushrooms
1 1/2 cups chicken stock

1 tablespoon cornstarch
1 cup cream cheese
1 thyme sprig
Salt and pepper to taste

Directions:
Heat the oil in a skillet and add the pork. Cook on all sides until golden then transfer in your crock pot.
Add the remaining ingredients and season with salt and pepper.
Cook on low settings for 5 hours and serve the stew warm and fresh.

Golden Maple Glazed Pork Chops

Time: 4 1/4 hours   Servings: 6

Ingredients:
6 pork chops
2 tablespoons canola oil
4 shallots, sliced
4 garlic cloves, chopped

3 tablespoons maple syrup
1/4 cup white wine
1/2 teaspoon chili powder
Salt and pepper to taste

Directions:
Heat the oil in a large frying pan and add the pork chops. Fry on high flame for a few minutes on both sides until golden then transfer in your slow cooker.
Add the remaining ingredients and adjust the taste with salt and pepper.
Cover with its lid and cook on low settings for 4 hours.
The chops are best served warm.

Autumn Pork Roast

Time: 6 1/2 hours   Servings: 6

Ingredients:
1 pound pork shoulder, cubed
1 pound fresh pork sausages, sliced
2 cups butternut squash cubes
2 sweet potatoes, peeled and cubed
2 cups chicken stock

2 thyme sprigs
1 bay leaf
1 star anise
1whole clove
Salt and pepper to taste

Directions:
Combine the pork and sausages with the remaining ingredients in a crock pot.
Add enough salt and pepper and cook on low settings for 6 hours.
Serve the pork roast warm and fresh.

Onion Pork Chops with Creamy Mustard Sauce

Time: 5 1/4 hours   Servings: 4

Ingredients:
4 pork chops, bone in
2 onions, finely chopped
4 garlic cloves, minced
1 teaspoon dried mustard
1/4 teaspoon cayenne pepper

1 tablespoon apple cider vinegar
1/2 cup white wine
2 tablespoons Dijon mustard
1/2 cup heavy cream
Salt and pepper to taste

Directions:
Combine the chops, onions, garlic, mustard, cayenne pepper, vinegar, wine and cream in your slow cooker.
Add salt and pepper to taste and cook on low settings for 5 hours.
Serve the dish warm and fresh.

Szechuan Roasted Pork

Time: 8 1/4 hours   Servings: 8

Ingredients:
4 pounds pork shoulder, trimmed
1 can (8 oz.) bamboo shoots
1 cup water chestnuts, chopped
2 shallots, sliced
1 tablespoon Worcestershire sauce
1/4 cup soy sauce

1 tablespoon rice vinegar
2 tablespoons red bean paste
1 teaspoon sesame oil
1 teaspoon garlic powder
1 teaspoon hot sauce
1 cup chicken stock

Directions:
Combine the pork shoulder and the rest of the ingredients in your crock pot.
Cover with a lid and cook on low settings for 8 hours.
Serve the pork shoulder and the sauce preferably warm and fresh.

Cola BBQ Pork Roast

Time: 8 1/4 hours   Servings: 6

Ingredients:

2 1/2 pounds pork shoulder, trimmed
1 cup BBQ sauce
1 cup cola drink
1 thyme sprig

1 red chili, chopped
1 rosemary sprig
2 onions, sliced
Salt and pepper to taste

Directions:

Combine all the ingredients in your crock pot.
Add salt and pepper to taste and cook the pork on low settings for 8 hours.
Serve the pork warm and fresh.

Filipino Adobo Pork

Time: 7 1/4 hours   Servings: 8

Ingredients:

4 pounds pork roast
1/4 cup red wine vinegar
1/4 cup soy sauce
1 cup water

2 bay leaves
1 chipotle pepper, chopped
6 garlic cloves, chopped
1/2 teaspoon chili powder

Directions:

Combine the vinegar, soy sauce, water, bay leaves, chipotle pepper, garlic and chili powder in a slow cooker.
Add the meat into this sauce and cover with a lid.
Cook on low settings for 7 hours and serve the pork warm and fresh.

Garlic Roasted Pork Belly

Time: 8 1/4 hours   Servings: 8

Ingredients:

4 pounds pork belly
8 garlic cloves
1 teaspoon cumin powder
1 teaspoon garlic powder

1 teaspoon cayenne pepper
Salt and pepper to taste
1 cup dry white wine

Directions:

Make a few holes in the pork meat and stuff them with garlic cloves.
Season the piece of meat with cumin, garlic powder, cayenne pepper, salt and pepper.
Place the pork belly in your slow cooker and add the wine.
Cook on low settings for 8 hours.
Serve the pork belly warm and fresh.

Sticky Glazed Pork Ribs

Time: 8 1/4 hours   Servings: 8

Ingredients:
6 pounds short pork ribs
1/2 cup hot ketchup
1/4 cup hoisin sauce
2 tablespoons maple syrup
1 teaspoon onion powder

1 teaspoon garlic powder
1 cup crushed pineapple in juice
2 shallots, chopped
1 teaspoon grated ginger
2 tablespoons soy sauce

Directions:
Combine all the ingredients in your slow cooker.
Mix until the ribs are evenly coated then cover with a lid and cook on low settings for 8 hours.
Serve the sticky ribs warm.

Kahlua Pulled Pork

Time: 8 1/4 hours   Servings: 6

Ingredients:
2 pounds pork shoulder
1/4 cup Kahlua liqueur
1/4 cup brewed coffee
1/2 cup chicken stock

2 bay leaves
1 chipotle peppers, chopped
1/2 teaspoon cumin seeds
Salt and pepper to taste

Directions:
Mix all the ingredients in your slow cooker. Adjust the taste with salt and pepper and cover with a lid.
Cook on low settings for 8 hours.
Serve the pork warm and fresh, shredded finely, either simple or in sandwiches.

Jerk Seasoning Pork Roast

Time: 6 1/4 hours   Servings: 6

Ingredients:
2 pounds pork roast
2 tablespoons Jamaican jerk seasoning
1 teaspoon dried thyme
1 teaspoon dried mint
1 large onion, sliced

4 garlic cloves, chopped
1 cup BBQ sauce
1/2 cup water
Salt and pepper to taste

Directions:
Season the pork with salt, pepper, mint, jerk seasoning and thyme.
Combine the onion, garlic, BBQ sauce and water in a slow cooker.
Place the pork over the sauce and cover with a lid.
Cook on low settings for 6 hours.
Serve the pork roast warm and fresh.

FRUITY PORK TENDERLOIN

Time: 8 1/4 hours   Servings: 8

Ingredients:

3 pounds pork tenderloin   1 onion, chopped
1/2 pound plums, pitted and sliced   1/2 teaspoon garlic powder
1/2 cup chopped dried apricots   1 cinnamon stick
1/2 cup frozen cranberries   1 star anise
1/2 cup golden raisins   Salt and pepper to taste
1 cup apple juice

Directions:

Combine the fruits, onion, garlic powder, spices, salt and pepper in your crock pot. Place the pork tenderloin on top and cover with a lid. Cook on low settings for 8 hours. Serve the pork roast tenderloin warm, topped with the fruits found in the pot.

CARIBBEAN STICKY PORK RIBS

Time: 7 1/4 hours   Servings: 8

Ingredients:

6 pounds pork ribs   1/2 teaspoon all spice powder
1 can crushed pineapple   1/4 teaspoon chili powder
2 tablespoons honey   2 onions, sliced
1 teaspoon hot sauce   2 garlic cloves, chopped
1 teaspoon Worcestershire sauce   Salt and pepper to taste

Directions:

Mix the pineapple, honey, hot sauce, Worcestershire sauce, all spice and chili powder, salt and pepper, as well as onions and garlic in your slow cooker. Place the pork ribs on top and drizzle them with the sauce found in the pot. Cover and cook on low settings for 7 hours. Serve the pork ribs warm and fresh.

PIZZA PORK CHOPS

Time: 6 1/2 hours   Servings: 6

Ingredients:

6 pork chops   1/2 cup pitted black olives, sliced
2 red bell peppers, cored and sliced   2 cups shredded mozzarella
1 1/2 cups tomato sauce   Salt and pepper to taste
1 teaspoon dried oregano

Directions:

Place the pork chops in your slow cooker.
Top with tomato sauce, oregano, black olives, salt and pepper.
Cover with a layer of shredded mozzarella and cook on low settings for 6 hours.
Serve the dish preferably warm while the cheese is still gooey.

APPLE CHERRY PORK CHOPS

Time: 3 1/4 hours   Servings: 6

Ingredients:
6 pork chops   1 onion, chopped
4 red, tart apples, cored and sliced 1 garlic clove, minced
1 cup frozen sour cherries   1 bay leaf
1/2 cup apple cider vinegar   Salt and pepper to taste
1/2 cup tomato sauce

Directions:
Combine the pork chops, apples, sour cherries, tomato sauce, onion, garlic and bay leaf in your slow cooker.
Add salt and pepper to taste and cook on high settings for 3 hours.
Serve the pork chops warm and fresh.

MANGO CHUTNEY PORK CHOPS

Time: 5 1/4 hours   Servings: 4

Ingredients:
4 pork chops   1 bay leaf
1 jar mango chutney   Salt and pepper to taste
3/4 cup chicken stock

Directions:
Combine all the ingredients in your crock pot.
Add enough salt and pepper and cook on low settings for 5 hours.
Serve the pork chops warm.

SMOKY APPLE BUTTER PORK CHOPS

Time: 4 1/2 hours   Servings: 4

Ingredients:
6 bacon slices, chopped   1 cup apple butter
1 tablespoon butter   1/2 cup tomato sauce
4 pork chops   1 bay leaf
1 teaspoon smoked paprika   Salt and pepper to taste

Directions:
Heat a frying pan over medium flame and add the bacon. Cook until crisp then add the butter and place the pork chops in the hot pan. Fry on each side for 2 minutes until golden then transfer in your slow cooker.
Add the rest of the ingredients and cook on low settings for 4 hours, making sure it has enough salt and pepper as well.

ROASTED ROSEMARY PORK AND POTATOES

Time: 6 1/2 hours   Servings: 6

Ingredients:
2 pounds pork roast, cubed   1 celery root, peeled and cubed
3 large carrots, sliced
1 1/2 pounds potatoes, peeled and cubed
2 rosemary sprigs   1 cup chicken stock
Salt and pepper to taste

Directions:
Combine the pork roast, carrots, celery, potatoes, rosemary and stock in your crock pot.
Add salt and pepper and cook on low settings for 6 hours.
Serve the dish warm and fresh.

THREE PEPPER ROASTED PORK TENDERLOIN

Time: 8 1/4 hours   Servings: 8

Ingredients:
3 pounds pork tenderloin   Salt and pepper to taste
2 tablespoons Dijon mustard   1 cup chicken stock
1/4 cup three pepper mix

Directions:
Season the pork with salt and pepper.
Brush the meat with mustard. Spread the pepper mix on your chopping board then roll the pork through this mixture, making sure to coat it well.
Place carefully in your crock pot and pour in the stock.
Cook on low settings for 8 hours.
Serve the pork tenderloin sliced and warm with your favorite side dish.

INTENSE MUSTARD PORK CHOPS

Time: 5 1/4 hours   Servings: 4

Ingredients:
4 pork chops   1 shallot, finely chopped
2 tablespoons Dijon mustard   4 garlic cloves, minced
1 tablespoon honey   1 cup chicken stock
2 tablespoons olive oil   Salt and pepper to taste

Directions:
Season the pork chops with salt and pepper and place them in your crock pot.
Add the rest of the ingredients and adjust the taste with salt and pepper.
Cover with a lid and cook on low settings for 5 hours.
Serve the pork chops and the sauce formed in the pan warm with your favorite side dish.

Cuban Style Pork Roast over Simple Black Beans

Time: 6 1/4 hours

Servings: 6

Ingredients:

2 pounds pork roast, trimmed and cubed
1/2 cup fresh orange juice
1/2 cup chicken stock
1 lime, juiced
1 large onion, sliced
4 garlic cloves, minced

1/2 teaspoon cumin powder
1/2 teaspoon chili powder
1 teaspoon smoked paprika
Salt and pepper to taste
Canned black beans for serving

Directions:

Combine the pork roast with the rest of the ingredients in your slow cooker.

Add enough salt and pepper and cook on low settings for 6 hours.

Serve the pork roast over canned black beans, topping the dish with plenty of sauce formed in the pan.

Honey Apple Pork Chops

Time: 5 1/4 hours

Servings: 4

Ingredients:

4 pork chops
2 red, tart apples, peeled, cored and cubed
1 shallot, chopped
2 garlic cloves, chopped
1 tablespoon olive oil

1 red chili, chopped
1 heirloom tomato, peeled and diced
1 cup apple cider
2 tablespoons honey
Salt and pepper to taste

Directions:

Mix all the ingredients in your crock pot.

Add salt and pepper to taste and cook on low settings for 5 hours.

Serve the chops warm and fresh.

Beef Recipes

Korean Beef Stew

Time: 8 1/4 hours

Servings: 6

Ingredients:
1 pound beef roast, cubed
2 tablespoons canola oil
1 pound baby carrots
1 large onion, chopped
4 garlic cloves, minced
1/2 cup tomato juice
3 tablespoons soy sauce

1 tablespoon brown sugar
1 teaspoon sesame oil
1 teaspoon hot sauce
1 cup diced tomatoes
Salt and pepper to taste
Cooked rice for serving

Directions:
Heat the canola oil in a frying pan and add the beef roast. Cook for a few minutes on all sides until golden then transfer the meat in your slow cooker. Add the rest of the ingredients in your crock pot and season with salt and pepper. Cover with a lid and cook on low settings for 8 hours. Serve the stew warm and fresh.

Beef Salsa Chili

Time: 7 1/2 hours

Servings: 8

Ingredients:
2 pounds beef roast, cubed
2 tablespoons canola oil
2 red onions, chopped
2 garlic cloves, chopped
2 carrots, diced
2 red bell peppers, cored and diced
1 leek, sliced

1 1/2 cups red salsa
1 bay leaf
1 teaspoon cumin seeds
1 teaspoon chili powder
2 cups dried black bean
4 cups chicken stock or water
Salt and pepper to taste

Directions:
Heat the oil in a skillet or frying pan and add the beef. Cook for a few minutes until golden brown then transfer in your crock pot. Add the rest of the ingredients and season with salt and pepper. Cook on low settings for 7 hours. The chili is best served warm, but it can also be re-heated.

Caramelized Onion Beef Pot Roast

Time: 8 1/2 hours

Servings: 8

Ingredients:
4 pounds beef roast
4 large onions, sliced
3 tablespoons canola oil
4 garlic cloves, chopped
2 carrots, sliced

1 celery root, peeled and cubed
2 large potatoes, peeled and cubed
1 cup beef stock
1/2 cup water
Salt and pepper to taste

Directions:

Heat the oil in a frying pan and add the onions. Cook for 10 minutes until golden brown, slightly caramelized.

Transfer in your slow cooker and add the rest of the ingredients.

Season with enough salt and pepper and cook on low settings for 8 hours.

Serve the pot roast warm.

*I*TALIAN BEEF SPAGHETTI SAUCE

Time: 8 1/2 hours   Servings: 10

Ingredients:

3 pounds ground beef
3 tablespoons canola oil
6 garlic cloves, minced
2 sweet onions, finely chopped
1/2 pound mushrooms, finely chopped
1 can fire roasted tomatoes

1 teaspoon chili powder
2 tablespoons tomato paste
1 teaspoon dried basil
1 teaspoon dried oregano
1 tablespoon balsamic vinegar
Salt and pepper to taste

Directions:

Heat the oil in a frying pan and add the beef. Cook on low flame for a few minutes, stirring often, then transfer the beef in your crock pot.

Add the garlic, onions, mushrooms, tomatoes, chili powder, tomato paste, basil, oregano, balsamic vinegar, salt and pepper.

Cover with a lid and cook on low settings for 8 hours.

Serve the sauce warm and fresh or freeze it into individual portions for later serving.

*O*LD FASHIONED BEEF STEW

Time: 7 1/4 hours   Servings: 6

Ingredients:

1 1/2 pounds beef roast, cubed
2 tablespoons all-purpose flour
2 tablespoons canola oil
1 onion, chopped
1 celery stalk, sliced
4 large carrots, sliced
2 parsnips, sliced

4 potatoes, peeled and cubed
1 cup diced tomatoes
1 1/2 cups beef stock
Salt and pepper to taste
1 bay leaf
1 thyme sprig

Directions:

Heat the oil in a frying pan. Sprinkle the meat with flour and place it in the hot oil. Fry on all sides until golden then transfer in your slow cooker.

Add the rest of the ingredients and season with salt and pepper.

Cook on low settings for 7 hours.

Serve the stew warm and fresh.

French Onion Sandwich Filling

Time: 9 1/4 hours   Servings: 10

Ingredients:
4 pounds beef roast
4 sweet onions, sliced
4 bacon slices, chopped
1 teaspoon garlic powder

1/2 cup white wine
Salt and pepper to taste
1 thyme sprig

Directions:
Combine all the ingredients in your crock pot.
Add salt and pepper to taste and cook on low settings for 9 hours.
When done, shred the meat into fine threads and use it as sandwich filling, warm or chilled.

Layered Enchilada Casserole

Time: 6 1/4 hours   Servings: 6

Ingredients:
1 pound ground beef
2 tablespoons canola oil
1 leek, sliced
1 shallot, chopped
4 garlic cloves, chopped

2 cups sliced mushrooms
2 cups enchilada sauce
6 flour tortillas, shredded
2 cups grated Cheddar
Salt and pepper to taste

Directions:
Heat the oil in a skillet and add the beef. Cook for a few minutes, stirring often then add the leek, shallot and garlic and remove from heat.
Layer the cooked beef, mushrooms, enchilada sauce and tortillas in your slow cooker.
Top with cheese and cook on low settings for 6 hours.
Serve the casserole warm.

Beef Roast with Shallots and Potatoes

Time: 7 1/2 hours   Servings: 6

Ingredients:
1 1/2 pounds beef chuck
2 large onions, sliced
1 1/2 pounds potatoes, peeled and halved
1 cup beef stock
1/2 cup white wine
1 thyme sprig

6 shallots, peeled

1 rosemary sprig
Salt and pepper to taste

Directions:
Combine all the ingredients in your crock pot. Add salt and pepper to taste and cook on low settings for 7 hours.
Serve the roast preferably warm.

Beef Roast with Shiitake Mushrooms

Time: 7 1/4 hours   Servings: 8

Ingredients:
3 pounds beef roast
1/2 pound shiitake mushrooms
1/2 pound baby carrots
1/4 cup low sodium soy sauce

1 tablespoon rice vinegar
1 1/2 cups beef stock
1 thyme sprig
Salt and pepper to taste

Directions:
Combine all the ingredients in your crock pot.
Add salt and pepper if needed and cook on low settings for 7 hours.
Serve the mushrooms warm or chilled.

Tangy Italian Shredded Beef

Time: 8 1/4 hours   Servings: 8

Ingredients:
4 pounds beef sirloin roast, trimmed of fat
1 lemon, juiced
1/4 cup white wine
1 tablespoon honey
1 teaspoon Italian seasoning

Salt and pepper to taste
1/2 cup tomato juice
1 rosemary sprig

Directions:
Mix all the ingredients in your crock pot.
Add enough salt and pepper and cook on low settings for 8 hours.
Serve the beef warm, finely shredded. It can be used in sandwiches or wraps if you want.

Southern Beef Pot Roast

Time: 8 1/4 hours   Servings: 8

Ingredients:
3 pounds beef sirloin roast
8 medium size potatoes, peeled and halved
1/2 pound baby carrots
1 cup red salsa

1 cup beef stock
Salt and pepper to taste
1 thyme sprig

Directions:
Mix all the ingredients in your slow cooker.
Add enough salt and pepper to taste and cook on low settings for 8 hours.
Serve the pot roast warm.

Beef Rice Stuffed Bell Peppers

Time: 6 1/2 hours   Servings: 6

Ingredients:

6 red bell peppers
1 pound ground beef
2 large onions, finely chopped
2 garlic cloves, minced
1 egg
1 cup white rice

2 tablespoons chopped parsley
1 tablespoon chopped dill
Salt and pepper to taste
1 1/2 cups beef stock
1 lemon, juiced

Directions:

Mix the beef, garlic, onions, egg, rice, parsley and dill in a bowl. Add salt and pepper to taste. Carefully cut the top of each bell pepper and stuff them with the beef and rice mix. Place the peppers in your crock pot and add the stock and lemon juice. Cover and cook on low settings for 6 hours. Serve the bell peppers warm and fresh or re-heat them later.

Beef Zucchini Stew

Time: 2 3/4 hours   Servings: 6

Ingredients:

1 pound ground beef
2 tablespoons canola oil
1 leek, sliced
2 garlic cloves, minced
3 zucchinis, sliced
1 can fire roasted tomatoes

1/2 cup beef stock
2 bay leaves
1/4 teaspoon paprika
1/4 teaspoon cumin seeds
Salt and pepper to taste

Directions:

Heat the oil in a skillet or frying pan and add the beef. Cook for a few minutes, stirring often, then transfer in your crock pot. Add the rest of the ingredients in a slow cooker. Adjust the taste with salt and pepper and cook on high settings for 2 1/2 hours. Serve the stew warm and fresh.

Beef Sloppy Joes

Time: 7 1/4 hours   Servings: 8

Ingredients:

2 pounds ground beef
2 large onions, finely chopped
1 tablespoon Worcestershire sauce
1/4 cup hot ketchup

1/2 cup tomato juice
1/2 cup beef stock
Salt and pepper to taste
Bread buns for serving

Directions:

Combine all the ingredients in your slow cooker. Add salt and pepper to taste and cook on low settings for 7 hours. When done, serve the dish in bread buns.

BBQ Beef Brisket

Time: 6 1/4 hours   Servings: 8

Ingredients:
4 pounds beef brisket
2 tablespoons brown sugar
1 teaspoon cumin powder
1 teaspoon smoked paprika
1 teaspoon chili powder
1 teaspoon celery seeds

1 teaspoon salt
1/4 cup apple cider vinegar
1/2 cup beef stock
1 cup ketchup
1 tablespoon Worcestershire sauce
2 tablespoons soy sauce

Directions:
Mix the sugar, cumin powder, paprika, chili powder, celery seeds and salt in a bowl. Spread the mix over the brisket and rub it well into the meat. Combine the vinegar, stock, ketchup, Worcestershire sauce and soy sauce in your crock pot. Add the beef and cook on low settings for 6 hours. Serve the beef brisket sliced and warm.

Vegetable Beef Roast with Horseradish

Time: 6 1/2 hours   Servings: 8

Ingredients:
4 pounds beef roast, trimmed of fat
4 large potatoes, peeled and halved
2 large carrots, sliced
2 onions, quartered
2 cups sliced mushrooms
2 cups snap peas

1 celery root, peeled and cubed
1 cup beef stock
1 cup water
Salt and pepper to taste
1/4 cup prepared horseradish for serving

Directions:
Mix all the ingredients in your crock pot, adding salt and pepper to taste. Cook on low settings for 6 hours. When done, serve the roast warm with prepared horseradish as sauce.

Cowboy Beef

Time: 6 1/4 hours   Servings: 6

Ingredients:
2 1/2 pounds beef sirloin roast
6 bacon slices, chopped
2 onions, sliced
4 garlic cloves, chopped
1 can (15 oz.) red beans, drained

1 cup BBQ sauce
1 teaspoon chili powder
Salt and pepper to taste
Coleslaw for serving

Directions:
Mix the beef sirloin, bacon, onions, garlic, red beans, BBQ sauce, chili powder, salt and pepper and cover with a lid. Cook on low settings for 6 hours.
Serve the beef warm and fresh, topped with fresh coleslaw.

Sweet and Tangy Short Ribs

Time: 9 1/4 hours

Servings: 8

Ingredients:

6 pounds beef short ribs
2 cups BBQ sauce
2 red onions, sliced
1/4 cup balsamic vinegar
1/4 cup brown sugar
2 tablespoons hot sauce

2 tablespoons apricot preserves
2 tablespoons Worcestershire sauce
1 tablespoon Dijon mustard
1 teaspoon garlic powder
1 teaspoon cumin powder
Salt and pepper to taste

Directions:

Mix the BBQ sauce, onions, vinegar, sugar, apricot preserved, Worcestershire sauce, mustard, garlic powder and cumin powder in your crock pot. Add the short ribs and coat them well. Cover the pot and cook on low settings for 9 hours. Serve the ribs warm.

Hungarian Beef Goulash

Time: 7 1/4 hours

Servings: 6

Ingredients:

2 pounds beef steak, cubed
2 tablespoons canola oil
2 red bell peppers, cored and diced
1 carrot, sliced
2 garlic cloves, chopped
1 red onion, chopped
1 can fire roasted tomatoes
2 tablespoons tomato paste

2 pounds potatoes, peeled and cubed
1 teaspoon smoked paprika
1 teaspoon cumin seeds
2 bay leaves
1 cup tomato sauce
1 cup beef stock
Salt and pepper to taste
Sour cream for serving

Directions:

Heat the canola oil in a frying pan and add the beef steak. Cook on all sides for a few minutes then transfer in your crock pot. Add the rest of the ingredients and adjust the taste with salt and pepper. Cover with a lid and cook on low settings for 7 hours. Serve the goulash warm and fresh, topped with sour cream.

Bavarian Beef Roast

Time: 10 1/4 hours

Servings: 6

Ingredients:

2 pounds beef roast
2 tablespoons all-purpose flour
2 tablespoons mustard seeds
1 teaspoon prepared horseradish

1 cup apple juice
1/2 cup beef stock
Salt and pepper to taste

Directions:

Season the beef with salt and pepper and sprinkle with flour. Combine the beef roast and the rest of the ingredients in your crock pot. Add salt and pepper as needed and cook on low settings for 10 hours. Serve the roast while still warm.

BEEF STROGANOFF

Time: 6 1/4 hours   Servings: 6

Ingredients:

1 1/2 pounds beef stew meat, cubed
1 large onion, chopped
4 garlic cloves, minced
1 tablespoon Worcestershire sauce

1/2 cup water
1 cup cream cheese
Salt and pepper to taste
Cooked pasta for serving

Directions:

Mix all the ingredients in a crock pot.
Add salt and pepper to taste and cook on low settings for 6 hours.
Serve the stroganoff warm and serve it with cooked pasta of your choice.

PEPPERONCINI BEEF STEW

Time: 7 1/4 hours   Servings: 8

Ingredients:

2 pounds beef roast, cubed
2 tablespoons canola oil
6 garlic cloves, minced
1 large onion, finely chopped
1 celery stalk, diced

4 red bell peppers, cored and sliced
1 jar pepperoncini
1 can fire roasted tomatoes
1 bay leaf
Salt and pepper to taste

Directions:

Heat the canola oil in a skillet or frying pan and add the beef roast. Cook on all sides until golden brown then transfer in your crock pot.
Add the rest of the ingredients in your crock pot.
Add salt and pepper to taste and cook on low settings for 7 hours.
Serve the stew warm and fresh.

CORNED BEEF WITH SAUERKRAUT

Time: 8 1/4 hours   Servings: 6

Ingredients:

3 pounds corned beef brisket
4 large carrot, sliced
1 pound sauerkraut, shredded
1 onion, sliced

1/2 teaspoon cumin seeds
1 cup beef stock
Salt and pepper to taste

Directions:

Combine all the ingredients in your crock pot.
Add salt and pepper to taste and cook on low settings for 8 hours.
Serve the beef sliced and warm, paired with the sauerkraut.

MEXICAN BRAISED BEEF

Time: 8 1/4 hours   Servings: 8

Ingredients:
4 pounds beef roast
2 chipotle peppers, chopped
1 teaspoon chili powder
1/2 teaspoon cayenne pepper
1/2 teaspoon cumin powder

1 can fire roasted tomatoes
1 cup frozen corn
1/2 teaspoon garlic powder
1 cup beef stock
Salt and pepper to taste

Directions:
Mix the peppers, chili powder, cayenne pepper, cumin powder, tomatoes, frozen corn, garlic powder and stock in your crock pot. Add salt and pepper to taste and cook on low settings for 8 hours. Serve the braised beef warm.

BEEF CABBAGE ROLLS

Time: 6 1/2 hours   Servings: 8

Ingredients:
16 green cabbage leaves
1 1/2 pounds ground beef
1/2 cup white rice
2 onions, finely chopped
2 garlic cloves, minced
2 tablespoons chopped parsley

1 egg
1 tablespoon all-purpose flour
Salt and pepper to taste
1 1/2 cups beef stock
2 lemons, juiced

Directions:
Bring a pot of water to a boil. Add the cabbage leaves and cook for 2 minutes just to soften them. Drain well and allow to cool. Mix the beef, rice, onions, garlic, parsley, egg and flour. Season with salt and pepper and mix well. Place the cabbage leaves on your working board and place a few spoonfuls of beef mixture at one end of each leaf. Roll the leaves tightly, hiding the ends in. Place the cabbage rolls in your crock pot. Add the stock and lemon juice and cook on low settings for 6 hours. Serve the rolls warm.

BELL PEPPER STEAK

Time: 6 1/4 hours   Servings: 4

Ingredients:
2 pounds beef sirloin, cut into thin strips
4 garlic cloves, chopped
2 shallots, sliced
2 red bell peppers, cored and sliced
2 yellow bell peppers, cored and sliced

1 tablespoon brown sugar
1 tablespoon apple cider vinegar
1 tablespoon soy sauce
Salt and pepper to taste

Directions:
Mix the beef sirloin, garlic, shallots, bell peppers, sugar, vinegar, soy sauce, salt and pepper in your crock pot. Cover with its lid and cook on low settings for 6 hours. Serve the beef sirloin warm.

BUTTON MUSHROOM BEEF STEW

Time: 6 1/2 hours

Servings: 6

Ingredients:

2 pounds beef roast, cubed
1 tablespoon all-purpose flour
2 tablespoons canola oil
2 carrots, diced
1 celery root, peeled and diced
1 can fire roasted tomatoes

1 pound button mushrooms
1 cup beef stock
2 bay leaves
1 red chili, chopped
Salt and pepper to taste

Directions:

Season the beef with salt and pepper and sprinkle it with flour. Heat the oil in a frying pan and add the beef. Cook for a few minutes until golden then transfer in your slow cooker. Add the rest of the ingredients and adjust the taste with salt and pepper. Cover and cook on low settings for 6 hours. Serve the stew warm or chilled.

THE ULTIMATE CHILI

Time: 7 1/4 hours

Servings: 8

Ingredients:

2 pounds ground beef
2 tablespoons canola oil
1 large onion, chopped
4 garlic cloves, chopped
2 cans (15 oz. each) kidney beans, drained
1 can fire roasted tomatoes
2 celery stalks, sliced

2 carrots, sliced
1 teaspoon chili powder
1 teaspoon cumin powder
1/4 cup red wine
1 cup beef stock
Salt and pepper to taste
Sour cream for serving

Directions:

Heat the oil in a skillet and add the ground beef. Cook for a few minutes, stirring often, then transfer in your slow cooker. Add the rest of the ingredients and season with salt and pepper. Cook on low settings for 7 hours. Serve the chili warm, topped with sour cream.

TOMATO BEEF STEW

Time: 5 1/4 hours

Servings: 6

Ingredients:

2 pounds beef roast, cubed
2 tablespoons canola oil
1 shallot, sliced
4 garlic cloves, minced
4 heirloom tomatoes, peeled and cubed

1 cup beef stock
1/2 teaspoon cumin powder
1/2 teaspoon dried oregano
Salt and pepper to taste

Directions:

Heat the oil in a frying pan and add the beef. Cook for 5 minutes until golden then transfer in your crock pot. Add the remaining ingredients and season well with salt and pepper. Cook for 5 hours on low settings. The stew is best served warm, although it can also be frozen into individual portions for later serving.

*B*EEF CURRY STEW

Time: 7 1/4 hours

Servings: 6

Ingredients:

2 tablespoons canola oil
2 pounds beef roast, cubed
2 garlic cloves, chopped
1 teaspoon grated ginger
1 sweet onion, chopped
1 jalapeno pepper, chopped
1 tablespoon curry powder

1 cup beef stock
1 cup diced tomatoes
1 cup green peas
1 bay leaf
1 lemongrass stalk, crushed
Salt and pepper to taste
Chopped cilantro for serving

Directions:

Heat the oil in a frying pan and add the beef. Cook for 5 minutes until golden then transfer in your crock pot.
Add the meat in your crock pot and stir in the rest of the ingredients.
Adjust the taste with salt and pepper and cook the stew on low settings for 7 hours.
Serve the stew warm and fresh, topped with chopped cilantro.

*B*EEF ROAST AU JUS

Time: 10 1/4 hours

Servings: 8

Ingredients:

4 pounds rump roast
1 tablespoon ground black pepper
1 tablespoon smoked paprika
1 teaspoon chili powder

1 teaspoon garlic powder
1 teaspoon mustard seeds
1 cup water
Salt and pepper to taste

Directions:

Mix the black pepper, paprika, chili powder, garlic powder, mustard seeds, salt and pepper in a bowl.
Spread this mixture over the beef and rub it well into the meat.
Place the beef on your crock pot and add the water.
Cover with its lid and cook on low settings for 10 hours.
Serve the beef roast sliced and warm.

*C*OFFEE BEEF ROAST

Time: 4 1/4 hours

Servings: 6

Ingredients:

2 pounds beef sirloin
2 tablespoons olive oil
4 garlic cloves, minced

1 cup strong brewed coffee
1/2 cup beef stock
Salt and pepper to taste

Directions:

Combine all the ingredients in your crock pot, adding salt and pepper to taste.
Cover with a lid and cook on high settings for 4 hours. Serve the roast warm and fresh with your favorite side dish.

Root Vegetable Beef Stew

Time: 8 1/2 hours   Servings: 8

Ingredients:

3 pounds beef sirloin roast, cubed
4 carrots, sliced
2 parsnips, sliced
1 celery root, peeled and cubed
4 garlic cloves, chopped
4 large potatoes, peeled and cubed

1 turnip, peeled and cubed
1 bay leaf
1 lemon, juiced
1 teaspoon Worcestershire sauce
1 cup beef stock
Salt and pepper to taste

Directions:

Combine the beef, carrots, parsnips, celery root, garlic, potatoes, turnip, bay leaf, lemon juice, Worcestershire sauce and stock in your crock pot. Add salt and pepper to taste and cover with its lid. Cook on low settings for 8 hours. Serve the roast and vegetables warm.

Beef Bolognese Sauce

Time: 6 1/4 hours   Servings: 6

Ingredients:

2 tablespoons canola oil
2 pounds ground beef
1 carrot, grated
1 celery stalk, finely chopped
4 garlic cloves, minced
1 can (15 oz.) diced tomatoes
2 tablespoons tomato paste

1/2 teaspoon dried oregano
1/2 teaspoon dried basil
1/4 cup red wine
1/2 cup beef stock
Salt and pepper to taste
Grated Parmesan cheese for serving
Cooked pasta of your choice for serving

Directions:

Heat the oil in a frying pan and add the ground beef. Cook for a few minutes then transfer in your slow cooker. Add the rest of the ingredients and adjust the taste with salt and pepper. Cook on low settings for 6 hours. Serve the sauce warm, over cooked past, topped with grated cheese or freeze the sauce into individual portions for later serving.

Hamburger Beef Casserole

Time: 7 1/2 hours   Servings: 6

Ingredients:

1 1/2 pounds beef sirloin, cut into thin trips
2 large potatoes, peeled and finely sliced
1 celery stalk, sliced
2 onions, sliced
1 cup green peas

1 can condensed cream of mushroom soup
Salt and pepper to taste
1 cup processed meat, shredded
1 cup grated Cheddar cheese

Directions:

Mix the beef, potatoes, celery stalk, green peas, mushroom soup, salt and pepper in your crock pot. Top with both cheeses and cover with a lid. Cook on low settings for 7 hours. Serve the casserole preferably warm.

Texas Style Braised Beef

Time: 8 1/4 hours   Servings: 8

Ingredients:

4 pounds beef sirloin roast
2 chipotle peppers, chopped
2 green chile peppers, chopped
1 shallot, chopped
1 cup BBQ sauce

2 tablespoons brown sugar
1/2 teaspoon garlic powder
1/2 teaspoon chili powder
Salt and pepper to taste

Directions:

Mix the chipotle peppers, green chile peppers, shallot, BBQ sauce, brown sugar, garlic powder, chili powder, salt and pepper to taste in your slow cooker. Add the beef and coat it well with this mix. Cover and cook on low settings for 8 hours. When done, slice and serve the beef warm with your favorite side dish.

Mediterranean Beef Stew

Time: 7 1/4 hours   Servings: 8

Ingredients:

2 pounds beef sirloin, cubed
2 tablespoons canola oil
1 large sweet onion, finely chopped
4 garlic cloves, minced
2 ripe tomatoes, peeled and diced
2 zucchinis, cubed
4 red bell peppers, cored and diced
1 cup tomato sauce

2 tablespoons tomato paste
1/2 cup fresh orange juice
1 teaspoon dried oregano
1/2 teaspoon dried basil
Salt and pepper to taste
1 bay leaf
1 thyme sprig
1 rosemary sprig

Directions:

Heat the oil in a frying pan and add the beef sirloin. Cook for a few minutes until golden then transfer in your slow cooker. Add the remaining ingredients in the recipe and season with salt and pepper. Cover the pot with a lid and cook on low settings for 8 hours. Serve the stew warm or chilled.

Beef Three Bean Casserole

Time: 6 1/4 hours   Servings: 8

Ingredients:

1 pound ground beef
4 bacon slices, chopped
2 tablespoons canola oil
1 can (15 oz.) black beans, drained
1 can (15 oz.) red beans, drained
1 can (15 oz.) kidney beans, drained
2 carrots, diced
1 celery stalk, diced

4 garlic cloves, chopped
1 tablespoon molasses
1/4 teaspoon cayenne pepper
1 cup beef stock
1/4 cup tomato paste
Salt and pepper to taste
1 1/2 cups grated Cheddar

Directions:

Heat the oil in a frying pan and add the beef and bacon. Cook for 5 minutes, stirring often then transfer the mixture in your slow cooker.

Add the beans, carrots, celery, garlic, molasses, cayenne, stock and tomato paste, as well as salt and pepper.

Top with Cheddar and cook on low settings for 6 hours.

The casserole is best served warm.

GARLICKY BEEF PASTA SAUCE

Time: 8 1/4 hours   Servings: 10

Ingredients:

2 pounds ground beef
1 pound pork sausages, casings removed
2 large onions, finely chopped
8 garlic cloves, minced
2 tablespoons olive oil
1 teaspoon Italian herbs
1/2 teaspoon dried marjoram

1 can (29 oz.) diced tomatoes
1 cup tomato juice
1/2 cup red wine
1/4 teaspoon cayenne pepper
1 tablespoon brown sugar
Salt and pepper to taste

Directions:

Combine the beef, sausages, onion, garlic, olive oil, herbs, tomatoes, tomato juice, red wine, cayenne and sugar in a slow cooker.

Add salt and pepper to taste and cover with a lid.

Cook on low settings for 8 hours.

Serve the sauce warm and fresh or freeze it into individual portions for later serving.

CROUTON BEEF STEW

Time: 5 1/4 hours   Servings: 6

Ingredients:

1 pound ground beef
2 tablespoons canola oil
1 shallot, chopped
2 garlic cloves, chopped
1 can fire roasted tomatoes
1 poblano pepper, chopped

1 cup beef stock
1 cup finely chopped mushrooms
2 celery stalks, chopped
2 carrots, sliced
Salt and pepper to taste
8 oz. bread croutons

Directions:

Heat the oil in a skillet and add the beef. Cook for a few minutes then transfer the meat in your slow cooker.

Add the shallot, garlic, tomatoes, poblano pepper, stock, mushrooms, celery and carrots, as well as salt and pepper.

Add salt and pepper as well.

Top with bread croutons and cover with a lid.

Cook on low settings for 5 hours.

Serve the stew warm and fresh.

SWISS STEAKS

Time: 8 1/4 hours   Servings: 4

Ingredients:
4 beef steaks
2 tablespoons all-purpose flour
2 tablespoons canola oil
2 red bell peppers, cored and sliced

1 shallot, sliced
1 can (15 oz.) diced tomatoes
Salt and pepper to taste

Directions:
Season the steaks with salt and pepper and sprinkle with flour. Heat the oil in a frying pan and add the steaks in the hot oil. Fry on each side until golden then place the steaks in your slow cooker. Add the remaining ingredients and add salt and pepper if needed. Cover and cook on low settings for 8 hours. Serve the steaks and sauce warm.

CARNE GUISADA

Time: 6 1/2 hours   Servings: 8

Ingredients:
3 pounds beef chuck roast, cut into small cubes
2 red bell peppers, cored and diced
2 shallots, chopped
3 garlic cloves, minced
4 medium size potatoes, peeled and cubed

1/4 teaspoon chili powder
1/2 teaspoon cumin powder
1 1/2 cups beef stock
1 cup tomato sauce
Salt and pepper to taste

Directions:
Combine the chuck roast, bell peppers, shallots, garlic, tomatoes, chili powder, cumin powder, stock and tomato sauce in your crock pot. Season with salt and pepper as needed and cook on low settings for 6 hours. The carne guisada is best served in burritos or tortillas.

RED WINE ONION BRAISED BEEF

Time: 7 1/4 hours   Servings: 8

Ingredients:
2 pounds beef chuck roast
1 cup red wine
2 red onions, sliced
1 thyme sprig

1 teaspoon ground coriander
1 teaspoon cumin powder
Salt and pepper to taste

Directions:
Season the beef roast with salt, pepper, coriander and cumin powder.
Place the meat in your crock pot and add the rest of the ingredients.
Cook on low settings for 7 hours.
Serve the beef roast sliced and warm.

Beer Braised Beef

Time: 8 1/4 hours   Servings: 6

Ingredients:

2 pounds beef sirloin
1/2 pound baby carrots
2 large potatoes, peeled and cubed
1 celery stalk, sliced
1 large sweet onion, chopped

4 garlic cloves, chopped
1 thyme sprig
1 cup dark beer
1/4 cup beef stock
Salt and pepper to taste

Directions:

Mix all the ingredients in your crock pot, adding salt and pepper to taste.
Cover the pot with its lid and cook on low settings for 8 hours.
Serve the beef and veggies warm and fresh.

Cabbage Rice Beef Stew

Time: 6 1/2 hours   Servings: 6

Ingredients:

1 pound beef roast, cut into thin strips
2 tablespoons canola oil
1 head green cabbage, shredded
1 large onion, chopped
1 large carrot, grated
2 ripe tomatoes, peeled and diced
1 cup white rice

1 cup beef stock
1/4 cup water
2 tablespoons tomato paste
1/2 teaspoon cumin seeds
1/2 teaspoon chili powder
Salt and pepper to taste

Directions:

Heat the oil in a frying pan and add the beef. Sauté for a few minutes on all sides then transfer in your crock pot. Add the cabbage, onion, carrot, tomatoes, rice, stock, water, tomato paste, cumin seeds and chili powder in your cooker as well. Adjust the taste with salt and pepper and cook on low settings for 6 hours. The stew is best served warm.

Marinara Flank Steaks

Time: 5 1/4 hours   Servings: 4

Ingredients:

4 flank steaks
2 cups marinara sauce
1 tablespoon balsamic vinegar

1 teaspoon dried Italian herbs
Salt and pepper to taste
1 cup shredded mozzarella

Directions:

Place the steaks in your slow cooker.
Add the marinara sauce, balsamic vinegar, Italian herbs, salt and pepper and mix well then top with the cheese.
Cover with a lid and cook on low settings for 5 hours.
Serve the steaks and sauce warm while the cheese is still gooey.

GROUND BEEF BBQ

Time: 7 1/4 hours

Servings: 8

Ingredients:

3 pounds ground beef
1 large onion, chopped
4 garlic cloves, chopped
2 celery stalks, chopped
1 tablespoon apple cider vinegar

1 teaspoon Dijon mustard
1 tablespoon brown sugar
1 1/2 cups BBQ sauce
1/2 cup beef sauce
Salt and pepper to taste

Directions:

Combine all the ingredients in your crock pot.
Season with salt and pepper and cook on low settings for 7 hours.
Serve the BBQ beef warm.

BEEF OKRA TOMATO STEW

Time: 6 1/4 hours

Servings: 6

Ingredients:

1 1/2 pounds beef roast, cut into thin strips
1 large onion, chopped
4 garlic cloves, minced
1 can (15 oz.) diced tomatoes
12 oz. frozen okra, chopped
Chopped parsley for serving

2 large potatoes, peeled and cubed
1 cup beef stock
1 thyme sprig
Salt and pepper to taste

Directions:

Combine the beef roast, onion, garlic, tomatoes, okra, potatoes, stock and thyme sprig in your crock pot.
Add salt and pepper to taste and cook on low settings for 6 hours.
Serve the stew warm and fresh or chilled, topped with chopped parsley.

BEEF BARBACOA

Time: 6 1/2 hours

Servings: 8

Ingredients:

4 pounds beef chuck roast
2 red onions, sliced
6 garlic cloves, chopped
3 tablespoons white wine vinegar

1 1/2 cups tomato sauce
1 1/2 teaspoons chili powder
Salt and pepper to taste

Directions:

Mix all the ingredients in your crock pot.
Add enough salt and pepper and cook on low settings for 6 hours.
Serve the beef barbacoa warm.

Caribe Pot Roast

Time: 8 1/4 hours   Servings: 8

Ingredients:

4 pounds boneless beef chuck roast
4 garlic cloves, chopped
2 large onions, sliced
1 celery stalk, sliced
2 tablespoons brown sugar
1 1/2 cups tomato sauce

1 tablespoon cocoa powder
1 teaspoon chili powder
1/2 teaspoon cumin powder
1/2 teaspoon dried oregano
Salt and pepper to taste

Directions:

Mix all the ingredients in your slow cooker. Add salt and pepper to taste and cover the pot with its lid. Cook on low settings for 8 hours . The pot roast can be served both warm and chilled.

Cajun Beef Stew

Time: 6 1/2 hours   Servings: 6

Ingredients:

1 1/2 pounds beef sirloin, cubed
4 bacon slices, chopped
2 tablespoons canola oil
1 tablespoon Cajun seasoning
1 teaspoon garlic powder

1/4 teaspoon chili powder
1 tablespoon apple cider vinegar
1 1/2 pounds potatoes, peeled and cubed
Salt and pepper to taste

Directions:

Heat the oil in a frying pan and add the bacon and beef. Cook for about 5 minutes until the beef begins to turn golden and the bacon crisp. Transfer in your crock pot and add the rest of the ingredients. Season with salt and pepper and cover with a lid. Cook on low settings for 6 hours. Serve the stew warm or chilled.

Everything But the Kitchen Sink Beef Stew

Time: 8 1/2 hours   Servings: 8

Ingredients:

2 pounds beef roast, cubed
1 large onion, chopped
2 carrots, sliced
1 can (15 oz.) white beans, drained
1 large zucchini, cubed
2 sweet potatoes, peeled and cubed
1 cup frozen corn
1 cup diced tomatoes

1 cup green peas
1/2 teaspoon chili powder
1 teaspoon dried oregano
1 teaspoon jerk seasoning
Salt and pepper to taste
1 1/2 cups beef stock
Sour cream for serving

Directions:

Combine the beef roast, onion, carrots, beans, zucchini, potatoes, corn, tomatoes, green peas, chili powder, oregano, jerk seasoning and stock in your crock pot. Add salt and pepper and mix well. Cover with its lid and cook on low settings for 8 hours. Serve the stew warm, topped with sour cream.

Stuffed Flank Steaks

Time: 6 1/2 hours   Servings: 2

Ingredients:

2 thick flank steaks
1/2 cup grated Cheddar
1/4 cup cream cheese

1 red bell pepper, cored and diced
Salt and pepper to taste
1/2 cup beef stock

Directions:

Mix the Cheddar with cream cheese, diced bell pepper, salt and pepper in a bowl.
Take each steak and make a small pocket into each one. Fill each steak with the cheese mix and secure the pocket with toothpicks.
Cover with a lid and place in your crock pot.
Add the stock and cook on low setting for 6 hours.
Serve the steaks warm with your favorite side dish.

Hominy Beef Chili

Time: 3 1/4 hours   Servings: 6

Ingredients:

1 pound ground beef
1 large onion, chopped
4 garlic cloves, chopped
2 carrots, diced
2 red bell peppers, cored and diced
1 can (15 oz.) hominy, drained
1 can fire roasted tomatoes

2 jalapeno peppers, chopped
1/2 teaspoon cumin powder
1 teaspoon chili powder
2 cups frozen corn
Salt and pepper to taste
1 bay leaf
Grated Cheddar for serving

Directions:

Mix the ground beef, onion, garlic, carrots, bell peppers, hominy, tomatoes, jalapeno peppers, cumin powder, chili powder and corn in your crock pot.
Add the bay leaf, salt and pepper to taste and cook on high settings for 3 hours.
Serve the chili warm, topped with grated Cheddar.

Mexican Beef Stuffed Bell Peppers

Time: 6 1/2 hours   Servings: 6

Ingredients:

6 green bell peppers
1 pound ground beef
1/2 cup white rice
1 cup frozen corn
1 tablespoon chopped parsley
1 chipotle pepper, chopped
1/2 teaspoon cumin powder

1/4 teaspoon chili powder
Salt and pepper to taste
1 cup tomato sauce
1 chipotle pepper, chopped
1 cup beef stock
1 lime, juiced
Sour cream for serving

Directions:

Cut the top of each bell pepper and remove the core carefully, making sure to leave the peppers intact.

In a bowl, mix the beef, rice, corn, parsley, chipotle pepper, cumin powder and chili powder. Add salt and pepper to taste then stuff each bell pepper with the mixture.

Place the bell peppers in your crock pot.

Add the tomato sauce, chipotle pepper, stock and lime juice then cover the pot and cook on low settings for 6 hours.

Serve the stuffed bell peppers warm, topped with sour cream.

Beef Macaroni

Time: 5 1/4 hours   Servings: 6

Ingredients:

1 pound ground beef
1 tablespoon canola oil
1 shallot, chopped
2 garlic cloves, minced
1 can (28 oz.) crushed tomatoes
1 cup beef stock

8 oz. macaroni pasta, cooked in a large pot of water
1/2 cup grated Parmesan
1 cup shredded mozzarella
Salt and pepper to taste

Directions:

Heat the oil in a skillet and add the beef. Cook for 2 minutes, stirring often then add the shallot and onion, as well as tomatoes. Cook for 5 minutes.

Transfer the beef mixture in your crock pot and add the rest of the ingredients.

Season with salt and pepper and cook on low settings for 5 hours.

Serve the macaroni warm.

Apple Corned Beef with Red Cabbage

Time: 6 1/2 hours   Servings: 6

Ingredients:

1 1/2 pounds beef chuck roast, cubed
1 red cabbage, shredded
1/2 teaspoon cumin seeds
1 cinnamon stick
1 star anise
1/2 cup red wine

1 tablespoon red wine vinegar
1/2 cup beef stock
2 red apples, cored and diced
1 bay leaf
Salt and pepper to taste

Directions:

Mix the chuck roast, cabbage, cumin seeds, cinnamon, star anise, red wine, vinegar, stock and apples in your crock pot.

Add the bay leaf, salt and pepper and cook on low settings for 6 hours.

The dish is best served warm.

Sweet Potato Shepherd's Pie

Time: 6 3/4 hours   Servings: 6

Ingredients:

1 pound ground beef
2 tablespoons canola oil
1 large onion, finely chopped
2 carrots, grated
2 celery stalks, chopped
4 garlic cloves, chopped

1 cup diced tomatoes
1/2 teaspoon chili powder
Salt and pepper to taste
2 pounds sweet potatoes, peeled and cubed
1/2 cup grated Parmesan

Directions:

Heat the oil in a skillet and add the beef. Cook for a few minutes, stirring often, then add then transfer in your crock pot. Add the onion, carrots, celery stalks, garlic and tomatoes, as well as chili powder, salt and pepper. Cook the sweet potatoes in a steamer for 15 minutes then mash them finely. Add salt and pepper to taste then spoon the sweet potatoes over the beef mixture. Top with grated cheese and cook on low settings for 6 hours. Serve the pie warm.

Chunky Beef Pasta Sauce

Time: 6 1/2 hours   Servings: 8

Ingredients:

2 pounds beef sirloin, cut into thin strips
1 carrot, diced
1 celery stalk, diced
2 garlic cloves, chopped
1 can (28 oz.) diced tomatoes

2 cups sliced mushrooms
1/4 cup red wine
1 cup tomato sauce
1 bay leaf
Salt and pepper to taste

Directions:

Combine the beef sirloin, carrot, celery, garlic, tomatoes, mushrooms, red wine, tomato sauce and bay leaf in your slow cooker. Add enough salt and pepper and cover with its lid. Cook on low settings for 6 hours. Serve the sauce right away with cooked pasta or freeze it into individual portions to serve later.

Hot Corned Beef

Time: 6 1/4 hours   Servings: 6

Ingredients:

2 pounds corned beef
1 cup beef stock
2 tablespoons balsamic vinegar

1 tablespoon Dijon mustard
2 chipotle peppers, chopped
Salt and pepper to taste

Directions:

Combine the stock, vinegar, mustard and chipotle peppers in your crock pot.
Place the corned beef in your slow cooker and place the beef in your pot.
Add salt and pepper if needed and cook on low settings for 6 hours.
Serve the beef warm and fresh.

MEDITERRANEAN BEEF BRISKET

Time: 7 1/2 hours   Servings: 8

Ingredients:

4 pounds beef brisket
1 can (15 oz.) diced tomatoes
1/2 cup dry red wine
1/2 cup pitted Kalamata olives, sliced

4 garlic cloves, chopped
1 rosemary sprig
1 thyme sprig
Salt and pepper to taste

Directions:

Mix the tomatoes, red wine, Kalamata olives, garlic, thyme sprig and rosemary sprig in your crock pot. Add salt and pepper to taste and cover with a lid. Cook on low settings for 7 hours. Serve the beef brisket and the sauce warm or chilled.

SRIRACHA STYLE CORNED BEEF

Time: 5 1/4 hours   Servings: 6

Ingredients:

2 pounds corned beef
1/4 cup low sodium soy sauce
2 tablespoons brown sugar
4 garlic cloves, chopped
1/2 teaspoon onion powder
1 tablespoon Sriracha

1 teaspoon sesame oil
1 tablespoon rice vinegar
2 shallots, sliced
1/2 cup beef stock
Salt and pepper to taste

Directions:

Mix the soy sauce, sugar, garlic, onion powder, Sriracha, sesame oil, vinegar, stock and shallots in your crock pot. Place the beef in the pot and coat it well with the sauce. Add salt and pepper if needed and cook on low settings for 5 hours. Serve the beef sliced and warm with your favorite side dish.

FRENCH STYLE BRAISED BEEF SIRLOIN

Time: 8 1/4 hours   Servings: 8

Ingredients:

4 pounds beef sirloin
1 cup dry white wine
4 large onions, sliced
6 garlic cloves, chopped
1/2 pound button mushrooms
2 carrots, sliced

1 celery stalk, sliced
1 cup beef stock
1 thyme sprig
1 rosemary sprig
Salt and pepper to taste

Directions:

Combine the wine, onions, garlic, mushrooms, carrots, celery stalk, beef stock, thyme and rosemary sprig in your crock pot. Season the beef with salt and pepper and place in the pot. Cover with its lid and cook on low settings for 8 hours. When done, slice the beef and serve it warm.

CLASSIC OSSO BUCO

Time: 7 1/4 hours   Servings: 4

Ingredients:

4 veal shanks
2 tablespoons all-purpose flour
2 tablespoon butter
2 red onions, chopped
1 can (15 oz.) diced tomatoes

1/4 cup red wine
1 teaspoon dried thyme
1/4 teaspoon cayenne pepper
1/2 teaspoon garlic powder
Salt and pepper to taste

Directions:

Season the veal shanks with salt and pepper and sprinkle them with flour. Melt the butter in a frying pan and add the veal shanks. Cook on all sides until golden. Mix the remaining ingredients in your crock pot then place the veal shanks on top. Cover with a lid and cook on low settings for 7 hours. Serve the osso bucco and the sauce formed in the pot warm and fresh.

CURRIED BEEF SHORT RIBS

Time: 8 1/4 hours   Servings: 6

Ingredients:

4 pounds beef short ribs
3 tablespoons red curry paste
1 cup tomato sauce
1 teaspoon curry powder
1/2 teaspoon garlic powder

2 shallots, chopped
1 teaspoon grated ginger
1 lime, juiced
Salt and pepper to taste

Directions:

Mix the curry paste, tomato sauce, curry powder, garlic powder, shallots, ginger and lime juice in a crock pot. Add salt and pepper then place the ribs in the pot as well. Coat the ribs well and cover with a lid. Cook on low settings for 8 hours. Serve the ribs warm and fresh.

BEEF BARLEY STEW

Time: 6 1/2 hours   Servings: 6

Ingredients:

1 pound beef chuck roast, cut into thin strips
2 tablespoons canola oil
1 shallot, chopped
2 garlic cloves, chopped
1 carrot, diced
1 celery stalk, diced

1 cup pearl barley
1/4 cup dried currants
1/4 cup pine nuts
2 cups beef stock
Salt and pepper to taste

Directions:

Heat the oil in a frying pan and add the beef. Cook for a few minutes on all sides then transfer in your crock pot. Add the shallot, garlic, carrot, celery, pearl barley, currants, pine nuts and stock. Add salt and pepper to taste and cook on low settings for 6 hours. The stew is great served both warm and chilled.

Beef Pot Roast with Turnip Greens

Time: 7 1/4 hours   Servings: 6

Ingredients:

1 1/2 pounds beef roast, cubed
2 tablespoons all-purpose flour
2 tablespoons canola oil
4 parsnips, peeled and chopped
1 shallot, chopped
1 garlic clove, chopped

1/2 cup red wine
2 tablespoons tomato paste
1 cup beef stock
1 bunch turnip greens, shredded
Salt and pepper to taste

Directions:

Season the beef with salt and pepper and sprinkle with flour. Heat the oil in a skillet and add the beef. Cook for a few minutes on each side then transfer in your crock pot. Add the rest of the ingredients and adjust the taste with salt and pepper. Cover with a lid and cook on low settings for 7 hours. Serve the dish warm.

Gruyere Flank Steaks

Time: 3 1/4 hours   Servings: 4

Ingredients:

4 flank steaks
Salt and pepper to taste
1 cup crumbled gruyere cheese
1/2 cup white wine

1 teaspoon Worcestershire sauce
1/2 cup cream cheese
1 teaspoon Dijon mustard
Salt and pepper to taste

Directions:

Season the steaks with salt and pepper. Place them in your slow cooker. Mix the rest of the ingredients in a bowl then spoon the mixture over the steaks. Cover the pot and cook on high settings for 3 hours. Serve the steaks warm with your favorite side dish.

Collard Green Feet Sauté

Time: 3 1/4 hours   Servings: 6

Ingredients:

1 1/2 pounds beef roast, cut into thin strips
1 tablespoon all-purpose flour
1/2 teaspoon cumin powder
2 tablespoons canola oil

2 bunches collard greens, shredded
1/4 cup beef stock
Salt and pepper to taste

Directions:

Season the beef with salt and pepper and sprinkle it with flour and cumin powder.
Heat the oil in a skillet and add the beef roast. Cook for a few minutes on all sides then transfer in your crock pot.
Add the rest of the ingredients and cover with a lid.
Cook on high settings for 3 hours.
Serve the dish warm and fresh.

Autumn Red Beef Curry

Time: 7 1/2 hours   Servings: 6

Ingredients:

1 1/2 pound beef roast, cubed
2 tablespoons coconut oil
1 shallot, chopped
4 garlic cloves, minced
2 cups butternut squash cubes
2 tomatoes, peeled and diced
1 sweet potato, peeled and cubed

1 star anise
1 cinnamon stick
1 bay leaf
3 red curry paste
1/2 teaspoon chili powder
1 1/2 cups coconut milk
Salt and pepper to taste

Directions:

Heat the oil in a skillet and add the beef. Cook on all sides until golden then transfer in your crock pot. Stir in the remaining ingredients and adjust the taste with salt and pepper. Cover and cook on low settings for 7 hours. Serve the curry warm and fresh.

Saffron Beef Tagine

Time: 7 1/4 hours   Servings: 6

Ingredients:

2 pounds beef sirloin, cubed
2 tablespoons olive oil
1 large onion, chopped
4 garlic clove, chopped
1 celery stalk, sliced
2 ripe tomatoes, peeled and diced
1 cup dried plums, chopped
1/2 teaspoon saffron threads

1/2 cup couscous
1 1/2 cups vegetable stock
Salt and pepper to taste
1 orange, sliced
2 tablespoons sliced almonds
Chopped parsley for serving
Lime juice for serving

Directions:

Heat the oil in a skillet and add the beef. Cook for a few minutes and transfer in your slow cooker. Stir in the remaining ingredients and season with salt and pepper. Cook the tagine on low settings for 7 hours and serve it warm and fresh, topped with chopped parsley and a drizzle of lime juice.

Jalapeno Braised Beef Flank Steaks

Time: 6 1/4 hours   Servings: 4

Ingredients:

4 flank steaks
4 jalapeno peppers, chopped
2 red bell peppers, cored and sliced
1 can fire roasted tomatoes

1/2 teaspoon cumin seeds
1/2 teaspoon mustard seeds
Salt and pepper to taste

Directions:

Mix all the ingredients in your crock pot, adding salt and pepper as needed. Cover the pot with its lid and cook on low settings for 6 hours. Serve the steaks warm.

VEAL PAPRIKASH

Time: 5 1/4 hours   Servings: 6

Ingredients:

2 pounds veal roast, cubed
2 tablespoons all-purpose flour
2 tablespoons butter
2 carrots, diced
1 celery stalk, diced
2 garlic cloves, sliced
1 teaspoon sweet paprika

1 teaspoon smoked paprika
2 tablespoons red pepper paste
1 can fire roasted tomatoes
1/2 cup beef stock
Salt and pepper to taste
2 bay leaves
Sour cream for serving

Directions:

Season the veal with salt and pepper and sprinkle it with flour. Heat the butter in a frying pan and add the veal. Cook for a few minutes then transfer in your slow cooker. Add the carrots, celery, garlic, paprika, red pepper paste, tomatoes and beef stock and season with salt and pepper. Throw in the bay leaves and cover the pot with a lid. Cook on low settings for 5 hours. Serve the paprikash warm, topped with a dollop of sour cream.

CURRIED YOGURT BRAISED BEEF

Time: 8 1/4 hours   Servings: 6

Ingredients:

2 pounds beef roast, cubed
1 1/2 cups plain yogurt
1 1/2 teaspoons curry powder
1/2 teaspoon cumin powder
1 teaspoon chili powder
1 teaspoon smoked paprika

1 teaspoon dried mint
2 tablespoons olive oil
Salt and pepper to taste
1/2 cup beef stock
Cooked basmati rice for serving

Directions:

Mix the beef roast, yogurt, curry powder, cumin powder, chili, paprika, mint and olive oil in a zip lock bag. Add salt and pepper to taste and mix well then seal the bag and place it in the fridge for 2 hours. Transfer the meat and sauce in your slow cooker. Add the stock then cook on low settings for 6 hours. Serve the beef over cooked basmati rice.

GINGER RUMP ROAST

Time: 6 1/4 hours   Servings: 6

Ingredients:

2 pounds rump roast
1 lemon, sliced
1 teaspoon grated ginger
4 black peppercorns
2 whole cloves

1 star anise
1 cinnamon stick
1 1/2 cups beef stock
Salt and pepper to taste

Directions:

Mix all the ingredients in your crock pot. Add salt and pepper to taste and cook on low settings for 6 hours. Serve the roast warm and fresh.

GARDEN BEEF STEW

Time: 7 1/4 hours   Servings: 8

Ingredients:

3 pounds beef roast, cubed
2 tablespoons canola oil
2 red bell peppers, cored and sliced
2 yellow bell peppers, cored and sliced
1 cup tomato sauce

2 cups cherry tomatoes
2 bay leaves
1 thyme sprig
1 pinch cayenne pepper
Salt to taste

Directions:

Heat the canola oil in a large frying pan and add the beef. Cook for a few minutes on all sides until golden then transfer in your slow cooker. Add the remaining ingredients and season with salt as needed. Cover the pot with its lid and cook on low settings for 7 hours. Serve the stew warm.

ROASTED GARLIC SHREDDED BEEF

Time: 9 1/4 hours   Servings: 8

Ingredients:

4 pounds beef roast
4 whole garlic heads, peeled
2 tablespoons olive oil
2 shallots, sliced

1 cup beef stock
Salt and pepper to taste
1 thyme sprig

Directions:

Combine the garlic and olive oil in a pot and add salt and pepper to taste. Cover with aluminum foil and cook in the preheated oven at 350F for 1 hour then transfer in your slow cooker. Add the rest of the ingredients and adjust the taste with salt and pepper if needed. Cover with a lid and cook on low settings for 8 hours. When done, shred the meat finely and serve it warm or chilled.

BEEF NACHO CASSEROLE

Time: 6 1/2 hours   Servings: 6

Ingredients:

1 pound ground beef
2 tablespoons canola oil
2 garlic cloves, minced
1 shallot, chopped
1 chipotle pepper, cored and chopped

1/2 cup tomato sauce
Salt and pepper to taste
12 oz. nachos
1 can (10 oz.) corn, drained
2 cups grated Cheddar

Directions:

Heat the canola oil and add the beef. Cook for 5 minutes then stir in the garlic, shallot and chipotle pepper, as well as tomato sauce, salt and pepper. Cook for another 5 minutes then remove from heat. Place the nachos in your crock pot. Top with the beef mixture, followed by the corn and cheese. Cover the pot with a lid and cook on low settings for 6 hours. Serve the nacho casserole warm.

Bacon Wrapped Beef Tenderloin

Time: 8 1/4 hours   Servings: 6

Ingredients:
2 pounds beef tenderloin
1 teaspoon cumin powder
1 teaspoon smoked paprika
1 teaspoon dried thyme

2 tablespoons olive oil
8 slices bacon
1 cup beef stock
Salt and pepper to taste

Directions:
Season the beef tenderloin with salt, pepper, cumin powder, paprika and thyme. Drizzle with olive oil and rub the meat well. Wrap the beef in bacon slices and place in your crock pot. Add the stock and cover the pot with its lid. Cook on low settings for 8 hours. When done, slice and serve the tenderloin warm with your favorite side dish.

Coffee Sriracha Roasted Beef

Time: 6 1/4 hours   Servings: 4

Ingredients:
1 1/2 pounds beef roast
1 cup freshly brewed coffee
1 teaspoon Worcestershire sauce
1 tablespoon Sriracha sauce

2 garlic cloves, minced
1/2 cup beef stock
Salt and pepper to taste

Directions:
Combine the beef roast, coffee, Worcestershire sauce, Sriracha sauce, garlic and stock in your crock pot.
Season the dish with salt and pepper and cook on low settings for 6 hours.
Serve the roasted beef warm with your favorite side dish.

Hard Cider Beef Pot Roast

Time: 6 1/2 hours   Servings: 6

Ingredients:
6 small shallots, peeled
2 pounds beef sirloin roast
6 oz. button mushrooms
1 pound small new potatoes, washed
1/2 pound baby carrots

1 thyme sprig
1 1/2 cups hard cider
1 bay leaf
Salt and pepper to taste

Directions:
Combine the shallots, beef, mushrooms, potatoes, baby carrots, thyme, hard cider, bay leaf, salt and pepper in your crock pot. Cover the pot and cook on low settings for 6 hours. Serve the pot roast warm.

Tangy Pomegranate Beef Short Ribs

Time: 6 1/4 hours

Servings: 6

Ingredients:

4 pounds beef short ribs
2 tablespoons olive oil
1 large onion, sliced
2 carrots, sliced
2 tablespoons brown sugar
1 cup fresh pomegranate juice

1/2 cup pomegranate kernels
1/4 cup low sodium soy sauce
1 teaspoon Worcestershire sauce
1 teaspoon dried thyme
1 rosemary sprig

Directions:

Combine all the ingredients in a slow cooker. Cover the pot with its lid and cook on low settings for 6 hours. Serve the short ribs warm and sticky.

Asian Style Beef Short Ribs

Time: 7 1/4 hours

Servings: 6

Ingredients:

4 pounds beef short ribs
1 large onion, sliced
1 carrot, sliced
1/2 cup light soy sauce
2 tablespoons brown sugar

4 garlic cloves, chopped
1 star anise
2 tablespoons rice vinegar
1 cup beef stock
2 green onions, chopped for serving

Directions:

Mix the onion, carrot, soy sauce, sugar, garlic, star anise, vinegar and stock in your slow cooker. Add the beef ribs and coat them well in the mixture. Cover with a lid and cook on low settings for 7 hours. When done, top with chopped green onions and serve right away.

Ginger Ale Beef Ribs

Time: 7 1/4 hours

Servings: 6

Ingredients:

4 pounds beef short ribs
1 teaspoon grated ginger
1/4 cup brown sugar
1 teaspoon cumin powder

1 1/2 cups ginger ale drink
1 rosemary sprig
Salt and pepper to taste

Directions:

Mix the ginger, brown sugar and cumin powder, as well as salt and pepper in a bowl. Spread this mix over the short ribs and rub them well into the meat. Transfer in your slow cooker and add the ginger ale. Cover the pot and cook on low settings for 7 hours. Serve the ribs warm and fresh.

Rich Stout Beef Casserole

Time: 8 1/4 hours   Servings: 8

Ingredients:

4 pounds beef roast, cubed
2 tablespoons canola oil
6 bacon slices, chopped
4 garlic cloves, minced
1 celery stalk, chopped
2 shallots, finely chopped

1 cup finely chopped mushrooms
1 1/2 cups brown stout
2 tablespoons tomato paste
1 teaspoon dried thyme
1/2 teaspoon chili powder
Salt and pepper to taste

Directions:

Heat the canola oil in your crock pot and add the beef and bacon. Cook for a few minutes until golden then transfer in your crock pot. Add the rest of the ingredients and adjust the taste with salt and pepper. Cook the beef on low settings for 8 hours. Serve the roast warm with your favorite side dish.

Five-Spice Beef Short Ribs

Time: 8 1/4 hours   Servings: 6

Ingredients:

4 pounds beef short ribs
1/4 cup molasses
1 tablespoon five-spice powder
1 teaspoon garlic powder
1 teaspoon chili powder

2 tablespoons peanut oil
2 tablespoons soy sauce
1 teaspoon fish sauce
8 green onions, chopped
1/2 cup beef stock

Directions:

Mix the molasses, five-spice powder, garlic powder, chili, peanut oil, soy sauce and fish sauce in a bowl. Spread this mix over the beef ribs and rub it well into the meat and bone. Place the ribs in your slow cooker. Add the green onions and stock and cover the pot with a lid. Cook on low settings for 8 hours. Serve the ribs warm and fresh.

Fruity Veal Shanks

Time: 3 1/4 hours   Servings: 4

Ingredients:

4 veal shanks
1 orange, zested and juiced
1/2 cup dried apricots, chopped
1/4 cup dried cranberries
1 cup beef stock

1 cup diced tomatoes
1 rosemary sprig
1 thyme sprig
Salt and pepper to taste
2 sweet potatoes, peeled and cubed

Directions:

Season the veal shanks with salt and pepper. Mix the orange juice, orange zest, apricots, cranberries, stock, tomatoes, rosemary and thyme in your crock pot. Add salt, pepper and the sweet potatoes and cook for 3 hours on high settings. The dish is best served warm, but it can also be re-heated.

Beef Lentil Stew with Goat Cheese

Time: 5 1/4 hours   Servings: 6

Ingredients:

1 pound beef roast, cut into thin strips
2 tablespoons canola oil
1 large onion, chopped
2 garlic cloves, minced
1 cup brown lentils
1/4 cup red lentils
1/2 teaspoon chili powder

1/2 teaspoon fennel seeds
1 cup diced tomatoes
1 cups beef stock
1 bay leaf
1 thyme sprig
Salt and pepper to taste
Crumbled goat cheese for serving

Directions:

Heat the canola oil in a skillet and add the beef. Cook for a few minutes on all sides then transfer in your crock pot. Add the rest of the ingredients and season with salt and pepper.
When done, pour the stew into serving plates and top with crumbled goat cheese while still warm. Serve right away.

Red Wine Braised Oxtail

Time: 6 1/4 hours   Servings: 4

Ingredients:

2 pounds oxtails, sliced
2 tablespoons olive oil
1 large onion, sliced
4 garlic cloves, chopped
1 carrot, sliced
1 parsnip, sliced

2 cups cherry tomatoes, halved
1 orange, juiced
1 bay leaf
1 rosemary sprig
Salt and pepper to taste

Directions:

Heat the oil in a skillet and add the oxtails. Fry on each side until golden then transfer in your crock pot. Add the remaining ingredients and season with salt and pepper. Cook on low settings for 6 hours and serve the dish warm.

Spiced Beef Tenderloin

Time: 7 1/4 hours   Servings: 8

Ingredients:

4 pounds beef tenderloin
1 tablespoon cumin powder
1 teaspoon chili powder
1 teaspoon smoked paprika
1 teaspoon ground ginger
2 tablespoons honey

2 tablespoons olive oil
1/2 teaspoon ground cloves
1/4 teaspoon nutmeg
1 teaspoon ground coriander
1 cup beef stock
1 1/2 teaspoon salt

Directions:

Mix the cumin powder, chili, paprika, ginger, honey, olive oil, cloves, nutmeg, salt and ground coriander in a bowl. Spread this mixture over the beef and rub it well into the meat with your fingertips. Place the beef in your crock pot and add the stock. Cover the pot and cook on low settings for 7 hours.

*B*EEF STRIPS WITH EGG NOODLES

Time: 5 1/4 hours   Servings: 6

*I*ngredients:

1 1/2 pounds beef roast, cut into thin strips
2 tablespoons peanut oil
1 shallot, sliced
2 red bell peppers, cored and sliced
1/2 teaspoon grated ginger
1/2 teaspoon chili powder
2 tablespoons soy sauce

1/2 cup tomato sauce
1 teaspoon Worcestershire sauce
1 teaspoon orange zest
1/4 cup fresh orange juice
Salt and pepper to taste
Cooked egg noodles for serving

*D*irections:

Heat the peanut oil in a frying pan. Add the beef roast and cook for 5 minutes on all sides then transfer in your crock pot. Add the shallot, bell peppers, ginger, chili powder, soy sauce, tomato sauce, Worcestershire sauce, orange zest, orange juice, salt and pepper. Cover the pot and cook on low settings for 5 hours. Serve the beef and the sauce warm over egg noodles.

*F*ENNEL OSSO BUCCO

Time: 6 1/4 hours   Servings: 4

*I*ngredients:

4 veal osso bucco pieces
1 tablespoon olive oil
2 garlic cloves, sliced
1 fennel bulb, sliced
1 orange, zested and juiced

2 tablespoons tomato paste
1/2 cup tomato sauce
1/4 cup beef stock
1 bay leaf
Salt and pepper to taste

*D*irections:

Combine all the ingredients in your crock pot, adding salt and pepper to taste. Cover the pot and cook on low settings for 6 hours. Osso bucco is best served warm.

*A*PPLE PARSNIP BEEF STEAKS

Time: 7 1/4 hours   Servings: 4

*I*ngredients:

4 flank steaks
4 red apples, peeled, cored and sliced
2 large parsnips, peeled and diced
2 large carrots, sliced
2 shallots, sliced

1/4 cup white wine
1 cup beef stock
1 rosemary sprig
Salt and pepper to taste

*D*irections:

Mix all the ingredients in your slow cooker. Add salt and pepper to taste and cover the pot with its lid. Cook for 7 hours on low settings and serve the steaks warm.

HEARTY BEEF BURRY

Time: 7 1/2 hours

Servings: 8

Ingredients:

1 1/2 pounds beef sirloin, cubed
2 tablespoons coconut oil
4 garlic cloves, chopped
1 shallot, chopped
2 carrots, sliced
3 cups cauliflower florets
2 red bell peppers, cored and diced
4 potatoes, peeled and cut into wedges
3 tablespoons red curry paste

2 tablespoons tomato paste
2 cardamom pods, crushed
2 kaffir lime leaves
1 lemongrass stalk, crushed
1 cup coconut milk
1 cup beef stock
1 tablespoon brown sugar
1 tablespoon lime juice
Salt and pepper to taste

Directions:

Heat the coconut oil in frying pan and add the beef. Cook for 5 minutes on all sides then transfer the beef in your crock pot.

Add the garlic, shallot, carrots, cauliflower, bell peppers, potatoes, curry paste, tomato paste, spices, coconut milk, stock, sugar and lime juice in the slow cooker as well.

Season with salt and pepper and cook for 7 hours on low settings.

Serve the curry warm or re-heat them later.

SPICY BEEF RAGU

Time: 6 1/4 hours

Servings: 6

Ingredients:

1 tablespoon canola oil
1 1/2 pounds ground beef
1 shallot, chopped
4 garlic cloves, chopped
1 teaspoon smoked paprika
2 tablespoons tomato paste
2 red bell peppers, finely chopped
1 cup finely chopped mushrooms

1 cup green peas
1 can fire roasted tomatoes
1 bay leaf
1 tablespoon red wine vinegar
Salt and pepper to taste
Grated Parmesan for serving
Cooked spaghetti or your favorite pasta for
  serving

Directions:

Heat the oil in a skillet and add the beef. Cook for a few minutes then transfer in your crock pot.

Add the rest of the ingredients in the slow cooker as well then cover and cook for 6 hours on low settings.

When done, serve the ragu warm with cooked pasta of your choice, preferably topped with grated Parmesan.

*B*EEF BROCCOLI SAUTÉ

Time: 2 1/4 hours   Servings: 4

Ingredients:

2 flank steaks, cut into thin strips
1 tablespoon peanut oil
1 pound broccoli florets
1/4 cup peanuts, chopped
1 tablespoon tomato paste
2 tablespoons soy sauce

1/4 cup beef stock
1 teaspoon hot sauce
1/2 teaspoon sesame oil
1 tablespoon sesame seeds
Salt and pepper to taste

Directions:

Combine all the ingredients in your crock pot. Add salt and pepper to taste and cook on high settings for 2 hours. Serve the sauté warm.

*J*ALAPENO MUSHROOM STEAKS

Time: 6 1/4 hours   Servings: 4

Ingredients:

4 beef steaks
2 red bell peppers, cored and diced
2 cups sliced mushrooms
2 tablespoons soy sauce
1 tablespoon hot sauce

2 large onions, sliced
1 teaspoon dried basil
Salt and pepper to taste
1/2 cup beef stock

Directions:

Mix the bell peppers, mushrooms, soy sauce, hot sauce, onions, basil, salt and pepper in a bowl. Season the steaks with salt and pepper and place them in your crock pot. Top each steak with the mushroom mixture and add the stock into the pot as well. Cover the pot and cook on low settings for 6 hours. Serve the steaks warm and fresh.

*H*ERBED BEEF TENDERLOIN

Time: 6 1/2 hours   Servings: 6

Ingredients:

2 pounds beef tenderloin
1 tablespoon dried rosemary
1 tablespoon dried basil
1 tablespoon dried oregano
2 tablespoons chopped parsley

2 tablespoons olive oil
1 tablespoon Dijon mustard
Salt and pepper to taste
1/4 cup white wine

Directions:

Brush the beef with mustard and olive oil then season it with salt and pepper. Mix the rosemary, basil, oregano and parsley on your chopping board and spread it into a thin layer. Place the beef on top and roll it carefully to evenly coat it in the herbs mixture. Place the beef in your crock pot and add the wine. Cover and cook on low settings for 6 hours.

KALE WHITE BEAN STEW

Time: 5 1/4 hours   Servings: 8

Ingredients:

2 pounds beef roast, cut into small cubes
2 tablespoons canola oil
2 cans (15 oz. each) white beans, drained
2 shallots, chopped
4 garlic cloves, chopped

1 teaspoon dried oregano
1/2 teaspoon dried sage
1 bunch kale, shredded
Salt and pepper to taste

Directions:

Heat the oil in a frying pan and add the beef. Cook for a few minutes on all sides then transfer in your crock pot. Add the remaining ingredients and season with salt and pepper. Cover the pot and cook for 5 hours on low settings. Serve the stew warm and fresh.

DIJON BEEF STEW

Time: 6 1/4 hours   Servings: 6

Ingredients:

2 pounds beef roast, cubed
2 tablespoons all-purpose flour
2 tablespoons canola oil
4 garlic cloves, chopped
2 cups finely chopped mushrooms

1 cup beef stock
1/2 cup white wine
2 tablespoons Dijon mustard
1 rosemary sprig
Salt and pepper to taste

Directions:

Season the beef with salt and pepper and sprinkle it with flour. Heat the oil in a frying pan and add the beef. Cook for a few minutes on all sides then transfer in your crock pot. Add the rest of the ingredients and adjust the taste with salt and pepper. Cook the stew on low settings for 6 hours. Serve the stew warm and fresh.

NEW POTATO BEEF STEW

Time: 5 1/2 hours   Servings: 8

Ingredients:

2 pounds beef roast, cubed
2 tablespoons canola oil
1 large onion, chopped
2 red bell peppers, cored and diced
2 carrots, diced
1 celery stalk, chopped

2 pounds small new potatoes, washed and
  cleaned
1 cup beef stock
1 cup tomato sauce
1 bay leaf
1 thyme sprig
Salt and pepper to taste

Directions:

Heat the oil in a frying pan and add the beef. Cook for a few minutes until golden then transfer in your crock pot. Add the rest of the ingredients and season well with salt and pepper. Cover the pot and cook on low settings for 5 hours. Serve the stew warm or chilled.

Rosemary Garlic Beef Stew

Time: 5 1/4 hours   Servings: 6

Ingredients:

2 pounds beef roast, cubed
1 celery stalk, sliced
1 sweet onion, sliced
1 leek, sliced
4 garlic cloves, minced
2 pounds red potatoes, peeled and cubed
1 tablespoon Dijon mustard
1 teaspoon Worcestershire sauce

1 tablespoon soy sauce
1 tablespoon brown sugar
1 tablespoon dried rosemary
1 cup diced tomatoes
1 cup beef stock
1 bay leaf
Salt and pepper to taste

Directions:

Mix all the ingredients in your slow cooker. Add enough salt and pepper and cook on low settings for 5 hours. The stew is best served warm.

Moroccan Beef Short Ribs

Time: 8 1/4 hours   Servings: 8

Ingredients:

6 pounds beef short ribs
1 tablespoon dried thyme
1 teaspoon ground ginger
1 teaspoon cinnamon powder
1 teaspoon chili powder

1 teaspoon cumin powder
2 tablespoon olive oil
1 can (15 oz.) diced tomatoes
1 lime, juiced
Salt and pepper to taste

Directions:

Mix the thyme, ginger, cinnamon, chili powder, cumin powder, olive oil, salt and pepper in a bowl. Spread this mixture over your ribs and rub them well into the meat. Place the ribs in your slow cooker and add the tomatoes and lime juice. Cover and cook on low settings for 8 hours.

Cuban Flank Steaks

Time: 8 1/4 hours   Servings: 6

Ingredients:

6 beef flank steaks
2 red onions, sliced
1 teaspoon cumin seeds
1 teaspoon chili powder
1 teaspoon dried oregano

1 cup beef stock
1 chipotle pepper, chopped
2 limes, juiced
Salt and pepper to taste

Directions:

Combine the steaks in your slow cooker and add salt and pepper. Cover and cook for 8 hours on low settings. Serve the steaks warm.

ORIENTAL BEEF BRISKET

Time: 8 1/4 hours   Servings: 8

Ingredients:

4 pounds beef brisket, cubed   1 teaspoon chili powder
1 tablespoon peanut oil   1 cup beef stock
1/4 cup hoisin sauce   1 bay leaf
1 cup red salsa   Salt and pepper to taste
1 teaspoon cumin seeds   Cooked rice for serving

Directions:

Combine all the ingredients in your crock pot, adding salt and pepper to taste
Cover and cook on low settings for 8 hours.
Serve the beef brisket warm over cooked rice.

Dessert Recipes

PEACH COBBLER

Time: 6 1/2 hours   Servings: 8

Ingredients:

2 pounds ripe peaches, pitted and sliced
1 tablespoon cornstarch
2 tablespoons brown sugar
1 1/2 cups all-purpose flour
1/2 teaspoon baking powder

1/4 teaspoon salt
1/4 cup sugar
1/2 cup butter, chilled and cubed
2/3 cup buttermilk, chilled

Directions:

Mix the peaches, cornstarch and brown sugar in your slow cooker. Combine the flour, baking powder, salt, sugar and butter in a bowl and rub the mixture well until sandy. Stir in the buttermilk and give it a quick mix then spoon the batter over the peaches. Cover and cook on low settings for 6 hours. The cobbler is best served slightly warm or chilled.

LAVENDER BLACKBERRY CRUMBLE

Time: 2 1/4 hours   Servings: 6

Ingredients:

1 1/2 pounds fresh blackberries
2 tablespoons cornstarch
1 teaspoon vanilla extract
1/4 cup white sugar

1 teaspoon dried lavender buds
1 cup all-purpose flour
1 pinch salt
1/2 cup butter, chilled and cubed

Directions:

Mix the blackberries, cornstarch, vanilla, sugar and lavender in your slow cooker. Combine the flour, salt and butter in a bowl and rub them well with your fingertips until the mixture looks grainy. Spread the mixture over the veggies and cook on high settings for 2 hours. Serve the crumble chilled.

RASPBERRY BROWNIE CAKE

Time: 3 1/4 hours   Servings: 10

Ingredients:

1 cup butter, cubed
1 1/2 cups dark chocolate, chopped
1 cup sugar
4 eggs

1/2 cup cocoa powder
1/2 cup all-purpose flour
1 pinch salt
1 1/2 cups fresh raspberries

Directions:

Mix the butter with chocolate in a bowl and place over a hot water bath and melt them together until smooth. Remove the bowl from heat and stir in the sugar and eggs. Add the cocoa powder, flour and salt and pour the batter in your greased crock pot. Top with raspberries and cover the pot. Cook on high settings for 3 hours. Allow the cake to cool before serving.

Banana Chunk Cake

Time: 3 1/4 hours   Servings: 10

Ingredients:

1/2 cup butter, softened
1/2 cup brown sugar
1/4 cup white sugar
2 eggs
2 tablespoons dark rum
1/4 cup milk

1 cup all-purpose flour
1 teaspoon baking powder
1/2 teaspoon salt
2 ripe bananas, sliced
1/2 cup dark chocolate chips

Directions:

Mix the butter and sugars in a bowl for a few minutes until creamy. Add the eggs, rum and milk and give it a quick mix. Fold in the flour, salt and baking powder then add the banana and chocolate chips. Pour the batter in your greased slow cooker and cook on high settings for 3 hours. Serve the cake chilled.

Apple Butter

Time: 8 1/4 hours   Servings: 12

Ingredients:

4 pounds Granny Smith apples, peeled and cored
2 pounds tart apples, peeled and cored
2 cups white sugar
1 cup fresh apple juice

1 teaspoon cinnamon powder
1/2 teaspoon ground ginger

Directions:

Combine all the ingredients in a slow cooker and mix well. Cover with a lid and cook on 8 hours. When done, puree the mixture with a hand blender and pour it into glass jars. Seal the jars and store them for up to a few months in your storage room.

Pineapple Upside Down Cake

Time: 5 1/4 hours   Servings: 10

Ingredients:

1 cup butter, softened
1/2 cup light brown sugar
1/2 cup white sugar
2 eggs
1 cup all-purpose flour
1/2 cup ground almonds

1 teaspoon baking powder
1/4 teaspoon salt
1/2 teaspoon cinnamon powder
2 tablespoons butter to grease the pot
1 can pineapple chunks, drained

Directions:

Grease the pot with butter then place the pineapple chunks in the pot. For the cake, mix the softened butter, brown sugar and white sugar in a bowl. Add the eggs, one by one, mixing well after each addition. Fold in the flour, almonds, baking powder and salt, as well as cinnamon. Pour the batter over the pineapple and bake for 5 hours on low settings.

PURE BERRY CRUMBLE

Time: 5 1/4 hours   Servings: **8**

Ingredients:

1 pound fresh mixed berries
1 tablespoon cornstarch
1/4 cup white sugar
1 teaspoon lemon zest
1 cup all-purpose flour

1/4 cup cornstarch
1 pinch salt
1/2 teaspoon baking powder
1/2 cup butter, chilled and cubed
2 tablespoons sugar

Directions:

Mix the berries, cornstarch, 1/4 cup sugar and lemon zest in your crock pot. For the topping, combine the flour, cornstarch, salt and baking powder in a bowl. Add the butter and mix well until the mixture is grainy. Spread the mixture over the berries and cook on low settings for 5 hours. Serve the crumble chilled.

APPLE SOUR CREAM CROSTATA

Time: 6 1/2 hours   Servings: **8**

Ingredients:

2 pounds Granny Smith apples, peeled, cored
   and sliced
1 tablespoon cornstarch
1 teaspoon cinnamon powder
1/4 cup light brown sugar

1 1/2 cups all-purpose flour
1/2 cup butter, chilled and cubed
1 pinch salt
2 tablespoons white sugar
1/2 cup sour cream

Directions:

Mix the butter, flour, salt and white sugar in a bowl. Rub the mix well with your fingertips until grainy then stir in the sour cream and knead for a few times. Roll the dough on a floured working surface to match the size of your crock pot. Transfer the dough in your slow cooker. For the topping, mix the apples, cornstarch, cinnamon and light brown sugar in a bowl. Place the mix over the dough. Cover the pot and cook on low settings for 6 hours. Serve the crostata chilled.

CRANBERRY STUFFED APPLES

Time: 4 1/4 hours   Servings: **4**

Ingredients:

4 large Granny Smith apples
1/2 cup dried cranberries
2 tablespoons honey
1/4 cup ground almonds

1/4 cup pecans, chopped
1/4 teaspoon cinnamon powder
1/2 cup apple cider

Directions:

Carefully remove the core of each apple and place them in your slow cooker. Mix the cranberries, honey, almonds, pecans and cinnamon in a bowl. Stuff the apples with this mixture then pour in the apple cider. Cover the pot and cook on low settings for 4 hours. The apples are best served warm.

Autumnal Bread Pudding

Time: 5 1/2 hours   Servings: 8

Ingredients:

16 oz. bread cubes
2 red apples, peeled and diced
2 pears, peeled and diced
1/2 cup golden raisins
1/4 cup butter, melted

2 cups whole milk
4 eggs, beaten
1/2 cup white sugar
1 teaspoon vanilla extract
1/2 teaspoon cinnamon powder

Directions:

Mix the bread cubes, apples, pears and raisins in your slow cooker.
Combine the butter, milk, eggs, sugar, vanilla and cinnamon in a bowl. Pour this mixture over the bread.
Cover the pot and cook on low settings for 5 hours.
Serve the bread pudding slightly warm.

Creamy Coconut Tapioca Pudding

Time: 4 1/4 hours   Servings: 6

Ingredients:

1 cup tapioca pearls
1 cup coconut flakes
2 cups coconut milk

1 cup water
1 teaspoon vanilla extract
1/2 cup coconut sugar

Directions:

Combine all the ingredients in your slow cooker.
Cover the pot and cook on low settings for 4 hours.
Serve the pudding warm or chilled.

Rich Chocolate Peanut Butter Cake

Time: 2 3/4 hours   Servings: 8

Ingredients:

1 1/2 cups all-purpose flour
1/4 cup cocoa powder
1 teaspoon baking powder
1/2 teaspoon baking soda
1/4 teaspoon salt

1 cup smooth peanut butter
1/4 cup butter, softened
3/4 cup white sugar
3 eggs
3/4 cup sour cream

Directions:

Mix the peanut butter, butter and sugar in a bowl until creamy. Add the eggs, one by one, then fold in the flour, cocoa powder, baking powder, baking soda and salt. Finally, add the sour cream and mix on high speed for 30 seconds.
Spoon the batter in your slow cooker and cook on high settings for 2 1/4 hours. The cake is best served chilled.

BLACK FOREST CAKE

Time: 4 1/4 hours

Servings: 8

Ingredients:

1 pound pitted cherries
2 tablespoons kirsch
1 tablespoon cornstarch
1/2 cup butter, softened
3/4 cup white sugar
1 teaspoon vanilla extract

3 eggs
1 cup all-purpose flour
1/2 cup cocoa powder
1/2 teaspoon salt
1 teaspoon baking powder
Whipped cream for serving

Directions:

Mix the cherries, kirsch and cornstarch in your slow cooker. For the batter, mix the butter, sugar and vanilla in a bowl until creamy. Add the eggs, one by one, then fold in the rest of the ingredients, trying to not over-mix the batter. Spoon the batter over the cherries and cook for 4 hours on low settings. Serve the cake chilled, topped with whipped cream.

ONE BOWL CHOCOLATE CAKE

Time: 4 1/4 hours

Servings: 10

Ingredients:

1 1/2 cups sugar
1 1/2 cups all-purpose flour
1/2 cup cocoa powder
1 teaspoon baking powder
1 teaspoon baking soda
1/2 teaspoon salt

2 eggs
1 cup whole milk
1/2 cup canola oil
1 teaspoon vanilla extract
1/2 cup brewed coffee

Directions:

Combine all the ingredients in a bowl and give it a quick mix. Pour the batter in your crock pot and cover the pot with its lid. Cook on low settings for 4 hours. Allow the cake to cool in the pot before slicing and serving.

OAT TOPPED APPLES

Time: 4 1/4 hours

Servings: 6

Ingredients:

6 Granny Smith apples
1 cup golden raisins
2 tablespoons brown sugar
1 cup rolled oats

1/4 cup all-purpose flour
1/4 cup butter, chilled and cubed
1/2 cup apple cider

Directions:

Carefully core the apples and place them in your slow cooker. Mix the raisins with brown sugar and stuff the apples with this mix. For the topping, combine the oats, flour and butter and mix well until grainy. Spoon the topping over each apple then pour the cider in the pot. Cook on low settings for 4 hours. Serve the apples chilled.

Apple Cinnamon Brioche Pudding

Time: 6 1/2 hours

Servings: 8

Ingredients:

16 oz. brioche bread, cubed
4 Granny Smith apples, peeled and cubed
1 teaspoon cinnamon powder
1/2 teaspoon ground ginger
2 tablespoons white sugar

1 cup evaporated milk
1 cup sweetened condensed milk
1 cup whole milk
4 eggs
1 teaspoon vanilla extract

Directions:

Mix the brioche bread, apples, cinnamon, ginger and sugar in your crock pot. Combine the three types of milk in a bowl. Add the eggs and vanilla and mix well. Pour this mix over the bread then cover the pot and cook for 6 hours on low settings. The pudding is best served slightly warm.

Apple Cherry Cobbler

Time: 4 1/2 hours

Servings: 10

Ingredients:

1 pound cherries, pitted
4 red apples, peeled and sliced
4 tablespoons maple syrup
2 tablespoons cornstarch
1 tablespoon lemon juice

1 1/4 cups all-purpose flour
1/2 cup butter, chilled and cubed
2 tablespoons white sugar
1/2 cup buttermilk, chilled

Directions:

Combine the cherries, apples, maple syrup, cornstarch and lemon juice in your crock pot. For the topping, mix the flour, butter and sugar in a bowl and rub the mix well with your fingertips until grainy. Stir in the buttermilk and give it a quick mix. Spoon the batter over the fruit mixture and bake on low settings for 4 hours. Serve the cobbler chilled.

Nutty Pear Streusel Dessert

Time: 4 1/2 hours

Servings: 4

Ingredients:

4 large apples, peeled and cubed
1/2 cup golden raisins
1 teaspoon cinnamon powder
1/2 cup pecans, chopped
1 cup ground almonds

2 tablespoons all-purpose flour
2 tablespoons melted butter
2 tablespoons brown sugar
1 pinch salt

Directions:

Mix the apples, raisins and cinnamon in your slow cooker. For the topping, combine the pecans, almonds, flour, melted butter, sugar and salt and rub the mix well with your fingertips. Spread this mixture over the pears and cook for 4 hours on low settings. This dessert is best served chilled.

PUMPKIN CROISSANT PUDDING

Time: 5 1/4 hours   Servings: 6

Ingredients:

6 large croissants, cubed
1 cup skim milk
1 1/2 cups pumpkin puree

3 eggs
1 teaspoon cinnamon powder
1/4 cup white sugar

Directions:

Place the croissants in your crock pot. Mix the milk, pumpkin puree, eggs, cinnamon and sugar in a bowl. Pour this mixture over the croissants. Cover the pot with its lid and cook on low settings for 5 hours. Serve the pudding chilled.

STRAWBERRY FUDGY BROWNIES

Time: 2 1/4 hours   Servings: 8

Ingredients:

1/2 cup butter, cubed
1 cup dark chocolate chips
2 eggs
1/2 cup white sugar
1/2 cup applesauce

1/4 cup cocoa powder
1/2 cup all-purpose flour
1 pinch salt
1 1/2 cups fresh strawberries, halved

Directions:

Mix the butter and chocolate in a bowl and place over a hot water bath to melt until smooth. Remove from heat and add the eggs, sugar and applesauce and give it a good mix. Fold in the cocoa powder, flour and salt and pour the mixture in your slow cooker. Top with strawberries and cook on high settings for 2 hours. Allow to cool before cutting into cubes and serving.

CARAMEL PEAR PUDDING CAKE

Time: 4 1/2 hours   Servings: 6

Ingredients:

2/3 cup all-purpose flour
1 teaspoon baking powder
1/2 cup sugar
1/4 teaspoon salt
1/2 teaspoon cinnamon powder

1/4 cup butter, melted
1/4 cup whole milk
4 ripe pears, cored and sliced
3/4 cup caramel sauce

Directions:

Mix the flour, baking powder, sugar, salt and cinnamon in a bowl. Add the butter and milk and give it a quick mix. Place the pears in your crock pot and top with the batter. Drizzle the batter with caramel sauce and cook on low settings for 4 hours. Allow the cake to cool before serving.

Walnut Apple Crisp

Time: 4 1/2 hours   Servings: 6

Ingredients:

1 1/2 pounds Granny Smith apples, peeled,
  cored and sliced
1 teaspoon cinnamon powder
1 teaspoon ground ginger
4 tablespoons light brown sugar
1 tablespoon lemon juice
1 tablespoon cornstarch

1/2 cup all-purpose flour
1 cup ground walnuts
2 tablespoons white sugar
1 pinch salt
1/4 cup butter, melted
Caramel sauce for serving

Directions:

Mix the apples, cinnamon, ginger, light brown sugar, lemon juice and cornstarch in your slow cooker.
For the topping, mix the flour, walnuts, white sugar, salt and butter in a bowl.
Spread this mixture over the apples and cover the pot. Cook on low settings for 4 hours.
Serve the crisp chilled.

Pumpkin Cheesecake

Time: 6 1/2 hours   Servings: 8

Ingredients:

Crust:

8 oz. graham crackers, crushed
1/2 cup butter, melted

Filling:

24 oz. cream cheese
1 1/2 cups pumpkin puree

3 eggs
2 tablespoons cornstarch
1/2 cup white sugar
1 teaspoon vanilla extract
1/2 teaspoon cinnamon powder
1/2 teaspoon ground ginger
1 pinch salt

Directions:

For the crust, mix the crackers with butter then transfer this mixture in your crock pot and press it well.
For the filling, combine all the ingredients in a bowl and mix well. Pour this mixture over the crust and cook on low settings for 6 hours.
Allow the cheesecake to cool in the pot before slicing and serving.

Lemon Berry Cake

Time: 4 1/2 hours   Servings: 10

Ingredients:

1 cup butter, softened
1 cup white sugar
1 teaspoon vanilla extract
2 teaspoons lemon zest
4 eggs

1 cup all-purpose flour
1 teaspoon baking powder
1/4 teaspoon salt
1 cup fresh mixed berries

Directions:

Mix the butter, sugar and vanilla in a bowl until creamy.

Add the eggs, one by one, as well as the lemon zest and mix for 1 minute on high speed.

Fold in the flour, baking powder and salt then spoon the batter in your slow cooker.

Cover the pot and cook for 4 hours on low settings.

Allow the cake to cool before serving.

SILKY CHOCOLATE FONDUE

Time: 2 1/4 hours   Servings: 6

Ingredients:

1 cup heavy cream
1/4 cup sweetened condensed milk
1/4 cup whole milk
1 1/2 cups dark chocolate chips

2 tablespoons dark rum
Fresh fruits of your choice for serving
(strawberries, grapes, bananas, kiwi fruits)

Directions:

Combine the cream, two types of milk, chocolate chips and rum in your slow cooker.

Cover and cook on low settings for 2 hours.

Serve the fondue by dipping fresh fruits into it.

ORANGE GINGER CHEESECAKE

Time: 7 1/2 hours   Servings: 8

Ingredients:

Crust:

6 oz. graham crackers, crushed
1/2 cup butter, melted
1 tablespoon grated orange zest

Filling:

20 oz. cream cheese

1 cup sour cream
4 eggs
1 tablespoon cornstarch
1 teaspoon grated ginger
1 teaspoon grated orange zest
1/2 cup white sugar
1 pinch salt

Directions:

For the crust, mix the two ingredients together in a bowl then transfer in your crock pot and press the mixture well on the bottom of the pot.

For the filling, mix all the ingredients in a bowl then pour the mix over the crust.

Cover the pot and cook on low settings for 7 hours.

Allow the cheesecake to cool before slicing and serving.

MOCHA CHOCOLATE BRIOCHE PUDDING

Time: 4 1/2 hours   Servings: 8

Ingredients:

8 cups brioche bread cubes
1 cup heavy cream
1 cup dark chocolate chips
1 1/2 cups whole milk
4 eggs

2 teaspoons instant coffee
1/4 cup light brown sugar
1 teaspoon orange zest
1/4 cup white chocolate chips

Directions:

Heat the cream in a saucepan to the boiling point then remove from heat and add the chocolate. Mix until melted then pour the mixture in a bowl and add the milk, eggs, coffee powder and sugar. Mix well. Combine the brioche cubes with white chocolate chips in your crock pot. Pour the milk and egg mixture over the brioche and cook on low settings for 4 hours. Serve the pudding slightly warm.

CHOCOLATE CHIPS PEANUT BUTTER CAKE

Time: 4 1/4 hours   Servings: 10

Ingredients:

1/2 cup butter, softened
1/2 cup smooth peanut butter
1/2 cup light brown sugar
3 eggs
1 teaspoon vanilla extract

1 cup all-purpose flour
1 teaspoon baking powder
1/4 teaspoon salt
1/2 cup dark chocolate chips

Directions:

Mix the butter, peanut butter and brown sugar in a bowl until creamy. Stir in the eggs, one by one, then add the vanilla. Fold in the flour, baking powder and salt and give it just a quick mix then stir in the chocolate chips. Spoon the batter in your slow cooker and cook on low settings for 4 hours. Allow the cake to cool before slicing and serving.

WHITE CHOCOLATE APRICOT BREAD PUDDING

Time: 5 1/2 hours   Servings: 8

Ingredients:

8 cups one day old bread cubes
1 cup dried apricots, diced
1 cup white chocolate chips
2 cups milk
1 cup heavy cream

4 eggs
1 teaspoon vanilla extract
1 teaspoon orange zest
1/2 cup white sugar

Directions:

Mix the bread, apricots and chocolate chips in your slow cooker. Combine the milk, cream, eggs, vanilla, orange zest and sugar in a bowl. Pour this mixture over the bread pudding then cover the pot with a lid and cook on low settings for 5 hours. The pudding is best served slightly warm.

Coconut Poached Pears

Time: 6 1/4 hours

Servings: 6

Ingredients:

6 ripe but firm pears
2 cups coconut milk
2 cups water
1 cinnamon stick

1 star anise
3/4 cup coconut sugar
2 lemon rings

Directions:

Carefully peel and core the pears and place them in your slow cooker. Add the rest of the ingredients and cover with a lid. Cook on low settings for 6 hours. Allow the pears to cool in the pot before serving.

Chocolate Walnut Bread

Time: 2 1/2 hours

Servings: 8

Ingredients:

1 cup whole milk
3 eggs
1/2 cup canola oil
1 teaspoon vanilla extract
1/4 cup sour cream
1/2 cup light brown sugar

1 cup all-purpose flour
1/2 cup cocoa powder
1/4 teaspoon salt
1 teaspoon baking powder
1 cup walnuts, chopped

Directions:

Mix the milk, eggs, canola oil, vanilla, sugar and sour cream in a bowl.
Add the remaining ingredients and stir quickly just until combined.
Pour the batter in your crock pot and cook on high settings for 2 hours.
Allow the bread to cool in the pot before serving.

Chocolate Pear Crumble

Time: 4 1/2 hours

Servings: 6

Ingredients:

6 ripe pears, peeled, cored and sliced
1/4 cup light brown sugar
1 tablespoon cornstarch
3/4 cup all-purpose flour

1/2 cup cocoa powder
1/4 teaspoon salt
1/2 teaspoon baking powder
1/2 cup butter, chilled and cubed

Directions:

Mix the pears, sugar and cornstarch in your slow cooker.
For the crumble topping, mix the flour, cocoa powder, salt and baking powder in a bowl.
Add the butter and mix well until the mixture looks grainy.
Spread this mixture over the pears then cover the pot and cook for 4 hours on low settings.
The dessert is best served slightly warm or chilled.

GINGER FRUIT COMPOTE

Time: 6 1/2 hours   Servings: 6

Ingredients:

2 ripe pears, peeled and cubed
2 red apples, peeled, cored and sliced
1/2 cup dried apricots, halved
4 slices fresh pineapple, cubed
1 cup fresh orange juice

3 tablespoons light brown sugar
2 cups water
1 star anise
1 cinnamon stick
2 whole cloves

Directions:

Combine all the ingredients in your slow cooker. Cover the pot and cook on low settings for 6 hours.
Allow the compote to cool before serving.

GINGERBREAD CAKE

Time: 2 1/2 hours   Servings: 8

Ingredients:

3/4 cup butter, softened
1/2 cup white sugar
1/2 cup dark brown sugar
3 eggs
1 teaspoon vanilla extract
1/2 cup buttermilk
1 1/4 cups all-purpose flour
1 tablespoon cocoa powder

1 teaspoon ground ginger
1 teaspoon cinnamon powder
1/4 teaspoon ground cloves
1 teaspoon baking powder
1/4 teaspoon baking soda
1/4 teaspoon salt
1/2 cup golden raisins

Directions:

Mix the butter and the two types of sugar in a bowl until creamy. Add the eggs, one by one, then the vanilla and mix
well. Stir in the vanilla and buttermilk. Fold in the remaining ingredients then spoon the batter in your crock pot.
Cover the pot and cook on high settings for 2 hours. Allow the cake to cool in the pot before slicing and serving.

EGYPTIAN RICE PUDDING

Time: 4 1/4 hours   Servings: 6

Ingredients:

1 1/2 cups white rice
4 cups whole milk
1 vanilla pod, cut in half lengthwise
2 tablespoons cornstarch

1/4 cup cold water
1/2 cup sugar
1 teaspoon cinnamon powder

Directions:

Mix the rice, milk, vanilla pod and sugar in your crock pot. Cook on low settings for 3 hours. Combine the water and
cornstarch in a bowl then pour this mixture over the rice pudding. Cover the pot again and cook on low settings for 1
additional hour. Serve the pudding warm or chilled, sprinkled with cinnamon powder.

Molten Chocolate Cake

Time: 2 1/2 hours   Servings: 6

Ingredients:

4 eggs
1/2 cup butter, melted
1 teaspoon vanilla extract
1 cup sugar

1 cup all-purpose flour
1/4 cup cocoa powder
1 teaspoon baking powder
1/4 teaspoon salt

Directions:

Mix the eggs, butter, vanilla and sugar in a bowl until creamy. Add the flour, cocoa powder and salt and give it just a quick mix, making sure not to over mix the batter. Pour the batter in your crock pot and cook on high settings for 2 hours. The cake is best served warm.

Amarena Cherry Cola Cake

Time: 4 1/4 hours   Servings: 8

Ingredients:

1 cup cola
1/4 cup light brown sugar
1/2 cup butter, melted
1 teaspoon vanilla extract
1/2 cup whole milk
1 1/2 cups all-purpose flour

1/4 cup cocoa powder
1/4 teaspoon salt
1/2 teaspoon baking powder
1/2 teaspoon baking soda
2 cups Amarena cherries, pitted

Directions:

Mix the cola, sugar, butter, vanilla and milk in a bowl. Add the flour, cocoa powder, salt, baking powder and baking soda and give it a quick mix. Fold in the cherries. Spoon the batter in your slow cooker and cook on low settings for 4 hours. Allow the cake to cool in the pot before slicing and serving.

Crock Pot Crème Brulee

Time: 6 1/4 hours   Servings: 4

Ingredients:

2 1/2 cups milk
1 1/2 cups heavy cream
2 egg yolks
2 whole eggs

1 teaspoon vanilla extract
2 tablespoons maple syrup
2 tablespoons white sugar
1 cup sugar for topping

Directions:

Mix the milk, cream, egg yolks, eggs, vanilla, maple syrup and white sugar in a bowl.
Pour the mixture in 4 ramekins and place the ramekins in your slow cooker.
Add water into the slow cooker, enough to cover the ramekins 3/4.
Cover the pot and cook on low settings for 6 hours.
When done, spoon the remaining sugar over the crème brulee and caramelize it using a blow torch.

No Crust Lemon Cheesecake

Time: 6 1/4 hours   Servings: 8

Ingredients:

24 oz. cream cheese
1/2 cup heavy cream
4 eggs
2 tablespoons cornstarch

1 lemon, zested and juiced
2/3 cup white sugar
1 teaspoon vanilla extract

Directions:

Combine all the ingredients in a bowl and mix well.
Pour the mixture in your greased slow cooker and cook for 6 hours on low settings.
Serve the cheesecake chilled.

Fudgy Peanut Butter Cake

Time: 2 1/4 hours   Servings: 8

Ingredients:

1/2 cup smooth peanut butter
1/4 cup canola oil
3/4 cup white sugar
1 teaspoon vanilla extract
2 eggs

1/4 cup whole milk
1 cup all-purpose flour
1/4 cup cocoa powder
1 teaspoon baking powder
1/4 teaspoon salt

Directions:

Mix the peanut butter, canola oil, sugar, vanilla and eggs in a bowl until smooth and creamy.
Add the milk then fold in the flour, cocoa powder, baking powder and salt.
Spoon the batter in your slow cooker and cook for 2 hours on high settings.
Allow the cake to cool in the pot before slicing and serving.

Spiced Rice Pudding

Time: 4 1/4 hours   Servings: 6

Ingredients:

1 cup Arborio rice
1/2 cup white sugar
3 cups whole milk
1 cinnamon stick

1 star anise
2 whole cloves
1/2-inch piece of ginger, sliced
1/2 teaspoon rose water

Directions:

Combine all the ingredients in your slow cooker.
Cover the pot and cook on low settings for 4 hours.
The pudding can be served both warm and chilled.

Spiced Poached Pears

Time: 6 1/2 hours

Servings: 6

Ingredients:

6 ripe but firm pears
2 cups white wine
1 1/2 cups water
3/4 cup white sugar
1 star anise

1-inch piece of ginger, sliced
4 whole cloves
2 cinnamon stick
2 cardamom pods, crushed

Directions:

Carefully peel and core the pears and place them in your crock pot. Add the remaining ingredients and cook on low settings for 6 hours. The pears are best served chilled.

White Chocolate Apple Cake

Time: 6 1/2 hours

Servings: 8

Ingredients:

5 eggs, separated
3/4 cup white sugar
1/2 cup butter, melted
1/2 cup whole milk
1 cup all-purpose flour

1 teaspoon baking powder
1/4 teaspoon salt
1/2 cup white chocolate chips
4 tart apples, peeled, cored and sliced
1/2 teaspoon cinnamon powder

Directions:

Mix the egg yolks with half of the sugar until double in volume. Stir in the butter and milk then fold in the flour, baking powder and salt. Whip the egg whites until stiff then add the remaining sugar and whip for a few minutes until glossy and stiff. Fold this meringue into the egg yolks and flour mixture then add the chocolate chips. Spoon the batter in your slow cooker and top with apple slices. Sprinkle with cinnamon and cook on low settings for 6 hours. Allow to cool before slicing and serving.

Tiramisu Bread Pudding

Time: 4 1/4 hours

Servings: 6

Ingredients:

6 cups bread cubes
1/4 cup white sugar
2 teaspoons coffee powder
2 tablespoons Kahlua

1/2 cup mascarpone cheese
1 1/2 cups milk
2 eggs
2 tablespoons cocoa powder

Directions:

Mix the sugar, coffee, Kahlua, mascarpone cheese, milk and eggs in a bowl.
Place the bread cubes in a slow cooker then pour the milk mixture over the bread.
Sprinkle with cocoa powder and cook on low settings for 4 hours.
Serve the pudding slightly warm.

Amaretti Cheesecake

Time: 6 1/2 hours   Servings: 8

Ingredients:

Crust:
6 oz. Amaretti cookies, crushed
1/4 cup butter, melted

Filling:
24 oz. cream cheese

1/2 cup sour cream
4 eggs
1/2 cup white sugar
1 tablespoon vanilla extract
1 tablespoon Amaretto liqueur

Directions:

Mix the crushed cookies with butter then transfer the mix in your crock pot and press it well on the bottom of the pot.
For the filling, mix the cream cheese, sour cream, eggs, sugar, vanilla and liqueur and give it a quick mix.
Pour the filling over the crust and cook for 6 hours on low settings.
Allow the cheesecake to cool before slicing and serving.

Brandied Brioche Pudding

Time: 6 1/2 hours   Servings: 8

Ingredients:

10 oz. brioche bread, cubed
4 eggs, beaten
2 cups whole milk

1/4 cup brandy
1/2 cup light brown sugar
1 teaspoon vanilla extract

Directions:

Place the brioche in a slow cooker.
Mix the eggs, milk, brandy, sugar and vanilla in a bowl then pour this mixture over the brioche.
Cover the pot and cook on low settings for 6 hours.
Serve the pudding slightly warm.

Vanilla Bean Caramel Custard

Time: 6 1/4 hours   Servings: 6

Ingredients:

1 cup white sugar for melting
4 cups whole milk
1 cup heavy cream
2 egg yolks

4 eggs
1 tablespoon vanilla bean paste
2 tablespoons white sugar

Directions:

Caramelize 1 cup of sugar in a thick saucepan until it has an amber color. Pour the caramel in your slow cooker and swirl to coat the bottom and sides as much as possible. Mix the milk, cream, egg yolks, eggs, vanilla bean paste and sugar in a bowl. Pour this mixture over the caramel. Cover the pot and cook on low settings for 6 hours.
Serve the custard chilled.

PINEAPPLE COCONUT TAPIOCA PUDDING

Time: 6 1/4 hours   Servings: 8

Ingredients:

1 1/2 cups tapioca pearls
2 cups coconut milk
1 cup sweetened condensed milk

1 can crushed pineapple
1/2 cup coconut flakes
1 teaspoon vanilla extract

Directions:

Combine all the ingredients in your crock pot.
Cover and cook for 6 hours on low settings.
The pudding is best served chilled.

CARDAMOM COCONUT RICE PUDDING

Time: 6 1/4 hours   Servings: 6

Ingredients:

1 1/4 cups Arborio rice
2 cups coconut milk
1 cup coconut water

1/2 cup coconut sugar
4 cardamom pods, crushed
Sliced peaches for serving

Directions:

Combine all the ingredients in your crock pot.
Cover the pot and cook on low settings for 6 hours.
The pudding is best served warm, although it tastes good chilled as well. For more flavor, top the pudding with sliced peaches just before serving.

ROCKY ROAD CHOCOLATE CAKE

Time: 4 1/2 hours   Servings: 10

Ingredients:

1 1/2 cups all-purpose flour
1/2 cup cocoa powder
1 teaspoon baking soda
1/2 teaspoon salt
1/2 cup canola oil
1 cup buttermilk

1/2 cup whole milk
1 teaspoon vanilla extract
2 eggs
1/2 cup mini marshmallows
1/2 cup pecans, chopped
1/2 cup white chocolate chips

Directions:

Mix the flour, cocoa powder, baking soda, salt, canola oil, buttermilk, milk, vanilla and eggs in a bowl. Give it a quick mix then pour the batter in your slow cooker.
Top the batter with mini marshmallows, pecans and chocolate chips.
Cover the pot and cook on low settings for 4 hours.
Allow the cake to cool completely before serving.

CARROT CAKE

Time: 2 3/4 hours   Servings: 12

Ingredients:

3/4 cup white sugar
1/4 cup dark brown sugar
2 eggs
1/2 cup canola oil
1 teaspoon vanilla extract
1 1/2 cups all-purpose flour
1 teaspoon baking powder
1/2 teaspoon baking soda

1/2 teaspoon ground ginger
1 teaspoon cinnamon powder
1/4 teaspoon cardamom powder
1/2 teaspoon salt
1 cup grated carrots
1 cup crushed pineapple, drained
1/2 cup pecans, chopped

Directions:

Mix the two types of sugar, eggs, canola oil and vanilla in a bowl until creamy.

Fold in the flour, baking powder, baking soda, ginger, cinnamon, cardamom powder and salt then add the carrots, crushed pineapple and pecans.

Pour the batter in your slow cooker and cook for 2 1/4 hours on high settings.

Allow the cake to cool in the pot before slicing and serving.

LEMON POPPY SEED CAKE

Time: 4 1/2 hours   Servings: 8

Ingredients:

3/4 cup butter, softened
3/4 cup white sugar
1 large lemon, zested and juiced
2 eggs
1 cup all-purpose flour
1/2 cup fine cornmeal

1 teaspoon baking soda
1/2 teaspoon baking powder
1/2 teaspoon salt
2 tablespoons poppy seeds
1 cup buttermilk

Directions:

Mix the flour, cornmeal, baking soda, baking powder, salt and poppy seeds in a bowl.

Combine the butter, sugar and lemon zest in a bowl and mix well for 5 minutes.

Add the eggs and lemon zest and mix well.

Fold in the flour mixture, alternating it with the buttermilk.

Spoon the batter in your crock pot and cook on low settings for 4 hours.

Allow the cake to cool in the pot before slicing and serving.

PEANUT BUTTER CHEESECAKE

Time: 8 1/2 hours

Servings: 10

Ingredients:

Crust:

8 oz. graham crackers, crushed
1/2 cup butter, melted

Filling:

20 oz. cream cheese

1 cup smooth peanut butter
1/2 cup sour cream
2/3 cup light brown sugar
1 teaspoon vanilla extract
4 eggs
1 pinch salt

Directions:

For the crust, mix the crackers with butter then transfer the mixture in your slow cooker and press it well on the bottom of the pot.

For the filling, mix the cream cheese, peanut butter, sour cream, sugar, vanilla, eggs and salt in a bowl.

Pour the filling over the crust and cook for 8 hours on low settings.

Allow the cheesecake to cool completely before serving.

RICOTTA LEMON CAKE

Time: 5 1/4 hours

Servings: 8

Ingredients:

1 1/2 cups ricotta cheese
1/4 cup butter, melted
1/2 cup white sugar
1 teaspoon vanilla extract
1 tablespoon lemon zest

4 eggs, separated
1 1/2 cups all-purpose flour
1 1/2 teaspoons baking powder
1/4 teaspoon salt

Directions:

Grease your slow cooker with butter.

Mix the ricotta, butter, sugar, egg yolks, vanilla and lemon zest in a bowl. Fold in the flour, baking powder and salt.

Whip the egg whites until stiff then fold them into the batter.

Pour the batter in your crock pot and cook on low settings for 5 hours.

Allow the cake to cool in the pot before slicing and serving.

Sour Cream Cheesecake

Time: 4 1/4 hours

Servings: 8

Ingredients:

Crust:

1 1/2 cups crushed graham crackers
1/2 cup butter, melted

Filling:

12 oz. cream cheese

12 oz. sour cream
4 eggs
1/2 cup white sugar
1 tablespoon cornstarch
1 tablespoon vanilla extract
1/2 teaspoon almond extract

Directions:

For the crust, mix the graham crackers with the butter in a bowl then transfer this mixture in a slow cooker and press it well in the pot. For the filling, combine the cream cheese, sour cream, eggs, sugar, cornstarch, vanilla and almond extract in a bowl. Pour the mixture over the crust. Cook for 4 hours on low settings. Allow the cheesecake to cool in the pot before slicing and serving.

Chocolate Chip Brownies

Time: 4 1/2 hours

Servings: 12

Ingredients:

1/2 cup butter
1 1/4 cups dark chocolate chips
3 eggs
1/2 cup white sugar
2 tablespoons dark brown sugar

1 cup all-purpose flour
1/2 cup cocoa powder
1/2 teaspoon salt
3/4 cup dark chocolate chips

Directions:

Mix the butter and 1 1/4 cups chocolate chips in a bowl and place over a hot water bath. Melt them until smooth then remove from heat. Add the eggs, the two types of sugar, flour, cocoa powder and salt and give it a quick mix. Fold in the chocolate chips then pour the batter in your greased slow cooker. Cover and cook on low settings for 4 hours. Allow to cool completely before serving.

Maple Roasted Pears

Time: 6 1/4 hours

Servings: 4

Ingredients:

4 ripe pears, carefully peeled and cored
1/4 cup maple syrup
1/4 cup white wine
1/2 cup water

1 teaspoon grated ginger
1 cinnamon stick
2 cardamom pods, crushed

Directions:

Combine all the ingredients in your slow cooker. Cover with a lid and cook on low settings for 6 hours. Allow to cool before serving.

APPLE GRANOLA CRUMBLE

Time: 6 1/4 hours   Servings: 4

Ingredients:

4 red apples, peeled, cored and sliced   1 1/2 cups granola
2 tablespoons honey   1/2 teaspoon cinnamon powder

Directions:

Mix the apples and honey in your crock pot. Top with the granola and sprinkle with cinnamon. Cover the pot and cook on low settings for 6 hours. Serve the crumble warm.

MIXED NUTS BROWNIES

Time: 4 1/4 hours   Servings: 12

Ingredients:

8 oz. dark chocolate, chopped   1 cup all-purpose flour
1/2 cup butter   1/2 cup cocoa powder
1 cup white sugar   1/2 teaspoon salt
3 eggs   1 cup mixed nuts, chopped
1 teaspoon vanilla extract

Directions:

Mix the chocolate and butter in a bowl and place over a hot water bath. Melt them together until smooth.
Remove from heat and add the eggs, vanilla, flour, cocoa powder and salt and mix gently.
Fold in the nuts then pour the batter in your slow cooker (greased or lined with baking paper).
Cover and bake for 4 hours on low settings.
Allow to cool before cutting into small squares.

TURTLE CAKE

Time: 4 1/2 hours   Servings: 12

Ingredients:

6 oz. dark chocolate, melted   1/4 teaspoon salt
1/2 cup butter, melted   1 cup crushed graham crackers
3/4 cup white sugar   1/2 cup mini marshmallows
2 eggs   1/2 cup mixed nuts, chopped
3/4 cup all-purpose flour   1/2 cup white chocolate chips
1 teaspoon baking powder   1/2 cup pretzels, chopped

Directions:

Mix the melted chocolate and butter in a bowl.
Stir in the sugar and eggs and give it a good mix then add the flour, baking powder and salt.
Pour the batter in a greased slow cooker and top with the remaining ingredients.
Cover and cook for 4 hours on low settings.
When chilled, cut into small squares and serve.

Peanut Butter Chocolate Chips Bars

Time: 2 1/4 hours   Servings: 12

Ingredients:

1/2 cup butter, melted
1/2 cup smooth peanut butter
2 eggs
1 cup light brown sugar

1 cup all-purpose flour
1/4 teaspoon salt
1 cup dark chocolate chips
1 cup pecans, chopped

Directions:

Mix the butter, peanut butter, eggs and brown sugar in a bowl until creamy and smooth.
Fold in the flour and salt then spoon the batter in your slow cooker/
Top with chocolate chips and pecans and cook on high settings fo2 hours.
Allow to cool in the pot before slicing and serving.

Cream Cheese Brownies

Time: 4 1/2 hours   Servings: 12

Ingredients:

1 cup dark chocolate chips
1/2 cup butter
3 eggs
1/2 cup sugar
1 cup all-purpose flour

1/4 teaspoon salt
2 cups cream cheese
1/4 cup white sugar
2 eggs
1 teaspoon vanilla extract

Directions:

Melt the chocolate chips and butter in a heatproof bowl over a hot water bath. Remove from heat and add the eggs and sugar and mix well. Fold in the flour and salt then pour the batter in your crock pot. For the cream cheese mix, combine the cream cheese, sugar, eggs and vanilla in a bowl. Drop spoonfuls of cream cheese over the chocolate batter and swirl it around with a fork. Cover the pot and cook on low settings for 4 hours. Allow the brownies to cool in the pot before serving.

Golden Raisin Brioche Pudding

Time: 2 1/2 hours   Servings: 6

Ingredients:

6 cups brioche cubes
1 cup golden raisins
2 tablespoons brandy

4 eggs
2 cups whole milk
1/4 cup white sugar

Directions:

Mix the brioche cubes and raisins in a slow cooker.
Combine the brandy, eggs, milk and sugar in a bowl then pour this mix over the brioche.
Cover the pot and cook on high settings for 2 hours.
The pudding is best served slightly warm.

Coconut Condensed Milk Custard

Time: 5 1/4 hours   Servings: 6

Ingredients:

6 eggs
1 can (15 oz.) coconut milk
1 1/4 cups sweetened condensed milk

1 tablespoon vanilla extract
1 teaspoon lime zest
1 cup evaporated milk

Directions:

Mix the eggs, coconut milk, condensed milk, vanilla, lime zest and evaporated milk in a bowl.
Pour the mixture in your slow cooker.
Cover and cook on low settings for 5 hours.
Allow to cool before serving.

Peppermint Chocolate Clusters

Time: 4 1/4 hours   Servings: 20

Ingredients:

2 cups pretzels, chopped
1 1/2 cups dark chocolate chips
1/2 cup milk chocolate chips

1 teaspoon peppermint extract
1 cup pecans, chopped

Directions:

Combine all the ingredients in your slow cooker.
Cover the pot and cook on low settings for 4 hours.
When done, drop small clusters of mixture on a baking tray lined with baking paper.
Allow to cool and set before serving.

Buttery Chocolate Cake

Time: 4 1/4 hours   Servings: 10

Ingredients:

3/4 cup butter, softened
3/4 cup light brown sugar
4 eggs
1 cup dark chocolate, melted and chilled
1/2 cup sour cream

1 1/4 cups all-purpose flour
1/4 cup cocoa powder
1 1/2 teaspoons baking powder
1/4 teaspoon salt

Directions:

Mix the butter and sugar in a bowl until creamy. Add the eggs, one by one, then stir in the melted chocolate and sour cream.
Fold in the flour, cocoa powder, baking powder and salt.
Spoon the batter in your slow cooker and cook on low settings for 4 hours.
Allow the cake to cool in the pot before serving.

S'MORES FONDUE

Time: 1 1/4 hours   Servings: 6

Ingredients:

1 can (15 oz.) sweetened condensed milk   1 1/2 cups dark chocolate chips
1/2 teaspoon all-spice powder   1 cup mini marshmallows
1/2 cup caramel sauce   Pretzels or fresh fruits for serving
1/2 cup heavy cream

Directions:

Mix the milk, all-spice powder, caramel sauce, cream, chocolate chips and marshmallows in your slow cooker.
Cover and cook for 1 hour on high settings.
Serve the fondue warm with pretzels of fresh fruits.

DOUBLE CHOCOLATE CAKE

Time: 4 1/4 hours   Servings: 8

Ingredients:

1 1/2 cups all-purpose flour   1 cup water
1 1/2 teaspoons baking powder   1 cup sour cream
1/4 teaspoon salt   4 eggs
1/4 cup cocoa powder   1 teaspoon vanilla extract
1/2 cup vegetable oil   1 cup dark chocolate chips

Directions:

Mix the flour, baking powder, salt, cocoa powder in a bowl.
Stir in the water, oil, sour cream, eggs, vanilla extract and give it a quick mix.
Pour the batter in your slow cooker and top with chocolate chips.
Cover and cook on low settings for 4 hours.
Allow the cake to cool before serving.

SAUCY APPLE AND PEARS

Time: 6 1/4 hours   Servings: 6

Ingredients:

4 ripe pears, peeled, cored and sliced   1 cup apple juice
2 Granny Smith apples, peeled, cored and   1 cup water
  sliced   1 cinnamon stick
1/4 cup light brown sugar   1 star anise
1/4 cup butter

Directions:

Combine all the ingredients in your crock pot.
Cover the pot and cook on low settings for 6 hours.
Allow the dessert to cool in the pot before serving.

BLUEBERRY DUMPLING PIE

Time: 5 1/2 hours

Servings: 8

Ingredients:

1 1/2 pounds fresh blueberries
2 tablespoons cornstarch
1/4 cup light brown sugar
1 tablespoon lemon zest
1/2 cup butter, chilled and cubed

1 1/2 cups all-purpose flour
1/2 teaspoon salt
1 teaspoon baking powder
2 tablespoons white sugar
2/3 cup buttermilk, chilled

Directions:

Mix the blueberries, cornstarch, brown sugar and lemon zest in your slow cooker.

For the dumpling topping, mix the flour, salt, baking powder, sugar and butter in a bowl and mix until sandy.

Stir in the buttermilk and give it a quick mix.

Drop spoonfuls of batter over the blueberries and cook on low settings for 5 hours.

Allow the dessert to cool completely before serving.

DRIED FRUIT RICE PUDDING

Time: 6 1/4 hours

Servings: 8

Ingredients:

2 cups white rice
1/2 cup golden raisins
1/2 cup dried apricots, chopped
1/4 cup dried cranberries

1/2 cup white sugar
3 cups whole milk
1 1/4 cups heavy cream
1 cinnamon stick

Directions:

Mix the rice, raisins, apricots, cranberries, sugar, milk, cream and cinnamon in your crock pot.

Cover the pot and cook for 6 hours on low settings.

The rice pudding is best served chilled.

HAZELNUT LIQUEUR CHEESECAKE

Time: 6 1/2 hours

Servings: 8

Ingredients:

Crust:

1 cup graham crackers, crushed
1 cup ground hazelnuts
1/4 cup butter, melted

Filling:

20 oz. cream cheese
1/2 cup hazelnut butter
1/4 cup hazelnut liqueur
1/4 cup light brown sugar

1/2 cup white sugar
4 eggs
1/2 cup heavy cream
1 pinch salt
1 teaspoon vanilla extract

Directions:

For the crust, mix the crackers, hazelnuts and butter in a bowl. Transfer the mix in your slow cooker and press it well on the bottom of the pot. For the filling, mix the cream cheese, hazelnut butter, liqueur, sugars, eggs, cream, salt and vanilla and mix well. Pour the mixture over the crust and cook in the covered pot for 6 hours on low settings. Serve the cheesecake chilled.

S'MORES BROWNIES

Time: 2 1/2 hours   Servings: 12

Ingredients:

1/4 cup butter, melted and chilled
1 cup dark chocolate chips, melted
4 eggs
1 cup white sugar
1 teaspoon vanilla extract
1 cup all-purpose flour

1/4 cup cocoa powder
1/2 teaspoon salt
1 1/2 cups mini marshmallows
1 cup dark chocolate chips
1 cup crushed graham crackers

Directions:

Mix the eggs and sugar in a bowl until tripled in volume. Stir in the melted butter and chocolate then add the vanilla. Fold in the flour, cocoa powder and salt then pour the batter in your crock pot. Top the batter with chocolate chips, graham crackers and mini marshmallows. Cover the pot and bake for 2 hours on high settings.

CHAI POACHED PEARS

Time: 6 1/2 hours   Servings: 6

Ingredients:

6 ripe but firm pears
1 cup water
1 cup whole milk
2 star anise

2 whole cloves
4 cardamom pods, crushed
1/4 cup maple syrup

Directions:

Mix the water, milk, maple syrup, star anise, cloves and cardamom in your crock pot.
Place the pears in the pot and cook on low settings for 6 hours.
Allow the pears to cool before serving.

STICKY CINNAMON ROLLS

Time: 6 1/2 hours   Servings: 8

Ingredients:

4 cups all-purpose flour
1/2 teaspoon salt
1 teaspoon active dry yeast
1 1/2 cups warm milk
2 eggs

1/4 cup melted butter
1 cup white sugar
1 teaspoon cinnamon powder
1 cup light brown sugar

Directions:

Mix the flour, salt and yeast in a bowl.

Add the warm milk, eggs and melted butter and knead the dough for 10 minutes until elastic and smooth.

Cover the bowl and allow the dough to rise for 1 hour.

Transfer the dough on a floured working surface and roll it into a thin sheet that has a rectangular shape.

Mix the white sugar with cinnamon and spread it over the dough then roll the dough tightly.

Carefully cut the roll of dough into thick slices.

Spread the brown sugar in your crock pot then arrange the dough rolls in your slow cooker, with the cut facing up.

Cover the pot and cook on low settings for 5 hours.

Serve the rolls warm.

CRUSTLESS PEACH PIE

Time: 4 1/4 hours   Servings: 8

Ingredients:

4 large peaches, pitted and sliced
1 1/4 cups all-purpose flour
1/2 cup ground almonds
1/4 cup white sugar

1/2 teaspoon cinnamon powder
1/2 teaspoon ground ginger
1 cup butter, melted

Directions:

Mix the peaches, flour, almonds, sugar, cinnamon and ginger in your crock pot.

Drizzle the butter over the pie and cook on low settings for 4 hours.

Serve the pie chilled.

MONKEY BREAD

Time: 5 1/4 hours   Servings: 8

Ingredients:

3 cups all-purpose flour
4 eggs
1/4 cup white sugar
1 teaspoon vanilla extract
1 1/4 cups warm milk

1 teaspoon active dry yeast
3/4 cup butter, melted
1 cup white sugar
1 1/2 teaspoons cinnamon powder

Directions:

Mix the flour, salt, eggs, 1/4 cup white sugar, warm milk, vanilla and active dry yeast in the bowl of your mixer and knead for 10 minutes. Allow the dough to rise for 1 hour.

Transfer the dough on a floured working surface and cut it into 24-30 small pieces of dough. Roll each piece of dough into a ball.

Mix the sugar with cinnamon powder.

To finish the bread, dip each ball of dough into melted butter then roll through the cinnamon sugar.

Grease your crock pot and place the dough balls in the pot.

Cook on low settings for 4 hours.

Allow to cool before serving.

Pumpkin Streusel Cake

Time: 6 1/2 hours

Servings: 8

Ingredients:

Streusel:

1/2 cup rolled oats
1/4 cup whole wheat flour
1 teaspoon cinnamon powder
2 tablespoons maple syrup
1/4 cup butter, melted

Cake:

1 3/4 cups all-purpose flour
1 1/2 teaspoons baking powder

1/4 teaspoon salt
1/2 teaspoon baking sods
1/2 teaspoon ground ginger
1/2 cup light brown sugar
1 cup pumpkin puree
1/2 cup fresh orange juice
1 tablespoon lemon juice
1/4 cup butter, melted
2 eggs
1/4 cup maple syrup

Directions:

For the topping, mix all the ingredients in a bowl and place aside. For the cake, combine all the dry ingredients in a bowl. Add the wet ingredients and give it a quick mix just until combined. Pour the batter in your crock pot and top with the streusel. Cover and cook on low settings for 6 hours. Allow the cake to cool in the pot before serving.

Spiced Raisins Tapioca Pudding

Time: 6 1/4 hours

Servings: 6

Ingredients:

1 cup tapioca pearls
3 cups whole milk
1 cup golden raisins
1 cinnamon stick

1 star anise
2 whole cloves
1/4 cup maple syrup

Directions:

Combine all the ingredients in your slow cooker.
Cover the pot and cook on low settings for 6 hours.
Allow the pudding to cool in the pot before serving.

Coconut Blueberry Crumble

Time: 2 1/4 hours

Servings: 6

Ingredients:

1 pound fresh blueberries
1 tablespoon cornstarch
1/4 cup white sugar
1 lemon, zested and juiced

1 cup shredded coconut
1/2 cup all-purpose flour
1/4 cup butter, chilled
2 tablespoons coconut milk, chilled

Directions:

Mix the blueberries, cornstarch, white sugar, lemon zest and lemon juice in your slow cooker.

For the topping, combine the coconut, flour and butter in a bowl. Mix until sandy then stir in the coconut milk.

Spread the mixture over the blueberries and cook on high settings for 2 hours.

Allow the crumble to cool before serving.

BLUEBERRY PRESERVE

Time: 4 1/4 hours   Servings: 8

Ingredients:

4 cups fresh or frozen blueberries   1 tablespoon lemon zest
2 cups white sugar   1 cinnamon stick

Directions:

Combine all the ingredients in your crock pot. Cover the pot and cook on low settings for 4 hours.

When done, pour the preserve into glass jars and cover them with a lid while still hot.

MANGO TAPIOCA PUDDING

Time: 6 1/4 hours   Servings: 6

Ingredients:

1 cup tapioca pearls   1/2 cup shredded coconut
2 cups coconut milk   1/4 cup white sugar
1 cup water   1 cinnamon stick
1 ripe mango, peeled and cubed

Directions:

Combine all the ingredients in your slow cooker.

Cover the pot and cook on low settings for 6 hours.

Allow the pudding to cool completely before serving.

NO CRUST LEMON CHEESECAKE

Time: 6 1/4 hours   Servings: 8

Ingredients:

24 oz. cream cheese   4 eggs
1 lemon, zested and juiced   1 teaspoon vanilla extract
2 tablespoons cornstarch   1/4 cup butter, melted
1/2 cup white sugar

Directions:

Mix all the ingredients in a bowl.

Pour the cheesecake mix in a greased slow cooker and cook on low settings for 6 hours.

Allow the cheesecake to cool in the pot before slicing and serving.

*U*PSIDE DOWN BANANA CAKE

Time: 4 1/2 hours   Servings: 8

Ingredients:

2 ripe bananas, sliced
1/2 cup light brown sugar
2 tablespoons brandy
1/2 cup butter
3/4 cup sugar
2 eggs

3/4 cup sour cream
1 teaspoon vanilla extract
1 cup all-purpose flour
1/4 cup cornstarch
1 teaspoon baking soda
1 pinch salt

Directions:

Spread the brown sugar in your slow cooker. Arrange the banana slices over the sugar and drizzle with brandy. For the cake, mix the butter and 3/4 cup sugar in a bowl until creamy, at least 3 minutes. Add the eggs, one by one, followed by the sour cream and vanilla. Fold in the flour, cornstarch, baking soda and salt then spoon the batter over the banana slices. Cover the pot and cook on low settings for 4 hours. Allow the cake to cool for 10 minutes then carefully turn it upside down on a platter. You can also slice it and serve it straight from the pot.

*D*ULCE DE LECHE

Time: 8 hours   Servings: 4

Ingredients:

1 can (14 oz.) sweetened condensed milk
Water as needed

Directions:

Make 2-3 holes in the condensed milk can, preferably on the top side.
Place the can in your slow cooker and add enough water to cover it 3/4.
Cover the crock pot with its lid and cook on low settings for 8 hours.
Serve the dulce de leche chilled.

*F*UDGE RASPBERRY CAKE

Time: 4 1/4 hours   Servings: 8

Ingredients:

1 cup all-purpose flour
1/4 cup cocoa powder
1 1/2 teaspoons baking powder
1/4 teaspoon salt
1 cup whole milk

1/2 cup canola oil
2 eggs
1/4 cup seedless raspberry jam
1 teaspoon vanilla extract

Directions:

Mix the flour, cocoa powder, baking powder and salt in a bowl. Add the remaining ingredients and give it a quick mix.
Pour the batter in a greased slow cooker and cook for 4 hours on low settings.
Allow the cake to cool before slicing and serving.

Gluten Free Blueberry Cake

Time: 5 1/4 hours

Servings: 6

Ingredients:

1/4 cup tapioca flour
1/2 cup white sorghum flour
1/4 cup quinoa flour
2 tablespoons ground flax seeds
1 1/2 teaspoons baking powder
3/4 cup coconut sugar

1/4 cup coconut oil, melted
1 cup coconut milk
2 eggs
1 teaspoon vanilla extract
1 cup fresh or frozen blueberries

Directions:

Mix the dry ingredients in a bowl. Add the wet ingredients and give it a quick mix. Fold in the blueberries then transfer the batter in your greased slow cooker. Cover the pot and cook on low settings for 5 hours. Allow the cake to cool in the pot before slicing and serving.

Caramel Peanut Butter Cheesecake

Time: 6 1/2 hours

Servings: 10

Ingredients:

Crust:

1 1/2 cups crushed graham crackers
1/2 cup butter, melted

Filling:

1/2 cup smooth peanut butter

1/2 cup caramel sauce
20 oz. cream cheese
4 eggs
1 tablespoon cornstarch
1 teaspoon vanilla extract
1/2 cup light brown sugar

Directions:

For the crust, mix the crackers and butter in a bowl. Transfer the mixture in your slow cooker and press it well. For the filling, combine the peanut butter, caramel sauce, cream cheese, eggs, cornstarch, vanilla and sugar in a bowl and give it a good mix. Pour the filling over the crust and cook on low settings for 6 hours. Allow the cheesecake to cool in the pot before slicing and serving.

Fudgy Raspberry Chocolate Bread Pudding

Time: 6 1/4 hours

Servings: 8

Ingredients:

6 cups bread cubes
1/4 cup cocoa powder
2 cups whole milk

1 cup heavy cream
1 1/2 cups fresh raspberries
1/2 cup white chocolate chips

Directions:

Mix the bread cubes, raspberries and white chocolate chips in your slow cooker. Combine the cocoa powder, milk and cream in a bowl and give it a good mix. Pour this mix over the bread cubes. Cover the pot with its lid and cook on low settings for 6 hours. Allow to cool slightly before serving.

Pear and Apple Butter

Time: 6 1/2 hours   Servings: 6 jars

Ingredients:

6 large red apples, peeled, cored and sliced
4 ripe pears, peeled, cored and sliced
1 1/2 cups fresh apple juice
1 cup white sugar

1 cup light brown sugar
1 cinnamon stick
4 cardamom pods, crushed

Directions:

Combine all the ingredients in your slow cooker. Cover the pot and cook on low settings for 6 hours. When done, pour the mixture into glass jars and seal them with a lid. Allow to cool before serving.

Cinnamon Coffee Cake

Time: 4 1/2 hours   Servings: 10

Ingredients:

Cinnamon streusel:

1 cup chopped walnuts
1/2 cup all-purpose flour
1/2 cup light brown sugar
1 teaspoon cinnamon powder

Cake:

3/4 cup butter, softened

3/4 cup sugar
4 eggs
1 teaspoon vanilla extract
1 1/2 cups all-purpose flour
1/2 teaspoon salt
1 1/2 teaspoons baking powder
1 cup sour cream

Directions:

For the streusel, mix all the ingredients in a bowl. Place aside. For the cake, mix the butter with sugar until creamy. Add the eggs, one by one, then stir in the vanilla. Fold in the flour, salt and baking powder then add the sour cream. Mix on high speed for 2 minutes then spoon half of the batter in your slow cooker. Top with the streusel and cover with the remaining batter. Bake on low settings for 4 hours. Allow the cake to cool in the pot before serving.

Spiced Applesauce Cake

Time: 4 1/2 hours   Servings: 10

Ingredients:

2 cups all-purpose flour
1 teaspoon baking soda
1/2 teaspoon baking powder
1 teaspoon cinnamon powder
1/2 teaspoon ground ginger
1/4 teaspoon ground whole cloves

1/2 cup butter, softened
1/2 cup white sugar
1/4 cup light brown sugar
2 eggs
1 cup applesauce

Directions:

Mix the dry ingredients in a bowl.

Mix the butter, sugar and eggs in a bowl until creamy.

Fold in the dry ingredients, alternating them with the applesauce.

Mix just until combined then transfer the batter in your slow cooker.

Cover the pot and bake on low settings for 4 hours.

Allow the cake to cool in the pot before slicing and serving.

RED VELVET BRIOCHE PUDDING

Time: 5 1/2 hours   Servings: 6

Ingredients:

5 cups brioche cubes
2 cups whole milk
1 cup cream cheese
1 teaspoon red food coloring

3 eggs
1/2 cup white sugar
1 teaspoon vanilla extract
1/2 cup white chocolate chips

Directions:

Mix the brioche and white chocolate chips in your crock pot.

Combine the milk, cream cheese, food coloring, eggs, sugar and vanilla in a bowl and mix well.

Pour this mixture over the brioche then cook on low settings for 5 hours.

The pudding is best served slightly warm.

CARAMEL MOCHA CHEESECAKE

Time: 6 1/2 hours   Servings: 10

Ingredients:

Crust:

1 1/2 cups crushed graham crackers
1/2 cup butter, melted

Filling:

18 oz. cream cheese

1 cup heavy cream
4 eggs
1/2 cup caramel sauce
1/4 cup strong espresso
1 pinch salt

Directions:

For the crust, mix the two ingredients in a bowl then transfer the mix in your slow cooker. Press the mixture well on the bottom of the pot.

For the filling, combine the rest of the ingredients in a bowl and mix well.

Pour the filling over the crust and cook on low settings for 6 hours.

Allow the cheesecake to cool before slicing and serving.

BUTTERSCOTCH SELF SAUCING PUDDING

Time: 2 1/4 hours   Servings: 6

Ingredients:

1/2 cup butter, melted
1 cup whole milk
1 teaspoon vanilla extract
1 cup white sugar
1 1/2 cups all-purpose flour

1/4 teaspoon salt
2 cups hot water
3/4 cup dark brown sugar
2 tablespoons golden syrup
2 tablespoons butter

Directions:

Make the butterscotch sauce by mixing the hot water, brown sugar, golden syrup and 2 tablespoons of butter in a saucepan. Cook over medium flame for 5-6 minutes until thickened then place aside. For the pudding, mix 1/2 cup butter, milk, vanilla, white sugar, flour and salt in a bowl. Pour the batter in a slow cooker. Drizzle the butterscotch sauce on top and cook on high settings for 2 hours. Serve the pudding slightly warm.

CREAMED RICE PUDDING

Time: 4 1/4 hours   Servings: 6

Ingredients:

1 cup white rice
1 cup evaporated milk
1/2 cup light brown sugar
2 cups whole milk

1 pinch nutmeg
1/2 cup golden raisins
1 teaspoon vanilla extract

Directions:

Combine all the ingredients in your crock pot.
Cover the pot and cook on low settings for 4 hours.
The pudding is best served slightly warm or chilled.

LEMON AND LIME QUICK PUDDING

Time: 4 1/4 hours   Servings: 8

Ingredients:

1 cup butter, softened
1 cup white sugar
3 egg yolks
2 tablespoons lemon juice
1 1/2 cups whole milk

1/3 cup self-raising powder
1 tablespoon lemon zest
1 tablespoon lime zest
4 egg whites
1 pinch cream of tartar

Directions:

Mix the butter and sugar in a bowl until creamy. Add the egg yolks, lemon juice and milk, as well as flour, lemon zest and lime zest. Whip the egg whites and cream of tartar in a bowl until stiff. Fold this meringue into the batter using a spatula. Pour the batter in a greased slow cooker and cook on low settings for 4 hours. Allow to cool before serving.

Dark Cherry Chocolate Cake

Time: 4 1/2 hours   Servings: 8

Ingredients:

2/3 cup butter, softened
2/3 cup white sugar
3 eggs
1 teaspoon vanilla extract
2/3 cup all-purpose flour
1 teaspoon baking powder

1/4 teaspoon salt
1/4 cup cocoa powder
1 1/2 cups dark cherries, pitted
1/2 cup water
1/2 cup dark chocolate chips

Directions:

Mix the butter and sugar in a bowl until creamy. Stir in the eggs and vanilla and mix well then fold in the flour, baking powder, salt, baking powder and cocoa. Pour the batter in your slow cooker and top with dark cherries. Mix the water and chocolate chips in a saucepan and cook over low heat until melted and smooth. Pour the hot sauce over the cherries and cook the cake on low settings for 4 hours. Allow the cake to cool in the pot before serving.

Overnight Plum Pudding

Time: 8 1/4 hours   Servings: 8

Ingredients:

1 1/2 cups all-purpose flour
1/4 cup dark brown sugar
1/2 teaspoon baking soda
4 tablespoons butter, softened

2 eggs
1 cup mixed dried fruits, chopped
1/2 cup dried plums, chopped
1 cup hot water

Directions:

Mix the dried fruits, plums and hot water in a bowl and allow to soak up for 10 minutes. Combine the flour, brown sugar, baking soda, butter, eggs and the dried fruits plus the water in a large bowl. Mix well with a spoon or spatula then spoon the batter in your crock pot. Cover and cook on low settings for 8 hours. Allow the pudding to cool in the pot before serving.

Golden Syrup Pudding

Time: 4 1/4 hours   Servings: 8

Ingredients:

1/2 cup golden syrup
1/2 cup butter, softened
1/4 cup light brown sugar
2 eggs

1 1/2 cups all-purpose flour
1/4 teaspoon salt
1/2 teaspoon baking soda
3/4 cup whole milk

Directions:

Mix the dry ingredients in a bowl and the wet ingredients in another bowl. Combine the dry and wet ingredients in a bowl and give it a quick mix. Spoon the batter in your slow cooker and bake on low settings for 4 hours. Allow the pudding cool before serving.

CHOCOLATE CHIP COOKIE BARS

Time: 2 3/4 hours

Servings: 12

Ingredients:

1 cup butter, softened
1 cup powdered sugar
2 egg yolks
1/2 cup ground almonds
1 cup all-purpose flour

1 pinch salt
1/2 teaspoon baking powder
1/4 cup heavy cream
1/2 cup dark chocolate chips

Directions:

Mix the butter and powdered sugar in a bowl until creamy. Add the egg yolks then fold in the almonds, flour, salt and baking powder, as well as the heavy cream. Stir in the chocolate chips. Spoon the dough in your slow cooker and level it well. Cover and bake for 2 1/2 hours on high settings. Allow to cool before cutting into squares.

BROWNED BUTTER PUMPKIN CHEESECAKE

Time: 6 1/2 hours

Servings: 8

Ingredients:

Crust:

1 1/4 cups crushed graham crackers
1/2 cup butter

Filling:

1 cup pumpkin puree
24 oz. cream cheese

4 eggs
1/2 cup light brown sugar
1 pinch salt
1 teaspoon cinnamon powder
1 teaspoon ground ginger
1/2 teaspoon cardamom powder
1/4 cup butter

Directions:

To make the curst, start by browning the butter. Place the butter in a saucepan and cook for a few minutes until it starts to look golden. Allow to cool slightly. Mix the browned butter with crushed crackers then transfer the mixture in your crock pot and press it well on the bottom of the pot. For the filling, brown 1/4 cup butter as described above then stir in the pumpkin puree, cream cheese, eggs, sugar, salt, cinnamon, ginger and cardamom. Pour the mixture over the curst and cook on low settings for 6 hours. Allow the cheesecake to cool down before slicing and serving.

BUTTERSCOTCH CAKE

Time: 4 1/2 hours

Servings: 8

Ingredients:

1/2 cup butter, softened
1/2 cup white sugar
1 cup butterscotch chocolate chips, melted
1/2 cup whole milk

1 cup hot water
1 1/2 cups all-purpose flour
1/2 teaspoon salt
1 teaspoon baking powder

Directions:

Mix the butter and sugar in a bowl until creamy, at least 5 minutes.

Add the melted butterscotch chips then stir in the milk and hot water.

Fold in the flour, salt and baking powder then pour the batter in your crock pot.

Bake for 4 hours on low settings.

Allow to cool completely before serving.

RICH BREAD PUDDING

Time: 6 1/2 hours   Servings: 6

Ingredients:

6 cups bread cubes   1 1/2 cups whole milk
1/4 cup golden raisins   1/2 cup heavy cream
1/2 cup dark chocolate chips   1 teaspoon vanilla extract
1/4 cup butter, melted   1 pinch cinnamon powder
4 eggs   2 tablespoons dark rum

Directions:

Mix the bread cubes, raisins and chocolate chips in your slow cooker.

Combine the butter, eggs, milk, cream, vanilla, cinnamon and dark rum and give it a good mix.

Pour the mixture over the bread and bake on low settings for 6 hours.

Serve the bread pudding slightly warm.

DULCE DE LECHE CHOCOLATE PIE

Time: 2 1/2 hours   Servings: 8

Ingredients:

Crust: 1/4 cup chilled milk
                                      2 tablespoons sugar
1/2 cup butter, chilled and cubed
1 cup all-purpose flour   **Filling:**
1 pinch salt   1 can (14 oz.) dulce de leche
1/4 teaspoon baking powder   2 cups dark chocolate chips

Directions:

To make the crust, combine the butter, flour, salt, baking powder and sugar in a food processor. Pulse until grainy.

Add the milk and pulse for a few seconds until it comes together.

Place the dough on a floured working surface and roll it into a round sheet.

Place the dough in your slow cooker.

Spoon the dulce de leche in the crust and top with chocolate chips.

Cook for 2 hours on high settings/

Allow to cool before slicing and serving.

GRAND MARNIER SOUFFLÉ

Time: 2 1/2 hours   Servings: 6

Ingredients:

1 large orange, zested
2/3 cup white sugar
1/2 cup all-purpose flour
8 egg yolks
1/4 cup butter, softened

1/4 cup Grand Marnier
10 egg whites
1 pinch salt
Butter to grease the pot

Directions:

Grease your slow cooker with butter. Mix the orange zest and sugar in a bowl and rub them together to release the flavor of the orange. Combine the sugar and milk in a saucepan and bring to the boiling point. Mix the egg yolks with flour until creamy then pour the hot milk over this mixture, stirring all the time. Return the mixture on low heat and cook for a few minutes, whisking all the time, until thickened. Remove from heat and stir in the butter and Grand Marnier then allow to cool. Whip the egg whites with a pinch of salt until stiff then fold this meringue into the orange mixture. Pour the batter in your slow cooker and bake for 2 hours on high settings. The soufflé is best served right away.

WHITE CHOCOLATE CHEESECAKE SOUFFLÉ

Time: 2 1/2 hours   Servings: 8

Ingredients:

1 1/2 cups white chocolate chips, melted
1 1/2 cups cream cheese, softened
4 egg yolks
1 teaspoon vanilla extract

4 egg whites
1 pinch salt
Butter to grease the pot

Directions:

Whip the egg whites with a pinch of salt until stiff. Combine the cream cheese, chocolate, egg yolks and vanilla in a bowl. Fold in the whipped egg whites then pour the batter in your slow cooker. Cook on high settings for 2 hours. The soufflé can be served both warm and chilled.

CHOCOLATE MOCHA BREAD PUDDING

Time: 4 1/4 hours   Servings: 6

Ingredients:

6 cups bread cubed
1 cup heavy cream
1 cup whole milk
1 cup brewed coffee

2 egg yolks
2 whole eggs
1/2 cup white sugar

Directions:

Mix the cream, milk, coffee, egg yolks, eggs and sugar in a bowl. Place the bread cubes in a slow cooker and pour the coffee mixture over it. Cover and cook on low settings for 4 hours. Allow the pudding to cool slightly before serving.

Chunky Pumpkin Cake

Time: 5 1/2 hours

Servings: 8

Ingredients:

3 eggs
1/2 cup canola oil
2/3 cup white sugar
1 cup sour cream
1 1/2 cups all-purpose flour
1 teaspoon baking powder

1/4 teaspoon salt
1/2 teaspoon cinnamon powder
1/4 teaspoon ground ginger
1/4 teaspoon ground cloves
2 cups pumpkin cubes

Directions:

Mix the eggs, sugar and oil in a bowl for 5 minutes until double in volume. Stir in the sour cream then add the flour, baking powder, salt and spices. Pour the batter in your crock pot. Top with pumpkin cubes and cook on low settings for 5 hours. Allow the cake to cool before slicing and serving.

Coconut Oatmeal Brownies

Time: 4 1/2 hours

Servings: 12

Ingredients:

1 cup all-purpose flour
1/2 cup cocoa powder
1/4 teaspoon salt
2 tablespoons powdered milk
1 cup shredded coconut

1/2 cup rolled oats
1/4 cup butter, melted
2 eggs
1 cup sweetened condensed milk
1/2 cup whole milk

Directions:

Mix the flour, cocoa powder, salt, powdered milk, shredded coconut and oats a bowl. Add the butter, eggs, whole milk and sweetened milk and give it a quick mix. Pour the batter in your slow cooker and bake for 4 hours on low settings. Allow the brownies to cool before cutting into small squares.

Swirled Peanut Butter Cake

Time: 5 1/2 hours

Servings: 10

Ingredients:

3/4 cup butter, softened
1 cup white sugar
3 eggs
1 teaspoon vanilla extract

1 cup all-purpose flour
1 teaspoon baking powder
1/4 teaspoon salt
1/2 cup smooth peanut butter, softened

Directions:

Mix the butter and sugar in a bowl for 5 minutes until creamy. Add the eggs, one by one and stir in the vanilla. Fold in the flour, baking powder and salt and mix gently. Pour half of the batter in your slow cooker. The remaining half, mix it with the peanut butter and spoon it into the pot. Bake for 5 hours on low settings. Allow the cake to cool completely before serving.

Lemon Buttermilk Cake

Time: 4 1/4 hours

Servings: 8

Ingredients:

4 eggs
1 cup buttermilk
3/4 cup white sugar
1 tablespoon lemon zest

2 tablespoons lemon juice
1/2 cup all-purpose flour
1/4 teaspoon salt
1 teaspoon baking powder

Directions:

Mix the eggs, buttermilk, sugar, lemon zest and lemon juice in a bowl.

Add the flour, salt and baking powder and give it a quick mix just until combined.

Pour the batter in your crock pot and bake for 4 hours on low settings.

Allow the cake to cool in the pot before slicing and serving.

Apple Dump Cake

Time: 4 1/2 hours

Servings: 8

Ingredients:

6 Granny Smith apples, peeled, cored and sliced
1/4 cup light brown sugar
1 teaspoon cinnamon

1 box yellow cake mix
1/2 cup butter, melted

Directions:

Mix the apples, brown sugar and cinnamon in a slow cooker.

Top with the cake mix and drizzle with butter.

Cover the pot and cook on low settings for 4 hours.

Allow the cake to cool in the pot before serving.

Butter Lime Cake

Time: 2 1/2 hours

Servings: 8

Ingredients:

1 cup butter, softened
1 1/4 cups white sugar
3 eggs
1 teaspoon vanilla extract
1 cup buttermilk

1 lime, zested and juiced
1 1/2 cups all-purpose flour
1 teaspoon baking powder
1/4 teaspoon salt

Directions:

Mix the butter and sugar in a bowl until creamy, for about 2 minutes.

Add the eggs, one by one, then stir in the vanilla, buttermilk, lime zest and lime juice.

Fold in the remaining ingredients then pour the batter in a greased slow cooker.

Cover and cook on high settings for 2 hours.

Allow the cake to cool in the pot before serving.

CARAMEL APPLE CRISP

Time: 6 1/2 hours   Servings: 8

Ingredients:

6 Granny Smith apples, peeled, cored and sliced
1/2 cup caramel sauce
1 tablespoon cornstarch
1/2 teaspoon cinnamon powder

1 cup all-purpose flour
1/2 cup rolled oats
1/4 cup butter, chilled
1 pinch salt

Directions:

Mix the apples, caramel sauce, cinnamon and cornstarch in your slow cooker.
For the topping, mix the flour, oats, butter and salt in a bowl until grainy.
Spread the topping over the apples and cook on low settings for 6 hours.
Allow the crisp to cool in the pot before serving.

PEAR BLUEBERRY CAKE

Time: 4 1/2 hours   Servings: 8

Ingredients:

3/4 cup butter, softened
1 cup white sugar
1 teaspoon vanilla extract
3 eggs
1 cup all-purpose flour

1/4 cup cornstarch
1 teaspoon baking powder
1/2 teaspoon salt
2 ripe pears, peeled, cored and diced
1 cup fresh or frozen blueberries

Directions:

Mix the butter, sugar and vanilla in a bowl for 5 minutes until creamy.
Stir in the eggs, one by one, then add the dry ingredients.
Fold in the pears and blueberries then spoon the batter in a greased slow cooker.
Cover the pot and cook on low settings for 4 hours.
Allow the cake to cool in the pot before serving.

AMARETTO PEAR BUTTER

Time: 6 1/2 hours   Servings: 6 jars

Ingredients:

4 pounds ripe pears, peeled, cored and sliced
1 1/2 cups white sugar
1/4 cup dark brown sugar

1/4 cup Amaretto liqueur
1/2 teaspoon cinnamon powder

Directions:

Combine all the ingredients in your slow cooker. Cover the pot and cook on low settings for 6 hours.
When done, pour the batter in your glass jars and seal with a lid while still hot.
Allow to cool before serving.

CHERRY DUMP CAKE

Time: 6 1/4 hours   Servings: 8-10

Ingredients:

1 1/2 pounds dark cherries, pitted
1 tablespoon cornstarch
1/4 cup white sugar
1 teaspoon lemon juice

1 cup all-purpose flour
1 cup ground almonds
1/4 teaspoon salt
1/2 cup butter, drizzled

Directions:

Mix the cherries, cornstarch, sugar and lemon juice in your slow cooker. Mix the flour, almonds and salt in a bowl. Spread this mixture over the cherries then drizzle with melted butter. Bake for 6 hours on low settings. Allow the cake to cool in the pot before serving.

CARDAMOM CARROT CAKE

Time: 4 1/2 hours   Servings: 8

Ingredients:

Cake:

4 eggs
1 cup white sugar
1 teaspoon vanilla extract
1/2 cup canola oil
1 cup crushed pineapple
1 1/2 cups grated carrot
1 1/2 teaspoons ground cardamom
1/2 teaspoon ground ginger

1 teaspoon cinnamon powder
1 1/2 cups all-purpose flour
1 teaspoon baking powder
1/2 teaspoon baking soda
1/2 teaspoon salt

Frosting:

1 cup mascarpone cream
1/4 cup powdered sugar
1/2 cup heavy cream, whipped

Directions:

Mix the eggs, sugar and vanilla in a bowl for 5-7 minutes until pale and fluffy.
Add the oil and mix well then stir in the pineapple, carrot, cardamom, finger and cinnamon.
In a bowl, sift the flour with baking powder, baking soda and salt then fold this dry mixture into the batter.
Pour the batter in your slow cooker and bake for 4 hours on low settings.
Allow the cake to cool completely when done.
For the frosting, mix the mascarpone cream with the sugar until fluffy. Fold in the whipped cream/
Top the cake with this frosting before serving.

HOT FUDGE CHOCOLATE CAKE

Time: 2 1/2 hours   Servings: 10

Ingredients:

1 cup cocoa powder
1 cup all-purpose flour

2 teaspoons baking powder
1/2 teaspoon salt

1 cup white sugar
1/4 cup butter, melted
2 eggs

1 teaspoon vanilla extract
1 cup plain yogurt
3/4 cup whole milk

Directions:

Mix the dry ingredients in a bowl then add the wet ingredients and give it a quick mix just until combined.

Pour the batter in your greased slow cooker.

Cover the pot and bake for 2 hours on high settings.

Allow the cake to cool completely before slicing and serving.

Cinnamon Rolls

Time: 6 hours   Servings: 8

Ingredients:

4 cups all-purpose flour
1/2 teaspoon salt
1 1/4 teaspoons active dry yeast
2 eggs
1 3/4 cups milk

1/4 cup sour cream
1/4 cup white sugar
1 cup light brown sugar
1 teaspoon cinnamon powder
1/2 cup butter, softened

Directions:

Mix the flour, salt and yeast in a bowl.

Add the eggs, milk, sour cream and white sugar and mix well with a spoon then knead for 10 minutes until elastic and smooth.

Allow the dough to rise for 40 minutes.

Transfer the dough on a floured working surface and roll it into a thin rectangle.

Spread the softened butter over the dough and top with brown sugar and cinnamon.

Roll the dough as tight as possible then cut the roll into thick slices and arrange them all in your slow cooker.

Allow to rise for 20 additional minutes then bake for 4 1/2 hours on low settings.

Serve warm or chilled.

Slow Cooker Fudge

Time: 1 1/4 hours   Servings: 12

Ingredients:

2 1/2 cups dark chocolate chips
1/2 cup heavy cream
1/2 cup honey

1 teaspoon vanilla extract
1/2 cup chopped walnuts

Directions:

Combine the dark chocolate chips, cream, honey and vanilla in your slow cooker.

Cover the pot and cook for 1 hour on high settings.

When done, stir in the walnuts and allow to cool completely and to set.

Cut into small squares and serve.

SPICED PLUM BUTTER

Time: 8 1/2 hours

Servings: 8 jars

Directions:
6 pounds ripe plums, pitted
3 cups white sugar
2 star anise

2 cinnamon stick
4 cardamom pods, crushed
2 whole cloves

Directions:
Combine all the ingredients in your slow cooker.

Cover the pot and cook on low settings for 8 hours.

Remove and discard the spices then pour the hot butter into glass jars and seal them with a lid.

SLOW COOKED CHOCOLATE CREAM

Time: 2 1/4 hours

Servings: 6

Ingredients:
1 1/2 cups dark chocolate chips
1 cup evaporated milk
1 cup heavy cream

1 teaspoon vanilla extract
2 tablespoons butter

Directions:
Mix all the ingredients in your slow cooker.

Cover and cook on low settings for 2 hours.

Allow the cream to cool before using as a filling or frosting for other desserts.

S'MORES BAKED SWEET POTATOES

Time: 3 1/2 hours

Servings: 8

Ingredients:
2 large sweet potatoes, peeled and diced
1 teaspoon cinnamon powder
2 tablespoons brown sugar
1 1/2 cups crushed graham crackers

1/4 cup butter, melted
1 1/2 cups dark chocolate chips
2 cups mini marshmallows

Directions:
Mix the crackers and butter in a bowl. Transfer this mixture in your slow cooker and press it well on the bottom of the pot.

Mix the sweet potatoes with the cinnamon and brown sugar then transfer this mix over the crackers crust.

Top the potatoes with chocolate chips, followed by marshmallows.

Cook on low settings for 3 hours.

Allow the dessert to cool down slightly before serving.

Sweet Potato Chocolate Cake

Time: 4 1/4 hours   Servings: 8

Ingredients:

1 cup all-purpose flour
1/2 cup cocoa powder
1 teaspoon baking soda
1/2 teaspoon salt
1 teaspoon cinnamon powder

2 eggs
1 cup buttermilk
1/2 cup canola oil
1cup sweet potato puree

Directions:

Mix the dry ingredients in a bowl then add the wet ingredients and mix with a whisk just until combined.
Pour the batter in your greased slow cooker and bake for 4 hours on low settings.
Allow the cake to cool in the pot before slicing and serving.

Dark Chocolate Almond Cake

Time: 4 1/2 hours   Servings: 10

Ingredients:

1 1/2 cups almond flour
1/2 cup cocoa powder
3/4 cup white sugar
1 1/2 teaspoons baking powder
1/4 teaspoon salt

1/2 cup butter, melted
2 eggs
1 cup almond milk
1 teaspoon vanilla extract
1/4 cup sliced almonds

Directions:

Mix the almond flour, cocoa powder, sugar, baking powder and salt in a bowl. Stir in the wet ingredients and mix well. Pour the batter in a greased slow cooker and top with sliced almonds. Bake for 4 hours on low settings. Allow the cake to cool completely before slicing and serving.

Honey Yogurt Cake

Time: 5 1/2 hours   Servings: 8

Ingredients:

1/2 cup butter, softened
1/4 cup honey
1/2 cup light brown sugar
1 teaspoon lemon zest
2 eggs

1 cup all-purpose flour
1 teaspoon baking powder
1/4 teaspoon salt
1/4 cup Greek yogurt

Directions:

Mix the butter, honey and sugar in a bowl for 5 minutes until pale and creamy. Stir in the lemon zest and eggs and mix well. Fold in the flour, baking powder and salt then add the yogurt. Spoon the batter in a greased slow cooker and bake for 5 hours on low settings. Allow the cake to cool in the pot before slicing and serving.

ONE LARGE VANILLA PANCAKE

Time: 2 1/4 hours   Servings: 6

Ingredients:

3/4 cup all-purpose flour
2 tablespoons white sugar
3/4 teaspoon baking powder
1/4 teaspoon baking soda
1/4 teaspoon salt

2 tablespoons butter, melted
1 teaspoon vanilla extract
2 eggs
1 cup buttermilk
Maple syrup for serving

Directions:

Mix all the ingredients in a bowl and give it a quick mix just until combined. Grease your slow cooker with butter then pour the batter in the pot. Cook for 2 hours on high settings. Serve the pancake with maple syrup if you want.

LEMON BARS

Time: 6 1/2 hours   Servings: 10

Ingredients:

Crust:

1/2 cup butter, softened
1/4 cup white sugar
2 egg yolks
1 teaspoon vanilla extract
1 1/2 cups all-purpose flour
1 pinch salt

1/4 teaspoon baking powder

Filling:

6 egg yolks
1/2 cup lemon juice
1 tablespoon lemon zest
2/3 cup white sugar

Directions:

To make the crust, mix the butter and sugar in a bowl for 5 minutes. Add the egg yolks and vanilla and give it a quick mix. Fold in the flour, salt and baking powder and knead the dough for a few times. Place the dough on a floured working surface then roll it into a thin sheet. Transfer in your slow cooker and trim the edges if needed. For the filling, mix the ingredients in a bowl. Pour the filling into the crust. Bake for 6 hours on low settings. Allow to cool in the pot before serving.

HAZELNUT CRUMBLE CHEESECAKE

Time: 6 1/2 hours   Servings: 8

Ingredients:

Crust and topping:

3/4 cup butter, chilled and cubed
1 1/4 cups all-purpose flour
1 cup ground hazelnuts
1/4 cup buttermilk
1 pinch salt
2 tablespoons light brown sugar

Filling:

20 oz. cream cheese
1/2 cup sour cream
1/2 cup white sugar
1 teaspoon vanilla extract
2 tablespoons Grand Marnier
1 tablespoon cornstarch
2 eggs

Directions:

For the crust and topping, combine all the ingredients in a food processor and pulse until a dough comes together.
Cut the dough in half. Wrap one half in plastic wrap and place in the fridge.
The remaining dough, roll it into a thin sheet and place it in your slow cooker, trimming the edges if needed.
For the filling, mix all the ingredients in a large bowl. Pour this mixture over the crust.
For the topping, remove the dough from the fridge then grate it on a large grater over the cheesecake filling.
Cover the pot and bake for 6 hours on low settings.
Allow to cool completely before slicing and serving.

Mexican Chocolate Cake

Time: 6 1/4 hours   Servings: 8

Ingredients:

1 cup all-purpose flour   1 cup buttermilk
1/2 cup cocoa powder   2 eggs
1 teaspoon baking soda   1/2 cup corn oil
1/4 teaspoon salt   1 teaspoon vanilla extract
1/4 teaspoon chili powder   1 cup dulce de leche to frost the cake

Directions:

Mix the dry ingredients in your slow cooker.
Add the wet ingredients and give it a quick mix just until combined.
Pour the batter in a grease slow cooker and bake for 6 hours on low settings.
Allow the cake to cool completely then frost it with dulce de leche.
Slice and serve fresh.

Boozy Bread Pudding

Time: 6 1/2 hours   Servings: 10

Ingredients:

8 cups bread cubes   1/2 cup brandy
1/4 cup dark chocolate chips   4 eggs
1/2 cup golden raisins   2 cups whole milk
1/2 cup dried apricots, chopped   1/2 cup fresh orange juice
1/2 cup dried cranberries   1/2 cup light brown sugar

Directions:

Combine the bread cubes and chocolate chips in your slow cooker.
Mix the raisins, apricots, cranberries and brandy in a bowl and allow to soak up for 30 minutes at least, preferably overnight.
In a bowl, mix the eggs, milk, orange juice and brown sugar.
Spoon the dried fruits and brandy over the bread cubes and top with the egg and milk mixture.
Cover the pot and bake for 6 hours on low settings.
The pudding is best served slightly warm.

Banana Walnut Cake

Time: 4 1/2 hours   Servings: 8

Ingredients:

1 cup white sugar
1/2 cup canola oil
2 eggs
1 teaspoon vanilla extract
4 small ripe bananas, mashed

1 1/4 cups all-purpose flour
1 teaspoon baking powder
1/4 teaspoon salt
1 cup chopped walnuts

Directions:

Mix the sugar and oil in a bowl for 2 minutes then add the eggs and continue mixing for a few minutes until fluffy.
Add the vanilla and bananas then fold in the flour, baking powder and salt, as well as walnuts.
Pour the batter in your slow cooker and bake for 4 hours on low settings.
Allow the cake to cool completely before slicing and serving.

Raspberry Poached Pears

Time: 6 1/2 hours   Servings: 6

Ingredients:

1 cup fresh or frozen raspberries
2 cups red wine
1 cup white sugar

1 vanilla bean, split in half lengthwise
6 ripe but firm pears, peeled and cored

Directions:

Combine all the ingredients in your slow cooker.
Cover and cook for 6 hours on low settings.
Allow the pears to cool down before serving. Drizzle them with the sauce formed in the pot before serving.

Saucy Peach and Apple Dessert

Time: 4 1/4 hours   Servings: 4

Ingredients:

2 Granny Smith apples, peeled, cored and sliced
2 ripe peaches, pitted and sliced
1 cinnamon stick
1 cup fresh orange juice
1 teaspoon orange zest

3 tablespoons honey
1 teaspoon cornstarch
Ice cream or whipped cream for serving

Directions:

Combine all the ingredients in your slow cooker.
Cover the pot and cook for 4 hours on low settings.
Allow the dessert to cool in the pot before serving.
Ice cream or whipped cream can be a great match for this dessert.

Turtle Upside Down Cake

Time: 6 1/2 hours   Servings: 10

Ingredients:

1/2 cup crushed pretzels
1/2 cup sliced almonds
1/2 cup pecans, chopped
1/2 cup caramel sauce
1/4 cup sweetened condensed milk
1 cup all-purpose flour
1/2 cup cocoa powder

1/2 cup light brown sugar
1 teaspoon baking soda
1/2 teaspoon salt
1 cup buttermilk
1/2 cup canola oil
2 eggs
1 teaspoon vanilla extract

Directions:

Mix the pretzels, almonds, pecans, caramel sauce and condensed milk in your crock pot.

Combine the flour, cocoa powder, sugar, baking soda and salt in a bowl.

Add the wet ingredients and give it a quick mix.

Pour the cake in your slow cooker, over the pretzel and caramel mix.

Cover the pot and cook for 6 hours on low settings.

When done, carefully turn the cake upside down on a platter.

Allow to cool before slicing and serving.

Indian Almond Pudding

Time: 6 1/2 hours   Servings: 6

Ingredients:

1 cup raw almonds, peeled and soaked overnight
5 cups whole milk
1/2 cup sugar

1/4 teaspoon cardamom powder
1 pinch saffron

Directions:

Mix all the ingredients in a blender and pulse until smooth.

Pour this mixture into the crock pot and cook for 6 hours on low settings.

Allow the pudding to cool in the pot before serving.

Triple Chocolate Brownies

Time: 4 1/2 hours   Servings: 12

Ingredients:

1 1/4 cups all-purpose flour
1/4 cup cocoa powder
1/2 teaspoon salt
1/2 cup butter, melted
8 oz. dark chocolate, chopped
1 cup sugar
2 eggs

1 egg yolk
1 teaspoon vanilla extract
1/2 cup dark chocolate chips

Directions:

Mix the dry ingredients in a bowl and place aside.

Combine the butter and 8 oz. chocolate in a heatproof bowl and place over a hot water bath. Melt them together until smooth.

Remove from heat and add the sugar, eggs, yolk and vanilla.

Fold in the flour mixture and the chocolate chips.

Pour the batter in your crock pot and bake for 4 hours on low settings.

Allow to cool in the pot before cutting into small squares and serving.

PEPITA PUMPKIN CAKE

Time: 5 1/4 hours   Servings: 8

Ingredients:

1 cup all-purpose flour
1 teaspoon baking powder
1/4 teaspoon salt
1/2 teaspoon cinnamon powder
1/2 teaspoon ground ginger
1 cup pumpkin puree

1/2 cup buttermilk
2 eggs
1/4 cup canola oil
1 teaspoon vanilla extract
1/4 cup pepitas (pumpkin seeds)

Directions:

Mix the flour, baking powder, salt and spices in a bowl.

Add the wet ingredients and give it a quick mix just until combined.

Fold in the pepitas and pour the batter in your slow cooker.

Cover and cook for 5 hours on low settings.

Allow the cake to cool in the pot before serving.

PUMPKIN BREAD

Time: 6 1/4 hours   Servings: 12

Ingredients:

1 1/2 cups white sugar
1/2 cup vegetable soil
2 eggs
1 cup pumpkin puree
1/2 cup buttermilk
1 1/2 cups all-purpose flour

1/2 cup almond flour
1/2 teaspoon cinnamon powder
1/2 teaspoon ground ginger
1 teaspoon baking soda
1/4 teaspoon salt

Directions:

Mix the sugar and oil in a bowl for 2 minutes, then add the eggs and give it a good mix for a few minutes.

Stir in the pumpkin puree and buttermilk then fold in the two types of flour, spices, baking soda and salt.

Pour the batter in your greased slow cooker and bake for 6 hours on low settings.

Allow the bread to cool before serving.

CINNAMON BANANA BREAD

Time: 3 1/4 hours   Servings: 8

Ingredients:
1/4 cup butter, melted
3 ripe bananas, mashed
1/2 cup light brown sugar
1 large egg
1 1/2 cups all-purpose flour

1 teaspoon baking soda
1/2 teaspoon salt
1 teaspoon cinnamon powder
1/2 cup dark chocolate chips

Directions:
Mix the butter, bananas, light brown sugar and egg in a bowl.
Add the dry ingredients and chocolate chips and mix just until combined.
Pour the batter in your slow cooker and bake for 3 hours on low settings.
Allow the bread to cool completely before serving.

CARAMEL SAUCE POACHED PEARS

Time: 6 1/2 hours   Servings: 6

Ingredients:
6 ripe but firm pears, peeled and cored
1 1/2 cups caramel sauce
1 1/2 cups white wine

1 cinnamon stick
1 pinch salt

Directions:
Combine all the ingredients in your crock pot.
Cover the pot and cook on low settings for 6 hours.
Allow the pears to cool in the cooking liquid before serving.

CARAMEL PEACH CRISP

Time: 4 1/2 hours   Servings: 6

Ingredients:
6 large peaches, pitted and sliced
1 tablespoon lemon juice
1/2 cup caramel sauce
1 cup all-purpose flour
1/4 teaspoon salt

1/4 cup butter, chilled and cubed
2 tablespoons light brown sugar
1 pinch nutmeg
1/4 teaspoon ground ginger

Directions:
Mix the peaches, lemon juice and caramel sauce in your slow cooker.
Combine the flour, salt, butter, sugar, nutmeg and ginger in a bowl and mix with your fingertips until sandy.
Spread this mixture over the peaches and bake for 4 hours on low settings.
Allow the crisp to cool completely before serving.

GRAIN FREE CHOCOLATE CAKE

Time: 6 1/4 hours   Servings: 10

Ingredients:

2 cups almond flour
1 cup shredded coconut
1/4 cup cocoa powder
1/2 cup xylitol powder
1 teaspoon baking soda
1 teaspoon baking powder

1/4 teaspoon salt
4 eggs
1/2 cup coconut oil, melted
1 cup coconut milk
1 teaspoon vanilla extract

Directions:

Mix the dry ingredients in your slow cooker. Add the remaining ingredients and mix well with a spatula. Cover the pot and bake for 6 hours on low settings. Allow the cake to cool completely before slicing and serving.

GLUTEN FREE COCONUT CAKE

Time: 2 1/4 hours   Servings: 8

Ingredients:

2 cups gluten free oat flour
1 cup coconut sugar
1/4 cup cocoa powder
1 teaspoon baking powder
1/2 teaspoon salt

1 cup coconut milk
2 eggs
1/4 cup butter, melted
1 teaspoon vanilla extract

Directions:

Mix the oat flour, coconut sugar, cocoa powder, baking powder and salt in a bowl.
Add the remaining ingredients and give it a quick mix.
Pour the batter in your greased slow cooker and bake for 2 hours on high settings.
Allow the cake to cool completely before slicing and serving.

CRANBERRY WALNUT BREAD

Time: 4 1/4 hours   Servings: 10

Ingredients:

1 cup all-purpose flour
1 cup ground walnuts
1 1/2 teaspoons baking powder
1/4 teaspoon salt

2 ripe bananas, mashed
2 eggs
1/2 cup buttermilk
1 cup frozen cranberries

Directions:

Mix the flour, walnuts, baking powder and salt in a bowl.
Add the bananas, eggs and buttermilk and mix well then fold in the cranberries.
Pour the bread in your slow cooker and bake for 4 hours on low settings.
Allow the bread to cool in the pot before slicing and serving.

TIPSY PUMPKIN BREAD PUDDING

Time: 6 1/2 hours

Servings: 8

Ingredients:

6 cups bread cubes
2 cups pumpkin cubes
1 teaspoon cinnamon powder
1 teaspoon ground ginger
4 eggs

1 cup pumpkin puree
1 1/2 cups whole milk
1/4 cup dark brown sugar
1 teaspoon vanilla extract
1/4 cup dark rum

Directions:

Mix the bread cubes, pumpkin cubes, cinnamon and ginger in your crock pot. Combine the eggs, pumpkin puree, milk, brown sugar, vanilla and rum in a bowl. Pour this mixture over the bread and bake for 6 hours on low settings. The pudding is best served slightly warm.

NUTELLA BREAD PUDDING

Time: 6 1/2 hours

Servings: 8

Ingredients:

8 cups bread cubes
1/2 cup dark chocolate chips
1/2 cup hazelnuts, chopped
2 tablespoons butter, melted

1/2 cup Nutella
2 cups whole milk
1/4 cup light brown sugar
1 teaspoon vanilla extract

Directions:

Mix the bread cubes, chocolate chips and hazelnuts in your slow cooker.
Combine the butter, Nutella, milk, sugar and vanilla in a bowl and mix well.
Pour this mixture over the bread cubes and cook on low settings for 6 hours.
Allow the pudding to cool down slightly before serving.

PEAR WALNUT CAKE

Time: 4 1/2 hours

Servings: 8

Ingredients:

1 cup butter, softened
1 cup white sugar
3 eggs
1 cup all-purpose flour
1 cup ground walnuts

1/4 cup cocoa powder
1/4 teaspoon salt
1 teaspoon baking powder
1/2 teaspoon cinnamon powder
4 ripe pears, peeled, cored and sliced

Directions:

Mix the butter and sugar in a bowl until creamy and pale. Add the eggs one by one and mix well.
Fold in the flour, walnuts, cocoa powder, salt, baking powder and cinnamon with a spatula.
Spoon the batter in your slow cooker and top with pear slices.
Bake in the crock pot for 4 hours on low settings. Allow the cake to cool in the pot before slicing.

CHOCOLATE CHIP COOKIE BARS

Time: 4 1/2 hours   Servings: 12

Ingredients:

1/2 cup butter, softened
1/4 cup dark brown sugar
1/2 cup white sugar
1 large egg
1 teaspoon vanilla extract

1 1/4 cups all-purpose flour
1/2 teaspoon sea salt
1 teaspoon baking powder
2/3 cup dark chocolate chips

Directions:

Mix the butter and the two types of sugar in a bowl until creamy.

Add the eggs and vanilla and mix well.

Fold in the remaining ingredients then spoon the dough in your slow cooker and spread it into an even layer with the back of a spoon.

Bake for 4 hours on low settings then allow to cool and cut into small bars.

Beverages

MULLED WINE

Time: 2 1/4 hours   Servings: 8

Ingredients:
6 cups sweet red wine   1 cinnamon stick
1 cup apple cider   4 whole cloves
1/4 cup light brown sugar   2 star anise
1 small orange, sliced   4 cardamom pods, crushed

Directions:
Combine all the ingredients in your slow cooker.
Cover the pot and cook for 2 hours on high settings.
The mulled wine is best served warm.

CRANBERRY SPICED TEA

Time: 2 1/4 hours   Servings: 6

Ingredients:
4 cups water   2 cinnamon stick
1 cup strong brewed black tea   2 star anise
1 cup cranberry juice   2 cardamom pods, crushed
1/2 cup white sugar   1 lemon, sliced

Directions:
Combine all the ingredients in your slow cooker.
Cook on high settings for 2 hours.
Serve the drink warm.

ROSEMARY MULLED CIDER

Time: 3 1/4 hours   Servings: 6

Ingredients:
4 cups apple cider   1/2 cup white sugar
2 cups rose wine   1 cinnamon stick
1 cup fresh or frozen cranberries   2 whole cloves
1 rosemary sprig

Directions:
Combine all the ingredients in your slow cooker.
Cover and cook for 3 hours on low settings.
Serve the beverage warm.

GINGERBREAD HOT CHOCOLATE

Time: 2 1/4 hours   Servings: 8

Ingredients:
6 cups whole milk   1/2 teaspoon ground ginger
1 cup dark chocolate chips   2 cinnamon stick
1 cup sweetened condensed milk   2 tablespoons maple syrup
2 tablespoons cocoa powder   1 pinch salt

Directions:
Combine all the ingredients in your slow cooker.
Cover the pot and cook for 2 hours on high settings.
Serve the hot chocolate warm.

GINGERBREAD MOCHA DRINK

Time: 1 3/4 hours   Servings: 6

Ingredients:
3 cups whole milk   1/2 teaspoon ground ginger
2 cups strongly brewed coffee   1/4 teaspoon cinnamon powder
1/2 cup sweetened condensed milk   1/4 teaspoon cardamom powder
1/4 cup light brown sugar

Directions:
Combine all the ingredients in a slow cooker.
Cover the pot and cook for 1 1/2 hours on low settings.
Serve the mocha drink warm.

SALTED CARAMEL MILK STEAMER

Time: 2 1/4 hours   Servings: 6

Ingredients:
4 cups whole milk   1/4 teaspoon salt
1 cup heavy cream   1/4 teaspoon ground ginger
1 cup caramel sauce   1 teaspoon vanilla extract

Directions:
Combine all the ingredients in your crock pot.
Cover the pot with its lid and cook for 2 hours on low settings.
Pour the steamer into glasses or mugs and serve right away.

*A*PPLE CHAI TEA

Time: 4 1/4 hours   Servings: 8

Ingredients:
4 cups brewed black tea
4 cups fresh apple juice
1/3 cup white sugar
2 red apples, cored and diced

2 cinnamon stick
1 star anise
2 whole cloves
2 cardamom pods, crushed

Directions:
Combine all the ingredients in your crock pot.
Cook the tea on low settings for 4 hours.
Serve the tea warm.

*G*INGER PUMPKIN LATTE

Time: 3 1/4 hours   Servings: 6

Ingredients:
4 cups whole milk
1 cup pumpkin puree
1 cup brewed coffee
1/4 cup dark brown sugar

1 teaspoon ground ginger
1 cinnamon stick
1 pinch nutmeg

Directions:
Combine all the ingredients in a slow cooker.
Cover the pot and cook for 3 hours on low settings.
Serve the latte warm.

*H*OT CARAMEL APPLE DRINK

Time: 2 1/4 hours   Servings: 8

Ingredients:
6 cups apple cider
1 cup apple liqueur
1 cup light rum

1/2 cup caramel syrup
2 red apples, cored and diced
2 cinnamon stick

Directions:
Mix all the ingredients in your slow cooker.
Cover the pot and cook for 2 hours on low settings.

Spiced White Chocolate

Time: 1 3/4 hours   Servings: 6

Ingredients:

4 cups whole milk
1 cup sweetened condensed milk
1 cup white chocolate chips
1 cinnamon stick

1 star anise
1/2-inch piece of ginger, sliced
1 pinch nutmeg

Directions:

Combine all the ingredients in your crock pot.
Cover the pot and cook for 1 1/2 hours on low settings.
Serve the drink hot.

Apple Bourbon Punch

Time: 2 1/4 hours   Servings: 4

Ingredients:

3 cups apple cider
1 cup bourbon
1/2 cup fresh or frozen cranberries

2 cinnamon stick
2 whole cloves
1/4 cup light brown sugar

Directions:

Combine all the ingredients in your crock pot and cook for 2 hours on low settings.
Serve the drink hot.

Maple Bourbon Mulled Cider

Time: 1 3/4 hours   Servings: 6

Ingredients:

5 cups apple cider
1/2 cup bourbon
1/2 cup fresh apple juice

1/4 cup maple syrup
2 star anise

Directions:

Mix all the ingredients in your slow cooker.
Cover the pot and cook for 1 1/2 hours on low settings.
Serve hot.

*A*UTUMN PUNCH

Time: 4 1/4 hours

Servings: 8

Ingredients:
6 cups red wine
1 cup bourbon
1 cup cranberry juice
1 vanilla bean, split in half lengthwise

2 red apples, cored and diced
1 ripe pear, cored and sliced
1 cinnamon stick
2 whole cloves

Directions:
Combine all the ingredients in your slow cooker.
Cover and cook for 4 hours on low settings.
The punch can be served both hot and chilled.

*H*OT SPICY APPLE CIDER

Time: 3 1/4 hours

Servings: 6

Ingredients:
5 cups apple cider
1 cup white rum
2 cinnamon stick

1/4 teaspoon chili powder
1 star anise
1 orange, sliced

Directions:
Combine all the ingredients in your crock pot.
Cover the pot and cook for 3 hours on low settings.
Serve the cider warm.

*B*OOZY HOT CHOCOLATE

Time: 4 1/4 hours

Servings: 6

Ingredients:
4 cups whole milk
1 cup sweetened condensed milk
1 cup dark chocolate chips

1/2 cup dark rum
1 cinnamon stick
2 tablespoons maple syrup

Directions:
Mix all the ingredients in your slow cooker.
Cover the pot and cook for 4 hours on low settings.
The drink is best served warm.

Vanilla Latte

Time: 2 1/4 hours

Servings: 6

Ingredients:
4 cups whole milk
2 cups brewed coffee

1 vanilla pod, split in half lengthwise
1/4 cup sweetened condensed milk

Directions:
Combine all the ingredients in your crock pot.
Cover and cook for 2 hours on low settings.
Serve the latte warm.

Apple Ginger Delight

Time: 1 3/4 hours

Servings: 6

Ingredients:
4 cups apple cider
1 cup ginger beer
1/2 cup bourbon

1-inch piece of ginger, sliced
1/4 cup light brown sugar
1 teaspoon dark molasses

Directions:
Combine all the ingredients in your slow cooker.
Cover and cook for 1 1/2 hours on low settings.
Serve the drink hot.

Eggnog Latte

Time: 2 1/4 hours

Servings: 6

Ingredients:
2 cups brewed coffe3
3 cups eggnog
1 cup whole milk

1/4 cup light brown sugar
1 teaspoon vanilla extract
1 pinch nutmeg

Directions:
Combine all the ingredients in your slow cooker.
Cook for 2 hours on low settings.
The latte can be served both warm and chilled.

CITRUS BOURBON COCKTAIL

Time: 3 1/4 hours   Servings: 6

Ingredients:
4 cups apple cider
1 cup fresh orange juice
1/4 cup white sugar
1 cinnamon stick

1 cup bourbon
1 small orange, sliced
1 lemon, sliced
1 small grapefruit, sliced

Directions:
Combine all the ingredients in your crock pot.
Cover the pot and cook for 3 hours on low settings.
The drink can be served both warm and chilled.

LEMONADE CIDER

Time: 1 1/2 hours   Servings: 6

Ingredients:
5 cups apple cider
1 cup ginger beer

1 large lemon, sliced
1/4 cup honey

Directions:
Combine all the ingredients in your slow cooker.
Cover and cook on low settings for 1 1/4 hours.
Serve the drink warm or chilled.

SPICED PUMPKIN TODDY

Time: 3 1/4 hours   Servings: 6

Ingredients:
1/2 cup pumpkin puree
1 cup bourbon
2 cups apple cider
2 cups water
1/4 cup maple syrup

1 cinnamon stick
1 star anise
2 orange peels
2 cardamom pods, crushed

Directions:
Combine all the ingredients in your slow cooker.
Cover the pot and cook for 3 hours on low settings.
Serve the toddy warm.

RASPBERRY HOT CHOCOLATE

Time: 2 1/4 hours

Servings: 8

Ingredients:

1 cup sweetened condensed milk
1 cup heavy cream
6 cups whole milk

1/2 cup seedless raspberry jam
1/4 cup cocoa powder
1 pinch salt

Directions:

Combine all the ingredients in your crock pot.
Cover and cook for 2 hours on low settings.
Serve the drink hot.

NUTELLA HOT CHOCOLATE

Time: 4 1/4 hours

Servings: 6

Ingredients:

5 cups whole milk
3/4 cup Nutella spread

1/4 cup heavy cream
1 cinnamon stick

Directions:

Mix all the ingredients in your slow cooker.
Cover the pot and cook for 4 hours on low settings.
Serve the drink hot.

MULLED CRANBERRY PUNCH

Time: 3 1/4 hours

Servings: 8

Ingredients:

4 cups cranberry juice
1 cup fresh or frozen cranberries
3 cups apple cider
1/2 cup bourbon

2 whole cloves
1 cinnamon stick
1 star anise
1/2 cup maple syrup

Directions:

Combine all the ingredients in your crock pot.
Cover and cook for 3 hours on low settings.
The punch can be served both warm and chilled.

Citrus Green Tea

Time: 1 3/4 hours

Servings: 6

Ingredients:

5 cups brewed green tea
1 cup fresh orange juice
1 lemon, sliced

1/4 cup honey
1/2-inch piece of ginger, sliced

Directions:

Combine all the ingredients in your slow cooker.
Cover and cook for 1 1/2 hours on low settings.
Serve the tea warm or chilled.

Whiskey Pumpkin Drink

Time: 2 1/4 hours

Servings: 6

Ingredients:

1 cup whiskey
1/2 cup pumpkin puree
1/4 cup maple syrup

1 cup ginger ale
3 cups water
1 cinnamon stick

Directions:

Mix all the ingredients in a slow cooker and cook for 2 hours on low settings.
Serve the drink warm or chilled.

Mulled Pink Wine

Time: 2 1/4 hours

Servings: 6

Ingredients:

6 cups rose wine
1 cup fresh raspberries

1/4 cup honey
2 cardamom pods, crushed

Directions:

Combine all the ingredients in your slow cooker.
Cover the pot with its lid and cook for 2 hours on low settings.
Serve the wine warm.

Black Tea Punch

Time: 4 1/4 hours   Servings: 8

Ingredients:
4 cups brewed black tea
2 cups cranberry juice
2 cups apple juice
1 orange, sliced

1 lemon, sliced
1 cinnamon stick
1/4 cup white sugar

Directions:
Combine all the ingredients in your slow cooker.
Cover the pot with a lid and cook for 4 hours on low settings.
The punch is best served warm.

Cherry Cider

Time: 1 3/4 hours   Servings: 8

Ingredients:
6 cups apple cider
2 cups cherry juice

2 cinnamon stick
1 star anise

Directions:
Combine all the ingredients in your slow cooker.
Cook for 1 1/2 hours on low settings.
Serve the cider warm.

Chocolate Hot Coffee

Time: 3 1/4 hours   Servings: 6

Ingredients:
4 cups brewed coffee
1 cup dark chocolate chips

1/2 cup chocolate syrup
1/2 cup heavy cream

Directions:
Combine all the ingredients in your crock pot.
Cover the pot and cook for 3 hours on low settings.
Serve the coffee hot.

SPICED COFFEE

Time: 2 1/4 hours

Servings: 6

Ingredients:
6 cups brewed coffee
1/4 cup chocolate syrup
1/4 cup white sugar
1 star anise

1 cinnamon stick
2 whole cloves
2 cardamom pods, crushed

Directions:
Mix the ingredients in a slow cooker and cook for 2 hours on low settings.
Serve the coffee warm.

KAHLUA COFFEE

Time: 1 1/4 hours

Servings: 6

Ingredients:
2 cups heavy cream
2 cups whole milk
2 cups water
1/4 cup Kahlua

2 teaspoons instant powder
1 teaspoon vanilla extract
1/4 cup white sugar

Directions:
Combine all the ingredients in your slow cooker.
Cover and cook on low settings for 1 hour.
Serve the coffee warm.

PEACHY CIDER

Time: 4 1/4 hours

Servings: 6

Ingredients:
2 cups peach nectar
2 cups apple juice
2 cups apple cider
1 cinnamon stick

1 pinch nutmeg
1 star anise
2 cardamom pods, crushed
2 tablespoons light brown sugar

Directions:
Combine all the ingredients in your slow cooker.
Cover and cook for 4 hours on low settings.
Serve the cider warm.

POMEGRANATE CIDER

Time: 2 1/4 hours

Servings: 6

Ingredients:

1 1/2 cups pomegranate juiced
4 cups apple cider
1/2 cup ginger ale
1/4 cup brown sugar

1 cinnamon stick
1 star anise
1 small orange, sliced

Directions:

Mix all the ingredients in your crock pot.
Cover and cook for 2 hours on low settings.
Serve the cider warm.

GINGER TEA DRINK

Time: 1 1/4 hours

Servings: 6

Ingredients:

6 cups water
6 green tea bags
1/4 cup honey

1-inch piece of ginger, sliced
1 lemon, sliced

Directions:

Mix all the ingredients in a slow cooker.
Cover the pot and cook for 1 hour on low settings.
Remove the lemon slices and tea bags and pour the drink in mugs.
Serve warm.

SPICED LEMON CIDER PUNCH

Time: 2 1/4 hours

Servings: 6

Ingredients:

4 cups apple cider
1 cup water
1 cup cranberry juice
1/4 cup lemon juice

1 lemon, sliced
1/4 cup honey
2 cardamom pods, crushed

Directions:

Mix the apple cider, water, cranberry juice, lemon juice, lemon slices, honey and cardamom pods in your slow cooker.
Cover the pot and cook for 2 hours on low settings.
Serve the punch warm.

BRANDIED MULLED WINE

Time: 1 3/4 hours

Servings: 8

Ingredients:
7 cups dry white wine
1 cup brandy
1/4 cup maple syrup
1 cinnamon stick

1 star anise
2 whole cloves
2 cardamom pods, crushed

Directions:
Mix all the ingredients in your crock pot.
Cover and cook for 1 1/2 hours on low settings.
Serve the wine warm.

HOT WHISKEY SOUR

Time: 2 1/4 hours

Servings: 6

Ingredients:
1 cup whiskey
1/2 cup lemon juice
1/2 cup white sugar

4 cups water
1 tablespoon honey

Directions:
Mix the ingredients in your crock pot.
Cover and cook for 2 hours on low settings.
Serve the drink warm.

CARAMEL HOT CHOCOLATE

Time: 4 1/4 hours

Servings: 6

Ingredients:
3/4 cup caramel sauce
4 cups whole milk
1 cup dark chocolate chips

1 cup evaporated milk
1 pinch salt

Directions:
Combine all the ingredients in your slow cooker.
Cover the pot and cook for 4 hours on low settings.
Serve the drink warm and hot.

Hot Marmalade Cider

Time: 1 1/4 hours

Servings: 6

Ingredients:
5 cups apple cider
1 cup fresh orange juice

1 orange, sliced
1/4 cup orange marmalade

Directions:
Mix all the ingredients in your crock pot.
Cover the pot with its lid and cook for 1 hour on high settings.
Serve the cider warm.

Peppermint Hot Chocolate

Time: 1 3/4 hours

Servings: 6

Ingredients:
4 cups whole milk
1 cup heavy cream
1 cup dark chocolate

1 pinch salt
1 teaspoon peppermint extract
1 tablespoon cocoa powder

Directions:
Mix all the ingredients in your slow cooker.
Cover the pot and cook for 1 1/2 hours on low settings.
Serve the chocolate warm.

Orange Brandy Hot Toddy

Time: 2 1/4 hours

Servings: 6

Ingredients:
4 cups brewed black tea
1 cup fresh orange juice
1 cup brandy
1 cinnamon stick

1/4 cup honey
1/2-inch piece of ginger, sliced
2 orange slices

Directions:
Combine all the ingredients in your slow cooker.
Cover the pot with its lid and cook for 2 hours on low settings.
Serve the toddy hot.

SPICY MULLED RED WINE

Time: 4 1/4 hours

Servings: 6

Ingredients:

6 cups red wine
1 teaspoon peppercorns
1/2 bay leaf
1 cinnamon stick

1 star anise
2 cardamom pods, crushed
1/2 cup white sugar

Directions:

Combine all the ingredients in your slow cooker.
Cover the pot and cook for 4 hours on low settings.
Serve the drink warm.

LEMON LIME JASMINE TEA

Time: 1 1/4 hours

Servings: 6

Ingredients:

6 cups water
2 tablespoons jasmine buds
1 lemon, sliced

1 lime, sliced
1/2 cup white sugar

Directions:

Combine all the ingredients in your crock pot.
Cook for 1 hour on high settings.
When done, strain and serve the tea hot.

PARTY CRANBERRY PUNCH

Time: 4 1/4 hours

Servings: 6

Ingredients:

2 cups cranberry juice
4 cups apple cider
1/2 cup fresh or frozen cranberries
1 small orange, sliced

1 red apple, cored and sliced
1 peach, pitted and sliced
2 tablespoons honey
2 cinnamon sticks

Directions:

Mix all the ingredients in your crock pot.
Cook for 4 hours on low settings and serve the drink warm.

CARAMEL CIDER

Time: 1 1/4 hours   Servings: 6

Ingredients:
1/2 cups white sugar   1 cup fresh orange juice
1/2 cup water   1 cinnamon stick
4 cups apple cider

Directions:
Melt the sugar in a saucepan until it has an amber color. Add the water and cook for 2 minutes until the sugar is melted.
Combine the caramel sauce with the remaining ingredients in your crock pot.
Cook for 1 hour on high settings.
Serve the cider warm.

HOT CRANBERRY TODDY

Time: 4 1/4 hours   Servings: 8

Ingredients:
6 cups apple cider   1/4 cup light brown sugar
2 cups cranberry juice   1/2 cup fresh or frozen cranberries
1/4 cup dark rum

Directions:
Mix all the ingredients in your crock pot.
Cook for 4 hours on low settings.
Serve the toddy warm.

THE ULTIMATE HOT CHOCOLATE

Time: 4 1/4 hours   Servings: 6

Ingredients:
4 cups whole milk   1 tablespoon cocoa powder
1 cup sweetened condensed milk   1 pinch salt
1 cup heavy cream   Mini marshmallows for serving
1 cup dark chocolate chips

Directions:
Mix all the ingredients in your crock pot.
Cover and cook for 4 hours on low settings.
Serve the drink hot, topped with marshmallows.

*B*UTTERED HOT RUM

Time: 4 1/4 hours

Servings: 6

Ingredients:

4 cups water
1 cup dark brown sugar
1/4 cup butter

2 cinnamon stick
1 whole clove
1 cup dark rum

Directions:

Mix the water, sugar, butter, cinnamon and whole clove in your slow cooker.
Cook for 4 hours on low settings.
When done, stir in the rum and serve right away.

*I*RISH CREAM COFFEE

Time: 3 1/4 hours

Servings: 4
3 cups brewed coffee
1/2 cup Irish cream liqueur
1/2 cup heavy cream
1 tablespoon cocoa powder
1/4 cup heavy cream

Directions:

Mix all the ingredients in your crock pot.
Cook for 3 hours on low settings.
Serve the coffee warm.

CONCLUSION

Crock pots surely are one of the most useful kitchen gadgets ever invented. They are capable of taking the most untalented, busy or lazy home cook to the next level by allowing food to cook slowly and develop intense flavor and amazing texture. Rushing to work? Late for a meeting? Too tired to cook tonight? Sick of cooking every single day? Slow cooking is the answer to all your problems!

Do yourself a favor and buy a crock pot then let yourself immerged into the world of slow cooking, discover amazing flavors, try great recipes, challenge yourself with unusual ingredients, step out of your comfort zone and do as little effort as possible – that's the religion of a crock pot! And it's all in your favor – you are the one enjoying healthy and nourishing meals, you are the one spoiling yourself with your favorite dishes, you are the one making sure your family and kids eat homemade food, you are the one controlling the ingredients used and the money spent!

Thank you again for purchasing this book!

Finally, if you enjoyed this book, please take the time to share your thoughts and post a review on Amazon. It'd be greatly appreciated!

Feel free to contact me at emma.katie@outlook.com

Check out more books by Emma Katie at:

www.amazon.com/author/emmakatie

Printed in Poland
by Amazon Fulfillment
Poland Sp. z o.o., Wrocław

35167213R00231